*Philosophical Anthropology
and Practical Politics*

Books by F. S. C. Northrop

The Meeting of East and West
Science and First Principles
The Logic of the Sciences and the Humanities
The Taming of the Nations
European Union and United States Foreign Policy
The Complexity of Legal and Ethical Experience
Editor, *Ideological Differences and World Order*
Co-Editor with Mason W. Gross, *Alfred North Whitehead, An Anthology*

Philosophical Anthropology and Practical Politics

F. S. C. NORTHROP

Sterling Professor of Philosophy and Law
Yale Law School

New York
The Macmillan Company
1960

First Printing

The Macmillan Company, New York
Brett-Macmillan Ltd., Galt, Ontario

Printed in the United States of America

Library of Congress catalog card number: 60-11611

Preface

This book describes several important recent discoveries in different natural and social sciences, submits the concepts of each to a careful epistemological analysis, thereby arriving at an empirically verifiable theory of what a human being is and what groups of human beings called nations are, and then applies this theory and the political methods which it prescribes to the description and suggested solution of some major political problems of today's world. The first two words of the book's title derive from the fact that one of these discoveries occurred in the science of cultural anthropology when scientists such as Paul Radin and Clyde Kluckhohn found that even people without a written language share a common, but by no means simple, philosophy, and that to determine objectively the culture of a particular people one must specify their predominant philosophy.

The science of sociological jurisprudence receives similar attention in this volume. Its political importance arises from the fact that it investigates the relation between the positive legal and political normative rules and decisions of the government of any people and their underlying social customs and then specifies the requirements which must be satisfied if the legal and political decisions of the public officials are to succeed. Knowledge of these requirements is especially necessary today, since the present failures of free democracy both at home and abroad arise in major part from a conflict between the norms of a free democratic nation and the normative customs of the people to whom free democratic legal and political institutions are being applied.

Two recent discoveries in neurophysiological psychology receive special attention also in Chapters 3 and 4. They are (1) the Mc-Culloch-Pitts theory of the neurophysiological correlate of intro-spected memory and ideas and (2) the cybernetic character of human nervous systems. Their importance for politics derives from the fact that, unless we have a complete and correct conception of what an individual person is, we are likely to have a mistaken theory of what any nation is and thereby fall into faulty political methods for either understanding nations or making trustworthy domestic or foreign policy decisions with respect to them. The writer is especially in-debted to Warren S. McCulloch for reading the manuscript of Chap-ter 3 and for suggesting several improvements in wording which the printed text contains. I am equally indebted to the Josiah Macy, Jr. Foundation and their research director, Dr. Frank Fremont-Smith, for the privilege of being a member of the conferences sponsored and called by them in which natural and social scientists and philosophers of science discussed the discoveries which Chapters 3 and 4 in part describe.

Similar thanks go to Mr. K. R. Dove for permission to publish here a description of his observations during a visit to the Soviet Union and for his reading and suggested improvements of Chapter 15. Appreciation is herewith expressed also to the anthropologist Mr. Tom Harrisson of Sarawak and to Professor W. R. Crocker, the present High Commissioner of Australia to India, for permitting me to write what appears concerning them at the beginning of Chap-ter 17. Special thanks are due also to Pearl Buck for her letter grant-ing me the right to quote in Chapter 16 from her autobiographical work *My Several Worlds,* and to Professor Sol Tax and Dr. Paul Fejos for their permission to quote in Chapter 15 from a letter of the former to the latter.

Grateful acknowledgment to the following is also made for per-mission to include here certain materials of the writer which origi-nally were published elsewhere. These materials and their respective sources are specified in each instance in the text: Liberal Arts Press, *Civilisations,* and the Hartford Theological Seminary, the Poly-technic Institute of Brooklyn, the American Academy of Political and Social Science, Evans Brothers, Ltd., London, and World Book Company, the University of Chicago Press, and the Wenner-Gren Foundation for Anthropological Research, Inc.

The writer is especially indebted to a grant from the Research Academy in the Philosophy of the Arts and the Sciences, made possible by the generosity of Mrs. William Hale Harkness, for completing the writing of this book. Without Helen H. Livingston's patience and expertness in checking all references, preparing the manuscript, and making the index, what appears here would have been impossible. To be acknowledged also with deepest gratitude is a grant made by the Wenner-Gren Foundation for Anthropological Research, Inc., to the Yale Law School which made Miss Livingston's assistance available. The patience of Mr. R. L. De Wilton and the care of Miss Ada Shearon in easing the way from the final manuscript to the printed page are also appreciated.

Readers whose interests are primarily practical and political may proceed directly from Chapters 1 and 2 via Chapter 5 of Part I to Parts II and III, reading Chapters 3, 4, 6 and 7 afterward. The latter chapters are of primary importance for anyone interested in (1) the cybernetic character of human nervous systems, (2) the relation of ideas and ideals to such nervous systems, (3) the methods of ethics and the normative social sciences or (4) the methodological justification for the political judgments made in Parts II and III.

F. S. C. NORTHROP

Rollins College
Winter Park, Florida
April 6, 1960

Contents

Part Three:

The Meaning and Methods of Any Free People

Philosophical Anthropology

and Practical Politics

1

A New Approach to Politics

Contemporary politics leaves much to be desired. Its shortcomings appear in both foreign and domestic policy.

The need to settle disputes between nations in an atomic age by peaceful rather than violent means is obvious. History gives no evidence, as Roscoe Pound reminds us, that even domestic social disagreements are resolved without recourse to fighting unless, in intervening periods when tempers are under control and passions are stilled, legal institutions and procedures are established.

Nevertheless, previous attempts to achieve an effective international legal order have been disheartening. Recall the disillusionment following the creation of the League of Nations at Versailles. Witness the present Cold War which followed so soon upon the high hopes for the United Nations that were publicly voiced and officially authorized at San Francisco.

Domestic politics also is not what it needs to be. The lack of foresight at both the state and federal levels in adjusting the cultural customs of the Old South to the unanimous decisions of the Justices of the Supreme Court of the United States in the desegregation cases and the resultant recourse to the military in full battle array with its breeding of bitterness suggest that the relation between legal decisions and social customs calls for more attention by ourselves and our politicians than it is now receiving.

Domestic events abroad reinforce this conclusion. Since World War II as Africans, Middle Easterners and Asians have freed themselves from Western imperialistic domination, they have not returned to their medieval political customs in which they were ruled by theocratic Hindu maharajas, caliphatic sultans, Judaic patriarchs

1

or African tribal chieftains. Instead, modern-minded leaders in the Westernized African, Islamic, Israeli and Asian cities have insisted on placing their domestic affairs under democratic control. To do this they have had to import modern Western constitutional, commercial and even family law. This law contains normative content which is incompatible at many points with the deepest beliefs, moral standards, marriage customs and familial and tribal loyalties of the masses of the people, most of whom live still in villages bound by customs that are tribally divisive, religiously and politically theocratic and socially laden with caste. The domestic politics of these contemporary nations is further complicated because the masses of the people in the villages, often 85 to 98 per cent of the population with these medieval and undemocratic customs, breed prolifically, whereas the few modern-minded leaders in the cities want small families, knowing that only if they keep their numbers small will they be able to provide a democratic and modern-minded education for their children. The result is the political paradox: The more these "democratic" governments are run by people who understand democracy and its modern ways and instruments, the less representative of their people their "democracy" is; conversely, the more the masses of the people truly express their own beliefs, values and customs in their government, the more family-centered, tribally divided and tribally led and dictatorial their new "democratic" nation becomes. This paradox defines the major domestic political problem of the nations of the world today, including, as Little Rock shows, even the United States.

That the present leaders of the nations of the free world do not know how to meet this situation is shown by the following recent events: During but the two months of November and December in 1958, the *New York Times* reported the following setbacks to free democracy: Military coups occurred, or a virtually permanent state of martial law was imposed, in Pakistan, Burma, Ceylon, Thailand, Iraq, French Algeria and the Sudan. At the same time, except for the temporary landing of United States troops, a military coup which in all likelihood would have removed the large Christian community from any role in the government was barely avoided in Lebanon. A few months later, at the point of the guns of the French military leaders of the Algerian coup and their military allies in France, the

French people were forced to choose between a civil war at home or the placing of a military man at the head of their government, whose condition for accepting office was that he be given powers which, if he uses them, are incompatible with free democratic legal and political practices. Simultaneously in Ghana, its first prime minister had no more than sworn, in accepting office, to uphold their many-party democratic constitution, than he proceeded, because opposition leaders in both the state and the federal governments were doing likewise, to behave like an African tribal chieftain, throwing into jail those who criticized him and his government.[1] At the same time the *New York Times* reported that one of the major handicaps of the foreign policy of the Western free nations with respect to Communism in Africa, the Middle East and Southeast Asia is the failure of the United States to live up to its democratic professions at home in its treatment of the Negro. Simultaneously, race riots occurred in England.

These domestic legal and political events at Little Rock, Karachi, Rangoon, Colombo, Bangkok, Baghdad, Khartoum, Algiers, Paris, Beirut, Accra and London have two things in common: First, they bespeak the fact that the present political and judicial leaders of the free democracies at home and throughout the world are facing bitter reactions and, in many cases, defeat in the application of free democratic legal and political norms to significant groups of their own people. Second, these defiances and defeats of the law have occurred when positive democratic legal norms were applied to a significant group of people in the nation whose living beliefs and customs embodied different norms.

The latter fact indicates that contemporary politics, both domestic and international, must pay more attention to cultural anthropology and the sociological conditions for effective law than has been the case in the recent past. The times seem ripe, therefore, for a turning aside momentarily from our present practical problems and politicians to see what cultural anthropology and sociological jurisprudence have to teach us about the conditions which must be satisfied if there is to be an effective domestic and international law and politics and if freedom is not to go down to defeat primarily because of the ineptness of the present political leadership of the "free" nations.

Sociologists of law have investigated the factor upon which the practical effectiveness of legal and political institutions depends. The findings can be stated most vividly in terms of the language of the Austro-Hungarian sociological jurist of the last generation—Eugen Ehrlich. In his classic work entitled *Fundamental Principles of the Sociology of Law,* Ehrlich distinguishes between the "positive law" and the "living law." By the former and its "norms for decision," [2] he meant the substantive normative content of the written constitution and the successive statutes of the political government as applied by the legally authorized judges to the settling of disputes between members of the legal and political community in question, and as implemented further by the legally authorized policemen. By the living law Ehrlich meant *the substantive normative content* of the spontaneously held beliefs and social habits and behavior of the people, or what most of them would do normatively even if there were little or no positive law.

Negatively stated, the sociological justists' finding is that positive law and politics will be ineffective if the substantive normative prescriptions of the positive legal decisions and political policies are not supported by the living personal morality and customs of a large percentage of the people. The failure of the Prohibition Amendment in the United States, even though it was legally passed, is a case in point. The failure of the still-persisting normative content of the living habits of the Africans of Ghana to conform to the norms of its duly passed, new positive contractual democratic constitution is another example, as in all likelihood are most of the other recent setbacks to free democracy noted above. The people of Africa, Israel, Islam and Asia undoubtedly want the democratic control of their own affairs that the modern peoples of the West enjoy, but most of them have little realization of the modifications in their present religious and moral practices and familial and tribal normative customs which an understanding of democratic contractual law and its effective practice entail.

Stated positively, the sociological jurists' *criterion of effective positive law and practical politics is that the substantive normative content of the positive law and the practical politicians' policies must for a considerable short run conform to the living law habits of the majority of people in the community in question.* It is because this condition is satisfied in the case of the unanimous positive legal decisions of the Justices of the Supreme Court of the United States for the living law of the American people as a whole but not satisfied for the living law of the Old South that these decisions have the support of the majority of the American people while at the same time engendering bitter reversion into old ways in a considerable number of the Southern states.

This sociological criterion of effective positive law and practical politics does not mean that positive law can never succeed in reforming the living law. To reach such a conclusion is to overlook the words "of the majority of the people" in the sentence italicized above. As the contemporary anthropologist E. A. Hoebel has pointed out in his recent study of the comparative living and positive laws of seven different so-called primitive societies,[3] never in any effective legal and political system do the living beliefs and normative habits of all the people conform to the norms of the positive law. For judicial decisions and political policies to be effective, it is necessary merely that their normative content be that of the living law of a statistically large proportion of the people. Then the morale of the community will sustain the policeman in his legally authorized execution of the courts' judgments. Hence, Professor Hoebel emphasizes that when a cultural anthropologist affirms that the legal norms of the people of a particular tribal nation or culture are such and such, he is making a statement which is in part *qualitative* and in part *quantitatively statistical*. The statement is *qualitative* in the sense that it describes the substantive content of the positive legal rules that are applied universally to everyone in the legal and political community in question. The statement is *quantitatively statistical* in the sense that only a *statistically* large proportion of the people embody these norms in their living beliefs and behavior.

This sociological and anthropological criterion of effective positive law and practical politics does not mean that *for a considerable short run* newly introduced positive legal and political normative rules and policies cannot succeed, even though the living beliefs and normative social habits of the majority of people in the community in question do not conform to them. To reach such an erroneous conclusion is to overlook the significance of the words "for a considerable short run" in the italicized definition above of the criterion of effective law and politics. What the sociological jurists' criterion does entail in such circumstances is that failure will ensue unless the practical politicians who are persuaded of, and are introducing, the new positive legal and political institutions, use their temporary position in office to educate their people in the basic beliefs and the objective reasons for those beliefs of the new positive legal system, thereby transforming the living law so that in the not too long run it will support the new positive law.

An example of such effective political statesmanship in transforming the old living law to bring it into accord with a new positive law is the "shift from status to contract" as described by Maine in his classic *Ancient Law*.[4] This transformation occurred when the Stoic Roman creators of the new positive law which is Western legal science made this new positive law effective in transforming the patriarchal and tribal living laws of the traditional Greek and Roman tribal nations. The key to their success is to be found in the Roman poets and educators who, collaborating with the practical politicians and the theoretical positive legal scientists, captured,[5] with their poetic imagery, the imaginations of more and more of the people for the new norms, thereby transforming the living law as the judges and politicians shifted the positive law from status towards contract.

How the Soviet and Chinese Communists have met this problem will concern us in Chapters 15 and 16. What the politicians of the free nations must do, if further setbacks to free democratic legal and political institutions are not to occur both at home and throughout the world, is, however, our major concern.

To this end, sociological jurisprudence has one important negative contribution to make. It removes the theoretical misconception which led so many of the elder generation of lawyers and legally educated secretaries of state and foreign policy advisers to take it for granted, as later chapters will show, that (a) international law is meaningless and therefore (b) the attempt to achieve it is the pursuit of a will-o'-the-wisp. This misconception is prevalent, not merely in the United States, Great Britain, Australia, Canada and New Zealand, but also in the African and Asian nations of the British Commonwealth.[6] It derives, in the case of the Americans, indirectly by way of the influence of Thayer of the pre-World War I Harvard Law School, and in the case of the others directly from the nineteenth century English jurist John Austin who derived it in turn from the seventeenth century English legal and political philosopher Hobbes. This positivistic theory is that legal and political acts owe both their justification and their effectiveness not to their normative content, but to the size of the policeman's or the soldier's club which the political executive has at his disposal. Austin gave expression to this power-politics theory in his famous definition of law. This definition is that to say that anything is "just" or, to use Austin's language, "laws proper, or properly so called," meaning thereby effective, rather than merely verbal, law, is equivalent to asserting that it is the command of a single unified political sovereign who has the physical power "to inflict an evil or pain" upon those who dissent from his commands.[7]

Note that the normative content of the command is irrelevant; the decisive factor defining both justice and effective law is physical power. Since on this definition, the physical power to enforce a command regardless of its normative content is what one means by both justice and effective law, it follows by definition, as Hobbes noted and affirmed,[8] that there is no such thing as an unjust political sovereign. The materialism of Marx has the same effect upon Communist law and foreign policy. From this concept of law arises the prevalent notion that the political sovereignty of any modern national state is absolute. It follows similarly by definition, as Austin noted and asserted, that the notion of international law to which the modern national states are even in part subject, is theoretically meaningless, and hence practically impossible since the notion of an absolute political sovereign who commands himself to dissent from his own absolute commands is self-contradictory.

Assuming their definition of law, their conclusions follow. But certainly definitions are not true *a priori*. Often they are merely conventions about the use of words. Isn't this a rather flimsy basis for condemning humanity to the game of power politics, played by national sovereigns laboring under the notion that the unilateral foreign policy decisions of each are absolute? Isn't it an equally questionable ground also for assigning any attempt to achieve effective international law to the realm of nonsense and defeat ahead of time? Need one wonder that one of the ablest lawyers of our century has described this *a priori* attitude as the "give-it-up-philosophy."[9]

The quantitatively larger striking power of the battle equipment which President Eisenhower dispatched to Little Rock, the embittered reaction into old customs throughout the South which ensued, and his subsequent decision not to seek the effectiveness of positive law in the size of the political sovereign's club, should give pause to those of our present elder generation of lawyers, legally educated secretaries of state and foreign policy advisers who hold this negative philosophy. In any event, sociological jurisprudence gives empirically verifiable reasons for believing that the definition of "laws proper, or properly so called" from which this negativism derives is spurious. The reason is that in the not too long run the policeman or the soldier gets his club and the political authorization to use it only if it is used in accord with the living law values of the people concerned. Consequently, it is not the physical power of the political executive President Eisenhower's battle equipment "to inflict an evil or pain" at Little Rock on those who dissent from his and the federal courts' commands that is the key to the justice or the effectiveness of those commands. Instead, it is the normative moral and social content of the customs of a statistically large proportion of the people that is the sanction for the positive law, the political sovereign's existence, the existence of his physical club and his effective practical use of that club. Later chapters will show that the Soviet Union and President Mao's China, notwithstanding their dictatorial methods and military might, are not exceptions to this rule.

This means that when, as at Little Rock, there is a conflict between the positive legal decisions of the Supreme Court of the United States and the positive legal and political decisions of the courts and government of Arkansas, the political problem involved in applying the federal courts' decisions to Arkansas is not fully envisioned by either the federal or the state executive, to say nothing about being effectively resolved, if it is thought of merely as a case of what the Supreme Court of the land has declared and the implementation of its declarations with physical force. There are also the two other more basic factors in the legal and political situation. One is the living law of the United States as a whole, including the Jeffersonian Declaration of Independence and Bill of Rights portion of the Old South. After all, Jefferson, who wrote the first of these two legal and political documents and insisted upon the second, was a Southerner, as is Mr. Justice Black. Undoubtedly, a quantitative statistical survey would show that the living law of the nation as a whole supports the Supreme Court in the desegregation decisions. This means, if sociologically jurisprudential political methods are used, that the unanimous decisions of the Supreme Court of the United States will win out. This is especially ensured because of the Jeffersonian component of the living law of the South. The other basic factor is the predominant Filmerian patriarchal white Christian component of the living law of the Old South. Effective political leadership must, therefore, devise a policy which attacks the problem at the deeper level of the conflict within the Southerner himself, between the Jeffersonian democratic and the Filmerian patriarchal components of his own living law, after the manner in which the creators of Western legal science succeeded in transforming the similarly patriarchal living law of the ancient Greek and Roman tribal nations from status towards contract. The methods for dealing with such political problems are the main concern of this book.

The success of the Stoic Romans in changing an old living law to conform to a new positive law is as important a clue to foreign policy as it is for domestic politics. Consider the international situation with which they began: Not only were there as many nations, each a law unto itself, within the area which is today Western Europe, North Africa and the Near and Middle East, as there were tribes (e.g., the tribes of Rome, Florence, Sparta, Thebes, Carthage, Israel, Burgundy, Anglia, etc.), but also there were as many different nations as there were different patriarchal family lines resulting from younger sons breaking away from the tribal family of the eldest son to set up tribal patriarchal family lines of their own. An example is the Filmerian Christian white man's patriarchalism which, through the first families of the Virginia Company, made the living law of the Old South so much what it is, as a recent study has shown.[10]

In the countless ancient patriarchal familial and tribal nations, the individual person's religious, moral, legal and political rights, privileges, obligations and duties were defined by one's sex (patriarchal or matriarchal national rule and family headship), the temporal order of one's birth (primogeniture) and most important of all the color of skin of one's tribal ancestors. This is what Sir Henry Maine meant by a law of status society. The living law of all the peoples of the world, before the Stoic Roman lawyers and philosophers discovered

Western contractual legal science, was of this character, as is most of the living law of the Africans, Middle Easterners and Asians today and, also, as noted above, the Filmerian Christian component of the Old South. The description of this pre-Stoic Roman living law of the ancient Western world is available for anyone to read in Fustel de Coulanges' *The Ancient City* [11] and C. W. Westrup's *Introduction to Early Roman Law*.[12]

Between these countless patriarchal and tribal nations of the ancient world, feuding and war were the methods of settling disputes. Each was most literally an absolute political sovereign, after the manner of Hobbes' and Austin's definition of justice and law, and hence a law unto itself in its foreign policy. The feuding patriarchal mountain-white families of West Virginia are a contemporary example. For a dramatic portrayal of the Christian patriarchalism of one of them, see Boyd Smith's play *The Patriarch*.[13]

Confronted with such warring nations, the legal theorists and practitioners of Stoic Rome came upon a new kind of law for relating human beings politically—the type which Sir Henry Maine has called law of contract; in short, they discovered Western legal science. According to this contractual theory, a person's social, religious, moral, legal and political rights and duties have nothing to do with sex, the temporal order of one's birth, or the color of skin of the tribe of one's ancestors. Instead, since legal and political obligations, rights, duties and privileges arise, in contractual law, only when human beings reach the maturity to enter into contractual relations with one another, it follows that all human beings the world over are born free and equal before the law and with respect to their legal and political rights and duties. This is what the Stoic Roman lawyers and philosophers meant when they said that moral, legal and political man is universal, ecumenical or cosmopolitan human being. This also is the root meaning of the word Catholic in Roman Catholic Christianity. It undoubtedly entered the Judaic-Christian living law tradition from Roman law. The American Declaration of Independence is its modern foreign policy expression, as the Bill of Rights is its domestic legal and political articulation.

The Stoic Romans' discovery of Western contractual legal science enabled them to see that human beings can be related legally and politically in a completely new way, cutting across the existing countless warring patriarchally familial and tribal nations, exactly after the manner in which Einstein's discovery of the mass-energy equation indicated that matter and energy can be related in a completely novel manner to produce the atomic bomb. Obviously at the beginning of the Stoic Roman experiment in legal and political engineering, their new contractual theory of domestic and foreign policy was merely a possible positive international law. The living law of their world was that of the countless warring patriarchal tribal nations. The establishment of Western contractual legal science as the *de facto* law of the Western world in both its civil and its common law versions is, therefore, not merely the story of "the shift from status to contract," but it is also the empirical demonstration that providing sociologically jurisprudential political methods are used an effective international law for achieving peace between countless previously warring nations can be created where none existed before.

The remarkable historical fact, moreover, is that the shift did not go first to the equivalent of the modern national states. Instead, it went directly to all the tribes of the Mediterranean area and its periphery, as the existence of the Roman, Eastern and Holy Roman empires shows. Nor was force, though present, the key to this notable success. Tribal nations sought to enter the Roman Empire. Because of its novel legal science, the Roman Empire was something unique in history. Previous tribal nations, when they conquered other tribal nations, tried to impose their provincial living law upon them. The Confucian patriarchal joint family Chinese absorbed both those they conquered and their conquerors by imposing Confucian joint family living customs and beliefs upon them. Not so these Stoic Romans. As the *Institutes of Gaius* show, the specific living and positive law of each conquered or welcomed tribal nation, called the *jus civile,* had the same status under Roman law as did the different *jus civile* of the tribes of Rome. Forthwith also, the common living law norms of the different instances of the *jus civile* of each old tribal nation were sought out and called the *jus gentium.* The quest first, therefore, was for the universal in the different living customs of the old warring tribal nations. Then within each specific *jus civile* the individual person was broken loose gradually from his familial and tribal living law ties and given the privilege of standing more and more equally, across the old tribal warring national boundaries, with all other human beings before a new and effective international common law. The final result was that Roman law achieved its most complete formulation far from Rome, under the direction of a legal and political leader who racially was not a Roman—namely, Justinian at Constantinople.

Even with the fall of the Roman, the Eastern and the Holy Roman empires, Western legal science did not die; instead its contractual internationalism for bringing the peace of legal institutions to the countless old patriarchal tribal warring nations continued to thrive, merely fragmenting with the Protestant Reformation into the relatively few modern contractually unified national states.[14] Never did the Roman positive legal internationalism of the original law of status patriarchal tribal nations decompose into their innumerable original warring nations. Hence, even the modern legal and political nations, each (following Hobbes, Austin or Marx) tending to conceive of itself as an absolute law unto itself, are a testimony to the effective political triumph of contractual legal internationalism over an original living law situation which was even more power-political, divisive and warful than is the case today.

There are independent reasons, given in the writer's *The Complexity of Legal and Ethical Experience,* for believing the even stronger conclusion that the present contractual domestic law of every modern nation, including even the Soviet Union, contains international legal and political principles which refer to and are valid for everyone. This fact has been obscured for two reasons. The first is the confusion of nation in the sense of the tribal nations of a law of status society with nation in the technical sense of any modern law of contract nation. The second reason is the failure of modern lawyers and politicians to analyze their abstract nouns. The result is that Western contractual legal science and domestic and foreign political policy have become filled by both Communists and democrats alike with law of status content that is quite incompatible with its basic concepts and principles.[15] When these two errors are avoided, it becomes evident that instead of national law being incompatible with either meaningful or effective international law, as Austin and the present elder generation of lawyers and politicians suppose, national law, when its incomplete symbols are analyzed, turns out to rest on an international legal and political principle.[16]

It follows that President Eisenhower was quite right in the Suez crisis when he appealed to international law in asking Israel, France and Great Britain to withdraw and that former Secretary of State Acheson was in error when later he described the international law to which the President appealed as "spurious."

It is, therefore, the present elder generation of lawyers and politicians, Communistic and freedom-loving alike, who, owing to their confusion of abstract nouns with concrete entities, are guilty of pursuing a will-o'-the-wisp when they suppose (a) negatively that there is and can be no such thing as international law and (b) positively that there is such a thing as an absolutely sovereign modern nation. The extent to which these ideas are still in our present statesmen, together with a description of the "hard cases" which mark a break with their thinking, will be described in Chapters 10, 11 and 17.

The success of Western European Union gives contemporary empirical confirmation of the conclusion that international and political legal institutions can be built where none existed before. Who would have dared predict in the midst of World War II that within fifteen years the soldiers of Germany, the Netherlands, Belgium, France, Luxembourg and Italy would be serving with West German soldiers under a German general in a common contractual international legal, political, military and atomic-energy community of these six groups of people? Yet this and much more has happened. British statesmen thought Continental European Union would not work, and counseled their Continental colleagues to be satisfied with merely consultative committees. The *Economist* of London of April 25, 1959, informs us that the main British concern now is lest it has worked too well.[17]

It would be a mistake, however, to conclude that an equally effective international law for the entire world can be achieved merely by drawing up international legal documents similar to those of the Schuman Plan for Coal and Steel, the Brussels Pact army, the Continental European Parliament and its Atomic Pool. Such a facile notion commits the mistake of seeing the problem of international peace as a merely positive legal problem. This is why the world constitution drawn up recently by Grenville Clark and Professor Louis Sohn has made such little impact on practical politicians.[18] It begins at the wrong end with an international positive law before one has taken the time and trouble to determine what the complex and diversified living law of the world is. Any experienced writer of legal prose can produce an international legal constitution; *the problem is to write one with the specific normative content that the living law of the world will support.*

The writer's firsthand study [19] in Europe of Western European Union shows that the political architects of this successful legal and political internationalism faced their problem at the living law level. Also, they had fortunate common differential as well as generic [20] living law factors in the six nations on their side. Their practical success occurred so quickly because they sought out these common differential as well as generic living law factors and built their positive international law and politics upon them.

The living law of the rest of the world is not identical with that of Western Continental Europe. Hence, if world-wide similarly effective international law or free democratic domestic national law is to be achieved, it must be tailor-made and fitted to the specific objectively determinable complex living law of each particular nation and cultural tradition.

For example, the problem of making contractual free democratic legal and political institutions work in Pakistan's India is far different and more difficult than is the case in New Delhi's India. First, the traditional living law of the latter India is quantitatively at least two-thirds Hindu, whereas that of Pakistan is at least 85 per cent Islamic; hence normative content in liberal democratic contractual positive law which draws upon Hindu traditions and symbols that support democracy is not likely to appeal to Muslims, and conversely. Second, New Delhi's India inherited from British India and the Princely States all the big cities. It is the cities that contain the modern-minded people who understand modern contractual, as distinct from ancient tribal and caste, legal and political ideals and institutions and have taken on modern Western ways in their daily living. The consequence is that New Delhi's India has had many leaders in every walk of life with the modern mentality and living experience necessary to give a freely democratic positive legal constitution of the British type a good chance of succeeding. Even so, Minister of Law Ambedkar told the writer in 1950 in New Delhi that they represent less than $3\frac{1}{2}$ per cent of the people. Pakistan, on the other hand, except for a few moderns in Lahore and Karachi, found herself with a living law composed almost entirely of old patriarchal patrician landowners and warring law of status tribal nations. Afghanistan is similar, as are most of the young nations of South Africa. To suppose that politics can be practical without facing such cultural facts is to live and operate in a fool's paradise.

What is true of the effective introduction of modern contractual freely democratic positive legal and political institutions into societies with an incompatible living law is true also of economic or technological aid, as Chapter 11 will show. The instruments of a people cannot be separated from their empirical scientific mentality and their cultural goal values. To send modern economic aid or technological instruments and "know-how" into a medieval community without a knowledge of its living law is to invite failure. This is why those politicians and economic "experts" who tell us that the foreign policy of the United States, for example, will succeed if power politics is soft-pedaled and the emphasis is put on economic and technological aid are, though more constructive in their intentions, as misguided as the power politicians and their colleagues the Divine interventionistic theologians. The political problems of today's world, both domestic and international, center in the mentalities and customs of people and only secondarily and afterwards in their tools—whether those tools be economic, military, technological or eschatological in the sense of the Reverend Reinhold Niebuhr. Since customs are anthropological and sociological, contemporary politics must be also.

As we turn to the practical methods of this approach to politics, certain errors into which one may easily fall are to be kept in mind and avoided. This approach in no way entails pacificism. Even the sleepiest domestic community in either Gandhi's India or Holderness, New Hampshire, has its policemen. Usually also the state militia are not far away. The fact that law and political policies receive both their justice and their effectiveness from the normative content of the living law and the living beliefs and habits of concrete men and women who together, in their individual creative thinking and acting, make that living law what it is, does not entail that physical implementation of both the living and the positive law is either misspent or unnecessary. The point, instead, is that a coordination of the normative content of the living law with that of the positive law and its policemen is necessary if either the positive law or the police-men with adequate physical instruments are to be forthcoming and be effective when positive legal processes authorize their use. Physical power is the product, not the cause, of effective law and politics either domestic or international.

Furthermore, the anthropological and sociological approach to politics forces one to center attention on the norms that define the association of the people in each particular nation or culture. Since the norms of Gandhi are quite different from those of Marx, a given number of military divisions in the hands of a government headed by a Gandhi would mean one thing; whereas that same number of divisions under the command of the head of any Communistic gov-ernment means something quite different. Only objective specific knowledge of the norms of Marxist Communism obtained by a read-ing of the Marxist classics and the successive commentaries upon, and application of, those classics to their own particular living law communities by Lenin, Stalin, Mao and now Khrushchev can enable one to predict what a given Communist leader is most likely to do, or to interpret correctly what his words, smiles and diplomatic ma-neuvers mean practically. In fact, this normative anthropological ap-proach to politics will cause one to take the Communistic physical threat to peace much more seriously [21] than some power politicians do. Therefore, one will be wise to keep one's powder both ample and dry until, by a laborious, but not necessarily lengthy, tapping of the potential resources of its living law, a world morale comes to ex-pression which will sustain an effective international law accom-panied by atomic disarmament.

Nevertheless, the present Communist threat to peace which, in the case of the Soviet Union, as Chapter 15 will show, is likely to persist, does not mean that an international law preserving peace is impos-sible today. Such pessimism overlooks the previously noted fact that in no domestic community where peace under law exists, do 100 per cent of the people believe in or behave according to the norms of the positive law; it is necessary merely that a quantitatively large pro-portion do. The percentage of the earth's nations that are officially Communistic is smaller than that of the free nations. Even more important, the percentage of the earth's inhabitants who are spon-taneous believing and behaving Communists is without question that of a small minority. Hence, notwithstanding the seriousness of the Communists' aims and their large military implementation of these aims, peace under effective international law is practically possible today providing the appropriate political methods for relating new positive law to old living law are used.

To this end, three things suggest themselves as immediately necessary and practical: (1) The freedom-loving people everywhere must recover their legal, political and religious normative idealism by means of an analytically precise and imaginatively captivating statement of what this idealism is. This will concern us in Part III. (2) Those in the non-Communist nations, and their modern-minded leaders, must succeed in their local national attempts at Little Rock, Accra, New Delhi, Karachi, Bangkok, Colombo, London and elsewhere freely to democratize and modernize their respective traditional societies, using methods which Part I will describe and Part II will apply in a preliminary way. In the latter process each nation will automatically provide the objective knowledge of its unique living law and the factors in it which will sustain both democracy and international law. (3) Then by bringing together objective knowledge of these national living law factors, it should be possible to write a positive legal constitution for the world that will specify and command the living law support that is necessary to make itself effective, thereby giving additional content to the basic international legal principle upon which any modern nation rests.

Since (1), (2) and (3) depend on the success of all for the success of any one, all three undertakings can and must go forward simultaneously, being approached from both the local national and the international standpoint. In fact, now that the notion of an absolute national political sovereign is, as noted above, demonstrably a will-o'-the-wisp, the situation is, both in theory and in fact, that there are very few domestic legal and political problems that are not international problems. Nor is there any "determinism of history" or eschatological sinfulness to ensure that such an undertaking will not alter the outlook of some Communistic dictators of the proletariat as well as many traditional chauvinistic or isolationistic "free democratic" political leaders.

But the converse is equally true. There are few international legal and political problems that are not also domestic problems in each and every nation. Certainly an effective international law that is compatible with the normative ordering relations of an association of free people will hardly be possible if the national attempts of freedom-loving statesmen to democratize and modernize their older societies in Free India, Pakistan, Burma, Thailand, Ghana, the United States and elsewhere end in failure. Also it is always wise scientific method to attack the complex problem in the simplest available instance, learning later how to combine the simpler to understand the more complex. Hence, this book will focus attention on the specific differing living laws of particular nations and cultures, the problems which arise and the tailor-made solutions that are necessary to successfully modernize each.

PART ONE

*Political Methods
and Their Basis*

2

The Need for More Objective Political Methods

An approach to anything is no better than its methods. What are the methods of politics?

More than one is required. As shown in the previous chapter, today's political problems call for three things: (1) The determination of the specific normative content of the living law in any particular nation; (2) the effective implanting of a new positive law in an old living law; (3) the evaluation of what in the old living law is to be retained and what discarded in such reform of an old society. Clearly the scientific method for determining the living law in any particular case must be different from the scientific method for evaluating it after it is once determined. The former we shall call the descriptive method; the latter the evaluative method of philosophical anthropology.

It is not being suggested that in this new approach to politics every politician be an expert in these methods. It is reasonable to expect, however, that he know the qualitative living and positive legal norms of his own nation. Chapters 10, 11 and 17 will show that this is far from being the case. Nor is it being suggested that every secretary of state, executive head of government and member of any committee on foreign affairs of the national legislature, or each foreign service, intelligence or military officer be an expert in and carry through the application of these methods to every nation of the world. What this sociologically jurisprudential approach to politics does require, however, is that all these topmost policy makers have experts in these methods constantly at their elbows in the Planning Board of the State Department, the Central Intelligence Office, the Foreign Service Institute, the National Security Council, the War Colleges and also in the Foreign Service College which in the United States, at least, still needs to be created.

It is reasonable also that each foreign service officer, including especially politically appointed amateurs to ambassadorships, become acquainted with the descriptive method for determining and distinguishing the living and the positive law of (a) his or her own nation and (b) at least one foreign nation. Without (a) no diplomat will be able to give the leaders and people of the nation to which he is assigned an image of his own nation in terms of its highest *de facto* living and positive legal, political, aesthetic and religious ideals, rather than in terms merely of its money-making, money-giving, bomb-shaking and foreign-base-demanding protection of those ideals. Briefing in the application of the descriptive method to at least one foreign nation is essential because otherwise (i) the foreign aid and the foreign military bases run great risk of being wasted, as Chapters 12 and 13 will show, and (ii) the foreign service officer will be quite incapable of sending back to his foreign minister or secretary of state politically objective reports on the nation to which he is assigned and on the most likely response of its leaders and people to any policy of his nation.

It is equally important that the latter reports be read and taken into account by the foreign minister or secretary of state when the reports arrive. This is not likely to occur unless these topmost officials and the chief executive are trained in at least the understanding of the descriptive method. This is especially true in nations such as the United States where there is a tradition of appointing as secretaries of state lawyers whose expertness is in the positive law of their own nation, and frequently only in that of the more lucrative corporation law. Why anyone should suppose that such expertness fits one for the quite different kind of skill involved in making political decisions concerning foreign policy is not clear.

With a State Department College, analogous to the War Colleges, and a Planning Board of the State Department composed of scientific experts in the methods of this new approach to politics, any foreign service officer upon a new assignment to a particular foreign nation could be briefed relatively quickly on its major sets of qualitative living law norms and the political parties and personalities representing each, together with their respective domestic and foreign policies and the latest quantitatively statistical support which each qualitative set of living law norms enjoys. The official's descriptive task abroad will then be to (a) use the operationally defined procedure of the descriptive method for following these quantitative shifts and the political changes accompanying them, and (b) report the findings to his own nation, while also (c) objectively and equally descriptively conveying to the nation of his assignment the living and positive ideals of his own nation, keeping them ever in the forefront of what he is doing.

To be sure, able diplomats do this. But often they have had to learn it the hard way over the years by firsthand experience with the different mentalities and cultural customs of other peoples. All too often their recommendations, when cabled daily to the Secretary of State, are ignored because the topmost policy makers are thinking in merely instrumental military, economic, demagogic domestic vote-catching or self-righteously religious or secular "know-how" terms. Even worse is the present all-black or all-white polar thinking which distorts the objective political fact that there are numerous other nations in the world than one's own nation and the Soviet Union and that the overwhelming majority of the earth's inhabitants live outside both of these nations. This polar distortion results in treating the entire very complex international political situation as if it involved merely the military postures of the United States of America and the Soviet Union with all other nations and peoples regarded as mere pawns, as if both they and their great civilizations do not matter. Domestic policy makers with such a mentality and the public opinion which they create will inevitably ignore the recommendations of an able ambassador which, if followed, could have prevented the self-defeating mistakes that later chapters of this book will describe.

What must be avoided by any topmost policy maker or any of his diplomats is the confusion of one's own personal political, religious or secular convictions with those of the living law customs and the positive political ideals of either one's own nation or the nation with which one is negotiating. For example, one's personal religious and political philosophy may be that of the theocratic and aristocratic Protestant Episcopalianism of Sir Robert Filmer or that of the similar Roman Catholic Christian philosophy of St. Thomas, but officially, as an ambassador of the United States of America, one represents the quite different political and religious philosophy of Locke and Jefferson as stated officially in the Declaration of Independence and the Constitution of the United States of America with its separation of church and state, its tolerative religious philosophy, its legally interpreted Bill of Rights and its "mixed theory" of democratic government which later chapters will describe in more detail. Such confusion of one's personal philosophy with one's official political philosophy is not easy to avoid. Many social scientists, as Chapter 1 has indicated, have fallen into this error, thereby confusing the living law as it is with what they personally think it ought to be. This is why the specification of objective methods and the distinction between the objective method for describing and the objective method for evaluating the living law of any nation are so important.

To be sure, each particular person's normative judgment is important and of the essence in any free society. But precisely for this reason it counts only as one in his nation and perhaps not at all in the living law and the positive politics of the nation to which he is officially assigned. Law and politics are concerned with the summations and interplay of private norms. Consequently, if lawyers and politicians are to deal with what their sciences and arts are about, they must have an objective method for determining the politically significant qualitative sets of norms in their quantitative summations. More also is involved to be sure, but it can be effective, as subsequent chapters will show, only if an objective description of the living law and positive political norms of each nation is made first. One cannot evaluate before one has objective knowledge of what one is evaluating.

Aesthetic as well as political considerations confirm this conclusion. In modernizing any medieval or ancient society, one is dealing, for all its shortcomings, with a very precious thing. Even our modern values have their origins in part of the living law of the ancient past. Most of our present religious beliefs and practices are still expressed in terms of ancient and medieval customs and symbols. Much of our painting and literature is similar. As noted in the previous chapter, a contemporary historian of seventeenth century England and its Virginia Company has shown recently that the earliest component of the present living law of the Old South was brought there from early seventeenth century Kent and Essex and expressed the white, aristocratic Christian Englishman's patriarchalism of Sir Robert Filmer and the living beliefs and customs of his predecessors Thomas Hooker and Queen Elizabeth I of which the literature of Shakespeare is the aesthetic expression.[1] Certainly there is something valuable and of high quality to be preserved in this England of Shakespeare, Elizabeth I, Sir Robert Filmer and the newer England of Virginia and the Old South. The great danger in modern political reform is that it pulls people away from their traditional civilized ways which, even though undemocratic, are of high quality, throwing the baby out with the bathwater, while at the same time never giving them a deep understanding of the cultural and philosophical political and religious ideals of the new. The result often is that in the name, but without the normative substance, of democracy and modernity, the best of both worlds is lost and a society results which is composed of individual citizens and politicians who are political chameleons with no deep convictions about anything, and little aesthetic, social or diplomatic good taste whatever. These dangers are very near in Africa, the Middle East and Asia, and much nearer at home, as Chapter 17 will show, than many of us like to believe. Such vulgar mediocrity, if not downright barbarism, can be avoided only if we know deeply and from within the living law of both the old and the new, thereby preserving respect for the quality of the old while reforming it in the light of the norms of equal quality of the new.

What is the objective descriptive method for doing this? In other words, what is the method for determining the living law of any culture or nation? Unfortunately, the sociological jurist Ehrlich left the answer to this question in an unsatisfactory state.[2] Nevertheless, he gave us two clues.

First, not everything with which the anthropologist or the sociologist concerns himself is relevant to the needs of the lawyer and the politician. The reason is that law and politics have to do with the intrinsic norms, or goal values, used by a people to order their relations to one another and to nature. Every political constitution or legislative statute specifies certain normative rules or procedures which serve as a normative measuring rod to distinguish the *de facto* behavior of the people in the nation in question which is permissible or to be encouraged from that which is prohibited and to be penalized. What the lawyer and politician, therefore, need to learn from the social scientist is the independent variable in any society which specifies this normative factor.

Ehrlich's second clue was that this independent variable is never a particular fact in the society in question, such as the physical terrain, the economic instruments, sex, pleasure, climate, hunger, etc.; instead, to use his language, it is the normative "inner order of the associations of human beings." [3] In other words, the normative factor in any nation is not any particular fact or class of facts, but the normative relatedness of all its particular people. It is the normative relatedness of these people, as embodied in their living law customs and articulated in their positive, legally defined political ideals and procedures that is a nation. Hence nations differ from one another as the normative contents of the relatedness of their associations differ from one another.

But how is the specific normative content of this relatedness to be determined? More specifically, what is the theoretically designatable and operationally determinable variable or set of independent variables, such that, when its empirical value or values for any given homogeneous culture are determined, the substantive content of its normative inner order is made determinate? Since a nation is usually a complex of different homogeneous cultures, this independent variable or set of independent variables will take on different values, each defining a qualitative set of norms for each homogeneous component of the complex culture of any nation. The Filmerian and the Jeffersonian components of the living law of the Old South are examples, since the qualitative sets of norms of each are different. The first suggestion of the answer to these questions came from the sociologist Pitirim Sorokin.[4]

Logico-Meaningful Social Causality

Causality is the name of the relation between the states of any system of entities as the system changes the inner order of these entities with time. In the systems of inorganic nature this relation is mechanical. The causality of any system of concrete entities is mechanical if (1) there is an indirectly and experimentally confirmed, deductively formulated and axiomatically constructed set of postulates (purporting to hold for any isolated system of the science in question) and if (2) this set of postulates specifies a very few independent variables, the empirical values of which at any moment of time t^1 (a) define the inner order or state of the system at that time, and then (b) enable one to calculate and predict ahead of time the empirical values the variables of state of the system will have at any specified later time t^2. Newton's mechanics, Einstein's special and general theories of relativity and in a slightly weaker form quantum mechanics are examples of such theories.[5] In Newton's mechanics, which is still valid to a first approximation within certain restrictions specified by relativity theory and quantum mechanics, the variables of state are the positions and the momenta of the masses of the system.

Requirement (1) above is important. It means that mechanical causality exists only for deductively formulated, indirectly confirmed theories of natural science. It means also that the theories of mathematical physics contain two different kinds of concepts which get their scientific meaning in quite different ways. There is the deductively formulated, theoretically postulated type of concept which being imageless has its meaning assigned to it purely formally by being constructed from the non-inductively given concepts of symbolic logic and pure mathematics. To find out what such a concept means it is of no use to look at anything given by the senses or to introspect the images of the imagination; instead, one must examine the formal properties or syntax of the relations or postulates of the specific deductively formulated scientific theory in question. Its theoretically designated scientific objects have only the properties that they derive from being relata in imageless mathematical relations which have the formal properties specified by the postulates of the theory. Concepts designating scientific objects, their properties and laws which are known in this way, the writer has called "concepts by postulation" or, more exactly, since such objects and laws are imageless, "concepts by postulation which are concepts by intellection." [6]

It is now generally recognized by informed mathematical physicists and philosophers of mathematical physics that all the theories of ancient Greek Democritean or Platonic and of modern mathematical physics contain such concepts. Another name for them is "incomplete symbols." [7] They are called "incomplete" because any one of them by itself is meaningless, since their meanings derive entirely from their formal logical or mathematical relation to one another in the postulates of the particular scientific theory in which they occur. Another name for concepts by postulation which are concepts by intellection is "constructs." [8]

The writer has shown recently that Western contractual legal science is constructed also of such concepts.[9] Since any modern nation is a legally contractual nation, we must expect in the sequel that incomplete symbols or concepts by contractual postulation which are concepts by intellection will be very important in contemporary politics.

But the theories of mathematical physics and contractual law and politics also contain complete symbols which get their meaning in the way most social scientists and laymen and most traditional philosophers suppose all concepts get their meaning—namely, by direct, denotative, purely inductive reference to something directly sensed or introspected or immediately experienced. Concepts referring to directly sensed "yellow," to an introspected pain, to any idea in one's mind, or to the directly inspectible operationally given lines on an experimental physicist's photographic plate are examples. Following Einstein's, Continental European and Oriental usage, the writer has called symbols which get their meaning *solely* in this way "concepts by intuition," [10] meaning thereby not concepts whose meaning is given mysteriously or by a hunch, but instead concepts whose complete meaning refers to something directly and denotatively observable or immediately experienceable. A radically empirical epistemology is one which affirms that all concepts are of this kind. The data referred to by concepts by intuition are equivalent to what the mathematical physicist Henry Margenau calls the "data of the P plane" of scientific knowledge.[11]

The significance of scientific concepts of the latter type is that, since they refer to the purely existential and directly observable empirical data, they make it possible, when appropriate relations between their data and that of concepts by postulation are specified ahead of time, to confirm indirectly and operationally the existence of the imageless, unobservable scientific objects and their mathematical laws that are designated by concepts by postulation which are concepts by intellection. Given experimentally confirmed theories of unobservable scientific objects, events and laws, it is then possible to create new technological instruments such as the atomic bomb of which "practical men" alone would never have dreamed, and to the existence of which politicians must adjust themselves. More important, however, for our present purposes is the fact that only scientific theory constructed out of concepts by postulation, which are appropriately related to directly observable data denoted by concepts by intuition, makes it possible to discover systems of concrete scientific objects whose causal changes of state are mechanical in the precise sense defined above.

Common-sense or natural-history scientific knowledge, which restricts itself to concepts by intuition and mere fact finding, has descriptive, but practically no predictive, power. Another advantage of a scientific method and theory which introduces concepts by postulation is the remarkable economy of thought with respect even to descriptive power that results. The mathematical physicist Ernst Mach has defined science as the economy of thought.[12] Only science using concepts by postulation achieves this. The reason is twofold: (1) Such theory defines many properties of its subject matter in terms of the smallest possible number of independent variables. As just noted with respect to Newton's mechanics, all the properties of any mechanical system anywhere in nature, however unique its observable properties may be, are known if merely the positions and momenta of the particular masses are determined empirically. (2) Since concepts by postulation are incomplete symbols, the meaning of any one symbol entails, through the postulates of the theory which define it, the meaning of many other symbols. This results in economy of thought.

With respect to directly observable data described by concepts by intuition, the opposite is the case. First, the number of different sensed facts in any subject matter is limitless. Hence, to describe them completely one needs to possess almost as many different ideas as there are different facts. Furthermore, concepts by intuition are complete symbols. This entails that one can find the meaning of any symbol, without considering its constitutively given theoretical relation to other symbols, solely by locating the observable fact in immediate experience to which it refers. This has the consequence that no symbol gives the meaning of any other symbol, since, as Hume noted, there is no sensed relation of necessary connection between immediately observed data. Such merely descriptive concepts do not provide economy of thought.

It is to be noted, however, that theories constructed of concepts by postulation achieve both their economy of descriptive power and their prodigious predictive power only if the unobservable scientific entities and laws to which they refer are "appropriately related" to the directly observable data denoted by concepts by intuition. What is this relation?

Since the entities which it relates are *known* in different ways and the science which describes knowing is called "epistemology," it is appropriate, in order to distinguish it from the relation of causality between the temporal states of entities known in the same way, to call this relation "epistemic correlation," as the writer first suggested in 1939,[13] or epistemic "rules of correspondence" if one prefers Professor Margenau's language.[14] Either expression is equivalent to what the late Hans Reichenbach called *Zuordnungsdefinition*.[15] The last word is, however, somewhat misleading, since any term in any epistemic correlation is irreducible to or indefinable in terms of its epistemic correlate. The important thing to keep in mind, if Professor Margenau's linguistic usage is preferred, is that these "rules of correspondence" are not causal relations between the temporal states of a system of entities in the same world of discourse, i.e., entities known epistemologically in the same way. Instead, they relate entities in different worlds of discourse, i.e., entities known epistemologically in two different ways. Similarly, the writer does not mean by "epistemic correlations" causal correlations, since the latter correlations apply only to entities in the same world of discourse. This is why it is important to speak either of epistemic correlations or of epistemic rules of correspondence. Otherwise these relations which occur only between entities in epistemologically different worlds of discourse are likely to be confused with causal relations between entities in the same world of discourse.

In this book we shall use the equivalent expressions "epistemic correlations" or "epistemic rules of correspondence" interchangeably. The sequel will show also that the "body-mind problem" is a pseudo-problem which arose because epistemic correlations between entities in epistemologically different worlds of discourse were confused with causal relations between entities in the same epistemological world of discourse.

This is not an easy error to avoid since every word that we use has different epistemological world-of-discourse meanings. For example, the word "yellow" has its immediately sensed, radically empirical epistemological meaning. "Yellow" in this sense is a concept by intuition, i.e., a concept the complete meaning of which is given by something that one can immediately sense, introspect or experience. The word "yellow" is also used to refer to the number of a wave length in the deductively formulated theory of Maxwell's electromagnetics and his electromagnetic equations. "Yellow" in this sense cannot be seen and is a concept by postulation that is a concept by intellection. Clearly "yellow" in these two different senses refers to quite different things and belongs epistemologically to different ways of knowing and hence to different worlds of discourse. The epistemological world of discourse of concepts by intuition has been called traditionally "radical empiricism." The different epistemological world of discourse of concepts by postulation which are concepts by intellection we shall henceforth call "logical realism," the adjective "logical" being used to distinguish this type of realism from the traditional realism which was called "naïve realism."

Realism is the thesis that in knowledge we know an object together with its defining properties and that both are independent of their relation to the observer; in other words we know a public, rather than merely a private, world. Naïve realism affirms that we know such a public self in a public world by direct observation. Logical realism affirms, with radical empiricism, that all directly observable items of knowledge are relative to one's frame of reference, to different observers at rest relatively to one another on the same frame of reference and to different sense organs of the same observer. Consequently, while still affirming realism, it rejects the naïve realist's thesis that either a public self or any other public object in a public world is directly sensed or introspected, affirming instead that it is knowable only by imageless, speculatively introduced concepts by postulation, the correctness of which is confirmable only indirectly and experimentally via recourse to epistemic rules of correspondence with radically empirically given relativistic sensed or introspected data.

Epistemic correlations or epistemic rules of correspondence are, therefore, epistemological relations, i.e., relations between entities in epistemologically different worlds of discourse. In other words, given an entity or a class of many entities denoted by concepts by intuition in the radically empirical epistemological mode of knowing, the epistemic rules of correspondence give its epistemic correlate in the indirectly confirmed, logically realistic mode of knowing, and conversely. To confuse these epistemic relations with causal relations which are meaningful only for entities in the same world of discourse is, therefore, to commit a very serious error. As the sequel will show, the pseudo-body-mind problem arose precisely because of this error. To confuse epistemic rules of correspondence between events or entities in different epistemological worlds of discourse with the predicate of a substance in a single epistemological world of discourse is to commit an equally serious mistake. We shall find that the commission of both of these errors has corrupted most traditional political theory and practice.

This becomes evident when one notes that all of the traditional modern ways of thinking about law and politics arose as the logical consequence of one or another of the traditional modern philosophies that were put forward as "the solution of the mind-body problem." Since this problem is a pseudoproblem, these modern conceptions of law and politics are pseudoconceptions also. For example, the power-political theory of both domestic legal obligation and foreign policy derives from Hobbes' pseudophilosophical answer to the pseudoproblem of the causal relation between body and mind.

A pseudoproblem or a pseudoanswer to a pseudoproblem is one that arises because the different epistemological meanings of "the same word" are not distinguished and thereby kept in their respective worlds of discourse with the result that epistemic correlations are confused with causal relations between entities in the same epistemological world of discourse. When this occurs, nonsense results. Politicians and other people then suppose that the following expressions are meaningful: "Electrons are pink." "Sensed objects are public objects." "Sensed simultaneity of spatially separated events is public simultaneity of spatially separated events." "Ideas are in the brain." "Dialectical logic causally determines the political triumph of the dictatorship of the proletariat." "Political power causally determines normative political decisions." "Economic facts decide political issues." Contemporary political discourse in "the free" as well as the Communist nations is full of such nonsense, as is much present so-called "social science."

It is practically impossible to avoid such nonsense unless two things are kept continuously in mind: First, objects of knowledge in different epistemological worlds of discourse are always related by epistemic correlations or epistemic rules of correspondence; never by the relation of causality or by the relation of a property to a substance. Second, when one reads any word, something equivalent to the writer's distinction between that word in its radically empirically known concept by intuition meaning and that word in its logically realistic epistemologically known concept by postulation meaning is necessary.

Another reason for keeping these epistemological relations and distinctions in mind is that otherwise we shall not understand the McCulloch and Pitts theory of "trapped universals" which is one basis for prescribing the descriptive method for politics which we are seeking. An additional reason is that without imageless concepts by postulation, the concept of mechanical causality cannot be distinguished from merely repetitive, directly observed temporal sequences, and, unless mechanical causality is correctly understood, the unique character of the causality of social and political systems will not be recognized.

Viewed from the standpoint of inorganic natural science, the concrete entity of any legal and political system is a particular human being, each with his or her proper name. As a merely bodily human being, each political person instances a concrete mass of Newton's physics. When, in Newton's mechanics, the positions and momenta of the concrete masses of any inorganic system are empirically determined at any given moment of time, the inner order or state of that system of concrete entities is specified. Moreover, because the causality is mechanical, their future inner order can be predicted provided during the interval external forces acting on the system are negligible. A theory of domestic legal obligation and a foreign policy based on normatively neutral, merely physical power considerations would be appropriate and valid were such the case for political persons and political systems. In fact, this is precisely what Hobbes, the first modern author of the power-political theory of legal obligation and of a just political sovereign assumed in his *Leviathan* when he wrote (italics mine):

> Liberty, or Freedom, signifieth, properly, the absence of opposition; by opposition, I mean external impediments of motion; *and may be applied no less to irrational, and inanimate creatures, than to rational.*[16]

Clearly, this confuses freedom in the concept by postulation realistic epistemological sense of a mass in public space-time moving according to Newton's first law of motion when that mass is not acted on by an external force, with the quite different meaning of the freedom of a "rational creature," i.e., a person in the concept by intuition meaning of the word "person" who introspects himself as freely assenting to a legal or political goal value principle to which he commits himself.

Moreover, empirically it simply is not the case that the mere specification of the momenta and positions of the living human bodies of any nation, considered merely as Galilean or Newtonian masses, is either a necessary or a sufficient condition for making determinate the normative political inner order of the associations of the people in that nation. The determination of the common introspected meanings that a statistically large proportion of any nation's people share is also essential. Hence, as Sorokin realized, the causality of political and other sociocultural systems is logico-meaningful rather than non-teleologically mechanical.

An example confirms this conclusion. For centuries in many village communities of British India before partition, Muslims and Hindus lived together. Most of the followers of Islam are converts from Hinduism; hence racially the two religious groups are, for the most part, identical. This means that the cultural differences which were so great as to break British India into the two nations, Pakistan and Free India, and to cause migration in large numbers from one nation to the other, are not to be explained by merely physical and racial considerations. The earlier differences in the momenta and positions

of the bodies of the Muslims and Hindus of the same village hardly
account for the differences in their later political behavior. If one
watched both groups walking down the village road in the prior nation that was British India, there might be slight variations in their
momenta, but hardly in amounts sufficient to account for the differences in their eating habits, religious practices, marriage customs and
later political incompatibilities. In fact one would suspect that where
variations in the velocities of Muslims and Hindus occurred, the
variations would be the effect rather than the cause of their cultural
and political differences. Clearly the cultural inner ordering relations
are not given after the manner in which the ordering relations of
non-teleologically mechanical inorganic systems are given.

An empirical consideration, previously noted, confirms this conclusion. As Ehrlich made clear and cultural anthropologists agree,[17]
the inner order of the concrete entities of any sociocultural system is
always normative in content; it prescribes an *ought-to-be*, it is never
a merely factual "is." The two independent variables "position" and
"momentum" which suffice to determine the inner order of the concrete entities of any inorganic system are non-normative, hence they
are quite incapable of describing an inner order which is normative.
For the latter type of system of concrete entities, ideas, ideals and
hence meanings are essential.

This is precisely the point of Sorokin's discovery that the causality
of human social systems is logico-meaningful. It amounts to the
thesis that the key variable, unique to social systems, is to be found
in the set of meanings that the concrete human beings making up any
society or culture hold in common and use to describe, order and
coordinate the raw data of their experience and to direct their motor
behavior normatively. It is because shared meanings are the independent variables defining the inner order or state of any human
social or political system that the relation governing the temporal
changes of state in such systems is appropriately called "logico-
meaningful causality."

Such causality entails that wherever there are two different homogeneous simple cultures or two different components of a complex culture or nation the people in these two cultural components or nations
are using, often quite unconsciously except in the case of the Founding Fathers, different sets of basic meanings or concepts to describe,

order and anticipate the facts of their experience. The Hindus in the British Indian villages, who knew little or nothing of the norms or habits of a free democratic contractual legal and political system, were using, or unconsciously behaving according to the meanings of Hindu philosophy and law; the Muslims, those of Islam. The British Raj, by applying Hindu positive law for the Hindu community and Muslim positive law for the Muslims, prevented the conflicting meanings from generating the bloody holy war that ensued the moment the British withdrew. Similarly the Soviet Russians are using the philosophical meanings of Marx as interpreted by Lenin, Stalin and more recently by Premier Khrushchev. Even the latter's article in *Foreign Affairs*,[18] which purported to separate "the relation of nations" from "ideological considerations," was in fact a description of the present international political situation and his conditions for avoiding an atomic war over peaceful Berlin, in the Marxist ideological terms of a polar issue between himself as the leader of the class of the proletariat and the American businessmen as the class of the bourgeoisie, with "the laws of history" giving Premier Khrushchev the political victory in the end.

The falsity of such a description of today's "political reality" becomes evident when one notes the following things. First, all other peoples, nations and cultures of the world except the United States and the Soviet Union are ignored (in typical power-political fashion) as if they do not exist or matter if they do exist. Second, there are countless ways of assigning the people of the world to different political groups, other than that of dividing them by thesis-antithesis polar thinking into the class of the workers led by the self-appointed leaders of the Communist party and the class of the American businessmen. Again it is as if all other classes of people do not exist or do not matter if they do exist. As a description of the present political situation of the entire world which purports to be realistic, isn't this a bit fanciful?

Certainly, none of the nations of the world are composed of people who fall politically into classes in this manner. The hundreds upon hundreds of millions of people in the law of status tribal nations and the patriarchal joint families of Africa, the Middle East and Asia know next to nothing of modern Western contractual legal and political nations, without which there is no industrial society either "capitalistic" or Communistic. Nevertheless these millions of people represent a majority of both the people and the nations in the world today. They are ignorant also of "the laws of history"; an ignorance perhaps for which they are to be congratulated. Similarly, Western European Union simply would not be, nor would it have succeeded politically as it has, if even the modern Western world's politics were what Mr. Khrushchev would have us believe. In fact, is not Western European Union the key to why peaceful Berlin, of a sudden, became in Mr. Khrushchev's mind such a threat to "the peace of the world"? The political realities in Western Continental Europe where common cultural and political norms, other than those of Communism, have made possible an effective Continental European international political, economic, military and atomic-pool community simply are not obeying Mr. Khrushchev's neat little antithesis between the American businessmen and himself as the self-appointed representative of the workers. In other words, the political facts are, to use a more concrete metaphor, thumbing their nose at "the laws of history."

Do not these considerations indicate another immediate political need? Napoleon once remarked that an able general never allows his opponent to pick the battlefield on which the decisive battle is to be fought. If this be true, then has not the time come for the free world's statesmen to stop agreeing to attend Summit Conferences in which the political facts of today's world and the issue of peace or war in an atomic age are stated in Mr. Khrushchev's objectively false political terms? Positively stated, isn't a new kind of political leader required in the free nations, who bases his political decisions on a more objectively determined description of the living law political realities of all the peoples, cultures and nations of the world? Such a leader should be able to devise an international political policy that will take the initiative with respect to peace away from the Communists by calling for Summit Conferences or, preferably, conferences in the United Nations which, because they have taken the living law loyalties of the majority of mankind into account, will have at least a three-to-one chance of political success.

In any event, the sociologist Sorokin is correct. In social systems, meanings do matter. Even Premier Khrushchev's Marxist unanalyzed abstract nouns determine "the facts" he picks out as politically important, the interpretation he puts on these facts and the political

policies which he proposes for dealing with them. It follows, therefore, if we are to be objective in our political descriptive judgments
of any nation or its political leaders that we must determine the set
of meanings that give the legal and political norms of that particular
nation their specific content and from the standpoint of which that
nation's representative politicians will make not merely their evaluative but also their descriptive political judgments.

The name for the subject which analyzes the subject matter of
any science to find its elementary meanings or concepts in terms of
which the facts of that subject matter are conceived or defined is
philosophy. Hence, any practical politician who would possess objective knowledge of the positive or living law of any nation must use
the descriptive method not merely of anthropology but of philosophical anthropology. At this point the findings of the anthropologist
Clyde Kluckhohn are most relevant.

The Philosophical Anthropology of the Navaho Indians

This American Indian tribal nation has no written literature. Even
so Professor Kluckhohn found that he did not understand what he
saw them doing until he teased out of them the way they, rather than
he, thought about what they were doing. When he did this he discovered that he was confronted with a unique, logically consistent
and very complex philosophy referring not merely to their normative
beliefs about how to order their political relations to one another, but
also to natural phenomena.[19] They have even a different way of
thinking about causality with respect to natural phenomena than
is used by their neighboring Americans.

This is but Sorokin's point proved over again in the science of
anthropology. Even a so-called primitive and very matter-of-fact
people order their relations to one another in terms of a specific set
of shared meanings, i.e., their particular philosophy. Moreover,
Kluckhohn was able to articulate the positive legal norms of the
Navaho and found them to be related essentially to their cognitive
natural philosophy.

He reconfirmed also that for most of the people their philosophy
is not consciously known, exactly as in the United States most people
are unaware of the fundamental role which the religious and political

philosophy of John Locke and Thomas Jefferson with its separation of church and state and its mixed theory of democratic legal and political government plays in their value judgments concerning political events both domestic and foreign. The fact, therefore, that most people think they have no philosophy and that they live "with their feet on the ground," concerned only with "facts," is no evidence whatever that this is the case. In fact, the only difference between a philosopher and anyone else is that the philosopher attempts to become conscious about what his philosophy is, getting it out into the open, comparing it with alternative theories and testing it with empirical evidence with respect to both its logical consistency and its compatibility.

Unless one is philosophical, one is likely, therefore, to be a mere puppet or loudspeaker for winds of doctrine and moods or passions of the moment; and, strictly speaking, one is not a free and creative human being, even though the living customs and positive political norms of one's nation as conceived by the consciously creative Founding Fathers be those of freedom. The anthropologists Kluckhohn and Kroeber have expressed the fact that for most people the norms of their nation or culture are not consciously evident to them by the distinction between those norms of any culture which are "covert" and those which are "overt." The Freudian distinction between the unconscious and the conscious self instances the same fact, even though Freud had little conception of the diversity and complexity of the substantive ideological content of the unconscious or covert self. In any person or nation, therefore, an implicit or explicit philosophy is present. Hence accompanying the sociological scientist Gregory Bateson's statement, "The human individual . . . constantly imposes on this environment his own constructions and meanings; these constructions and meanings are characteristic of one culture as opposed to another," [20] the anthropologist Kluckhohn writes: "Every people has its characteristic set of 'primitive postulates,'" [21] where by "primitive" is meant their shared assumed propositions from which other propositions in their belief system are deduced or interpreted and evaluated.

In identifying the independent variable which, when its empirical content is determined, defines the living law of a given culture or nation as a set of postulates, one caution is to be noted. This does not mean that the philosophy of every culture is one containing concepts by postulation in the technical sense defined a few pages earlier. Such will be the case only for those cultures which in their natural science or law have discovered and use concepts by postulation that are imageless concepts by intellection. Hence, in speaking of any culture as possessing its unique set of elementary assumptions or postulates, the question is left open as to the type or types of concepts which are present.

Failure to keep in mind this distinction between "postulate set in the generic sense" of any set of assumptions whatever regardless of the type of concept used and "postulate set in the specific sense" of a particular set of postulates which in whole or part contain concepts by postulation which are concepts by intellection has caused many people to misunderstand the thesis of the writer's *The Meeting of East and West* [22] with respect to the difference between classical Oriental and Occidental science and philosophy. The thesis is not that the Oriental does not have a postulate set defining very elaborate, even mathematically scientific and philosophical theories. Of course they do, just as do the Navaho Indians, since every society does. The thesis instead is that all cultures containing or influenced by Democritean, Platonic or modern science and philosophy and Stoic Roman contractual law think in terms of concepts by postulation which are concepts by intellection; whereas the elaborate scientific, philosophical, legal and political theories of classically Oriental peoples and nations contain only the concepts by intuition of either a radically empirical or a naïvely realistic set of shared meanings. We shall find in later chapters that the recognition of this distinction is one of the major keys to the effective introduction of Stoic Roman and modern Western contractual free legal and political institutions and modern mathematically defined technology into non-modern African, Middle Eastern and Asian societies or any medieval-minded Western society.

That the Communists recognized this is shown by the tremendous emphasis which they place, from the beginning to the end of their educational system, on imageless mathematical thinking. Covertly at least, they appreciate the importance of concepts by postulation that are imageless concepts by intellection for industrial and military engineering. Like non-Communist political leaders, however, they have failed to appreciate the equal importance of such concepts in the Western contractual legal science by means of which all modern political nations, whether free democratic or Communistic, are built. When this failure is avoided, present Communistic and non-Communistic politicians will realize that many of their present political notions and policies arise from semantic nonsense, due to their error of confusing the word "nation" in its concept by intuition or naïve realistic epistemological meaning with the word "nation" in its concept by postulation Stoic Roman and modern law of contract meaning. For the legal content of these two quite different meanings of the word "nation" and some political implications for both domestic and international law, the reader is referred to the last chapter of the writer's *The Complexity of Legal and Ethical Experience.*

But how can philosophy and especially concept by postulation, imageless mathematical or contractual legal philosophy have such practical technological and political significance? Is not the behavioristic motor response to physical stimuli the determining factor in both human behavior and politics, with meanings, and especially philosophical meanings, a mere "epiphenomenon" or "rationalization of no importance after the fact"? In other words, does not power politics determine what the politically significant philosophical meanings are? At this point certain recent discoveries concerning events in and the neural connections of any human nervous system take on considerable political as well as psychological importance.

3

The Neurological Epistemic Correlates of Introspected Ideas

Two recent scientific developments have necessitated a revision of the traditional modern conception of the relation between introspectively known ideas and human behavior in the public world of mathematically designated, indirectly verified space-time. These two developments are: (1) Dr. Warren S. McCulloch and Walter Pitts' indirectly confirmed theory of neurologically "trapped universals." (2) Arturo Rosenblueth, Norbert Wiener and Julian Bigelow's distinction between non-teleological and teleological mechanisms, together with the demonstration that all human nervous systems are mechanisms of the latter type.

If the import of these discoveries is to be appreciated, two historical facts must be kept in mind. First, they passed through the most exacting analyses by experimental and theoretical natural and social scientists from a score of different sciences over a period of some fifteen years in a series of annual conferences called by Dr. Frank Fremont-Smith of the Josiah Macy, Jr. Foundation and presided over by Dr. McCulloch. Second, before McCulloch coined the expression "trapped universals," he was well aware, as the sequel will show, of three things: (i) The writer's distinction, described in the previous chapter, between any word in its concept by intuition radically empirical epistemological meaning and that same word in its imageless, formally constructed concept by postulation logically realistic epistemological meaning. (ii) The relation between what is denoted by the concept by intuition meaning of any word and what is desig-

42

nated by its concept by postulation meaning is not that of the predicate of a substance or that of causal interaction. Instead it is that of epistemic correlation, or what the mathematical physicist Margenau called "rules of correspondence." (iii) The writer's application of (i) and (ii) to the clarification of the relation between (a) the concept by intuition words and data of introspective and psychoanalytic psychology and (b) the required concept by postulation theory and data of neurological and behavioristic psychology. This application was presented to the Symposium on Mind and Body of the Association for Research in Nervous and Mental Disease at its meeting in New York City in 1938.[1]

It was McCulloch's recognition that any scientifically clear theory of the public person must be an imageless, formally constructed concept by postulation that is a concept by intellection, which caused him to collaborate with the symbolic logician Walter Pitts in the statement of their theory of "trapped universals."[2] McCulloch's contribution consisted in discovering the theory and bringing forth evidence from experimental neural physiology in its support.

Similarly, it was McCulloch's acceptance of directly known, radical empiricism in epistemic correlation with indirectly confirmed logical realism as the epistemology required to distinguish and correctly relate the different types of concepts of the experimentally verified theories of both common-sense knowledge and mathematical physics which made him aware from the outset that his and Pitts' expression "trapped universals" is elliptical. In other words, it is a shorthand for a much more complex expression. Unless the reader keeps this continuously in mind, he will be guilty of falling into mixed epistemological worlds-of-discourse nonsense in his interpretation of what follows.

That such is the case becomes evident when one notes that, if taken literally as non-elliptical, the expression "trapped universals" is nonsensical. As will be shown in a moment, the word "trapped" refers to a physical impulse which is passed continuously around a circle of nerve cells in the public space-time of the logically realistic epistemological world of discourse of neural physiology and mathematical natural science. The word "universal," on the other hand, refers to a species of conceptual meaning in the radically empirical world of discourse of introspective psychology. Consequently, to use the epistemological language of the previous chapter, the concept "universal," regardless of its content, refers to an idea or meaning the content of which (though not the truth or falsity) is introspected, and hence is a concept by intuition, whereas the concept "trapped" refers to an unobservable, theoretically designated entity in the indirectly confirmed public world of natural science and is, therefore, a concept by postulation which is a concept by intellection. Whenever a concept by postulation referring to the public world of discourse is predicated of an entity denoted by a concept by intuition in the directly sensed or introspected radically empirical world of discourse, or conversely, nonsense results. Examples, in addition to those given in the previous chapter, are "Physical power causes legal obligation," "That electromagnetic wave is yellow," "Photons are particle-like," "Meanings are spatially extended," "Facts are true" and "The idea of a universal is in the brain." As McCulloch was well aware from the beginning, the expression "trapped universals" would be similarly nonsensical were it not an elliptical shorthand symbol for a much more epistemologically complex expression. To understand what this complex expression is, it will be wise for us to begin with the empirical considerations in introspective and behavioristic psychology and in neural physiology which led McCulloch and others to the theory of trapped universals.

He began his postgraduate work in the eclecticism of the traditional introspective, behavioristic and analytic psychology and turned later to medicine to specialize in experimental research on the neuronic firings of the motor area of the cortex under electrical stimulation and pickup with implanted electrodes. He came to realize early, as did von Neumann in the building of calculating machines, that were the relation between in-put stimulus and out-put behavioristic motor response in the human nervous system merely the mechanical linear transmission of the stimulating cause to the motor effect, there would be no such thing as "memory" in either a human being or a calculating machine. Neither could possess or recall the data fed into it inductively as stimulus or "information." Nor could any person or calculating machine be "programmed" to deduce consequences, i.e., calculate in a specified way from the "information" fed into it.

Since it is an indubitable fact of introspective and psychoanalytic psychology that people do remember and forget, and recall in many cases what they have temporarily forgotten, McCulloch's task as a neurological psychologist became that of discovering and confirming a speculatively introduced theory of the concept by postulation neurophysiological epistemic correlates of remembered ideas. This discovery involved also the specification of epistemic correlations or "rules of correspondence" which epistemically related a particular idea in the concept by intuition meaning of radically empirical introspective and psychoanalytic psychology to its epistemic correlate in the logically realistic public self world of discourse of neurological and behavioristic psychology and of mathematical physics and physiology generally.

We can most easily understand the McCulloch-Pitts theory of trapped universals if we approach it by way of the route which McCulloch actually traveled in its discovery. As a student who took considerable philosophy as well as psychology, mathematics and mathematical physics in Yale College, the young McCulloch became intimately acquainted with the major systems of modern epistemology, psychology and philosophy. Upon receiving his B.A. he pursued graduate studies in psychology. There he encountered the eclecticism of the psychology of that time, an eclecticism composed of introspective, psychoanalytic and behavioristic components all of them tending to fight one another. This eclecticism convinced him that one should not pursue psychology further without obtaining the most thoroughgoing knowledge of the human nervous system and its brain. He noted, as did Norbert Wiener, that what behavioristic psychology did was to treat the human body as a box, the internal contents of which in its brain were disregarded or assumed to remain a constant. Then the behavioristic psychologist attempts to find laws connecting a stimulus introduced on the sensory neuronic side of this box to the box's motor neuronic response on its other side. This was thoroughly scientific as far as it went. It seemed unreasonable, however, to suppose that any adequate or complete theory of the public self could be obtained without also looking inside the box to learn what were the entities, neural connections and events that occurred there.

Consequently, McCulloch decided to enter medical school where he received his M.D. at the College of Physicians and Surgeons. Even then he did not believe that he had even the beginnings of enough knowledge to construct a neurological and behavioristic psychological theory of the public self. He decided, therefore, to do two things: (1) acquaint himself with neurological disorders by pursuing a neurological internship in residency in Bellevue Hospital and (2) when this was completed get the tools for the theoretical concept by postulation side of his problem by studying mathematical physics at New York University. When these two things were accomplished, he then went to Rockland State Hospital for two years to acquaint himself, as one of the hospital's physicians, with the more extreme forms of neurological and mental disorders. There he found himself associated with one of the outstanding diagnosticians of schizophrenia, Dr. Eilhard von Domarus, who took his M.D. in Germany and who had written a thesis under the direction of the writer on "The Logical Structure of the Mind" for which he received the Ph.D. in Philosophy at Yale University in 1930. From von Domarus McCulloch became acquainted for the first time with the writer's epistemological theory of radical empiricism in epistemic correlation with logical realism which was described in the previous chapter.

With all these symbolic logical, mathematically theoretical, neurologically clinical and epistemological distinctions and materials in hand, McCulloch then localized his problem in research work, concentrating on experimental study of the relation between neuronic firings in the cortical neurons and in the motor areas of any animal's cortex. To this end he shifted to the Yale Medical School, carrying on his research in the laboratory of the Dutch neurologist, Dusser de Barenne, who had been trained under Rudolf Magnus who was famous for his work on the "physiological *a priori*," i.e., the theory that the person does not come as a Lockean blank tablet to the data given to him by his senses, but instead brings a certain relational structure within his nervous system to the interpretation which he puts on the sensuous data. The analogy with the epistemology of Kant's *Critique of Pure Reason* is obvious and was not overlooked by Dusser de Barenne. It was while carrying on his experiments that McCulloch, together with Clark Hull, H. S. Burr, Mark A. May, John Dollard, Leonard Doob, Henry Margenau and Frederic B. Fitch, decided to launch a research scientist's seminar in the analysis of the theories and methods of mathematical physics which they asked the writer to guide. It was in this period that McCulloch came again upon the writer's theory of epistemic correlations for escaping the pseudo-body-mind problem and bringing the data of neurological behavioristic, introspective and psychoanalytic psychology into an epistemologically meaningful relation to one another. This also is the reason why, when Doctors Fremont-Smith and McCulloch organized the later Macy Foundation conferences,[3] the writer was made a continuous member from the outset.

One evening at a meeting of this Yale scientific research group, the symbolic logician, Frederic B. Fitch, gave a descriptive report of the primitive concepts and postulates of the theory of deduction and mathematical calculation in Whitehead and Russell's *Principia Mathematica*. McCulloch read the latter treatise before he was graduated from Yale College in 1921. He also was introduced, while an undergraduate, to the imageless constructs of Einstein's theory of relativity during this period by the Yale physical chemist Professor Boltwood. McCulloch also began, as early as 1923, to envisage the ordering of nerve cells and the neural firings in any animal's cortex as ordered in ways that possess the logical and mathematical formal properties of the primitive logical relations of *Principia Mathematica*. If so, the neurological reason becomes evident why human beings can carry through calculations and logical deductions when their brains are healthy and cannot do so if the neural connections in those brains are destroyed by cancer, a lesion or from any other cause. Immediately, therefore, upon the presentation by Fitch to the Yale research group in the 1930's, McCulloch urged Fitch to work on the symbolic logical formulation of neural nets and attended advanced lectures by Fitch on certain logical operators. McCulloch learned also from Fitch how to think with formal logical rigor about discontinuous and continuous processes. Only later did Fitch carry through McCulloch's suggestion.[4] Hence the earliest formulation of the formal logical structure of neural nets was by McCulloch and Pitts. Meantime, McCulloch intensified his thinking of the firings which he induced or picked up with electrodes in the cortex of a monkey or cat from the standpoint of the formal proper-

ties of the logical relatedness of these events and the logical relatedness of the neural nets within which the experimentally confirmable
events occurred.

Note what he now had. An epistemic rule of correspondence exists
between the introspected primitive ideas and postulates of symbolic
logic, Boolean algebra or *Principia Mathematica* and the logical relatedness of nerve cells and events in the human nervous system and
especially in its cortex. The unique character of this particular
correspondence will concern us in Chapter 7.

One key problem, however, remained unsolved. The concept by
postulation theory, with its epistemic rules of correspondence, provided no neurological and physiological epistemic correlate for
consciously introspected memory. What is this correlate? If it can be
found, then calculating machines built with mechanical units and
their events that are related by a relation with the same formal
properties as that of this neurological factor in human nervous systems will have the capacity to retain the information fed into them.
In short, it will be possible, to use von Neumann's language, to build
"memories" into calculating machines. It is such considerations that
brought together experimental neurologists and the designers of
calculating machines in the Macy conferences, as von Neumann's
posthumous book *The Computer and the Brain* confirms.

The clue, as far as McCulloch and the psychoanalytic psychiatrist
Dr. Lawrence Kubie were concerned, came when they noted that the
Spanish experimental neurologist, Lorente de Nó, who is now in the
medical institute of the Rockefeller Foundation in New York City,
gave anatomical experimental reasons for believing that the nerve
cells in cortical neural nets are ordered in circles as well as through-
ways. It was McCulloch's and Pitts' genius to have realized that this
neural possibility permitted one to have the neural physiological
public epistemic correlate of a privately introspected and remembered idea.

To see why this is the case, let us examine the previous theory of
the ordering of sensory, cortical and motor neurons in any nervous
system, whether it be that of lower animals or of human beings. This
theory was that its nerve cells, i.e., neurons, were ordered linearly
from the sensory neuron through the cortical neurons to the motor
neuron after the manner of the abbreviated model of Diagram I:

DIAGRAM I

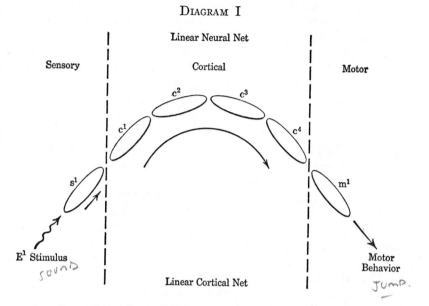

Linear Neural Net

Sensory

Cortical

Motor

c^2 c^3

c^1 c^4

s^1 m^1

E^1 Stimulus

sound

Motor
Behavior

JUMP.

Linear Cortical Net

Were this the case, McCulloch, Kubie and von Neumann among others noted that no human nervous system or mechanically equivalent calculating machine could retain the data fed in by the sensory neurons as "information." In the concept by intuition language of introspective psychology, memory would be impossible.

The reason has to do with the explosions or firings of nerve cells under stimulation. Any nerve cell when stimulated usually fires on the all-or-none principle. In other words it behaves discontinuously and hence digitally. If the stimulation is not sufficient to fire it completely, it fires not at all. And if the stimulation is sufficient to fire it at all, it fires completely. Formally this means that the nerve cells have the property of a two-valued logic.[5] Also, any nerve cell has what is called its *refractory phase*. This is the definite amount of time it takes after it has been stimulated to fire the first time, before continuous stimulation will fire it a second time. The reason for this measurable temporal delay is that in order for any nerve cell to fire it must contain stored potential energy. Its explosion uses up this energy. Hence, the nerve cell cannot fire again until the metabolic *energy to free nerve cells*

processes of the body have restored its potential energy. The length of time of this refractory phase is a definite measurable finite interval of about one millisecond. Let us call it n^r.

With this in mind, turn back to the linearly ordered neural net represented by Diagram I. Assume a single event E^1 which is an explosion in the public neighborhood of one's body and that this physical event in public mathematical space-time emits sound waves which mechanically cause the sensory auditory neuron s^1 from one's ear to one's brain, to fire releasing its potential energy. Assume also, as can be shown neurologically to be the case with electrode pickups, that the firing of the sensory neuron s^1 mechanically causes the cortical neuron c^1 to fire, which in turn causes sequentially firings of cortical neurons c^2, c^3 and c^4 whose firing in turn causes the motor neuron m^1 to fire. The firing of m^1 causes one's muscles to contract quickly and in one's epistemically correlated concept by intuition experience one immediately apprehends a loud noise, a sense of fear and that one has jumped.

After the number of milliseconds n^r have elapsed, following upon the firing of the motor nerve cell m^1, all the nerve cells in the entire neural net will have their energy completely restored. The entire neural net will be, therefore, exactly as it was before the explosion occurred. Hence, there will be no trace of the fact of the past explosion persisting in the nervous system. Such a nervous system, or a calculating machine built similarly, could, therefore, have nothing in it to represent any past stimulus or any past information fed into it. In short, it would have no neural physiological or mechanical epistemic correlate of one's directly inspected memory of the past explosion. For such a nervous system or calculating machine, the fact of memory or of retaining its previously received information would have to be brushed aside as an "epiphenomenon."

It follows, therefore, that if the introspected fact of memory is not to be dismissed as an epiphenomenon or if calculating machines are to retain the information "fed into them" at least long enough to carry through calculations on this information, both they and human nervous systems must have some of their mechanical units or their nerve cells ordered in loops, circles or reentrant paths. Even so, how is a neurophysiological epistemic correlate of a persisting and remembered idea possible?

R. Lorente de Nó's evidence for believing that cortical nerve cells in a nervous system may be ordered in a circle gave McCulloch and Kubie an answer. To see why, another experimentally verified neurological fact must be noted and then related to the neural net portrayed in Diagram II (page 52).

This additional neurological fact is that if any nerve cell's firing causes a neighboring nerve cell in its neural net to fire, a definite measurable lapse of time occurs between the first nerve cell's firing and its neighbor's firing. This is the amount of time, so to speak, that it takes the firing of one neuron to jump the gap between it and its neighbor and thereby cause the neighbor to fire. The name for this gap between any two neighboring nerve cells in the same neural net is "synapse." Hence this measurable finite amount of time is called the "synaptic time." It also is a definite finite interval of about a millisecond. Let us call this number of milliseconds n^s.

Consider now the neural net in Diagram II. Let us assume that the actual event E^1 is the same explosion we described in connection with Diagram I and that the sensory and motor neurons s^1 and m^1 and the cortical neurons c^1, c^2, c^3 and c^4 are identical with those in Diagram I. Then, as before, the actual explosion will set in causal sequence a chain of events beginning with the explosion of sensory nerve cell s^1 and ending with the later firing of motor nerve cell m^1. Upon the lapse of n^r milliseconds of time following the final firing of the motor neuron m^1, the entire neural net composed only of s^1, c^1, c^2, c^3 and c^4 and m^1 will be exactly as before. No persisting trace of the effect of the past explosion will remain.

It was because Bergson assumed that a publicly meaningful neurological epistemic correlate of introspected memory is impossible to find that he relapsed into his purely intuitive philosophy which accounted for impressionistic art and the introspected private flow of time which he confused with public time and called "durée," but which left no meaning for public space and time, the public events and objects in it or a public self, all of which he called "falsifications of fact" or the "misuse of mind." That fact in part is intuitively known will be shown in Chapters 14 and 19; but that it is also much more than Bergson's or any other intuitive existential philosophy permits it to be, the following considerations indicate. For there is a publicly meaningful, theoretically designated and experimentally confirmed neurophysiological epistemic correlate of the introspected memory of a particular introspected meaning or idea. This becomes evident when one considers the following diagram:

Diagram II

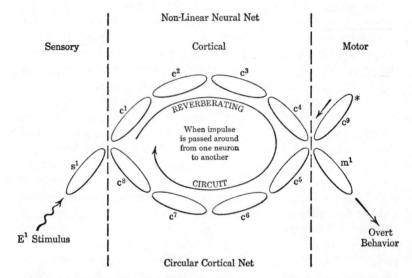

* This addition of c^9 expresses the fact that motor neuron m^1 will not fire unless c^4 and c^9 fire simultaneously. Otherwise motor neuron m^1 would fire (and in case of event E^1 being the aforementioned explosion, the person would jump) every time the impulse traverses the circle to fire c^4.

The presence of cortical neurons c^5, c^6, c^7, and c^8 circularly ordered with respect to c^1, c^2, c^3 and c^4 throws an entirely different complexion on the situation, for the firing of c^4 will fire c^5, as well as m^1 and c^5's firing will explode c^6 which in turn causes c^7 and c^8 to fire. Note that there are eight synaptic gaps between the eight circularly arranged cortical neurons. This means that between the time when c^1 fires and the time when c^8 fires at least seven units of synaptic time, $7n^s$ will have elapsed. But the sum of seven units of synaptic time is much longer than one unit n^r of refractory phase time. Hence, by the time c^8 fires, its neighbor c^1 will have its energy completely restored. Consequently the firing of c^8 will cause a second firing of c^1. But by this time c^2 will have its energy restored, so the firing of c^1 will fire c^2, and so on continuously for all the other cells. In short, for the lifetime of the organism, as long as the metabolic processes of the body restore the energy of any nerve cell in the re-fractory phase amount of time n^r, the impulse will be passed around the circuit. It is the temporal figure of such impulses that McCulloch called a "trapped impulse." A circle of cortical neurons containing such a persisting trapped figure of impulses, neurologists called a "reverberating circuit." This trapped form of impulses persisting in the nervous system and representing uniquely the persisting effect of the past explosion is assumed to be the epistemic correlate in the public self of the directly introspected idea, the awareness of which today we call "the memory of yesterday's immediately heard ex-plosion."

As von Neumann states in his *The Computer and the Brain,* one way of bringing memory into calculating machines is by ordering in circles the mechanical units that fire on the all-or-none principle and then trapping in one of the circuits an impulse which is the unique persisting causal effect of one of the bits of information that is fed into the calculating machine.[6] There are other ways of preserving the unique persisting representatives of past events or bits of informa-tion in calculating machines. Undoubtedly the brain uses these and additional ways also. Otherwise the brain would have to be larger than it is. Dr. Ralph Gerard has also given experimental evidence which suggests that the brains of animals must contain persisting representatives of past stimuli other than trapped impulses in re-verberating circuits.[7] Upon one fact all builders of calculating ma-chines and students of the nervous system are, however, agreed. A neural net of sequentially firing nerve cells as simple as that of a reverberating circuit does have the formal properties necessary to be the epistemic neurophysiological correlate of the introspected mem-ory of a particular meaning or idea. The reiterative procedure of such a circle of neurons accounts for *the primary recognition* of objects immediately on presentation of the image which was noted by Whitehead in his *Principles of Natural Knowledge.*

The formal equivalence, let it be noted, is the important fact. The reason is that in any concept by postulation theory of any kind, whether it be of scientific objects other than the public self or of one's

public nervous system, what we know, as Bertrand Russell has emphasized, is a relatedness with certain formal properties. Thus he writes: "Mathematical logic is used in creating structures . . . [and] theoretical physics . . . lays down fundamental equations which enable it to deal with the logical structure of events, while leaving it completely unknown what is the intrinsic character of the events that have the structure."[8] All the objects and their properties and the events and their properties within the relation are what they are in the logically realistic component of their meaning solely because of the formal properties of the relatedness within which they function as relata or terms. This is why all scientific objects and events in concept by postulation theory, whether it be that of mathematical physics, neural and behavioristic psychology or contractual law, are incomplete symbols. In other words, they are symbols which by themselves are meaningless and only take on meaning as terms or relata in a relatedness the formal logical properties of which are knowable only as specified theoretically by an imageless symbolical logically or mathematically constructed particular set of postulates.

McCulloch noted a second formal property of any neural net, the relatedness of which is that of Diagram II. Assuming that only the sensory nerve cell s^1, can fire the cortical nerve cell c^1, the trapped figure of impulses is not merely the persisting causal effect of the outer past event, E^1, but also it represents that event and that event only. When any fact stands in such a one-one relation to a fact other than itself, it has the formal properties of a symbol. The trapped impulses in the neural net above fit the formal requirement necessary, therefore, to be the concept by postulation epistemic correlate of the concept by intuition meaning which in introspective psychology we call the "remembered idea of the past explosion." We have now the epistemic correspondence rule that connects the unobservable impulse in the reverberating circuit described just above to the immediately and consciously experienced and remembered idea of that particular past explosion E^1. Note, as indicated a few pages earlier, that only the radically empirically experienced epistemic correlate of the latter fact is directly sensed.

Since there was but one explosion, the trapped impulse may be regarded as the concept by postulation epistemic correlate of an introspected remembered idea that is a nominalistic particular, i.e., the idea of the one and only event now perished with the proper name E^1. Suppose, however, that several later explosions fire the sensory neuron s^1 of Diagram II. The trapped figure of circulating impulses will then have the formal property of representing a class of similar particulars, the similarity being guaranteed by the neurological fact that sensory neuron s^1 will fire only if stimulated by a sound wave of a specific wave length and intensity. The trapped figure of impulses now has the formal property of a concept by intuition which is a nominalistic class concept, or, in other words, a nominalistic universal. This is why McCulloch called these trapped impulses "trapped universals."

As noted earlier, McCulloch's expression, "trapped universal," is elliptical. Always the reader must think of it as expanded to read, the "trapped figure of impulses in a reverberating circuit, or its formal mechanical equivalent, which is the physiological realistic epistemological correlate of a private, introspected, radically empirically known idea."

McCulloch noted also that there are different sensory neurons epistemically corresponding to the different species of images that one senses and introspects. Neural physiologists call these species "auditory neurons," "tactile neurons," "visual neurons," "taste receptors," etc. Assuming a reverberating circuit for each species of these sensory nerve cells, the concept by postulation correlates of the various species of concept by intuition universals are discovered. Once such epistemic correlations are fixed between the physiological events in the concept by postulation world of discourse of neurological and behavioristic psychology and the concept by intuition world of discourse of introspective psychology, one can use the latter to identify its epistemic correlates in the former, and conversely. Then the following conclusions become reasonable.

There must be an area in the cortex, the concept by postulation "conscious" area, where cortical neurons are fired simultaneously by many different species of sensory neurons. The concept by intuition epistemic correlate of this is one's conscious, differentiated specious present, i.e., what the writer in *The Meeting of East and West* called the "differentiations of the differentiated aesthetic continuum." [9] Otherwise, one would not hear a sound while seeing a color, introspecting a pain and entertaining an idea.

From this "conscious cortical area," the impulses are abstracted by cortical neurons that are fired by the physiological epistemic representatives of the specious-present conscious events and then trapped in the "auditory," "olfactory" and other spatially separated "sensory" areas of the cortex, thereby making possible the memory of the disjunctively related ideas which Whitehead in *Process and Reality* [10] called "eternal objects." * This abstracting and trapping is, for the most part, done unconsciously. These cortical abstractive areas are known. As indicated previously, stimulation of any one of these areas by Penfield when the patient's brain is exposed for an operation has the effect in the patient's concept by intuition consciousness of his sensing the species of sensuous image that is epistemically correlated with the brain area in question. Again McCulloch's epistemic rules of correspondence are experimentally confirmed. The patient reports that he introspects what the physiological events and the epistemic rules of correspondence call for.

From these separated abstraction areas cortical neurons converge to an "association area" of the brain. In this area different trapped universals are spontaneously combined. Without this association area, imagination, the novelist's fantasies, detective stories and, even more important, scientific and philosophical theories and any knowledge of either ourselves as a public person or our external world would be impossible, for all that is given to us inductively as "facts" on the sensory side of our nervous systems and in our immediate, differentiated consciousness are the impressionistic effects of both one's theoretically known own public self and the external world upon one's

---

* From the standpoint of the theory of the public self of this book, Whitehead's "eternal objects" are not, as he supposed or at least suggests, part of the furniture of the public universe. Instead, they are the sometimes consciously rememberable epistemic correlates of the persisting impulses trapped in a particular person's cortex and in some cases conveyed to and trapped in another person's cortex either by interpersonal communication or by the two people quite independently trapping as primitive the same impulse to account for the incoming sensory "information" or "data." These "eternal objects" do, however, function constantly through time insofar as similar independent trappings occur and insofar as they are passed covertly in any culture or nation from generation to generation. Hence, they are part of the furniture of the second order factual cultural world but not of the first order factual natural universe, except as their epistemically correlated impulses are trapped in particular human nervous systems. For the distinctions between first order and second order facts see Ch. XIX in *The Complexity of Legal and Ethical Experience* and later chapters of the present book.

theoretically known self. This is why the practical fellow who dismisses ideas and theories as irrelevant and tells us he *believes* in "keeping his feet on the ground" is usually in fact living in fairyland; moreover, one that can be fatally dangerous for everyone in this atomic age. Without these association areas in human brains there could be no military, power-political or any other kind of planning; or any of the errors and sins that arise when one's motor neurons are fired by impulses, trapped in reverberating circuits, that are the concept by postulation epistemic correlates of false theories or semantically confused nonsensical notions.

Hence, there is nothing esoteric about sin or evil or legal and political injustice. In the concept by postulation realistic epistemological world of discourse, it is, as Chapter 7 will show, motor behavior conditioned by the neurological epistemic correlates of false theory. Conversely, goodness or virtue or justice is motor behavior conditioned by the most empirically verified and logically consistent theory available. This is why scientists, artists, philosophers and saints who use the creatively imaginative association areas of the brains God gave them to acquire more and more empirically confirmed and logically consistent theory in order to account for all the relativistic and impressionistic data fed in on the sensory side of human nervous systems are the *true* leaders of mankind in the only sense the word "true" has. To be sure, the soldier, the labor leader, the political leaders of the proletariat and the businessmen who are concerned with expertness in instrumental values have their necessary place in any good society, i.e., one based on empirically confirmed and logically consistent "trapped universals," but that place is as an instrument of the good life and not as the epitome of or the end-all and be-all of human existence.

But let us return to McCulloch. He inferred also that the trapping of the physiological epistemic correlates of compound or defined ideas as well as simple ideas, such as "bang," "yellow," "sensed," "round," "earlier than," "to the left of," must be achieved in the association areas of the brain as follows: Assume an empty circle C^c of cortical neurons to which two in-put neurons come, one each, from two other empty circles of neurons C^a and C^b. Assume now that an impulse representing epistemically the concept by intuition "yellow" becomes trapped in circuit C^a and that another impulse representing epistemically the concept by intuition idea of a sensed circle becomes trapped in circuit C^b. Assume also that any cortical neuron in circuit C^c will fire only if both the in-put neurons from circuits C^a and C^b fire simultaneously or temporally very near together. Then this ordering of the three circuits in a single neural net has the formal property of a definition since it ensures that the impulse trapped in circuit C^c is the physiological epistemic correlate of the definable compound idea "yellow circle" which is defined in terms of the undefined ideas "yellow" and "sensed circle" assumed as undefined or primitive concepts.

By such compoundings of different circular neural nets, compound ideas, propositions and theories of any degree of complexity are made possible. This requires that in the so-called "higher areas" of the cortex the empty, circularly ordered neural nets or their formal equivalents are so laid down at birth or earlier before anything is trapped in them that they are related hierarchically. In his book *The Computer and the Brain,* von Neumann tells us that this is the case for part of both the human nervous system and calculating machines.[11] Otherwise in our immediate consciousness we would not be able to separate elementary ideas and assumptions of our belief system from the more complex, defined ideas and deduced propositions to achieve the economy of thought which is scientific, common-sense or any other kind of useful knowledge. Also, all the ideas of all the endless facts of our experience would be on the same level of importance and our information as it increased would overwhelm us.

There is no reason also why there are not figures of impulses trapped in reverberating circuits or their formal equivalents that are the epistemic correlates of the complex of ideas which we call a "proposition." Substituting proposition p^1 and proposition p^2 in the empty circuits C^a and C^b referred to above, one then obtains the formal logical relation of "If p^1 and p^2, then p^3 the conjunct of p^1 and p^2." McCulloch noted also that in *Principia Mathematica* Russell and Whitehead have given the formal logical imageless primitive ideas and propositions necessary and sufficient to carry through any deduction of the most complex common-sense or mathematical calculations. It is, moreover, relatively easy, as McCulloch and Pitts saw, to relate reverberating circuits to one another in different neural nets which have the formal properties of all these primitive logical relations of *Principia Mathematica*. This makes deductive reasoning or calculation possible. More specifically it enables one, given the trapped figure of impulses that are the epistemic correlates of a minimum set of introspected, assumed propositions called postulates, to deduce as their necessary consequence a very much larger number of proved propositions called "theorems." Moreover, when the mechanical equivalents of the figures of impulses trapped in neural reverberating circuits are ordered in calculating machines by these symbolically logical, imageless relations, machines result which can calculate and deduce theorems from a given set of minimal propositional premises fed into them.

There are, to be sure, formal differences as well as identities between the logic of any human being's central nervous system and the logic of calculating machines. For these differences, the reader is referred to the latter portion of von Neumann's *The Computer and the Brain*. There are also analog as distinct from digital computers.

Those factors which both human nervous systems and computers have in common can now be summarized from the foregoing description. The final ordering of trapped impulses is hierarchical. This necessitates that the association areas of the cortex must try out different abstracted "trapped universals" as candidates for being trapped at the top of the cortical hierarchy as the primitive concepts and propositions in terms of which all the other impulses epistemically representing other ideas and propositions are to be "defined" or from which they are to be "deduced." The test of which set of candidates may be finally selected and trapped at the top of the cortical hierarchy of ideas (as ordered by the relations of definitions between elementary and defined concepts and implication between postulates and theorems) may be the pragmatic trial-and-error pursuit of rival sets to their respective deductive consequences to determine which accounts most adequately for all the incoming sensory data. At least this would seem to be the case for all self-critical people who do not allow the final set of impulses that is trapped at the top of their neural cortical hierarchy to be determined for them by others, or merely covertly and unconsciously by their culture. The content of these final elementary concepts and propositions defines, therefore, any particular person's philosophy, since philosophy is but the name for the elementary concepts and propositions of any logically analyzed subject.

The aforementioned distinction between (1) primitive or elementary concepts and assumed propositions or postulates and (2) defined concepts and deduced propositions and theorems will take on practical political importance after we become clear about what a nation is and begin in Chapters 6 and 7 to specify the methods of philosophical anthropology for first describing and then evaluating nations. Were it not for the distinction between (1) and (2), neither a science nor an art of politics would be possible.

The importance of the imageless concepts of symbolic logic for the understanding of the relatedness of any human nervous system and for the construction of calculating machines has been noted. Being imageless, the existence of such concepts is evidence also that some minds have discovered, memorized and can use imageless concepts by postulation that are concepts by intellection. It is the thesis of the writer's *The Meeting of East and West* that such concepts were first discovered by the Greek mathematical physicists Democritus, Theaetetus, Plato and Eudoxus. In the more recent *The Complexity of Legal and Ethical Experience*, reasons have been given for believing that their discovery was made use of by the Stoic Roman lawyers and philosophers to create Western contractual legal science. If this be true, the importance of such concepts for politics is inescapable since all modern nations, whether Communistic or freely democratic, are contractually constructed nations. The existence in some minds of such concepts tells us, therefore, that there are some ideas in some intellects that are not first in the senses, since everything given by the senses is imageful, and concepts by formal postulational construction are not. Expressed neurologically, this entails (if any introspected idea in the mind has its unique epistemically correlated trapped impulse in the brain) that the association areas of the cortex need not be limited in their self-initiating activities to the mere recombining of impulses trapped as the effects of sensory stimuli after the manner of Diagram II. In addition in some persons such as Democritus, Theaetetus, Plato, Eudoxus, Galilei, Newton, Maxwell, Gibbs, Einstein, Russell, Whitehead, Schroedinger, Heisenberg and von Neumann, the association areas of the cortex have trapped unique elementary impulses of their own. Then, as von Neumann writes, "the orders are ideal entities." [12] Otherwise, there would not be the imageless elementary concepts of symbolic logic, pure mathematics, the mathematically theoretical part of mathematical physics and contractual legal and political science.

Aristotle, however, returned Greek and medieval science to universals, the content of which is given through the senses. Thus he, and St. Thomas following him, affirmed that there are no ideas in the intellect that are not first in the senses. The existence of the concepts by postulation that are imageless concepts by intellection in symbolic logic, pure mathematics and the theoretically known part of mathematical physics, gives the lie to this doctrine; as does also contractual legal and political science. Modern physics arose when Galilei and Newton returned Western mathematical physical theory to imageless, formally and postulationally constructed concepts. Contemporary quantum mechanics is self-contradictory unless the complete dropping of images, either particle-like or wave-like as the predicates of scientific objects, is recognized. Again Lord Russell's observation is to the point that what we know in mathematical physics is an imageless relatedness with very complex formal logical properties, the entity variables of which are what we mean by scientific objects.

As shown above and in the previous chapter, it is only by recourse to logically realistic concepts by postulation that are concepts by intellection, indirectly tested (via antecedently specified epistemic rules of correspondence) by appeal to what is given directly through the senses or introspectively, that one can know either one's public self or the public spatiotemporal world of nature within which this public self and other public objects are located. It happens that Pitts and McCulloch have succeeded in formally constructing a neural net with the relatedness such that it can take the trapped persisting representatives of the various relativistic sensed impressions and introspected feelings and images varying from individual to individual, frame of reference to frame of reference and sense organ to sense organ, and from this relativistic and disjunctively related set of data, construct invariant spatiotemporal relations and objects. They have also given reasons for believing that such an ordering of nerve cells exists in human nervous systems [13] even though it was not until the ancient Greek mathematicians that this portion of any human being's nervous system was used to trap the impulses that are the neurological epistemic correlates of the imageless concept by postulation ratios and propositions of Eudoxian mathematical physics, as instanced by Definition 5, Book V, of Euclid. In any event, we are now able to understand why Einstein was correct when he said that man gains knowledge of an external public world only by speculative means.[14] What this means neurophysiologically is that knowledge of an external world is not given as signals stimulating the sensory neurons of the nervous system but is instead the result of the spontaneous self-creation activity of the association areas of one's own cortex.

To Einstein's correct observation, it should be added that man also gets knowledge of his public self, thereby escaping from his own private solipsistic conscious interior, only by such a self-creative method. As Earl (Bertrand) Russell has written, "The inference to your own eyes . . . is essentially of the same sort as the physicist's inference to electrons, . . . and, if you are going to deny validity to the physicist's inferences, you ought also to deny that you know you have visible eyes—which is absurd, as Euclid would say." [15] This means that any objective natural knowledge of either one's own self as a public person or of other public objects in nature, that does not commit the nonsense of predicating relative private concept by intuition properties of public concept by postulation objects, must be a combination of theoretically known invariant imageless objects and their relatedness in epistemic correspondence with private relativistic consciously immediate data.

But the impulses trapped in some figure in any brain can fire motor neurons, thereby causing muscles to contract and bodily behavior to occur in the public world of politics and nature. An electrode implanted in the motor area of the brain of a monkey can emit an electrical stimulus which causes a neuron in the motor area of the monkey's cortex to fire, thereby causing the monkey's muscles to contract suddenly. The figure of impulses trapped in the brain, which are the epistemic correlates of consciously and unconsciously persisting ideas, can, therefore, mechanically cause a determinate kind of human behavior to occur.

But the query immediately arises: This means that mechanical causation is present. Is not mechanical causation incompatible with ideologically purposeful and self-directed human behavior? At this point, the investigations of Rosenblueth, Wiener and Bigelow become of critical importance.

Before turning to their work, one caution is to be noted. It would be an error to conclude, as some have done, that this conception of human nature is false because it is excessively rationalistic. Whether the content of a person's conscious mind or unconscious "trappings" are rationalistic or not depends upon the content of what is trapped. As psychoanalysis shows, one can trap the epistemic representative of a passion, an emotional disturbance, a sexual feeling, an obsession or any other emotively charged past experience or image as easily, if not more easily, than one can trap the epistemic representative of a fence post, a piece of granite or the mass of an external object which we call the moon. Consequently, this theory permits one to be as emotive, aesthetically sensitive and even passionate as the sensed and introspected facts require. In later chapters we shall give evidence to suggest that any adequate philosophy of human experience must root itself in the aesthetically immediate and emotive as well as in the theoretically constructed and the contractual. Intuitive scientific and philosophical theories are no more or no less conceptual and rationalistic than are non-intuitive ones. What the theories refer to is merely different in content in the two cases.

4

The Self-Regulation of Human Behavior by Means of the Epistemic Correlates of Ideas

To appreciate the importance of the article by Rosenblueth, Wiener and Bigelow entitled "Behavior, Purpose and Teleology"[1] one must recall two major reasons why many modern natural scientists, psychologists, philosophers and politicians came to the conclusion that ideas are "mere epiphenomena" incapable of having any significance for the motor behavior of human beings and hence irrelevant to what they actually do in their political decisions and behavior.

The first reason is that the earlier scientists and philosophers, such as Hobbes, Locke, Descartes, Haeckel and Marx, who broke from the naïve realistic concepts of Aristotle and St. Thomas, interpreted the imageless concept by postulation masses of Newton's physics as little imageful concept by intuition billiard balls which they supposed they directly sensed in the aggregate if not individually. Thus the notion, of the modern man of "common sense," arose of directly sensed material substances obeying the mechanically causal rules of Newton's physics.

Upon these unconscious, colorless and hence unaesthetic material substances, conscious minds, conceived as mental substances or windowless spiritual monads with their ideas and normative purposes, could have no influence. Otherwise the principle of the conservation of mass and energy would be violated. Moreover, the mathematical

64

physicist Leibniz pointed out that material substances are located in the space and time of Newton's physics, whereas mental substances are not in space and time, but instead, so to speak, contain space and time as mere items of awareness within each conscious mind's purely private and introspective windowless interior. Hence, to talk about a conscious mind and its ideas, all of which are not in space and time, causally acting upon material substances which are in space and time is to talk about the meaningless since causality by definition is a relation between factors in time. It follows, therefore, if the bodies of human beings are supposed to be aggregates of material substances, that any person's conscious ideas and purposes are irrelevant to his specific spatiotemporal behavior, since they can never contact it causally or in any other way.

Applied to politics, this gives Hobbes' statement, quoted in Chapter 2, that men are doomed to collide mechanically with one another and that, therefore, the natural state of mankind is war. In order, however, to account for why ordered political governments rather than anarchy and war exist domestically, Hobbes introduced the additional confused and *ad hoc* hypothesis that every human being, by some self-initiating miracle which Hobbes never explained, hands over the determination of all his personal political sovereign rights, privileges, obligations and duties to a single, undivided political sovereign who is identified with any modern political nation and whose political power, being thus one, undivided and unlimited, is absolute. For such a modern nation it follows that to talk about international law, i.e., about a modern nation being subject in the slightest part even to a law beyond itself, is to talk about the self-contradictory and hence the legally and politically meaningless.

This entire complex of confused notions is seen to be the meaningless nonsense which it is when the different epistemological meanings of the words used to state it are distinguished and then epistemically related in the way which was described in the previous chapters. First, one does not immediately introspect oneself as a mental substance or a self-conscious windowless monad as the spiritualists supposed. Nor does one immediately sense imageful material substances either individually or in aggregate as the free democratic Hobbesian or the Marxist Communistic power politicians suppose. The reason in both cases is, as Hume pointed out, that neither introspective consciousness nor sense awareness acquaints one with a substance. Also, as the theoretical physicist Ernst Mach made clear, "the masses" and "forces" of Newton's mechanics or of any other modern theory of mathematical physics are not naïve realistic epistemological substances defined in terms of either sensed or imagined properties; instead their scientific properties are imageless and are constitutively and postulationally assigned to them relationally by the formal properties of the imageless mathematical equations and laws in which they function as the related terms. In short, mass is a relational concept. It is not a substance with fixed sense predicates attached to it. Nor is force, i.e., the acceleration of the mass, an immediately felt push or pull that is similarly fastened to a material substance with its subject-predicate grammar and its Aristotelian type of logic, as the Aryan group of cultural languages led the Mimamsa Aryan Hindu philosophers, Aristotle, St. Thomas, Hobbes, Sir Robert Filmer, Feuerbach, Marx and the contemporary philosopher Paul Weiss in his *Essential Mode of Being* to suppose.

Moreover, any naïve realistic epistemological concept of the public self or any public object is self-contradictory. The mark of such an epistemology is that it attempts to define the purportedly public substances in terms of directly sensed or introspected properties. But all sensed or imagined items of knowledge are imageful and all images are relative, not merely to the observer's frame of reference and to the percipient, but even, as Democritus, Galilei, Newton and Berkeley pointed out, to different sense organs and moments of perception of the same percipient. The naïve realist means, however, by his public substances something that exists with its determinate imageful properties independently of its relation to any observer. Clearly, therefore, it is self-contradictory to define an object existing independently of its relation to the observer in terms of sensed or introspected imageful properties all of which are relative to the perceiver.

What has to be realized, therefore, if words like "mass" and "force" in mathematical physics are to be understood is that its logic is not the subject-predicate logic of ordinary Aryan linguistic prose; instead, it is that of symbolic logic with its symbols that do not conjure up either sensed or introspected images; more particularly it is that of the formal logic of relations. This is why the mechanics of Einstein, notwithstanding the fact that it escapes all the afore-mentioned relativity of sensed or imagined items of knowledge to achieve greater objectivity (i.e., invariants) for the public scientific objects of space-time of nature than was the case in any previous theory, is called "the theory of relativity." The latter name expresses the fact that in all theories of non-Aristotelian and non-naïvely realistic Western physics all entity and property concepts are rela-tionally defined in imageless, formally constructed symbolical logic or mathematical relational terms. In other words, the indirectly and experimentally confirmed theories of modern mathematical physics affirm the relational theory of mass and of space-time.

The importance of Ernst Mach, whom Einstein recognized as his precursor, is that Mach showed this to be true even for the so-called particle physics of Newton. We now see more clearly why the ma-terialistic Communist Lenin attacked Mach so furiously. The ma-terialism of a Marxist Communist or of a free democratic power politician rests on the notion of material substances of a naïve realistic epistemology. Mach showed that one completely misunder-stands what one means by mass or force in modern physics if one thinks of either in this way. They are logical realistic concepts by postulation which are concept by intellection relational concepts; they are not naïvely realistic directly sensed substantive things.

The first reason, therefore, why early modern physicists, psycholo-gists, philosophers and political thinkers supposed that ideas and the normative purposes of people could have no significance for their public human and political behavior is now known, therefore, to have no basis in either fact or theory. This notion of material sub-stances, which a mind conceived as a mental substance could not contact, rests on the epistemologically confused, empirically false and self-contradictory notions of a naïve realistic epistemology.

The second reason why modern scientists and philosophers sup-posed that ideas could have no significant effect upon the behavior of peoples and nations is that if such were the case, the causality governing publicly meaningful human behavior would have to be purposeful or teleological, whereas modern mathematical physics shows conclusively that publicly meaningful physical systems change their states with time mechanically rather than teleologically. Rosen-blueth, Wiener and Bigelow have shown, however, that this supposition is a mistake, due to the failure to distinguish two kinds of mechanical systems; the one non-teleological, the other teleological in its behavior. The latter type contains a negative feedback from both (a) its target and (b) its motor response to the target. The other type of mechanism does not contain such a feedback.

One example of a negative feedback mechanism is any healthy human being's nervous system. Another example is an antiaircraft gun which (1) fires a projectile at an airplane, (2) has within itself an apparatus which receives electromagnetic waves from its own moving projectile and from the continuously moving airplane and (3) mechanically self-corrects the direction in which the next projectile is fired if the data of (2) indicate that the previously fired projectile is missing its target. When, on the other hand, no miss is occurring, the old motor response is reinforced and the feedback is positive. The notable characteristic of such a mechanism is that it mechanically self-directs and corrects its own motor responses with respect to stimuli received from some target and from the machine's projected response to that target in such a way that any discrepancy between the projected motor response and the target mechanically causes the present or later response to hit the target. In short, by means of mechanical causality alone a miss mechanically necessitates a later hit. Because such negative feedback mechanisms are self-governing, Norbert Wiener created the word "cybernetics," [2] taken from the Greek word for "helmsman," to denote the science that studies them.

It is to be noted also that in any negative feedback mechanism, the final state of the entire system is a mechanically causal function of both the target or goal and the intervening states of the motor response of the system. Since teleological behavior is behavior in which the final state is a function not merely of the initial state of the system but also of its later future states, such a mechanical system behaves teleologically and is, therefore, appropriately called a "teleological mechanism."

Providing the reader does not have Parkinson's disease or some other similar breakdown in the negative feedback mechanism of his nervous system, he can test for himself, by performing the two following simple experiments, that his own nervous system is such a mechanism. Place a watch within reach on a table at which you seat yourself. Proceed then to pick up the watch with your thumb and forefinger, keeping your attention fixed on both the watch and on your hand as it approaches the watch. You will find that your thumb and forefinger converge practically exactly on the circular edge of the watch. Repeat the experiment with your head turned away. Your hand will arrive near the watch, but not with the previous precision. The reason is not merely that "You did not keep your eye on the ball," but also that, with your head turned to one side, there was no feedback to your brain via light waves from both your moving hand and the watch. Hence, the negative feedback mechanism in your central nervous system was not mechanically caused, by the incoming sensory data, to correct the discrepancy between your hand as it moved near the watch and the watch itself.

There is an even more important fact that the second of these two experiments demonstrates. You, the reader, consciously entertained the idea of picking up your watch. A moment later you were conscious also of your decision to implement this idea, thereby turning it into an objective actuality. Since both your initial entertainment of this idea and your later conscious experience of the decision to realize it were immediately experienced conscious events, these events are entities denoted by concepts by intuition, i.e., concepts the entire meaning of which is to be found in immediately and consciously experienced items of knowledge. Your direct sensing of the later images of your thumb and forefinger and watch together in the final state of the first experiment and separated slightly in the final state of the second experiment mean also that these later different sensed images are entities denoted by concepts by intuition.

However, the correction of your motor responses en route to the final state in the first experiment was not consciously experienced. Nor was the impossibility of making such a correction consciously experienced in the second experiment. The reason, as shown by Penfield's operations on the human brain when the patient is conscious, is that we are not conscious of our own brains. We are not conscious of our nervous system itself, since apparently consciousness is reserved for the immediately experienced concept by intuition epistemic correlates of but some of the theoretically known concept by postulation signals fed into the nervous system to be later represented by trapped impulses. This means that the portion of one's publicly meaningful self, which is one's own nervous system in its automatic mechanically self-regulatory neurological and muscular behavior, can be known only by speculatively introduced theory stated in terms of concepts by postulation that are concepts by intellection. It means also that such theory can be confirmed only indirectly by appeal to epistemic rules of correspondence with directly sensed or introspected private and subjective relativistic data denoted by concepts by intuition.

Similarly one does not sense or introspect one's own body in its publicly meaningful nature for the very simple reason that neither sensing nor introspecting gives one any datum which is invariant from sense organ to sense organ, from observer to observer and from frame of reference to frame of reference. Nor does anyone sense public space-time. This means, as emphasized in the previous chapter, that one's public bodily self, like any other public object, can be known only by theory stated in non-sensuous or non-imageful concepts by postulation that are concepts by intellection. It is precisely such a theory of the publicly meaningful person in the world of public nature which is provided by the theory that anyone's public self is in part at least a teleological mechanism. The reader, moreover, has experimentally confirmed the correctness of this theory for himself. There are countless other confirmations known to neurophysiologists. The second reason for believing that the ideas and consciously entertained purposes of human beings could have no bearing on what they actually do as public persons in the public space-time of world politics and spatiotemporal nature is, therefore, also groundless. This second reason, let it be recalled, was that were the ideas and consciously entertained purposes of people significant with respect to their public behavior, they would have to be teleologically behaving beings, and modern physics has shown that this is not the case. The error arose from failing to note that there are two different types of mechanical systems, one of which does not behave teleologically and the other of which does. Publicly meaningful, i.e., logically realistic, human beings are mechanisms of the latter type. In short, any human being is a cybernetic creature.

But, it will be said, "Self-regulating antiaircraft guns are also, and certainly there is a difference between such a teleological mechanism and a human being." This is unquestionably true. One of the major differences is that whereas the teleological mechanism which is the antiaircraft gun must have its target selected for it by some human being and its inner negative feedback mechanism designed for such a target, human beings select their own targets and also, unlike calculating machines, self-select in part the data and information that is fed into them and also the normative procedural rules for not merely describing but also for evaluating this data. How can this be?

This question brings us to the writer's paper published in *Science* in 1947.[3] Its major thesis is relatively simple and can be put in the form of a question: Why can't the target of the negative feedback mechanism which is a particular human nervous system be the hierarchically ordered, cortically trapped persisting impulses that are the epistemic correlates of that particular person's set of elemental concepts and postulates, i.e., his cognitively true or false philosophy? Were such the case, then the negative feedback mechanism which is the human nervous system would self-correct mechanically its motor responses to any stimulus to make these motor responses conform more and more to that cortically trapped set of reverberating circuit impulses, the epistemic correlates of which are the elementary concepts of that person's covertly or consciously affirmed and entertained philosophy.

There is no reason whatever why such is not the case. In fact, combining the theory of trapped impulses of McCulloch and Pitts with the theory of the nervous system as a self-regulating negative feedback teleological mechanism, as clarified by Rosenblueth, Wiener and Bigelow, it must be the case. Forthwith also Kluckhohn's findings with respect to the essential relation between the behavior of the Navaho Indians and their common philosophy becomes intelligible in consistent introspective, neurological, behavioristic and psychoanalytic psychological terms.

Certain facts in the reader's second experiment confirm this conclusion. To be sure, your hand did not converge on the watch in this case with the accuracy of the attainment of its target that occurred in the first experiment. Nevertheless, merely the introspected idea, entertained in your private consciousness, of picking up the watch and of where the watch was remembered to be, sufficed to enable you, without looking at either the watch or your hand, to almost hit your target. This simple fact, therefore, in your second attempt to pick up your watch, shows that the target of the human being's realistic publicly conceived negative feedback mechanism need not be some realistic epistemological natural object such as the airplane or the watch, outside the human nervous system; it can instead be and, in the case of the normative ideas and ideals of all political and legal systems, is some particular set of trapped impulses within the negative feedback human nervous system itself that are the neurophysiological epistemic correlates of otherwise private, purely subjective consciously entertained ideas. These trapped epistemic correlates and unique representatives of consciously entertained ideas *mechanically must* inhibit or reinforce the firing of motor neurons to give determinate content to one's public objective behavior.

The behavior of calculating machines provides another independent confirmation of this conclusion. In such a teleological mechanism also the target is not an object outside the mechanism; instead it is given by the normative rules for calculating that are fed into the machine by some human being or in some cases built into it in its very construction. These procedural rules function in the machine as norms from which it cannot depart in any motor response to the data or information which is fed into the machine as stimuli.

At long last we are in a position to see why the descriptive and evaluative methods of philosophical anthropology are what Chapters 6 and 7 will indicate them to be. Even so, if politicians are to believe that these methods are relevant to their practical problems, they and we must first become clear about what the abstract noun "nation" means.

5

What Is a Nation?

Before there can be a theory, to say nothing of a science, of domestic or international politics, one must first have a clear conception of a nation. To find the guiding principles for putting a special class of things together in an effective manner, the kind of thing one is putting together must be known. Then one must describe the various species of this kind of thing and determine the scientific method for doing this. Otherwise, the student of either domestic policy or international relations does not know either the subject matter or the method of his subject.

Suppose the chemists claimed to know what they were talking about when they stated a policy for combining the different kinds of chemical elements, but had no clear theory of what a chemical element is or what the scientific method is for determining the properties of the different species of chemical atoms. Suppose also such a chemist regarded the physical weight of the different chemical compounds as the only relevant thing about them, thereby neglecting to pay attention to the properties which differentiate a pound of nitroglycerin, let us say, from a pound of fresh spring water. If, having thus treated nitroglycerin as if it were merely so much weighty matter and then blowing up both his laboratory and his neighbors', he then blamed one of his neighbors for what happened, we would not think very highly of his expertness in interchemical relations. Yet this treatment of different nations, peoples and cultures as if they were merely so much weighty physical power is precisely what present "experts" in international relations, such as Professor Hans Morgenthau and Mr. George F. Kennan, do when, deprecating the "moral-legal approach" to international relations, they treat nations merely as so much quantitative physical power. If, on the other hand, a chemist took very seriously the specific chemical properties of one element, let us say hydrogen, and then proceeded to combine hydrogen with the other chemical elements as if they possessed the same properties as hydrogen, or indulged in outraged religious and moral indignation if they did not, then also we would be justified in concluding that we could well dispose of him as a policy maker in the interrelations of the chemical elements. Yet when President Eisenhower and his Secretary of State, Mr. Dulles, reacting from Mr. Kennan's rejection of the political significance of the moral and legal properties of nations in foreign policy decisions, built a United States foreign policy on a "roll-back crusade" of the Judaic-Christian American way of life alone, precisely this relating of many different things upon the basis of the knowledge of some of the properties of but one of those things is occurring.

We need hardly be surprised, therefore, as Chapters 10, 11 and 17 will document, that the results of both Mr. Kennan's and Secretary Dulles' theory and practice in international relations were self-defeating with respect to the relating of the nations as they would be were such procedures applied to the combining of the chemical elements. Both schools of thought—the power politicians who would keep the moral-legal mentality out of foreign policy decisions and the Eisenhower-Dullesites who would keep the Judaic-Christian American way of life in such decisions—were guilty of the same error. Both plunged into the specification of the procedure for relating the nations before they were clear about either (a) what any nation is, or (b) what the particular objective method is for determining the specific properties which make one species of nation different from another.

It may be said: "But everybody knows what a nation is. There is the United States. There is the Soviet Union. There is Free India. There is, or there was, Free Pakistan." This seems to be the case. But the necessary qualification "there was" with respect to Free Pakistan suggests that the matter is not such a simple and empirically self-evident thing as at first appears. Is Pakistan under a military dictatorship the same nation as Pakistan under a free democratic, modernized Islamic theory of goal values? To be sure, the concrete people are bodily the same, the two widely separated geographical terrains in which they reside are the same and their military power is the same, but does this suffice to make the nation the same before and after the military coup? Also, the bodies of the people are concrete and the two geographical areas are concrete, as are the military weapons, but in what does the concreteness of the nation consist? Clearly, the bodies of the people and the geography are not enough to answer this question. Nor is the answer empirically self-evident. Hence our query, "What is a nation?" is not merely a real question, but also a difficult one to answer.

This becomes more evident if we consider another aspect of the recent military coup in Pakistan. Some say that this marks the beginning of the breakdown of Pakistan as a nation. Whether this is the case or not is irrelevant to our present concern. That such might be the eventuality is, however, most relevant. Any theory of what a nation is must provide meaning for a nation passing out of being when the concrete people, the concrete geography and the concrete military soldiers and weapons with which it was previously associated remain.

In the case of Pakistan, there is physical power. Certainly a military leader is not devoid of that. Yet with all of these three physical things—the people's bodies, the geographical terrain and the physical power—Pakistan as a nation may, nevertheless, disappear. Obviously, therefore, whatever a nation is, it is something apparently very abstract and empirically very elusive.

These considerations mean that when we, or our "experts" in international relations, suppose that we know what a nation is, we are guilty of confusing abstract nouns such as "nation," "national interest" or "national power" with concrete entities. This occurs when one puts the word "the" before such abstract nouns to produce expressions such as "the nation," "the national interest" or "the major powers" and then supposes, without further reduction of these abstract expressions to empirically verifiable concrete entities, that one knows what one is talking about.

The word "the" is meaningless unless it refers to an empirically observable or indirectly and experimentally confirmable scientifically designated particular entity, but the words "nation," "national interest" and "major powers" by themselves do not refer to concrete entities. Thus when taken by themselves as the elementary concepts in foreign policy or international relations, as is done by Professor

Morgenthau and Mr. Kennan, instead of being realistic or scientific concepts such expressions are abstract words that are confused with concrete things. Until a reduction of such otherwise meaningless abstract nouns to empirically verifiable concrete entities is given, the expertness of present professors of international relations and of other similar foreign policy decision makers is spurious.

At this point we of the older generation can learn something very important from the younger generation of Anglo-American analytic philosophers. This something is to be exceedingly suspicious of abstract nouns unless statements containing them are reduced to at least indirectly testable empirical statements about concrete entities and events. To confuse an abstract noun with a concrete entity by putting the word "the" before it and then supposing that one is talking about something realistic and meaningful is what Whitehead called the "fallacy of misplaced concreteness." This does not mean that abstract nouns like "nation," "culture," "the living law," "legal system" or "pattern of a culture," "a great power" or "national interest" must be thrown away. It does mean, however, that, before we can know what we are talking about when we use them, we must translate them into theoretically precise and direct or indirect empirically confirmable statements about concrete entities and find the specific concrete entities in terms of which such a translation can be made. Until this occurs, we shall do well to trust our domestic and foreign policy to our most experienced diplomats and domestic politicians, probably also to those who do not theorize too much about foreign policy, rather than to professors of international relations or of "social science," or to the graduates of our traditional law schools where only the positive law of one particular nation is taught.

Even so, the crucial question remains, What is a nation? In other words, What are the concrete entities and events in terms of which the abstract noun "nation" is to be analyzed? It is unlikely that even politicians with lengthy experience or career diplomats can avoid self-defeating decisions involving other nations unless they, as well as we, become clear about the answer to this question. Is there any clue?

A more concrete understanding of the difficulty which the question raises will become evident if we compare the unity of the group of concrete human bodies making up a nation with the quite different anatomical unity of any one of these concrete individual human bodies. Looked at comparatively in this manner, the existence of a nation appears as almost a miracle. In the case of any individual man or woman, the anatomical parts are physically held together by physical bones, nerves, muscles and tendons. Consequently no person with all his or her anatomical parts intact can move one part of his or her body without that anatomical part physically pulling all the other parts along. The unity of the concrete people who make up the nation which is the United States of America or the Soviet Union is, however, something quite different from this. There are no material wires, bones, muscles or tendons physically connecting all the bodies of the individual American people in such a manner that, if one of the bodies responds in a certain way, the bodies of all the others must do the same. Nevertheless such a unified response is what occurs when any people form a nation or when a majority of them or any group of them respond with a common domestic or foreign policy. How is this possible? This is our question.

Thirty years ago a satisfactory answer could not have been given. Since then the indirectly confirmed scientific theory described in the previous chapter has been discovered. This experimentally testable theory makes possible the escape from the fallacy of misplaced concreteness with respect to the meaning of the word "nation."

Stated as briefly as possible, *a "nation" is any group of concrete, particular human beings who possess in the hierarchically ordered neural nets of their brains a similar set of elementary trapped impulses* (which are the physiological epistemic correlates of consciously or unconsciously memorized elementary ideas and postulates) *for firing or inhibiting their motor neurons and thereby mechanically causing a similar cognitive behavioristic living law response to any given stimulus.* As indicated in the two previous chapters, what is trapped, as the neurological epistemic correlate of any particular directly introspected or unconsciously held idea, is an impulse that is passed around a circular neural net or some neural physiological formal equivalent of such a persisting impulse. The entire hierarchically ordered system of such neurophysiological surrogates of a particular person's immediately conscious or covertly retained ideas is, like the events of any other theory of mathematical natural science, not directly sensed. Instead, it is known only by theoretically con-

structed imageless theory and its existence is confirmed only indirectly by way of epistemic correlations or epistemic rules of correspondence with the directly experienced meanings, ideas and other
data of awareness and introspected consciousness that are denoted
by concepts by intuition.

The advantage of supplementing the bare data, ideas and theories
of radically empirical introspective psychological consciousness with
such a concept by postulation theory of neurophysiological events,
only some of which possess directly inspectable epistemic correlates
in the domain of immediate conscious experience, is identical with
the advantage of mathematical chemistry over merely sensed chemistry or of mathematical electromagnetic theory with its spectrum
of electromagnetic waves, extending far beyond the so-called visible
range. The psychology of the unconscious and the anthropology of
the covert, as well as the psychology of the immediately conscious
and the anthropologically overt, are thereby given public logically
realistic neurological and behavioristic psychological meaning.

Conversely, such a concept by postulation neurophysiological theory enables one to use objectively given physical cultural artifacts
and spatiotemporally measured bodily public human behavior when
antecedently specified epistemic rules of correspondence with immediately introspected or sensed data are also given, to test operationally in the case of a given culture, people or nation whether one
has inferred the correct consciously or covertly held ideas and political intentions that are behind their immediately sensed smiles and
their behavioristic deeds and overt cultural customs. Thus an end is
put to the feud between the introspective, neurological and behavioristic psychologists, the analytic psychiatrists and the cultural anthropology of the covertly unconscious by separating out the logically
realistic concept by postulation and the radically empirical concept
by intuition worlds of discourse in which all operate and then, after
the manner of the empirically verified theories of the objective
methods of mathematical physics, bringing these two ways of knowing anything and their respective domains of discourse into harmo-
nious and precise relation to one another by means of epistemic rules
of correspondence. Thereby a complete, consistent analysis of what
it means to be a concrete particular person is for the first time at
hand.

Since the concreteness of any nation must be explicated in terms of the concreteness of the people making it up, important implications for politics become evident immediately. First, the concreteness of a particular nation finds its unity and the organic tie of its concrete persons in the high-frequency state of shared meanings or ideas (covert or overt) of its people. The problem, therefore, of explaining how the people of any nation can respond as a unit in its domestic or foreign policy notwithstanding the fact that there are no physical ties, such as muscles, bones and tendons between them, is, therefore, solved. This is especially the case when communication by means of symbols occurs. Second, as suggested in Chapter 3, any directly introspected idea, whether it be that of a concept by intuition or a concept by postulation and its epistemologically corresponding trapped impulses, is elementary, primitive or basic if it is an idea that is used to define other ideas but is not itself defined in terms of other ideas. Similarly, any compounding of ideas expressed as a proposition is elementary, primitive, or, in other words, a postulate if it is an assumed proposition not deducible from any other proposition in the belief system, from which, together with other postulates, additional propositions called theorems can be deduced. Since the word "philosophy" is but the name for the elementary concepts and postulates of any subject matter, it follows that a legal and political nation is a group of particular persons locatable in the public space-time of nature, each with a nominalistic proper name, who have trapped in the hierarchically ordered reverberating circuits of their brains persisting impulses or their formal, analytic, physiological equivalents which are the concept by postulation epistemic correlates of the elementary concepts and propositions or postulates of a consciously or covertly held common philosophy to which they have committed themselves and of which they may or may not be introspectively conscious. In order, therefore, to know what a particular nation is, the descriptive method of philosophical anthropology must determine, in a manner that is empirically confirmable by anyone, its particular high-frequency common philosophy.

This criterion of a legal and political nation leaves open for the descriptive method to determine in any particular nation the substantive content of its predominant philosophy or its predominant sets of philosophies. Its predominant philosophy may be pluralistic and eclectic, skeptical of systematic doctrine after the manner of William James, and a piecemeal and pragmatic approach to political problems. It may, on the other hand, be systematic and monistic after the manner of a medieval Thomistic theocratic Christian nation such as the Mexico of Cortes or the Filmerian patriarchal Christian theocratic nation of early seventeenth century England, a naïvely realistic and materialistic Marxist Communist nation, or a Hegelian Prussian German dialectically idealistic nation and *Kultur*. It may also be, as later chapters will show often is the case, that a particular nation is a complex of different, even incompatible, cultural philosophies. Such nations are likely to be unstable politically.

But it will be said: "The ideas in people's minds are subjective things. When one looks at any person, considering that person as an object, one cannot see his or her ideas. Hence to talk about an objective determination of another person's or a foreign people's philosophy is to talk about the impossible." This would be the case were there no scientific method for empirically confirming theories that refer to unobservable entities and relations. But we have such a scientific method. In mathematical physics its scientific objects and laws, being imageless, are not directly observable. No one has ever seen the four-dimensional Riemannian space-time of Einstein's general theory of relativity. Nor has anyone seen an electron or an electromagnetic wave which travels at approximately 186,000 miles per second. Nor, as Einstein has made evident quite independently of the theory of physics, does anyone directly sense the logically realistic public simultaneity of spatially separated events. This, however, presents no difficulty providing, by recourse to epistemic rules of correspondence with directly inspectable empirical data, one deduces the logical consequences of the imageless, theoretically designated, unobservable scientific events, objects and laws to test whether one's theoretical specification of what they are is correct, by means of recourse to operationally defined experiments that are directly inspectable and repeatable by anyone. Obviously, philosophical anthropology must proceed in the same way in its determination of the quantitative set of elementary common ideas in the minds of the people of any particular nation. Because also its analysis of any particular person exhibits one's introspective consciousness and its ideational and emotive content as irreducible, introspective psychological reports, either by speech or the symbols of the printed pages of the national and cultural classics of a people, provide the most obvious and easiest way to determine the high-frequency philosophy which defines the political properties of that particular nation. The epistemic rules of correspondence that relate this introspectively given high-frequency philosophy to the trapped impulses in the brains of particular people then take on a secondary, but none the less very important, role. This role is in part operational and in part psychoanalytically psychological and covertly anthropological.

Operationally the trapped impulses in the brains of a group of people in a particular nation and the one-one epistemic correlation of these impulses with the introspectively meaningful ideas of their shared national philosophy define the scientific method by means of which the cultural anthropologist or comparative cultural philosopher confirms or disconfirms whether he has found the correct set of postulates for describing the high-frequency philosophy of that particular nation. Consider, for example, Kluckhohn's set of postulates for the tribal nation of the Navaho Indians. Even though the philosophy which he concludes to be theirs is not his, how can he or we be sure that in emotively trying to put himself inside their national philosophical mentality he has not surreptitiously confused a mere product of his own imagination with what they in fact think or covertly assume and believe? It is at this point that the epistemic rules of correspondence with events in the logically realistic public nervous system and its overt public behavior become important. These epistemic rules and neurobehavioristic correlates permit a rigorous scientific method to be formulated such that when Kluckhohn's imaginatively proposed description of the Navaho philosophy is given in his set of philosophical postulates, if this is in fact their philosophy, then anthropologists other than he can confirm his descriptive set of Navaho postulates by observing in crucial experimental situations what must be observable if his descriptive philosophical theory and the antecedently specified epistemic rules of correspondence are the correct ones. Only with antecedently specified epistemic rules of correspondence that relate introspected ideas and meanings in the unobservable private consciousness of particular Navahos (via the target-trapped impulses in their brains) to the observable (by anyone) sensed epistemic correlates of their overt behavior, can this operational requirement for even a descriptive science of cultural anthropology and of nations be met.

Psychoanalytically and cultural anthropologically the need for supplementing introspective psychological data and their ideological meanings with epistemically correlated trapped impulses and behavioristically conditioned reflexes and habits is equally important. Otherwise one's capacity to recall today the name which one could not recall yesterday remains an utter mystery. Unless there are persisting representatives somewhere of a consciously known person's consciously known name of which he was conscious in the past but could not recall yesterday, then his capacity to have that name return to his consciousness today is left without any theoretical meaning. Similarly, the psychoanalytic psychiatrist's demonstration of the persisting influence of past conscious experiences on a person's present mental disturbances, even though the person is quite unconscious now of his past experiences, becomes equally unintelligible if one restricts one's psychological and philosophical theory of any person solely to the conscious person. Likewise the cultural anthropologists' agreement that most of the values and beliefs of a cultural nation or a people are covert or unconscious becomes meaningless if introspective conscious psychology and its radically empirical epistemology alone are taken as the whole of psychology and of the conceptually meaningful.

These operational, psychoanalytical and culturally anthropological considerations indicate that the method of descriptive philosophical anthropology as applied to politics must, therefore, have three parts which give: (1) The specific qualitative set of postulates that define a particular nation's most elementary common philosophy or complex of common philosophies; (2) the quantitatively statistical support that each qualitative set of philosophical principles enjoys and (3) empirical operational criteria for confirming that (1) has been specified correctly.

Requirement (2) is important for it reminds us of the point made in Chapter 1 that never in any culture or nation do all the people hold the same philosophy, the physiological epistemic correlates of which fire their motor neurons to condition a common living law behavior. To say that people of a particular nation share a common philosophy which has, via its physiological epistemic correlates, behavioristically conditioned their communal customs is to make a quantitatively statistical statement. Similarly even for those people in a given nation who share a common philosophy, never is there agreement on all the ideas which they hold. Otherwise, within any nation there would not be differences of religious affiliation or of scientific and other opinions; nor would there be different political parties. All, therefore, that is being affirmed when it is said that a nation exists is that a statistically large group of its people hold at least some elementary philosophical beliefs in common.

The problem of designing a foreign policy to achieve peace becomes that of describing the specific anthropologically philosophical properties of each of the world's nations, including one's own, and then putting together these nations with their diverse philosophical properties as they are today (not as one might like to have them be) in such a way that political nitroglycerin is not exploded. An example of such political nitroglycerin will be the topic of Chapter 13.

The foregoing reduction of the abstract noun "nation" to (a) the concrete negative feedback mechanisms which are the nervous systems of its people and (b) the similar persisting impulses trapped in the cortical hierarchies of a statistically large proportion of those different particular nervous systems, where (c) the similar elementary trapped impulses are the one-one physiological epistemic correlates of similar consciously or unconsciously remembered elementary ideas and propositions, enables one to account for the following political facts: (1) Why people can respond politically as a national unit even though they are not physically connected to one another by bones, wires, tendons, muscles and other physical tissues. (2) Why a nation can come into being, as in the case of Pakistan, Free India and Ghana, where none existed before. All that is required is what they find by intercommunication that they can share a common set of elemental ideas and propositions for ordering their relations to one another. As noted previously, only when the leaders of a people are creating a new nation are they consciously aware of the common philosophy which they use to order themselves legally and politically with respect to one another, thereby giving that nation its special legal and political properties.

Our analysis of the meaning of the word "nation" explains also why one nation can go out of existence to be replaced by a different nation or by two or more different nations when the geographical area, the people's bodies and the military physical power remain constant. The division of British India into Free India and Pakistan is an example. The breakup of the Holy Roman Empire into the modern national states, when the divisive ideas of the Protestant Reformation entered people's minds to capture their motor religious and political commitments, is another example.

Conversely, we can understand why one nation can replace many different nations. The bringing of the many different Princely States of India, as well as those states inherited from the British, into Free India is an example. The shift from status to contract described in Chapter 1 in which the countless tribal nations of the Western European world were replaced by the one nation called the Roman Empire is another instance. We can understand also why, because of the common norms provided by Islam and by modern contractual legal and political theory and its institutions, Pakistan could come into being as a single nation following World War II notwithstanding the geographical fact that East Pakistan is one thousand miles from West Pakistan and that the masses of the people in East Pakistan speak a different language from that of West Pakistan. It becomes clear, also, why the Muslim Indians and the Hindu Indians created two different nations upon the withdrawal of the British even though, from a geographical, economic or power-political standpoint such a partition into Pakistan and Free India makes little if any sense. The reason is ideologically cultural. It is that in a unified over-all Free India which was based on a homogeneous, secular, positive, free democratic constitution, the Hindus would outnumber and outvote the Muslims by more than two to one. Consequently, the geographically localized, overwhelmingly Muslim communities of East and West Pakistan felt that they would lack sufficient control of their nation and have little to say about what happened politically in it; nor would their Islamic living law values be taken sufficiently into account if they agreed to become members of an over-all Indian secular state.

Prime Minister Nehru's first Minister of Law, the late Dr. Bhimrao Ramji Ambedkar, who was chairman of the committee that wrote Free India's constitution and who was the leader of India's Hindu Untouchables, in the end felt precisely the same way about the preponderance of high-caste Hindus in the top decision-making posts of Prime Minister Nehru's secular state. This is a major reason why Dr. Ambedkar later resigned from the Nehru government. Not to pay attention to the *de facto* beliefs in the minds of people and to the religious and social customs and political choices which these beliefs have behavioristically conditioned is simply not to understand recent political events.

It was suggested also in Chapters 3 and 4 that any person's set of covertly or overtly persisting ideas functions as a censor or conscience determining for any given stimulus what motor, political or other responses are permitted or positively reinforced and what possible motor responses to that stimulus are inhibited. This is why any national people's preponderant common set of "trapped universals" is their normative criterion of the politically good, the legally just, the economically and militarily feasible and the aesthetically beautiful.

The attempt, therefore, to remove moral or philosophically anthropological considerations from either domestic or international politics, basing the subject solely on "power balancing," is impossible. For there is no nation except as a people in part consciously and in major part unconsciously share at least a minimal common set of elementary ideas and propositions for inhibiting or conditioning and reinforcing their motor responses to any stimulus. The epistemological distinctions which were described in previous chapters and shown to be indispensable, if nonsense in discourse is not to occur, provide a semantic reason why such is the case. Note first that, like any other political policy, power politics is a theory, the physiological epistemic correlates of which are trapped, unfortunately, in many people's brains. Moreover, power politics is a very specific philosophical theory—namely, the naïvely realistic imageful confused notion of material substances called materialism that derives in modern times from Hobbes, John Austin and Marx's theory of legal and political obligation, in medieval times from Machiavelli and in ancient times from the patriarchal familial and tribally focused customs and religion of a law of racially bred status society. Philosophically it rests on the materialistic metaphysical notion that the "real" as distinct from the "epiphenomenal" human being is merely an unconscious, yet directly sensed aggregate of imageful billiard-ball-like material substances which are pushed around by sensuously felt materialistic forces after the manner of the now out-moded billiard-ball physics of the seventeenth century when Hobbes wrote his political philosophy and the mid-nineteenth century when Marx and the legally positivistic English jurist Austin wrote theirs. The welter of conceptual confusions which this theory contains have been exposed in a previous chapter.

Later chapters will show that similar confusions occur in the philosophical assumptions of any medieval or ancient law of status society or tribal nation and in the theory of mental or spiritual substances of those nations of Latin America during the nineteenth century whose political philosophy was called *Espiritualismo,* one example of which is described in Chapter 8.

Such spiritualistic national politicians were correct in their emphasis upon the political citizen or leader being an indubitably conscious being for whom philosophical ideas and political ideals are of the essence. These indubitable facts must be taken care of in some other manner than by Leibniz and Lotze's assignment of them to the interior of a windowless mental substance, thereby turning a nation into a mere aggregate of insulated atoms or particles of consciousness each incapable of contacting any other in any conceivable manner. How this is to be done will concern us in Chapters 14, 18 and 19.

The Hobbesian and Austinian free democratic and the Marxist Communistic power politicians were correct in their recognition that both people and nations are realistically epistemological, neurological and behavioristic things. This experimentally confirmable fact must be taken care of in some way other than by appeal to Hobbes', Feuerbach's and Marx's equally confused notions of naïvely realistic sensed material substances and then being forced to assign one's indubitable consciousness and its ideas and ideals to the realm of limbo. How the truth in materialism and power-political nationalism without its confused worlds-of-discourse nonsense is to be cared for has been shown in the two previous chapters. Epistemologically stated, the answer is that radical empiricism related to logical realism by epistemic rules of correspondence is substituted for the naïve realism of either spiritual substances or material substances.

Even so, as we now turn to the more precise methods for describing the properties of any particular species of nation and then evaluating the properties of this nation as so described, the aforementioned distinctions between different political philosophies such as naïvely realistic power-political materialism, introspectively naïve realistic personalistic spiritualism, mental substance-material substance causally interacting ontological dualism, radically empirical introspective moral, legal and political positivism and logically realistic imageless concept by postulation mathematical physics and contractual legal and political science must be kept continuously in mind. Otherwise we will not be able to identify the particular species of nation in any particular instance of a nation that is before us.

Because political leaders in Africa, the Middle East and Asia are now importing Western technological instruments and Western contractual legal and political institutions, both of which derive from a logical, rather than a naïvely realistic, epistemology, whereas the ways of thinking and living of their own people express both (a) the naïvely realistic mode of thought and customs of a patriarchal joint familial or tribally focused law of racially bred status nation and (b) the intuitive aesthetic religious and mediational legal values of a radically empirical mentality and behavior, we shall not be too surprised at the recent failures of free democracy in these areas, which were noted in Chapter 1, or at the unsolved political problems that exist which will be described in Chapters 12 and 13. Nor will we be unduly pessimistic over these recent political failures providing our methods can remove the causes which brought them about. We cannot be too careful, therefore, about making these methods clear.

In attempting to do so, we shall take initially as our example in Chapter 8 a nation which illustrates the simple homogeneous case, exactly as in physics one assumes the ideal gas or the frictionless machine in the statement of one's empirically verified theory. This does not mean that we shall leave out of account the diversity and heterogeneity of ideas and propositional beliefs in the minds of men on the earth's surface, any more than the physicist's theory and method leaves out of account complex gases or friction. In the sequel, we shall demonstrate again and again the heterogeneity and even incompatibility of the diverse elementary beliefs of particular people, groups of people and of nations. One must, however, begin with the homogeneous case and with the specification of many different homogeneous cases, leaving until later the description of the heterogeneous and the complex as the compounding of different, simpler legal, political and national philosophies.

Furthermore, in dealing with domestic or international political questions we must avoid confusing the objective description of what the philosophical properties of a given nation are, or what the complex of philosophical properties of that nation is, with the quite different question of evaluating what we have thus described. The unfortunate fact is that politicians, laymen and many social scientists corrupt their descriptive judgments because their descriptive method is so intuitive and nebulous that they surreptitiously and frequently quite unconsciously smuggle in evaluative judgments of their own political party or nation or school of "social science" when they are purporting merely to be describing another party or nation. We cannot be too careful, therefore, in specifying in further detail the descriptive method of philosophical anthropology as applied to politics. Only if it is made clear and then distinguished from the evaluative method can any social scientist's or politician's judgments be based on objective evidence concerning what the other nations or his own nation is, rather than on what he feels or thinks it ought to be.

6

The Descriptive Method

It has been noted that any nation or its culture is known only when the complex postulate set which describes the covert or overt norms of its living and positive law is determined. Hence the descriptive method of philosophical anthropology and its practical politics must include deductive and theoretical as well as inductive operational and fact-finding procedures. In different nations and cultures the postulate sets are different. Also in some nations, as for example classical Buddhist Burma, its postulate set has been found [1] when checked by suitable operational tests to be composed only of concepts by intuition in the sense defined in Chapters 2 and 3. In other nations and civilizations, such as those under the significant influence of imageless mathematical physics and Stoic Roman contractual legal science, their postulate sets will be found to contain concepts by postulation which are concepts by intellection in epistemic correlation with concepts by intuition.

Operational definitions for testing whether one's descriptive method has designated the correct postulate set in describing any particular nation or culture are yet to be developed by cultural anthropologists. This book, for the most part, will not attempt to improve on present methods. Nor is such improvement immediately necessary, as the sequel will show. As suggested in the previous chapter, by interrogating its citizens or by reading the philosophical or other classics of any nation or political party and their positive legal constitutions and consciously expressed political policies, one can determine their respective philosophical assumptions to a first degree of approximation that is sufficient for most practical purposes.

Even so, one example of a more precise operational criterion for determining whether one has designated the correct set of postulates in any particular nation or political party is worth indicating here. This example was suggested to the writer by the following experience of two American soldiers in North Africa during World War II. They found themselves billeted with African villagers whose life and mentality were apparently quite simple. Sitting beside "common-sense objects," these soldiers chatted with the villagers for months. One of them painted one of these "common-sense" objects in the classical Western manner. To his surprise he found that his fellow Africans hung the painting upside down. Moreover, when he turned the painting "right side up" and told them such was the way to hang it and look at it, it was equally clear that it signified no more than the two-dimensional impressionistic collection of colors which they saw when they hung it upside down or sideways. They simply did not have the previous education in the elementary propositions of Euclidian three-dimensional geometry that must be trapped in the association areas of any person's brain if he is to "see" the modern man's "common-sense" objects or even to "see" the modern man of "common sense" himself with "his feet on the ground."

Rorschach tests applied by Mr. Carter Zeleznik to the local people of Abyssinia suggest additional operational and experimental criteria for determining whether the people of any culture or any nation have merely the psychological epistemic correlates of concepts by intuition trapped in their brains or also concepts by postulation which are in part at least concepts by intellection of a Euclidian three-dimensionally proportional kind.

These differences in the kinds and the content of the covertly or consciously held beliefs in the minds of people are not hereditary. Their physiological correlates may all be personally and culturally trapped or untrapped and changed with appropriate educational techniques. They can even be brought out into the open and examined with respect to their cognitive truth or falsity. Many people who previously thought of the sensed and introspected data of their experience only in terms of concepts by intuition have mastered the imageless concepts by postulation which are concepts by intellection of the symbolic logical and axiomatically constructed, deductively formulated mathematical physics. Conversely, many modern Westerners who do not realize the degree to which they think and behave both consciously and unconsciously largely in terms of formal theoretical scientific and legal constructs, are now learning to feel, think and behave from the standpoint of concepts by intuition and the emotive and impressionistically aesthetic component of themselves and of nature which concepts by intuition denote. Impressionistic painting and the present interest in Zen Buddhism and in Oriental art and culture generally instance this fact.

It remains to specify the theoretical, as distinct from the operational, part of the descriptive method of philosophical anthropology. To this end mathematical logic, especially that of the Harvard Professor of Philosophy Emeritus Henry M. Sheffer, contributes information that is exceedingly important. He showed that science has a systematic as well as an analytic side.*

The analytic emphasis has been appreciated and pursued from the very beginning. It encourages the departmentalization of knowledge, the investigation of specific problems in logic and empirical science, and the conception of philosophy as analysis. The latter conception of philosophy tends to take the meaningfulness of a proposition as given and to conceive of philosophy as the analysis of the proposition to render its meaning in an expanded and literal form.

The systematic emphasis in mathematical logic notes that not merely individual propositions but bodies of propositions—or in other words systems, to use Henry Sheffer's earlier language, or doctrines, to use Cassius Keyser's terminology—have formal properties. From this standpoint, the meaning of an individual proposition cannot be fully understood apart from the formal properties of the systematic body of propositions of the deductively formulated theory of which it is a part. From this viewpoint, the conception of philosophy as the analysis of an individual proposition as given appears to be exceedingly naïve. Certainly, if a proposition is in a deductively formulated theory, any concept in the proposition is either a logical constant, a primitive concept, or a defined concept—that is, a concept that is defined in terms of primitive concepts and logical constants; and, since any primitive concept in a deductively formulated theory

* What follows is an abridged version of the essay "The Importance of Deductively Formulated Theory in Ethics and Social and Legal Science," published in *Structure, Method, and Meaning: Essays in Honor of Henry M. Sheffer,* eds., Paul Henie, *et al.* (New York, 1951), pp. 99 ff. Reprinted by permission of the publishers, The Liberal Arts Press, Inc., New York.

depends for its essential, syntactically given meaning upon all the postulates within which it is a term, it follows that the attempt to find the complete meaning of any proposition merely by analyzing it in isolation is incompatible with the way in which the primitive and defined concepts of a deductively formulated theory get their meaning.

It is very important to realize that a primitive or undefined concept in a deductively formulated theory is not a meaningless concept, even when it has no meaning given to it apart from the deductive theory, in the form of concept by intuition knowledge by acquaintance; it is meaningless only when considered by itself, apart from the postulate set in which it is a term. But within the postulate set, it has meaning assigned to it by the way in which it is related to other concepts by all the postulates and deduced theorems, not merely by one of them. For example, the primitive concept "point" represented by an entity variable has a quite different concept by postulation meaning in the postulate set of Euclid's geometry from what it has in any postulate set of Riemann's geometry, even though apart from any postulate set it is without meaning and even though the empirical question is not raised concerning whether there is a concept by intuition empirical epistemic correlate of it in the empirical world. Similarly, it is possible to formulate the theory of the "electron" with the postulate set either of Lorentz or of quantum mechanics, treating the concept by postulation "electron" as a primitive concept. This does not mean, however, that the primitive concept "electron" within the postulates of either theory is meaningless until denotative concept by intuition correlates for it are found in the empirical world. Quite apart from these empirical concept by intuition correlates, the primitive concept "electron" has a meaning given to it syntactically by the postulates in which it appears as a term. That this is the case is shown by the fact that the denotative concept by intuition meaning of electron, as illustrated in the Wilson cloud chamber experiment, is the same for the Lorentzian as for the quantum mechanical theory, whereas the concept by postulation meaning of the primitive concept "electron" is fundamentally different in the two cases. In the Lorentzian theory the primitive concept "electron" is by postulation an entity which has a sharp position and momentum at one and the same time. In quantum mechanics, on the other hand, the primitive concept "electron" is given a concept by postulation meaning by the basic postulates of the theory such that it is impossible for it to have both a sharp position and a sharp velocity at one and the same time. It must not be thought, therefore, that the so-called undefined or primitive concepts in a deductively formulated theory, even when considered wholly apart from the question of empirical applications of the theory, are without meaning. All the postulates of the theory prescribe their meaning syntactically. When an undefined or primitive concept appears within the postulates or theorems of a deductively formulated theory, that "undefined" entity takes on all the meanings assigned to it by satisfying that particular postulate set and its deduced theorems. As stated in the previous chapter, it is impossible in the analysis of scientific theory and method to avoid confusion on this point unless the denotative, operationally defined meaning of a scientific concept in a deductively formulated theory is clearly distinguished from the scientifically constructed postulationally designated meaning. To this end the distinction which I have introduced between concepts by intuition designating the purely empirical, operationally given meaning and concepts by postulation designating the syntactical theoretically given meaning is essential. A concept by intuition is one the complete meaning of which is given by something that can be immediately apprehended. A concept by postulation is one the meaning of which in whole or part is proposed for it syntactically by the postulate set of some specific deductively formulated theory in which it functions as a term.

Once this systematic character of the meaning of any single proposition is realized, one's conception of science and philosophy undergoes a sea change. No proposition in a deductively formulated theory can be analyzed apart from a consideration of all the primitive propositions of the deductive theory as a whole. This conception of philosophy, while keeping analysis, at the same time puts an equal emphasis upon science and philosophy as systematic thinking. In fact, it entails that analysis of any single proposition of a deductively formulated theory is never exact or complete unless the formal properties of any such theory as a whole which relate the proposition being analyzed to all the other propositions of the theory are kept constantly in mind. . . .

Not only does deductively formulated knowledge enable us with precision to designate and formulate the part in its relation to the whole, thereby giving us the conception of science and philosophy as system, but also, because of the fact that there are many possible deductively formulated theories, it gives us the conception of the heart of science and philosophy as the definition and resolution of the theoretic problems to which the different postulate sets of the different deductively formulated theories are different answers.

Once this point is grasped, it becomes evident that the key to a genuine understanding of either empirical science or philosophy is neither a knowledge of facts alone nor a knowledge of theories succeeding one another in time alone, but an understanding of the basic *theoretically defined* problems which the inductively given facts and the many deductively formulated theories together generate. In this connection, the writer is reminded of a report given him by Professor John Dewey of a conversation which Professor Dewey had in the 1920's with a European physicist of unquestioned distinction, objectivity, and integrity. The conversation occurred the night before this physicist sailed for Europe, after having returned from a trip which had taken him to the major physics departments and laboratories of the United States. Professor Dewey asked the physicist what he thought of American physics, as the result of his observations. The European physicist replied as follows, "I take it you want a frank answer. It is my opinion that in about fifty years there will be some first-rate physics in the United States." One may well ask, as Professor Dewey did, why, with the many laboratories, their powerful and refined apparatus, and the greater amount of experimentation, this should be the verdict. The reply was, "I believe that we in Europe have a better understanding of the basic theoretical problems."

In this statement, the European scientist showed that his judgment was not born, as one might at first suppose, of the provincialism of a foreigner, but resulted from his having put his finger on the objective heart of the matter. Western scientific knowledge, when it is most effective, is deductively formulated knowledge indirectly verified * experimentally. This being the case, unless one has learned to think

---

* By "indirect verification" is meant the confirmation of a deductively formulated theory, not by verifying its postulates, but by verifying merely some of its deduced theorems.

deductively and systematically, considering in relation to one another and the experimental evidence the three major deductively formulated theories of modern physics—particle physics, field physics and quantum mechanics—thereby revealing the basic theoretical problems to which the rival postulate sets of these three theories give different answers, one literally does not even know what the basic problems of contemporary physics are, to say nothing about having first-rate science.

Deductively formulated theory is equally important for the social sciences. In considering them, it is necessary to keep two types of social theory in mind. Since the social sciences are facing normative problems of value as well as problems of fact, two quite different types of theory are required. The one type, appropriately termed "factual or descriptive social theory," attempts, after the manner of natural science, to obtain an empirically verified deductively formulated theory of society as it is in fact. The other type, appropriately called "normative social theory," attempts to specify a deductively formulated theory of society as it ought to be. Marxist Communism and the democracy of Locke, Jefferson, Lincoln, Bentham, Mill and Jevons are theories of the latter type.

Only certain of the social sciences have to date achieved deductively formulated factual social theory. Economics has such theory in the case of W. Stanley Jevons' formulation of the science,[2] and also in the case of the very similar theory of the Austrian school.[3] Even so, deductively formulated factual economic theory has been achieved only for statics, and not for dynamics.[4] What this means is that the postulates of the deductive theory enable one, when empirical values of theoretically specified variables defining the present state of an economic system are determined, to deduce other characteristics which the state of the economic system must have at that same time; the postulates do not enable one, given the aforementioned empirical values of the present state of an economic system, to deduce the future state of that economic system.[5] Sociology to date has not achieved a deductively formulated factual social theory, even for statics.[6]

In normative social theory and in philosophy, on the other hand, many deductively formulated theories, or theories which even though written in ordinary prose are only understood with precision when their primitive ideas and postulates and attendant theorems are brought out into the open, have been formulated. Roman legal science, with its doctrine of *jus gentium* grounded in *jus naturae,* was such a normative theory. The Marxist ideology is another such theory. Thomistic philosophy is a third instance. Hume's philosophy, as worked out by Bentham and Austin for law and politics and by Jevons for economic science, is a fourth.

The empirical sociologists and anthropologists of the nineteenth and twentieth centuries, influenced as they were by positivism and British empirical philosophy, supposed that they could obtain an objective understanding of a foreign people or culture observed in the field if they honestly described the facts which they saw. This mentality is now perhaps more prevalent among philosophers than among social scientists. Actual experience in the field shows it to rest on the naïve assumption that one can have facts in a form which makes them of use for science without having ideas and concepts. It is possible, of course, by sense awareness to apprehend directly inspectable data and, in this sense, to obtain facts without ideas. Unfortunately, however, such knowledge is of little use to science, because it cannot be conveyed to other scientists and reconfirmed as to its objectivity by them. To convey observed data to other scientists, one must report it at scientific meetings or record it in scientific publications; and the moment one speaks or writes, one no longer has pure facts. Instead one has described facts; and the instant one has described facts, one has concepts, and hence ideas and theory.

Long ago, therefore, the natural scientists learned that the way to be objective is not to try to get along without concepts and theory, but to get the concepts and theory which one is using out into the open, so that nothing is being smuggled in surreptitiously and everyone can see precisely what the ideas or concepts are. The scientific method for doing this most effectively is the method of deductively formulated theory. This method forces one to specify the primitive concepts designating the elementary entities and relations in terms of which all the observed and inferred data in one's subject matter are being described. In short, the way to keep facts from being corrupted by faulty ideas and bad theory is not to be hard-boiled and attempt to get along without ideas by restricting oneself to pure fact alone, but to pay as much attention to the ideas or concepts one uses to describe the facts as one does to the facts being described.

Such considerations indicate that the objective social scientist or politician is not the hard-boiled, positivistic empiricist who would get nothing but facts; or even he who, adding description to observation of the facts, would still use only inductive methods. Instead, the objective social scientist is the one who makes sure that the conceptualization of the facts of a foreign culture which he portrays is the conceptualization of the people in that culture, rather than his own. To do this, he must, by conversation with them and by reading their written documents, discover their basic covert and overt concepts or ideology, as well as observe their overt behavior and institutions; and he must supplement induction with deductively formulated theory presenting each culture as its particular observable data conceptualized by its particular set of primitive concepts and propositions.

7

The Evaluative Method

It is generally recognized that there is a cognitive method for describing the normative judgments of a person or a group of people with common normative customs and political ideals. The crucial question is whether there is a cognitive method for evaluating such normative judgments, customs and political ideals once they are objectively described.

By a cognitive, or scientific, method is meant one which, when applied to the living and positive legal norms of a given person, people or nation, gives a conclusion of which it is significant to say that it is true or false in a sense which can be confirmed by anyone in that or any other culture or nation. For example, that Hitler's normative judgments and the customs of his followers were such and such can be determined by reading his *Mein Kampf* and his speeches and comparing what he wrote and said with what he and the quantitative majority of his contemporary Germans did or approved. The result of this descriptive method will be a set of statements of which it is significant to say that they are true. Moreover, they are true in the descriptive sense that, were Hitler alive or were a Hitlerian present now to read these statements, he as well as we would agree that they are empirically confirmed and in this sense cognitively true. The question which this chapter is asking has to do with whether in precisely this same sense of being valid for him as well as for us there is a cognitive method for evaluating the normative judgments and living law behavior of Hitler's Germany, once any Hitlerian and we have agreed that it has been correctly described.

That there is a method for doing this, providing one assumes the descriptively true normative premises of a free democratic society with its legal Bill of Rights protecting minority groups, no one is likely to deny. Conversely, assuming Hitler's norms as described correctly in the sense of the previous paragraph, then, as so measured, a free democratic society which protects minority groups is similarly a false or evil society composed of morally spineless individuals who prefer to die in bed instead of shouting and fighting passionately for the romantically Wagnerian demands of the purely bred, law of biological status "rights of the German *Volk.*"

But our present question probes deeper than this. Given two such different correctly described normative nations, it asks whether there is a cognitive method which, when applied to both of them, enables one to say *in a sense which anyone anywhere can confirm* that the philosophy which correctly describes one of these nation's goal value beliefs and behavior is true and that the quite incompatible, different philosophy of that of the other nation is false?

The words in italics in the last sentence are very important. Unless they are taken seriously, the reader will erroneously interpret this chapter. The writer speaks from concrete experience when he issues this important caution. Before publishing what follows in this chapter, he read an earlier, abridged version to a small group of very able philosophers, all of whom have thought deeply and at length on these matters. Many of them reached the conclusion in their initial comments afterwards that the evaluative method described here cannot be the correct one, and even if it were a correct one, it is unnecessary. The major reason given was that certainly each one of us knows that he can and does evaluate conduct, such as that of Hitler, without the use of the elaborate method described in this chapter. Of course this is the case if one means by "evaluate," an evaluation that is true merely as judged by me, or as judged from the standpoint of the norms of my culture or the legal and political normative principles of my nation, or the assumption of my particular ethical and political philosophy. But to assume that this shows that the evaluative method described here is, therefore, either false or unnecessary is to overlook what this method is introduced to do—namely, specify an evaluative method, the application of which can give an evaluative judgment in the sense of the words in italics in the previous paragraph. In short, we are seeking for a method for evaluating Hitler's Germany which will be not merely intuitively convincing in its findings for those in nations holding different political norms, but which also will give a conclusion that can be confirmed by *anyone anywhere* whether he be a follower of Hitler, a Marxist dialectically materialistic Communist, one who believes in the free democratic political philosophy of Locke and Jefferson, a classically Confucian Chinese gentleman, or a contemporary British analytically and radically empirical philosopher.

Another reason which some may give for saying that the evaluative method about to be described is unnecessary is that one can test the different national normative political philosophies pragmatically after the manner in which different non-normatively worded theories in the natural sciences are confirmed or disconfirmed. By a non-normatively worded theory of natural science we mean one in which aesthetic, ethical, legal or political normative words such as "beautiful," "ugly," "good," "bad," "just," "unjust," "murder," "traitor," "political rights" or "political duties" do not occur. By a normatively worded theory we mean one in which such words do occur. We shall find that there is a sense in which even for normatively worded theory the pragmatist's thesis is correct. But there is also a very important sense, which is the heart of the difficulty, in which this is not the case.

The latter sense is twofold. The reasons for it have been stated very clearly in A. J. Ayer's *Language, Truth and Logic* where he distinguishes, as we have done, (1) between (a) describing a norm and (b) evaluating a norm that has been correctly described and (2) between (a) instrumental norms or instrumental values and (b) intrinsic norms or goal values.[1] Ethical words which merely describe some *de facto* set of ethical norms Ayer calls "descriptive ethical symbols."[2] Ethical words, however, which evaluate the descriptive ethical symbols, he calls "normative ethical symbols."[3]

The pragmatist's method of confirming a theory indirectly and hence pragmatically by way of its inspectable deductive practical consequences is necessary and sufficient to confirm cognitively that one's description of the normative philosophical character of a particular *de facto* nation is correct. But as Professor Ayer's distinction between descriptive normative words and evaluative normative words makes clear, the describing of any nation's norms with cognitive correctness by the pragmatic test and the evaluating of those correctly described norms by the pragmatic method are two quite different things.

The difficulty is that any nation's normative political philosophy does not merely conform to what happens pragmatically in practice; it also evaluates it, sending to jail or even to the electric chair many who do not conform to the nation's normative ideals and also using its normative ideal to measure the precise sense in which what has happened pragmatically in practice has fallen short of the national legal and political ideal. In other words, political norms measure what happens pragmatically in practice. They do not merely conform completely, after the manner of the theories of natural science, to *all* the operationally given data that are found to be the case pragmatically in fact.

Also, with respect to those cases noted in Chapter 1 in which free democratic legal and political norms have failed when put to a pragmatic test, we do want it to be cognitively meaningful to say that free democratic norms are none the less the cognitively correct ones in the sense of cognitive correctness which can be confirmed by *anyone anywhere* today without waiting for further pragmatic appeal to what may or may not happen in the future. If so, then some political method other than that of mere pragmatic political experimentation is required to evaluate, as distinct from merely to describe, what happens when the pragmatic experiment has been performed.

The usual way to avoid this conclusion is to add onto the pragmatic test the words "in the long run." This recourse makes the pragmatic method worthless for evaluating any normative political theory today. Furthermore, it makes the pragmatist's evaluative method scientifically spurious, since whatever turns out to be the case pragmatically with respect to the normative theory with which one is experimenting, one can always save the theory. If the normative theory works, then one says, "It is pragmatically confirmed." If it doesn't work, then one says, "Even so, but it will work in the long run." Suppose also that one tests the Communistic theory in this pragmatic manner, as many "open-minded" Asians are now inclined to do, by giving the Communists a chance to try their Communistic experiment in one's nation. If this pragmatic experiment is to be a real one, the Communists would have to be given complete control. Then, however, all experimentation might very well be over, since, if you, the private citizen, found that the Communist theory did not work for you, it would in all likelihood be you rather than the theory that would be liquidated as a result of the pragmatic experiment.

Professor Ayer's use of G. E. Moore's well-known distinction between (a) instrumental norms and values and (b) intrinsic or goal values is equally important. It cuts to the heart of the present practical political question concerning whether merely instrumental economic or military aid can solve today's political problems either at home or abroad. It also points up another difficulty in the assumption that the pragmatic method can evaluate as well as describe *de facto* national political norms. As Professor Ayer notes, if the norms are instrumental to a given person or a given nation's intrinsic or goal values, then, assuming those intrinsic goal values, of course it can. But the question with which evaluative as distinct from merely descriptive ethics, law and politics are concerned is whether there is a method for evaluating the described personal intrinsic goal value norms which the pragmatist's descriptive method has assumed. That the pragmatist's method cannot do the evaluative job is implicit in the pragmatic method itself, since, as Dewey himself tells us, there is no meaning to any pragmatic operation or experiment except with respect to an "end-in-view." [4] A method which must assume an end-in-view in order to be, clearly, therefore, cannot evaluate the end-in-view itself.

We accept, therefore, the validity of the pragmatic method for doing two things with respect to normatively worded theory: (1) It can confirm the cognitive correctness of any theoretical description of any particular person's or nation's political and living law norms, after the manner described in the previous chapter with respect to Kluckhohn's philosophy of the Navaho nation. Also, (2) assuming a given correctly described intrinsic normative political end-in-view of any particular nation, it can determine the most efficient economic or military instrumental values for achieving or protecting that particular normative political aim. What it cannot do is to evaluate the correctly described aim itself.

G. E. Moore's intuitive method is invalid for different reasons. According to this theory the word "good" is an indefinable ethical predicate similar to the predicate "yellow" in impressionistic art. It is by no means self-evident that there is such an ethical predicate. Assuming, however, for the purposes of argument, that such a predicate exists, it is of no practical use, since possessing such an atomic meaning gives one no criterion for determining when it is to be predicated correctly of anything. Not being empirically given as a naturalistic predicate of the object, after the manner of "yellow," examining the object being evaluated will tell one nothing about whether it should be affirmed to be good or bad.

In fact, as the late Professor Felix Cohen, who held Moore's theory in order to avoid "the naturalistic fallacy," [5] noted, unless one has some other criterion such as "pleasure" for telling one when the indefinable ethical predicate "good" is correctly affirmed of anything, this intuitive method for evaluating ethical, legal and political norms is more likely to be an excuse for bigotry or the mere expression of the culturally relative norms of one's own people or nation in the name of one's indefinable and irreducible moral intuition than an elucidation of what the word "good" means. Cohen tried to overcome this likely danger in any intuitive theory of ethics by agreeing with G. E. Moore about what the word "good" means theoretically, and adding Bentham's "greatest pleasure for the greatest number" as the operational criterion for predicating the indefinable ethical predicate "good" of anything. But if one has to resort to hedonism to protect intuitive ethics from itself, why have intuitive ethics at all?

Nor is hedonism by itself any improvement as an evaluative method. As Judge Learned Hand replied to Senator Paul Douglas when questioned about Bentham's principle,[6] this evaluative method is more clever in theory than it is usable in practice for the very simple reason that there is no objective method of either getting inside another person's private, introspective consciousness to find out what pleases him or of adding up all these different amounts of pleasantness for the majority of people even if one could find out what each is. What happens in practice with the hedonistic method is that one surreptitiously shifts from pleasantness judged en masse by everybody or by the majority, to pleasantness as judged by me. Otherwise, the hedonist would not have been justified in judging the majority-pleasing statutes of Congress, with respect to the treatment of the minority American Indians, to be bad, as Felix Cohen did, notwithstanding the likelihood that the total quantity of pleasure which the majority in Congress and the people behind them ex-

pressed, was larger in quantity than the amount of pleasure the relatively small number of American Indians would have enjoyed had not
the majority in Congress been pleased to act as they did by taking
away from them their land as granted in a treaty.

Other introspective psychological theories of evaluative ethics and
politics are similar. Such theories are that to say of anything that
it is good is equivalent to saying that it is approved by the majority
or that it is an interest of the majority. There are two fatal weaknesses in any of these introspective psychological normative theories:
(1) Even if one assumes the theory, it gives an evaluation which is
cognitively true merely as judged by me or by the majority of people
in my nation; it does not give an evaluative judgment in the sense of
the italicized words in the paragraph above. (2) The question with
which this chapter is concerned is, however, whether the hedonistic
definition of intrinsic value is the correct one or whether the Marxist's, Hitler's or some other normative theory such as the ethic of
Christ's sacrifice on the Cross, in which pain clearly outweighed pleasure, is the cognitively correct one *in the sense of being confirmable by
anybody anywhere.* Clearly, as the normative non-cognitivists Stevenson, Ayer and Alf Ross have shown, all introspective psychological
theories for evaluating correctly described personal or political norms
beg the question. Assuming any one of them to be true, they, of
course, give evaluative judgments that are cognitively true or false
in a sense which can be confirmed by anyone anywhere. But the
question at issue is whether there is any meaning for saying, in a
sense which can be confirmed by anyone anywhere, that the definition
of the meaning of "ethically good" or "politically good" that is assumed is cognitively true or false. We conclude, therefore, that unless
some new method is specified for cognitively evaluating correctly
described personal or political intrinsic goal values, the non-
cognitivists Stevenson, Ayer and Alf Ross, who affirm that descriptive but not evaluative ethics, law and politics are cognitive, have
said the last word in this most difficult of all subjects.

Nevertheless, the scientific findings and the philosophical analyses
described in the previous chapters indicate that there is a cognitive
method for evaluating *in a sense which can be confirmed by anyone
anywhere,* the correctly described intrinsic goal value norms of any
particular person or nation. Having gone to great length to become

clear concerning what the precise question is to which our evaluative method is attempting to give the answer, the time has now come to specify this method.

Two preliminary observations are in order. First, much of present analytic philosophy has approached this problem with two surreptitious cultural assumptions. These two assumptions are British empirical philosophy and radically empirical introspective psychology. In the writer's recent *Complexity of Legal and Ethical Experience,* he has attempted to justify the evaluative method of this chapter as far as possible within these traditional Anglo-American cultural assumptions. In the present chapter, however, we are approaching evaluative ethics and politics from the standpoint of the richer epistemological and psychological theory of Chapters 3, 4, 5 and 6. This richer theory accepts the radical empiricism and introspective psychology of modern British empirical philosophy as irreducible while adding to it the equally irreducible concepts by postulation that are concepts by intellection of a logically realistic epistemology. Thereby the directly and radically empirically known data and ideas of one's private, introspectively psychological self are epistemically correlated with the logically realistic, indirectly confirmed data of one's public, neurological and behavioristic psychological self. This permits us to give an independent validation of the evaluative method of philosophical anthropology. It also gives us a public person, rather than merely a private, introspective self.

What this richer epistemological and psychological theory does is to accept the radical empiricism of Locke's *Essay Concerning Human Understanding* and of Hume the radically empirical theoretician, while also substituting logical realism that is indirectly confirmed via epistemic rules of correspondence for the naïve realism of the earlier Locke, what Hume believed "in practice," and G. E. Moore.

Thereby their inconsistency is avoided of oscillating back and forth as Anglo-American empirical philosophy since Hume has done between (1) the radical empiricism of Locke of the *Essay* and of Hume in theory, which rejects naïve realism and (2) the naïve realism of the earlier Locke, of Hume in practice and of G. E. Moore. This traditional inconsistency in modern Anglo-American empirical philosophy since Hume, which oscillates between (a) a radical empiricism that rejects naïve realism only to find that it cannot live

with nothing but its radical empiricism and then (b) reverts "in practice" surreptitiously to naïve realism, is appropriately called *the fallacy of the Humean oscillator*. Radical empiricism epistemically correlated with indirectly confirmed logical realism avoids this fallacy.

One brief caution is necessary. In what follows and in later chapters we shall not always use the lengthy, expanded expression "the neurologically trapped impulses that are the epistemic correlates of introspected ideas." Instead, we shall sometimes use, in quotes, McCulloch and Pitts' briefer elliptical expression "trapped universals." The quotes express the fact that this shorter expression is elliptical and, therefore, must always be thought of by the reader as a shorthand for the longer, expanded expression. Otherwise, as emphasized in Chapters 2 and 3, the two words "trapped" and "universals" which belong to epistemologically different worlds of discourse are likely to be combined in the reader's mind as if they referred to items of knowledge in the same epistemological world of discourse, in which case nonsense will be the result.

Our reason for using the richer theory of conceptual meaning and of the psychological person is twofold: First, as Chapters 14 and 18 will show, neither mathematical physics and its technology nor any modern nation whose law and politics are contractual can be understood without (1) the incomplete symbols, or concepts by postulation that are concepts by intellection of a logically realistic epistemology in (2) epistemic correlation with (3) the concepts of intuition of a radically empirical epistemology. Second, as Chapters 11 and 17 will indicate, a major theory of politics in both the free and the Communist world has been the Hobbesian or Marxist materialistic power-political theory of both domestic legal obligation and foreign policy in which "international law" is a self-contradictory notion. As shown by the quotation from Hobbes in Chapter 2, this theory rests on the conception of the public self as merely a public material mass governed only by Galilei's law of inertia. With the Marxist it rests also on the behavioristic psychology of Pavlov. Both of these concepts of the public person confuse any person's teleologically mechanical public self with the non-teleological mechanisms of early seventeenth century physics. They also completely neglect (a) the role of trapped impulses serving as the inner target of any human nervous system

and (b) the self-initiating activities of the association areas of the cortex in determining what are the unique trapped impulses of any particular person's nervous system. Thus in terms of the power politician's concept of a person as merely the physical, neurologically behavioristic public person, his theory is false.

Even so, Hobbes, Marx, Watson, Pavlov and the power politicians are correct against the morally intuitive introspectionists in realizing that in law and politics the willful killing of another person must take place in the public world of the motor neuronic behavioristic responses of the public person before that person is guilty of murder. For this reason, a realistic epistemological theory of the person is required to account for normative second-order factual deeds such as murder.

But there is more to murder than this. For murder is also such realistic public behavior of the public person in the public space-time of natural science as measured normatively by the domestic legal and political ideals and normative prescriptions of some particular nation. Normative ideals entail private, introspective psychology with its radically empirical epistemology. A nation similarly is such a radically empirical, introspectively psychological private personal thing. What the power politician does is to omit the private, introspective psychological moral, legal, political person and nation, restricting himself to the public Pavlovian non-teleologically mechanical entities. When he does this, he ceases to have either a person or a nation.

Conversely, the traditional introspective, moral and ideological politician had a private moral, religious and political person and nation, but one which was wholly private to him. Furthermore, he had no theoretical conception or operational method for relating his private, introspective moral or religious convictions to the public selves and people of his nation. The consequence frequently was that the more religiously serious and morally principled the latter type of private, introspective politician was on Sunday morning when in church, the less he knew what to do with his morality and religion as applied to particulars in public space and time when he arrived at his desk in the Department of State on Monday morning. The result in some instances, at least, as Chapter 11 will show, was that between the avowed power politician and the traditional private, introspective

morally and religiously principled statesman there was little difference in practice, for all their verbal incompatibilities. The plain fact
was that neither knew how to put his private, introspected moral,
religious and political self and his public, neurologically behavioristic
self together.

Clearly what is needed in contemporary psychology, morality and
politics is a theory and a practice which can get (1) the morally
normative, introspectively psychological private self and nation and
(2) the neurologically and behavioristically meaningful public self,
person and nation together, specifying the cognitively verifiable
substantive content of the normative ideals of what (1) must be if
they are to be cognitively true in a sense that can be confirmed by
anyone anywhere. Only a psychological theory of the person which
is such that it can be confirmed by anyone anywhere can do this.
Moreover, this psychological theory cannot be a merely introspective
one; otherwise there will be no public self capable of committing
murder in public space-time and no public nation capable of aggressive war at some particular point with a quantitatively specific
amount of military weapons in astronomically determined and operationally confirmed Greenwich time. Nor can this psychological
theory be merely that of the neurologically behavioristic public
person in public space and time; otherwise nations would not differ
normatively because of their different philosophically defined, introspectively known and private personal goal-value political propositions. Furthermore, the relation between self or nation in the latter,
directly introspective, normative and ideational meaning and person
or nation in the public, theoretically designated, indirectly and experimentally confirmed sense must be described. Otherwise the unbridgeable gulf between what the citizen or the politician professes
morally and normatively and what he does behavioristically and
power-politically will continue to be unbridgeable. It is the merit of
the theory of the epistemological and psychological theory of the self
of Chapter 4 that it meets these conditions.

In other words (1) it accepts the introspective and directly known
private self with its personal and national ideals for the indubitable
fact that it is, as real as anything else that is real; not describing it
as an epiphenomenon, whatever that word may mean, if it means
anything. Any person anywhere is such a private, conscious self with

his or her particular ideas, ideals and moral, political and religious commitments. Any nation, moreover, as Chapter 5 has shown, is a quantitatively large group of such private selves sharing a common philosophy with its specific aesthetic, emotive, theoretical, religious and secular content for defining the normative political properties of their nation. (2) The psychological theory of Chapter 4 introduces and accepts also a richer and more adequate neurological and behavioristic psychological theory of the public person and of the nation in the sense of a group of public people located and behaving somewhere and somewhen in the public space and time of natural science. (3) It specifies that the relation between the directly known facts of (1) and the imageless, theoretically postulated, indirectly and experimentally confirmed facts of (2) are epistemic rules of correspondence rather than that of the relation of a predicate to its substance or of causal relations between different kinds of substances.

It affirms also that the antecedently specified epistemic rules of correspondence between the directly inspected, radically empirical facts of (1) and the indirectly confirmed, logically realistic facts of (2) are different when (a) the public object in (2) is an object other than the public self, than what the epistemic rules are when (b) the public object is one's public self. In the former case, (a), the epistemic rules of correspondence are many-one; in the latter case, (b) they are one-one.

The many-oneness in the case of (a) expresses the fact that the relatedness of the radically empirically observed events, objects and properties, all of which are relative to each observer, is not isomorphic with the relatedness of logical realistically known, indirectly confirmed invariant events, objects and properties in public space-time. Newton expressed this non-isomorphism between sensed and public space and time when, in the first Scholium at the beginning of his *Principia,* he warned his readers against "certain prejudices" [7] of confusing the two. Einstein made this non-isomorphism even more evident when he noted that the public simultaneity of spatially separated events, in the sense of being the same for all observers even on the same frame of reference, is not directly sensed. Quantum theory has made the difference between the relatedness of invariant public nature and the imageful relativity of radically empirical sensed nature even more evident when it finds that not merely sensed, but also even imaginable images must be dismissed from the determination of the state function in any mechanical system.

It is this non-isomorphism of the relatedness of directly sensed nature and the relatedness of invariant public nature which the many-oneness of the epistemic rules of correspondence between the two expresses that dooms to failure all Aristotelian or Weissian naïve realistic abstractive theories of science, natural philosophy and ontological metaphysics. This is why also the even more sophisticated "method of extensive abstraction" of Whitehead will not work.[8]

Of equal significance is the one-oneness of the epistemic rules of correspondence when they relate the introspective self and its emotions, ideas and ideals to the events within the object in public space-time which is one's public self. This one-oneness of the epistemic correlations expresses the fact that the relatedness of sensed nature which any person immediately observes is not the relatedness of the invariant external world but is instead the effect of the casual action of objects and events in public nature other than one's public self, upon one's own particular public self. Hence it is only (1) by taking as clues the sensed effects of the external world upon one's own public nervous system and its brain and (2) by using self-initiatively and actively the association areas of one's brain and its epistemically correlated private conscious mind to construct a hypothetically introduced theory of the external public source of these clues that one can (3) hypothetically and imagelessly postulate and then (4) by appeal to epistemic rules of correspondence, (5) confirm operationally and thereby know either the public world of nature or one's public self as a member of that public world.

Positively, this one-oneness of the epistemic rules of correspondence between one's radically empirical private, introspected self and one's indirectly confirmed logically realistic, theoretically known public self means that the relatedness of introspected meanings and of sensed events in the former is isomorphic with the relatedness of neurophysiological objects and events in the latter. This isomorphism between the relatedness of the data of one's private introspective self and the relatedness of the data of one's public self means not merely that one's introspected ideational self, with its conscious or covertly known or testable philosophy, is irreducible, but also that it has as its one-one epistemic correlate and instrument a brain containing as its inner target trapped impulses that are isomorphic in their behavior with the private conscious self's ideational activities. In other words, the one-one epistemic rules of correspondence between the introspective philosophical ideas in one's private, subjective consciousness and the trapped impulses in the imaginative association areas of one's cortex and in the hierarchy of its final trappings ensure that one's conscious, private, philosophically-minded self has a one-one surrogate in one's public self by means of which it can inhibit or reinforce one's motor neuronic behavioristic responses to any stimulus in public space and time and communicate with other private conscious selves to share commonly agreed upon ideas and ideals, thereby making nations possible. This follows, let it be noted, from two things: (i) Any completely known being is its radically empirical irreducible component and its equally irreducible, logically realistic, indirectly confirmed component joined by epistemic rules of correspondence. (ii) In the case of the completely known self, these epistemic rules of correspondence are one-one.

In grasping all the implications of the last paragraph, two points established in Chapters 3 and 4 are to be kept in mind. First, any person's public self is a teleological mechanism with an inner, self-contained target that is determinable, in the case at least of creative persons, by that person's own speculatively introduced and indirectly confirmed philosophy. Second, once the impulses that are the one-one neural physiological epistemic correlates of that person's elemental postulate set are assigned to and trapped hierarchically, the negative feedback mechanism which is one's nervous system takes over. This ensures mechanically that one's overt behavior, which is a function of (a) the stimulus of the moment and (b) the feedback from the inner target, approximates nearer and nearer to the hitting of the target.

The crucial point to note with respect to the evaluative method in ethics and politics is that any trapped impulses whatever which define this inner target will have this prescriptive effect upon motor behavior. Whether the particular hierarchically trapped impulses which define the inner target are the epistemic correlates of normative or non-normative ideas is irrelevant.

Consider Adam and Eve. Being the first human beings on earth, there were no previous man-made cultural (i.e., second-order) facts antecedent to their eating of the fruit of the tree of knowledge. Hence the only ideas possible for them to trap epistemically in their brains were ideas expressed as propositions (because without propositions there is no knowledge either true or false) which referred to the first-order facts * of non-man-made nature or of non-man-made (i.e., natural) man. (Without this distinction between first-order and second-order facts, our evaluative method would be circularly question-begging, appealing to cultural facts that presuppose pro or con the very cultural or national goal-value philosophy that one is evaluating.) Such a theory will be non-normatively worded and hence cognitively testable by anyone anywhere by appeal to first-order factual data given by his senses or introspectively. In short, the normative words "true" and "false" of cognitive science will apply to the sentences of such a theory. However, relative to the motor side of their nervous systems, this first non-normatively worded first-order factual cognitive philosophy of Adam and Eve, being epistemically the inner target of their own teleologically mechanical nervous systems, would be *prescriptive,* either inhibiting or reinforcing their motor responses to any stimulus of the moment. But *prescriptions* causally determined by the trapped epistemic correlates of a non-normatively worded set of primitive propositions concerning first-order factual nature and natural man give for motor behavior an *ought* or an *ought not,* just as, relative to the first-order factual sensory signals, this same non-normatively worded set of propositions is *true* or *false,* or *more probably confirmed* or *less probably confirmed* than any alternative cognitive theory. It is because non-normatively worded first-order factual theory is *prescriptive* with regard to the motor side of any person's public self and *cognitively true* or *false* in a way that can be tested by anyone anywhere by appeal to the first-order factual data on the introspective and sensory side of anyone's nervous system, that an evaluative, as distinct from a merely descriptive, method for ethics and politics is

* For a fuller account of the distinction between first-order facts which are temporally and logically antecedent to the propositional beliefs of any person and second-order man-made cultural artifacts which in part at least are what they are because of the beliefs of people concerning first-order non-man-made facts, see Chapter XIX in Northrop, *The Complexity of Legal and Ethical Experience,* Little, Brown, Boston, 1959.

possible and can be specified with operational as well as theoretical exactitude.

Theoretically it is possible because in addition to the radically empirical private, subjective introspected self there is the logically realistic, indirectly confirmed public teleologically mechanical neurological self with its three sensory, cortical and motor neural components. So far as the introspected self alone is concerned, it is impossible, as Hume, Kant, G. E. Moore and the normative non-cognitivists Ayer, Stevenson and Alf Ross noted, to derive an "ought" from the "is" of any introspectively entertained non-normatively worded theory. But no person is merely his private introspected self with the mere "is" of its introspectively entertained ideas and evaluations; he is also his logically realistic public self in one-one epistemic correlation with his private self, and this public self, because of its inner target which is the one-one epistemic correlate of that person's elemental philosophy of first-order facts, does mechanically entail that this non-normatively worded theory of what "is," prescribes an "ought" for measuring that person's motor response to any stimulus of the moment.

Even so, there is a sense in which even this theory does not define away normative ethical and political words in terms of non-normative words. This becomes evident when one considers non-normatively worded scientifically testable philosophy by itself introspectively or via its epistemically trapped impulses in the human cortex. Qua theory by itself, unless all its postulates are analytic, such theory is no more true or false than it is good or bad. Only relative to anyone's incoming sensory signals of first-order facts is it true or false in a sense that can be confirmed by anyone anywhere; just as only relative to the motor responses of the individual person's nervous system to any stimulus of the moment is it prescriptively good or bad, an "ought" or an "ought not" for reinforcing or inhibiting one's *de facto* motor behavior. Hence non-normatively worded first-order factual theory of nature and natural man is normative, but its normative words are "true" or "false" or "more probably confirmed" or "less probably confirmed."

What our evaluative method does theoretically, therefore, is two-fold: (1) Assuming the bare "is" of a particular non-normatively worded theory of first-order factual nature and natural man, considered either merely as introspectively entertained or as its epistemically correlated impulse trapped hierarchically in one's cortex, the theory of our evaluative method does not define away "ought" in terms of this bare "is"; instead, it defines "ought" as imposing something on this "is," namely, its teleologically mechanical causal efficacy as the inner target of one's public self in prescriptively inhibiting or reinforcing one's motor response to any stimulus of the moment. Since in any simple or complex moral and political goal value choice one's *de facto* behavior is the mechanical product of (a) the attention-absorbing stimuli of the moment and (b) one's covert first-order factual philosophy, i.e., one's epistemically correlated inner target, there is usually a discrepancy between what the target calls for and what one does. This discrepancy appears in introspective consciousness as conscience and as the existentialist philosopher's and theologian's sense of sin or *Sorge*. (2) Evaluating, however, rather than merely assuming, the bare "is" of a particular non-normatively worded scientifically testable philosophy of first-order factual nature and natural man, our evaluative method for cognitively determining the truth or falsity of a correctly described, normatively worded national political philosophy defines away the "ought" or "ought not" for motor conduct in terms of the "true" or "false" for its cognitively testable non-normatively worded epistemological and psychological assumptions as judged by appeal to first-order factual, radically empirical, introspected and sensory data.

The twofold theoretical distinctions (1) and (2) just above specify the operational procedures of our evaluative method, given any correctly described normatively worded personal ethics with content or any nation's specific, intrinsic, normatively worded political philosophy. Theoretical principle (1) tells us that to talk about any normative words such as "ought," "ought not," "good," "bad," "politically good" or "politically bad" without specifying the non-normatively worded, cognitively testable philosophy of first-order factual nature and natural man for which this specific normatively worded content is the case is as meaningless as it would be in contemporary mathematical physics to say that two spatially separated events in invariant public space-time occurred simultaneously without also specifying the frame of reference for which this is the case. Consequently, given any normatively worded national political philosophy of any particular nation, such as that of the Declaration of Independence and the Constitution and Bill of Rights in the case of the United States of America or the Marxist Communistic philosophy and its Communist Manifesto in the case of the Soviet Union, our first operational prescription is to bring out into the open the respective non-normatively worded theory of first-order factual nature and psychological man which each implicitly and frequently explicitly assumes. This is usually done to a sufficient degree of accuracy for most practical purposes when the epistemological theory of conceptual meaning and the psychological theory of the first-order factual person are made determinate.

Then for any theory two possibilities may occur. Either the epistemological and psychological non-normatively worded premises of the national philosophy in question will be logically inconsistent or they will be logically consistent. If the former is the case, then the normatively worded natural philosophy will be demonstrably false in a sense which anyone anywhere can confirm on logical grounds. If, however, the latter alternative is the case, then theoretical principle (2) must be brought into play. In other words, by appeal to the first-order factual data of any person's experience anywhere, it must be determined whether the consistent epistemological and psychological theory in question is confirmed empirically and, if so, whether its assumptions are not merely necessary but also sufficient to account for all the first-order factual, introspected and sensed data.

To make the latter evaluative method clear, consider two different non-normatively worded epistemological and first-order factual psychological theories of the person, T^1 and T^2. To say that T^1 is false is equivalent to finding one first-order fact with respect to conceptual meaning or to the first-order factual theory of any psychological person which is incompatible with some deductive consequence of theory T^1. Similarly, to say that theory T^2 is confirmed with a greater degree of probability than is the case with theory T^1 is equivalent to saying that T^2 accounts for every first-order fact for which T^1 accounts and also for at least one such fact for which T^1 does not account.

It remains to apply this evaluative method to some concrete cases. Suppose that the descriptive method has determined that a given patriarchally tribal law of status nation affirms as a non-cognitively worded postulate of their empirical theory of heredity that all the inherited qualities of people pass to the children only through the male line, the mother being merely a passive receptacle, and that they present this empirically confirmable, cognitive theory as the justification for affirming that any person's political rights, obligations and duties have nothing to do with their being "born free and equal" as the American Declaration of Independence affirms, but are instead determined temporally antecedent to anyone's birth by the patriarchal line of breeding in a pure male line from the original patriarchal leader of the tribe. Let T^1 represent this cognitive thesis. When, therefore, more recent experimentation in the science of genetics leads to a conclusion, which can be cognitively confirmed by anyone, that the patriarchal political leaders' cognitive premise concerning heredity is false, then we have a cognitive proof that his patriarchally tribal political norms are false also, insofar as they refer, after the manner of Aeschylus, to this cognitive frame of reference for their cognitive justification.

Going a little deeper into the concepts of any person or nation's normative political philosophy, let us suppose that the descriptive method of philosophical anthropology has confirmed that the political philosophy of that nation assumes a naïve realistic epistemology. Then the proof that that normative theory in its cognitive frame of reference is false requires appeal to no empirical facts whatever, since, as was shown in the previous chapters and as has been shown in greater detail elsewhere,[9] any naïve realistic epistemological theory of conceptual meaning is self-contradictory.

The proof is as follows: To affirm a naïve realistic epistemology is to say that every cognitively meaningful proposition gives knowledge of a substance existing independently of its relation to the perceiver, and that all the knowable persisting, defining properties of this substance exist also as predicates of the object, independently of their relation to the observer and are naïvely known, i.e., directly sensed or introspected. But as shown above, every sensed quality, whether primary, secondary or tertiary, is not merely relative to different frames of reference and to different observers on the same frame of reference, but also to different sense organs of the same observer. It is, therefore, self-contradictory and hence meaningless to define an object of knowledge which is affirmed to exist and possess its defining properties independently of its relation to the perceiver in terms of either sensed or imageful qualities, any and all of which are relative to the perceiver.

This cognitively demonstrated proposition gives the reason why the following *de facto* cultures of the world reject a naïve realistic epistemology: (1) Chinese Confucian culture in its first-best method for settling disputes between either people or nations,[10] (2) any non-realistic Buddhist culture,[11] (3) unqualified non-dualistic Vedanta Hindu culture,[12] (4) Democritean and Platonic Greek mathematical physics [13] and (5) modern mathematical physics since Galilei, Descartes and Newton.[14] But if the naïve realistic epistemology is cognitively self-contradictory and hence meaningless, then the sensed color-of-skin law of biological-status ethic and politics which makes the purity of one's tribal biology of birth the criterion of anyone's political rights, privileges, obligations and duties is false also. Since universal affirmative propositions do not convert simply, it does not follow that because a person believes in a naïve realistic epistemology he will, therefore, affirm a law of biological-status personal and political philosophy.

Is this not, moreover, precisely the inarticulate covert cognitive premise which is implicit in the normative judgment of anyone who affirms that the social customs of the white Christian patriarchal Southerners in the United States are bad and unjust? In short, does not anyone who judges such a caste and tribal society to be bad and unjust believe that this judgment is correct because of his cognitive belief that sensed color of skin is not an essential part of the scientific definition of any truly known person? Were this not the case, he would hardly believe that color of skin is irrelevant as the criterion of the moral qualities and the legal and educational status of a given person.

The same argument applies to the Marxist philosophy of goal values, since it rests epistemologically for its certainty concerning its materialism on the naïve realistic epistemology which it took over from the German theologian Feuerbach when it rejected the idealistic epistemology of the modern mathematical physicist and philosopher Kant and his successor Hegel. The same cognitive consideration applies in part to the philosophy of goal values of any introspective psychological theory of ethics used as the approval theory, or the theory that "x is good as judged by p" is equivalent to "x interests p." For any such introspective psychological theory makes the same mistake as does a naïve realistic epistemology of basing one's judgment about an objective person not on the objective scientific properties of the person himself, but merely upon the subjectively introspected psychological effect of the objective person upon the observer. There is, of course, nothing self-contradictory about a radically empirical theory of conceptual meaning. It is true as far as it goes, but, because of its neglect of irreducible concepts by postulation, it is incomplete. We conclude, therefore, that cognitively a subjective, introspective psychological theory of ethics, law and politics, such as the one held by Judge Learned Hand, William James, Ralph Barton Perry, David Hume, Jeremy Bentham or Bertrand Russell, is a cognitively incomplete theory for the same reason that a law-of-status ethics is a cognitively false one.

But our evaluative method is not merely a standard for measuring traditional moral and political goal-value philosophies and norms of the *de facto* nations. It also prescribes what to do to determine the ideal nation. Its procedure consists in determining two things: (1) The present epistemological theory of conceptual meaning in first-order factual natural and psychological science, and (2) the present first-order factual psychological theory of the person. Both of these things have already been done in Chapters 2 to 5.

The cognitively testable epistemological theory (1) tells us that any completely known thing is known in two ways which are irreducible the one to the other and that the relation between these two radically empirical and logically realistic components of anything is neither that of causality nor of a predicate to a substance but instead is that of epistemic rules of correspondence which are many-one when the logically realistic object is other than oneself and one-one when it is one's public self. The cognitively testable psychological theory (2) tells us that any human being whatever is his or her private, radically empirical concept by intuition introspective psychological self with all its directly known ideas, ideals, frustrations, evaluations and emotions in one-one epistemic correlation with one's public self which is a teleologically mechanical nervous system the inner target of which is a set of hierarchically trapped impulses that are the one-one epistemic correlates of that person's covert or overt philosophy.

To be sure, many more deductions from these two theoretical premises and their epistemic rules of correspondence need to be made and put to experimental tests. Undoubtedly, as these tests are performed, modifications in this theory on its indirectly confirmed concept by postulation which is a concept by intellection side will have to be made, as has been the case with all such theories in the past. But this very likelihood proves that it meets the test of a cognitive method for determining the criterion of a positive normative theory that is confirmable by anyone anywhere.

Our evaluative method, therefore, warrants us in taking this epistemological and psychological theory as the non-normatively worded cognitive reference frame for evaluating and reforming the *de facto* intrinsic political goal-value ideals of one's own nation or any other nation when those ideals have been correctly described. This follows, let it be noted, because our non-normatively worded epistemological and psychological theory of any first-order factual person is empirically verifiable in a sense which can be confirmed by anyone anywhere who takes the trouble to test it by appeal to the first-order factual data of his immediate experience or who trusts other people called scientists or sages who have the time to do so for him.

Even so, one caution is necessary. We would fail practically in our politics if we took this cognitively testable, non-normatively worded scientific philosophy of conceptual meaning and of any person as the sole political instrument. The reason is the sociologically jurisprudential one that we have to work with the nations and peoples of the world as they are, adjusting what ought to be as prescribed by our evaluative method to what is as determined by our descriptive method. To get the former far ahead of the latter is to fail because the new positive moral and legal ideal which the evaluative method enables us to define with precision then fails to enjoy the support of the traditional beliefs and customs which are still in the minds and habits of humanity and which are necessary to make any positive ideal effective.

How to devise a politics which combines the results of our descrip-

tive method with the ideal political standard given by our evaluative
method will be the major concern of the remainder of this book. We
shall find that the descriptive method alone will at least enable us
to understand and go a long way toward resolving many of our
present domestic and international political problems without having
to wait for our cognitive theory of conceptual meaning and the first-
order factual psychological theory of any person to become trapped
epistemically in the brains of the majority of men and women on the
surface of this earth. Part II will reveal, however, that one-one conscious or covert epistemic correlates of parts of this theory are already trapped there. Hence, immediately practical political progress
from what is to what ought to be can be made without any violation
of the sociological jurisprudential principle that any ideal positive
legal and political norm will be effective only if it is supported by the
de facto living law of the particular people to whom it is applied.

Summary of Part I: A person (and hence a nation) is an epistemologically complex item of knowledge. One exemplifies not merely
(1) one's private introspected covert and overt non-normatively
worded theory of first-order factual man and nature, but also (2)
its one-one epistemic correlate which is the inner hierarchically
trapped target of one's public teleologically mechanical nervous
system and its motor behavior as mechanically inhibited or reinforced prescriptively by this target. Hence, although by itself the
philosophy of (1), being non-normatively worded, does not imply
an ought for human behavior, nevertheless, when considered in its
one-one epistemic relation to its formal equivalent (2), it does.
Normative prescriptive words refer therefore not to items of knowledge, but to the relation between non-normatively described items
of knowledge and their epistemically correlated target effect upon
human behavior. Consequently evaluative, as well as descriptive,
morality and politics is a science. Its method consists in finding the
non-normatively worded first-order factual assumptions of any personal or national philosophy, apart from which its normative words
are devoid of content, and then examining these assumptions with
respect both to (a) their logical consistency and (b) empirical
data inspectable *by anyone anywhere,* to test their truth or falsity.

PART TWO

Some Applications

8

The Nation of Uruguay's Batlle y Ordóñez

In international politics one can never tell where a given set of trapped universals will turn up to become politically significant. The political policy of Uruguay's greatest recent statesman José Batlle y Ordóñez, is an example. We shall approach him and the Uruguay of his time through their wider Latin American and European context.*

One of the most remarkable characteristics of Latin America is the far-reaching and detailed respect in which major political events, parties and statesmen have been guided by philosophical ideas. This guidance is both implicit and explicit.[1]

An ideological determination is implicit when it operates through a tradition so long established that its members are unaware of its explicit ideological origin and content. Latin American examples are: (1) The native American Indian culture, (2) the Negro culture and mentality of Brazil and the Caribbean, and (3) the colonial Spanish or Portuguese Roman Catholic theocratic and hierarchical institutions. An ideological determination is explicit if its effect upon governments, political parties or cultural institutions is consciously recognized and expressed. Explicit ideological determination occurs of necessity in any revolution, since a revolution by its very nature rejects the customary social order and its traditional implicit norms to put different explicit, consciously stated norms in their stead.

* What follows is reprinted here from *Civilisations*, Vol. 5, No. 4, 1955, pp. 525–539, with the permission of the Hartford Theological Seminary, where it was first presented as part of a conference on Latin American culture and politics.

Examples in Latin America are: French Cartesian and Encyclopedist philosophy in the Mexican revolution of 1810; the ideas of Thomas Paine in the Venezuelan revolution of 1810 and the Uruguayan revolution under Artigas in the same period; Comtian positivism in Mexico's Díaz dictatorship at the end of the nineteenth century; in the Brazilian governments inspired by Benjamin Constant in 1889 and headed in very recent times by Vargas; and organic spiritual personalism in the Uruguay of Batlle y Ordóñez and his present successors.

These and other implicit and explicit ideological factors constitute the variegated cultural complex which negatively, by contrast to the United States and Canada, and positively, because of the Roman Catholic component of its Spanish and Portuguese colonial period and the French influence of the nineteenth century, is called Latin America.

One must not forget, however, that the Roman factor spent itself at the end of the eighteenth century as did the French factor at the end of the nineteenth. This means that today, if we speak strictly, "Latin" is a misnomer for the culture of our neighbors to the south of the Rio Grande. In Mexico the native Indian component, either directly or through its mixture with the Spanish, is coming to expression, as the paintings and the political influence of Diego Rivera and Orozco clearly show. The Negro and Creole component is similarly significant in Brazil and the Caribbean. Also, North American commercialism with its more laissez-faire economic and political norms, derived from a British empirical modern philosophy, is now transforming Latin America, as Mexico City, Havana, São Paulo, Montevideo and even Lima demonstrate.

But in recognizing that the Latin component from either Catholic Rome or nineteenth century Paris does not now dominate, one must not go to the error of the other extreme to conclude that the traditional cultural influences from medieval or modern Continental Europe no longer matter. No people can escape completely from their past. Moreover, each of the aforementioned implicit or explicit traditions has present passionate believers and is implemented by entrenched interests in the form of influential newspapers, open political parties, hidden pressure groups and able writers and painters of great popular appeal.

To understand the complicated culture to the south of Key West and the Rio Grande it is necessary, therefore, to know something about the ideological content of all of the traditional implicit and explicit cultural components. Except for novel contemporary influences, it is merely the ratios of these components to one another, their relative weights that have changed, not the persisting significance of the components themselves. For this reason, as well as the difficulty of changing North American linguistic usage, we shall refer to the culture of this area as Latin American.

Initially, the values and institutions of the native American Indians predominated. To speak of this culture as one is, of course, misleading, as becomes evident when the Inca remains in the Peruvian high Andes are compared with those of the Mayas in Yucatan and the Aztecs and Toltecs in the valley of Mexico City. In the sixteenth and seventeenth centuries the Portuguese and Spaniards consolidated their imperial conquests, thereby ensuring the dominance of their values in the colonial period. At the same time the Negro culture from Africa came into Brazil and the Caribbean. The product of the impact of Spanish or Portuguese colonialism upon the native Indian cultures and values varied in different places. Under the wise missionary guidance of Las Casas there was a genuine synthesis in parts of Mexico and the Caribbean as illustrated at Cholula and Tepotzotlan.[2] At Peruvian Cuzco, in the famous Cuzco madonnas, there was a similar but much more localized synthesis in which the Spanish Roman Catholic factor played a larger part than did the Indian. For the most part, however, in Peru the Indians and the Spaniards remained apart, with the former living their lives undisturbed in the high Andes and the Spaniards expressing purely Spanish Roman Catholic values of an exceptionally high quality in Lima. Only in our time do the native Indians and the aristocratic Spanish Roman Catholics mingle at Lima in the single community of a commercial society heavily under the influence of the United States. The result tends to be a corruption of both the Indian and the Spanish Christian values and their displacement by individual self-seeking commercialism, uncontrolled by the religious and secular philosophical norms at the foundation of the culture of the United States. The popular political criticism of the United States in Latin America cannot be understood unless this fact is appreciated. The Communists play upon this cultural fact; they do not, however, create it. In Uruguay native Indians were defeated by the Spanish conquerors and destroyed or pushed away. Brazil, under the Portuguese, was much the same except that the Indians in the western and northwestern areas remained within the national boundaries. Argentina, although Spanish, gives much the same picture.

The presence, by 1890, of the Negro in Brazil in numbers greater than that of the Indians and their location in the seaboard areas makes the cultural complexion of this nation unique. Its cultural future lies more, therefore, in a synthesis between Negro, Portuguese and North American industrial and commercial values than in a merging of Portuguese and Indian cultural norms.

The major ideological story of the Latin American world since the early 1800's does not have as its theme, however, the issue between the Spanish, Portuguese or other Continental European Latin Americans and the native Indians or the entrenched African Negroes. Instead, its theme is the triumph of modern philosophical, political, economic, anticlerical and even antireligious ideas over those of Spanish and Portuguese medieval Roman Catholic Europe. In this respect, except for anticlericalism, modern Latin America is similar to the culture of the United States. Both cultures, since 1776 and 1810, express the triumph of modern philosophical ideas and the political, economic and legal institutions and values which modern philosophy prescribes.

There are, however, two differences between the modern cultures of the United States and Latin America. The Christian religious faith of the majority of people north of the Rio Grande is Protestant. That of those to the south is Roman Catholic. This means that the North Americans had passed through the Protestant Reformation before they were captured by modern philosophy and its educational, political and economic theories. This undoubtedly gave them a better preparation in their religious thinking for rejecting Aristotelian and medieval hierarchical philosophical ideas in their secular institutions without, at the same time, rejecting their religion and its institutions. This permitted them to escape the anticlericalism and even the atheism which accompanied modern democracy in Continental Europe [3] and in Latin America. The second difference is that the modern philosophical, political, economic and legal thinking of the United

States and British Canada is that of British empirical philosophy and the more inductive English type of law, whereas the modern thinking of Latin Americans is that of continental Rationalistic or Comtian positivistic philosophy and the more deductive Continental code type of law.

To be sure, the Latin Americans, during a brief period in the early nineteenth century and in recent decades, have been influenced by the United States. Its Federal Constitution, the Constitution of Massachusetts, Thomas Paine and William James have been important, as the sequel will show. Also, the British empirical and positivistic thinking of Newton, Locke, Hume, Spencer and Bain had significant influence in Latin America in the nineteenth century. It is to be remembered, however, that Voltaire brought this early British empirical way of thinking to the Continent. From this importation, the French Encyclopedists derive. It is largely, therefore, by way of France, rather than directly, as in the case of the United States and British Canada, that modern British empirical philosophy has, upon occasion, determined the curricula of the universities or influenced the course of political and social events in Latin America.

Because the Latin Americans looked to France for their intellectual and spiritual inspiration throughout the nineteenth century, the political, architectural, educational and economic institutions created in this period in all the Latin American nations derived in major part from the four following philosophical movements which dominated the northern portion of Continental Europe at the time: (1) Continental Rationalism, beginning with Descartes, culminating in Kant and Hegel, and including German Romanticism and *Historismus*,[4] (2) French Encyclopedism, including British empirical philosophical ideas by way of Voltaire, (3) the personalistic pluralistic continental idealism of which Cousin was the exponent in France and Kraus and Ahrens the proponents in Germany, Belgium and France and, through their translated works, in Spain and Latin America. This movement was quite vigorous in Belgium, France and Spain during the nineteenth century. It is known throughout Latin America as Krausism or philosophical spiritualism or spiritual eclecticism.[5] The curriculum of the University of Mexico in the third quarter of the nineteenth century, before the coming of the Díaz dictatorship and its Comtian positivism, was dominated by this philosophical spiritualism of

Kraus. It also dominated the philosophical teaching, the editorial writing and the political and economic program of the greatest of Uruguayan statesmen, Batlle y Ordóñez.[6]

(4) The fourth major Continental European philosophy to influence Latin America is the French positivism deriving from Saint-Simon and Comte.[7] Not only did it determine the educational reforms of the party of the "scientificos" in Mexico, under Díaz, from 1877 to 1910, but it also influenced the intellectual and cultural life of Argentina through the writings of J. Alfredo Ferreira,[8] affected the literature and educational curriculum of Chile,[9] Cuba and Bolivia,[10] and dominated Brazil intellectually and politically in its first modern government and through the administrations of the late President Vargas.[11] The words "Order and Progress" on the flag of Brazil express the slogan of Comtian positivism and the fact that "positivism in Brazil is inseparable from the proclamation of the Republic in November, 1889." [12] In Rio de Janeiro today the Comtian positivistic church still functions. Not only were the leaders of Brazil's democratic revolution of 1889 Comtian positivists, but this mode of thinking still dominates Brazil's southernmost province, Rió Grande do Sul. The late President Vargas came from there. This means that the Brazilian government has been under major Comtian direction from 1889 to 1954 at least.

Another effect of French influence upon Latin America was the intuitive philosophy of Bergson. It combined with the radical empirical psychology and philosophy of William James. This philosophical combination was especially significant in Uruguay due to the influence of the philosopher Carlos Vaz Ferreira, as the sequel will show.

Generally throughout Latin America in the last quarter of the nineteenth century and the first decade of the present century, French Comtian positivism was in the ascendancy. Its authoritarian, undemocratic political philosophy and its dictatorial political practices had the effect over time of consolidating all other philosophical movements in Latin America against itself. The result was a new synthetic Latin American philosophy called Humanism. The political consequences of this new humanism appeared in the second democratic revolutions which occurred throughout Latin America during the second decade of the twentieth century.

The immediate philosophical inspiration of this Latin American humanism was the German *Historismus* which was the nineteenth century derivative of non-dialectical post-Hegelian Continental Rationalistic philosophy. This philosophical *Historismus* was an effective ideology for attacking positivism since it made every dimension of human experience, every period of human culture, every civilization of the world and every department in the university curriculum, rather than merely the modern ideas of the French Comtian social scientists, the criterion of the good for man's personal life, his educational curriculum and his cultural and legal institutions.

It is not an accident, therefore, that the humanistic, democratic Mexican revolution of 1910, which overthrew the positivistic Díaz dictatorship, had its inspiration in the leadership of two philosophers, Antonio Caso and José Vasconcelos, who took the whole history of the world's philosophy as their province, and a distinguished poet and scholar, Alfonso Reyes, who turned to the classical Greek philosophical texts for his criterion of the beautiful.[13] The ideal political and cultural forms were to be found in all of man's cultural creations throughout human history, not merely in the pseudoscientific concepts of nineteenth century French sociologists. This is why the large Secretariat of Public Education building in Mexico City, which was the creation of the new democratic government brought into being by the humanistic revolution of 1910, contains the following four figures, one in each corner of the large high court immediately within its main entrance—Quetzalcoatl, representing the American Indian and so-called primitive man generally; Las Casas, who exemplifies the synthesis between medieval Spanish Roman Catholic Christian values and native Indian norms; Plato, who represents the classical Western tradition generally; and the Buddha, who stands for the intuitive, religious and human values of Asia.[14]

The great Latin American liberal humanist Francisco Romero, who dominated the liberal intellectual and political life of Argentina before the coming of Perón, expresses the same philosophical humanism except that, like Batlle y Ordóñez of Uruguay, Romero draws more fully, because of his personalistic spiritualism, upon the Krausian component of Continental Rationalistic philosophy than upon its *Historismus*.[15] José Enrique Rodó of Uruguay is perhaps nearer the Mexican humanists.[16]

Between World Wars I and II, through Ortega y Gasset and others, the phenomenological philosophy of the German Husserl entered every Latin American university. Its influence upon legal thinking has been great. In more recent times, the existentialism of Heidigger and Sartre has swept over Latin America. It has much in common with the passionate Spanish individualism of the colonial era that is embodied in the bullfight.[17]

Simultaneously, the commercialism of the United States has impinged. Its values tend to be incompatible, not merely with those of the current popular existentialism, but also with the major Latin American cultural traditions other than positivism. In this incompatibility the neutralism and negativism with respect to the culture of the United States of Latin American intellectuals and those Latin American political leaders who gain popular support by attacking the United States have their major basis.

The foregoing considerations make it clear that, whereas the culture of the United States has been dominated by but three major philosophical and social movements, each of which has developed from within out of its own Anglo-American heritage, the social and cultural life of all the Latin American nations is the product of at least eleven different cultural factors, mostly derived from abroad and to a great extent incompatible one with another. These eleven ideological factors are: (1) The native American Indian culture, (2) the Spanish theocratic, imperialistic Roman Catholic culture, (3) the Portuguese theocratic Roman Catholic culture, (4) the African Negro patriarchal law of status culture, (5) the early French Cartesian and Encyclopedist modern philosophy, (6) the spiritual eclecticism of Cousin, Kraus and Ahrens, (7) French Comtian positivism, (8) the aesthetic intuitive empiricism of James and Bergson, (9) German *Historismus* and the new humanism, (10) phenomenology and existentialism, and (11) contemporary North American commercialism.

To these conflicting intellectual, cultural and political influences have been added differences in blood or race and with respect to belief in religion. Neither the Indian nor the Negro is prepared for Western philosophical, political and economic ways of thinking, whether these ways derive from colonial Roman Catholic medieval values, the modern British philosophical empiricism and pragmatism of the Anglo-Americans or the rationalism, spiritualism and social positivism of the Continental Europeans. Need one wonder, therefore, at the intellectual and political upheavals in the Latin American universities and the Latin American governments?

From the foregoing eleven major conflicting intellectual and cultural traditions, each with its differing practical consequences for government, politics, law, education and the economics of daily life, the many different Latin American people have drawn in each nation and at different times in differing ways. Because the established, diverse cultural components, from which the selection at any time must be made, are incompatible, no selection tends to be permanent. Consequently, whereas in the United States there has been but one revolution, the history of Latin America is the story of a sequence of revolutions. Also, whereas in the United States a university professor has security of tenure through changes of political administrations in Washington, his colleagues in Latin America tend to be forced into exile or seclusion with the frequent revolutionary changes in political administration in the national capital.

Such a complex of conflicting cultural traditions and influences has its potential assets as well as its actual liabilities. The creativity of ancient Athens undoubtedly derived in major part from the crossroads of diverse and conflicting cultural traditions and influences at which it stood. Genuine creation consists in the modification or rejection of traditional assumptions. In a culture such as that of the United States, in which there is a relatively indigenous and homogeneous cultural tradition largely Anglo-American in content, the tendency to be satisfied with the implicit traditional norms is difficult to escape. In a culture such as that of any Latin American people, in which there are incompatible, yet inescapable, conflicting norms for ordering one's educational, political and cultural institutions, the impulse to attempt a new creative synthesis is well-nigh inescapable. It is from this fact, undoubtedly, that the imaginative daring and passion of Mexican painting and architecture and the vitality of its contemporary social and spiritual life derives. The story of Mexico's unique attempt at a creative synthesis which probes the emotional, aesthetic and metaphysical depths of human nature and the diverse, conflicting norms of human culture has been sketched elsewhere.[18]

By way of contrast, therefore, it seems wise to choose, for detailed analysis, a Latin American culture which, while selecting from approximately the same initial diverse components, arrives at a quite different result—one almost the polar opposite of contemporary Mexico. This culture is that of Uruguay.

Uruguay, like other Latin American nations, has had its sequence of revolutions. It also has had its Spanish Roman Catholic colonial period, its democratic revolution near the end of the first decade of the nineteenth century, its subsequent fifteen years of ideological and legal influences from the United States and its seventy-five years of nineteenth century French influence, dominated by the spiritual pluralism and eclecticism of Cousin, Kraus and Ahrens in its third quarter and by positivism in the final quarter. Also, at the beginning of the twentieth century, like the other Latin American nations, its spiritual personalism combined with an expanded humanism, under Batlle y Ordóñez, to repudiate positivism in both education and government and to launch its continuous liberal democratic constitutional era of the present century.

Why, then, after all these similarities, is the result today in Uruguay so different from that in Mexico or, as the sequel will show, in Peru across the Andes? One's first inclination is to find the answer in geographical terrains and distances. This answer will, however, not do. There is an equally great difference between the present culture of Uruguay and that of Argentina or of the Brazilian state of Río Grande do Sul, both of which border on Uruguay and are identical in being portions with Uruguay of a common plain.

The correct answer centers in historical and cultural factors which make Uruguay unique in its selection from the many ideological components common to the Latin American world. First is the relation of the Spanish conquerors of Uruguay to the native Indians. As in the case of the North Americans, the Spanish founders of Uruguay either slaughtered the native Indians or pushed them, for the most part, beyond the local national frontiers. Consequently, Uruguay, like the United States, never faced in any serious way the problem of combining the values of the incoming Europeans and their progeny with the values of the native American Indians. This was not the case in Mexico, the Caribbean or with the Indians of Peru at Cuzco in the high Andes. Consequently the people of Uruguay, largely European by blood or birth, were free to build in the Southern Hemisphere a new culture and society largely in the light of merely European traditions and ideas. Their only question was, with time, whether the European ideas would be medieval or modern.

The first major cultural problem for the vast majority of the Uruguayan people did not come, therefore, until the modern scientific and philosophical ideas of Descartes, Newton, Locke, Voltaire and the French Encyclopedists captured the minds of the Franciscan priests and more and more people to make them question the traditional theocratic and imperial institutions and norms of the Spanish colonial conquerors and the Roman Catholic hierarchy. Forthwith not merely their traditional Spanish political rulers but also their traditional Roman Catholic hierarchical religious norms and institutions were brought into question. Historical evidence concerning Uruguay and Mexico, at least, shows that the Roman Catholic priests fell into two groups—one group composed of Dominicans or Jesuits, associating themselves with the orthodox Aristotelian and Thomistic regal and hierarchical ideas of the colonial period and the landowners in their haciendas; the other group, made up largely of Franciscans, associated themselves with the democratic revolution. Evidence shows that there are two reasons for this. One is that the Franciscans had read and been persuaded by the modern Continental Rationalistic philosophy of Descartes and the later Encyclopedists. The other reason is that it was of the essence of the teaching of St. Francis that Christian love entailed a warm, intimate human affection for all human beings and all living creatures. This, together with the new Cartesianism and Encyclopedism, is undoubtedly what swung their teaching and influence, in both rural Mexico and in Uruguay in favor of the democratic revolution and against the Dominicans and Jesuits with their hierarchical values.

For all these identities between the roles of Roman Catholic priests in the first democratic revolutions of Mexico and Uruguay, there was, however, one difference. The leaders of the democratic revolution in Mexico had the rural priests on their side, but the Dominican priests associated with the hierarchy in Mexico City were in opposition. In Uruguay's democratic revolution, however, Artigas and his Franciscan secretary found the majority of priests in Montevideo on their side. Thus the first Uruguayan democratic revolution obtained a much easier victory than was the case in Mexico.

Also, the Roman Catholic hierarchy in southern South America had not set up a separate organization for Uruguay. Instead it put Uruguay and Argentina under a single hierarchy centered at Buenos Aires. This had the practical effect in the revolution, with its nationalistic as well as democratic overtones, of turning the democratic revolution against the hierarchy at Buenos Aires and of giving the Franciscans an influence in Montevideo which they did not have in other major Latin American colonial cities. Furthermore, the Jesuits, who were associated with the hierarchy, had been expelled from Uruguay in the previous century. At the time of the expulsion there was a Franciscan pope, the influence of the Freemasons was very strong, and a liberal Bourbon dynasty in Europe was expelling the Jesuits from Spain, Naples, and Portugal. Charles III of Spain was heavily under the influence of the French Encyclopedist ideas. In fact, these Encyclopedist ideas were the inspiration of the brief Spanish liberal democratic revolution centered at Cádiz which preceeded and was the prime inspiration for the liberal democratic revolution led by Artigas in Uruguay.

Although the Uruguayan revolution derived initially from French Cartesian and Encyclopedist ideas and was inspired by the Spanish revolution at Cádiz, it was carried through and ended under the influence of Thomas Paine and the Constitution of Massachusetts. It seems that Artigas' Franciscan secretary called his attention to the ideas of Thomas Paine and in particular to a book written by a Venezuelan and published in Spanish at Philadelphia in 1811. This book was read widely in both Venezuela and Uruguay. Artigas urged his people to read both it and the Massachusetts Constitution. Consequently the Venezuelan democratic revolution began and ended under these influences from the United States and modeled its final constitution on the Federal Constitution of the United States; whereas its counterpart in Uruguay began under the influence of French Encyclopedist ideas, as expressed in the Spanish revolution at Cádiz, and ended under North American influence, modeling its final constitution on that of Massachusetts.

Why did Artigas choose the Constitution of Massachusetts as his model? The democratic constitution of Cádiz had been strongly federal. The twenty towns in Uruguay which participated in its democratic revolution, however did not want to be strongly federated. The Constitution of Massachusetts expressed a similar sentiment.

There were, however, deeper reasons for choosing it. Artigas felt that in Latin America the presidency invites to anarchy and to dictatorships. He also felt that the living law habits and inclinations of the strong and localized rural landowners were such as to cause them (a) to resist federal control if a non-landowner became president, thereby producing anarchy, or (b) to rule as a dictator if a landowner of the Spanish colonial type obtained the presidency. As a consequence, there has been a tradition in Uruguay against the United States institution of the presidency and for an executive council instead. In 1953 Professor Hugo Ferñandez Artucio, one of Uruguay's educators and editorialists, said to the writer, "It is a basic idea in Uruguay that one of the deepest dangers of ordered government is the institution of the presidency." In no other American nation, to the writer's knowledge, does this idea exist.

This tradition reached its most striking expression at the beginning of this century when Uruguay's greatest statesman, Batlle y Ordóñez, came to power. Immediately events forced him to use strong executive powers. The Spanish landowners, still dominated by the hierarchical values of the colonial period and known politically as the Blancos, were engaging in military skirmishes with Brazilian revolutionary troops from Río Grande do Sul. Batlle immediately dispatched national troops to bring order, declaring that when national jurisdiction is in danger, sovereignty is one. By this means he dispersed the Brazilians and put down the Blancos' domestic revolution. At the same time there was no revenge. Instead, a genuine secret ballot was introduced and the Blancos were taken into the Executive Council. Every Batllista president since then has promised, in accepting office, to suppress the presidency. On December 16, 1951, this occurred. An Executive Council of nine now administers the government, and Batlle's hope that its head could bicycle through the streets of Montevideo without being noticed by the populace has been realized.

Events seem to confirm the correctness of the Uruguayan judgment that the institution of the presidency is a danger to constitutional democracy in the Latin American world. Certainly coups, dictatorships and periods of anarchy have been frequent. Why this contrast with the experience of the United States? May it not be due to Spanish ethics and the type of moral and political individualism that it generates? The Spaniard, Madariaga, in his *Englishmen,*

Frenchmen, Spaniards,[19] has noted that, whereas British mentality is governed by empiricism and utilitarian pragmatism and French thinking is guided by logic and the clarity and distinctness of ideas, the Spaniard is dominated by passion. This shows, as has been noted elsewhere, in the Spanish and Mexican bullfight, in the books of Unamuno, and in the paintings of the Mexicans—Orozco, Rivera and Siqueiros.[20]

According to this ethics of passionate Spanish individualism, the morality of man consists in his freedom of choice. By freedom of choice that is moral, the Spaniard means a choice which is made solely because one has made it and not for a hedonistically or rationalistically calculated reason. From this Spanish point of view, to make a choice for an empirical or rationalistic reason is to be a calculating machine rather than a moral or spiritual agent. The basis for the moral choice must be in the voluntaristic act of one's own free will and in staying passionately, and without deviation or compromise, with one's commitment. The proof of one's morality, the "moment of truth" of the Spanish bullfight, must be tragic, moreover, to be authentic. Otherwise one can never be sure that the choice was not made for the reward at the end rather than merely because, in one's God-given freedom, one has made it.

From such a standpoint, conforming one's own opinions to those of the majority after free debate is the very antithesis of moral and political leadership. The moral and respected leader, instead, is one who makes his choice solely because he makes it and then pursues it with passionate uninhibited grace of form and absolute seriousness to its tragic consequences, pushing all opposition and any conformity to other people's opinions and choices aside. This uncompromising moral individualism inherent in the Spanish spirit and temperament is hardly compatible with the restraints upon the presidency which stable democratic constitutional government requires if dictators are not to be regarded even by the people as the only truly moral and principled statesmen.

In any event, Uruguay's tradition of suppression of the presidency and substitution of an Executive Council is one way to relate Spanish passion and Spanish moral individualism to democratic constitutional processes without having the former destroy the latter. This is, at least, one reason, in addition to the influence of Thomas Paine and the Constitution of Massachusetts, why the democratic climate of opinion in Uruguay today is so similar to that in the United States, notwithstanding its different theory of the executive branch of constitutional democratic government.

There is another reason for this similarity. At the time of the failure of the Cádiz revolution in Spain, many liberals emigrated from there to Uruguay. When similar liberal democratic revolutions failed later in Germany and Italy, liberals emigrated from those countries to Uruguay and also to the United States. Thus by a process of automatic cultural selection, the populations of the United States and Uruguay are heavily composed of liberal democrats. When one recalls that the population of Uruguay at the beginning of the nineteenth century comprised only a few tens of thousands, the significance of this factor becomes evident.

The fourth quarter of the nineteenth century was characterized throughout Latin America by the dominance of French positivism, in particular that of Comte. This influence was felt in Uruguay also, in the press and in the curriculum of its university.[21] Uruguayan positivism, however, was British rather than French in character. The difference is exceedingly important. British positivism is rooted in British empirical philosophy. It is liberally democratic. The French positivism of Comte, however, affirms that society is a complicated system which only social scientists are competent to comprehend and operate. From this, the French positivists draw the conclusion that the criterion for good government cannot be found in an appeal to the people; instead, even though a legislature may be introduced, the guidance of the government must be in the hands of the party of the social "scientificos." The logical and *de facto* consequence of this is a one-party state and dictatorship. Because Uruguay's positivism was British rather than French, she escaped the Comtian type of dictatorship that appeared in Mexico and Brazil. Instead she was dominated by the same British empirical philosophy which has determined political, economic and legal thinking in the United States.

The similarity with the United States during this period became even more marked due to the influence upon the educational curriculum and public opinion of the Uruguayan professor of philosophy, Dr. Vaz Ferreira. Starting as an English Spencerian positivist, he soon embraced the philosophy of William James and introduced the ideas of James' psychology and instrumental pragmatic theory of conceptual meaning into the curriculum of every university-educated Uruguayan. Up to a few years ago, these ideas of Vaz Ferreira and his pupils dominated the educational system of Uruguay.[22]

The major influence, however, in Uruguay, since the opening of this century, came from another philosopher who later became Uruguay's greatest statesman, Batlle y Ordóñez. We have already noted his legal and political ideas with respect to the national executive of any Latin American government and his implementation of these ideas during his first term in office from 1903 to 1907. Since the Uruguayan constitution prevented him from having a consecutive second term as the chairman of the Executive Council, he went, in 1907, to Europe. Upon his return in 1911 he again became head of the Executive Council and introduced democratically legislated reforms as far-reaching in the fiscal and economic field as his previous reforms had been in the political and legal domain. These reforms and the ideas behind them have dominated Uruguayan social life to the present moment. They mark him also as one of the greatest statesmen in Latin American history. Batlle's political, fiscal and economic reforms have been described for English readers at great length elsewhere.[23] Unfortunately these writers have supposed that in his political, fiscal and economic reforms Batlle was guided by merely practical considerations. Consequently they ignore the philosophy, regarded by Batlle as of the essence, that was behind his practical deeds. Without knowledge of this philosophy and the acceptance of it by his people, Batlle's political, legal, fiscal and economic policies cannot be understood; nor is it likely that they would have become effective!

Batlle's trip to Europe in 1907 was not his first visit there. In 1883 he had made a previous intellectual sojourn at Paris. At that time he met Thiers and the builders of the French Third Republic. He also became acquainted with the leaders and ideas of French positivism and, most important of all, he studied and became converted to the eclectic spiritualism of Cousin, Kraus and Ahrens. From Cousin, Batlle derived the idea of the moral, religious and political person as a conscious spiritual entity. The pluralism of such autonomous spiritual persons was one cornerstone of Batlle's liberal democracy. From the post-Kantian idealist, Kraus, Batlle derived (1) the pluralistic idea of the autonomy of the different dimensions of the human spirit and the corresponding different associations of persons in society, as terms in (2) the organic unity which is the unity of the complete personality and the complete society. From Ahrens, who was a follower of Kraus and who worked out the practical implications for law and for social institutions of this Krausian spiritual philosophy which was at once both autonomously personalistic and monistically organic, Batlle derived, he tells us, "My criterion of law and . . . my guide in my public life." [24] The detailed account of Batlle's philosophy and the way in which, through his lectures in philosophy and his newspaper editorials, he informed public opinion over the years since 1872 has been recorded by the contemporary Uruguayan lawyer and philosopher Arturo Ardao, in his *Espiritualismo y Positivismo en el Uruguay* and *Batlle y Ordóñez y el Positivismo Filosófico*.

The heart of Batlle's thought and conduct is expressed by two words of his philosophy—"organic autonomy." By this Kraus, Ahrens and Batlle meant, "A federative system of all the spheres of life and of culture." What distinguished Kraus' spiritualism from that of Hegel was that in Hegel's state, the organicism tended to destroy the autonomy, whereas for Kraus, due to his personalistic pluralism, the pluralism of the autonomy of the different dimensions of the human spirit and the monism of the organicism were kept more nearly in equilibrium. Kraus, Ahrens and Batlle achieved this equilibrium (1) by making the state unequivocally democratic and only one of the social expressions of the different autonomous dimensions of the human spirit, and (2) by locating the unifying organic contribution of the state in the free wills of the many spiritual individuals as expressed through a legislature elected by secret ballot. If such an organic pluralism was to work politically and economically, Batlle believed that the free individuals had to be educated in a personalistic philosophy which was organic as well as pluralistic. This is why his philosophical lectures at the University Club and his philosophical editorials in the press over a period of thirty years before he became President in 1903 were an essential basis for (*a*) Batlle's success as a statesman and (*b*) the unique direction which his political and economic policies took. The living law was being transformed to prepare the way for his later positive legal, political and economic policies.

The organicism in the spiritual personalism of Kraus, Ahrens and Batlle was as basic a cornerstone of his political, legal, fiscal and economic policies as was its autonomous pluralism. With personalistic pluralism only, Batlle saw that his practical policies would be laissez-faire. The organicism of his philosophy required, however, that the autonomous freedom of the individual only justified itself if the result politically, economically and culturally was one in which every dimension of human experience came to fulfillment. The end of good government was not merely the freedom of the individual to express himself but also a social expression in such a way that every member of the community, and not merely the freely enterprising fortunate few, had a real, *de facto* opportunity to live a fully rounded and complete life. For this the economic needs of all must be satisfied and as far as possible manufactured domestically. Insofar as the latter organic social ideal was not actualized, the autonomous human spirits must operate democratically through the federal legislature to create the necessary industries and fiscal and economic policies. It is not an accident, therefore, nor the mere result of practical expediency that Batlle y Ordóñez replaced the individualism of the presidency with the organic pluralism of an Executive Council in his political reforms and that he brought individual free enterprise and even many industries under organic control by means not merely of fiscal and welfare legislation but also of government ownership. Such is the way in which the organic personalistic philosophy, which Latin American writers refer to as *espiritualismo,* determined the practical policies of Batlle y Ordóñez to make Uruguay most like the United States in its liberal democratic climate of opinion, yet at the same time unique among the nations of the Pan American world.

At a third corner of the Latin American triangle, composed of Mexico and Uruguay, there stands Peru. Uruguay represents a selection of Spanish colonial and diverse modern norms and values with little if any Indian component. Mexico expresses a conflicting merging of Spanish colonial and modern philosophical values with the native American Indian ways. In Peru, the Indian as well as the medieval and modern European values are present, but as previously noted, geographical isolation tended to prevent them from mixing, and even in Cuzco, where synthesis occurred, the Spanish Baroque values predominated. The consequence is that of all the Latin

American countries, Peru is the most purely Spanish and the most orthodoxly Roman Catholic. At least, this was true of the Peru of Lima before the commercialism of the United States reached its present intensity. It is doubtful if anywhere in the world, even in Madrid or Rome, one can find the carving and the painting and the rich gorgeousness in the orthodox Roman Catholic and Spanish tradition which exists in the sacristies, inner chapels and the cloisters of the Roman Catholic churches of Lima. To fly, as one can, from Montevideo yesterday to Lima today is literally to breathe the cultural climates of two different spiritual worlds, both of which are Spanish American. The cultural climate of Montevideo is spiritual, liberal and even religious, but with a liberalism which is largely secular and a religion that has little to do with ecclesiastical institutions. To move through the cloisters of the Spanish Roman Catholic Peru of Lima's yesterday, still present today, is to be perhaps nearer the authentic spirit and aesthetic quality of Baroque Spain and Catholic Rome than it is now possible to be in either of these two places themselves.

This relative purity of Lima's orthodox Spanish and Roman Catholic tradition distinguishes the culture of Peru as sharply from that of Mexico as it does from that of Uruguay, notwithstanding the fact that Peru includes the same Indian, colonial European and modern philosophical components as Mexico. The purity of the orthodox Roman Catholic Spanish tradition was impossible to preserve in Mexico because geography and the volume of population made some kind of a conflicting synthesis inescapable.

Nonetheless, one of the most creative, open-hearted and open-minded Latin American syntheses has come from the pen of a Peruvian—Dr. Victor Andrés Belaunde—presently the Ambassador of the Peruvian government to, and in 1959 President of the Assembly of the United Nations. Liberal democracy and the free inquiry of the human spirit have no more able a champion. Born and reared a Spanish Roman Catholic, in love, after the manner of Santayana, with the beauty of its ritual, this spirit has also passed through, and even in its youth embraced, the skepticism and the religious disillusionment of the modern positivistic secular liberal. He has known also what it means to go to prison and to the very edge of death for his liberal democratic political convictions. Only exile from his country freed him from prison. During this exile at Williamstown, Massachusetts, he observed Protestant Christianity at first hand and studied its literature. It seemed initially to offer the way of synthesizing his Christian religious tradition with his modern philosophical liberalism. Several years of study and life with it revealed, however, that as an adequate synthesis for the Latin American, Protestant Christianity will not do. Its absence of passion, its blank beauty, its omission of the Virgin and its calculated practicality, when put beside the metaphysical depth and the rich beauty of the Baroque Roman Catholic architecture and the Roman Catholic ritual, left him, when finally he was permitted to return home, with the conviction that liberal North American Protestantism leaves out too much. The need was for a fresh synthesis. There followed a re-examination of the spiritual roots of the Roman Catholic tradition and its metaphysical doctrine of the Trinity, stripped of the political apparatus of its hierarchy and brought to terms with modern philosophical liberalism and humanism. The final conclusion bears the title *The Living Synthesis*.[25]

Brazil with its Portuguese colonial background, its native Indians in the hinterland, its contemporary North American commercialism at São Paulo and its Negro component, coming directly from Africa and indirectly through the mixed blood of the conquerors from southern Portugal, constitutes another unique chapter in the Latin American story. Such a chapter must include the differences as well as the identities between the Spanish and the Portuguese mentality. These differences show in their bullfights and in the influence of the French Renaissance on Portuguese architecture when compared with the Spanish Baroque. So one should proceed from one people and nation and cultural component to another.

Clearly the entire culture of the world to the south of Key West and the Rio Grande is a most complex one—a remarkably rich manifestation of differences within identity, where even the generic identity embraces conflicting philosophies from which ever new selections must be made, none of which is yet stable. In this philosophical and moral conflict within the Latin American's very being, the instability of his political, religious and educational institutions, and his explicit awareness of the inescapable role of philosophy in his practical decisions, have their basis.

900n.

Marx's
Evolution and
the Cold War

9
_____

*The Nineteenth Century Background of Contemporary Politics** *

Three events make the domestic and international politics of the century in which we live unique. These are: (1) the Cold War, (2) the release of atomic energy and (3) the political rise and cultural resurgence of Africa, Islam and Asia. The "trapped universals" essential for an understanding of (3) will concern us in Chapters 10, 12, 13, 14, 16 and 19. Events (1) and (2) derive from sets of cognitive philosophical premises that were discovered and formulated in the nineteenth century, the one in the natural-history biological and social sciences with their more inductive naïve realistic concepts, the other in mathematical physics with its formal theoretical constructs or concepts by postulation that are concepts by intellection.

Nineteenth century biological and social thought was dominated by the idea of evolution. This idea took on two antithetical formulations in different portions of the modern Western world. The first formulation derives from Hegel and tends to dominate thinking and action in Germany and eastward. The second formulation derives from Darwin and dominates all Anglo-American thought and most Continental European thinking west of the Rhine.

The Hegelian concept of evolution operates through theses and conflicting antitheses governed by the logic of negation. Hence it is appropriately called "dialectical evolution." The Darwinian concept of evolution adjusts organism to environment by operating on rare

---

*An address delivered at the Polytechnic Institute of Brooklyn on October 8, 1955, and reprinted here from the *Proceedings of the Centennial Convocation.*

mutations or slight chance variations. Because of the hundreds of centuries of time required in order to generate a new species, it is appropriately called "gradualistic evolution."

Viewed negatively, the Hegelian and Darwinian conceptions of evolution have one thing in common. Both reject the monistic, teleological evolution of medieval scholasticism and Aristotelian natural science. According to this medieval and Aristotelian doctrine, evolution is to be thought of as the slow imposition through time of a single thesis, termed the timeless final cause, or essential nature of all creation, upon formless matter. Hegelian dialectical evolution denies this monistic teleology for the middle states of temporal change by affirming that evolution entails a battle between two temporary final causes, one of which is termed the thesis, the other the antithesis. Darwinian gradualistic evolution departs from the orthodox Roman Catholic and Aristotelian concept by rejecting any teleology: Evolution is the product of neither a single purpose nor a dialectical conflict of antithetical purposes, or theses, working towards a final synthesis; it is, instead, a gradual mechanical interplay between countless internal and external factors operating imperceptibly slowly over hundreds of centuries of time upon genetical mutations or slight variations.

If, as the Hegelians and Marxists maintain, dialectic is of the essence of change in nature and in society, then contradiction and conflict, the essence of cold war, is natural even to times of peace. Furthermore, if evolution always involves theses and countertheses, termed antitheses, then wholesale planning upon the basis of the conflicting, rival theses is essential to social progress and to social wisdom. Evolution is not something outside human control that occurred some hundreds of thousands of years ago with the appearance of Neanderthal man. It is instead a dramatic, inevitable conflict of rationally articulatible theses which can be intensified in their opposition, thereby forcing a resolution here and now. Moreover, to intensify the conflict and force its revolutionary resolution is good. Hence, both the doctrinaire and the contemporary revolutionary character of world Communism with its dialectical theory of evolution.

If, on the other hand, evolution is the result of countless factors within individual organisms and their environment which are too many in number and too variable in place and time for human knowledge to record and relate in a neat thesis, then in one's approach to the complexity of human and social living one will tend to be suspicious of rationally articulated theses and antitheses and the reification of the logical principle of negation and the law of contradiction into an ontological power. Hence the Englishman's native suspicion of doctrinaire solutions to social problems—a suspicion which clearly distinguishes even the British Labour Party from the anti-Communistic Socialist parties on the Continent. Hence also the Anglo-American similar, more gradualistic trial-and-error, pragmatic and parliamentary approach to life and to politics.

There is a second factor in the nineteenth century's conflicting concept of evolution which throws light upon the deep intellectual and cultural roots of the contemporary Cold War. This second factor is the modification in Hegel's thinking which was made by Karl Marx, the founder of dialectical Communism. Marx kept Hegel's dialectical theory of evolution but rejected Hegel's idealistic theory of knowledge, substituting for it the naïve realistic epistemology which Marx derived from the German theologian Feuerbach. Marx uses this naïve realistic epistemology negatively against idealism to reject the role of ideas in human and social affairs and positively to establish the primacy of external material objects and of materialism. Hence the designation of Hegel's theory of evolution as dialectical idealism and of Marxism as dialectical materialism. According to the latter theory, the basis of dialectical evolution centers in matter and more particularly in the need of the organized matter of human bodies for energy, in order to survive, which only the material environment can provide. This turns the dynamics of social evolution into the biological struggle for environmental energy. At this point Marxist social theory comes close to the biochemical and thermodynamic knowledge of non-Marxist scientists. To this extent the Marxist realistic epistemology and materialism assert something that is experimentally verified. To this extent also it is a healthy theory of evolution since it avoids confusing the logical relation of negation and the law of contradiction with an ontological power in nature and in society. But were the Marxist to stop at this scientifically valid point in his theory of man and society he would have a statement of what is, but he would hardly have a utopia defining what ought to be. He would be entirely without a theory of reform and of revolution. In short, he would not be a Communist. Nor would his theory of evolution be dialectical. Consequently, to keep his theory of revolution he must smuggle his dialectical logic into his biochemistry and his thermodynamics—a very unrealistic and a very unmaterialistic procedure. This confusion of logical, ethical and physical categories he attempts to cover up by talk about "the physical production relations" and the antithetical classes of owners and proletariat which these physical production relations are supposed dialectically, by the logic of negation, to generate.

This Marxist Communist dialectical materialistic theory of evolution might be dismissed as the intellectual confusion of logical, ethical and physical concepts which it is, were it not for the fact that its materialism as well as its doctrinaire revolutionary dialectic is so widely believed and practiced by important political decision makers in the contemporary world. Its dialectical revolutionary component gives it its simple-minded doctrinaire claim to be able to produce quick results here and now. Its materialism, dressed up to look like social idealism, due to its confusion of ethical, logical and physical categories, gives it the appearance of morality while in fact taking matter and the struggle for power as the criterion of the good.

A third factor distinguishes the Hegelian and Marxist theory of evolution from the Darwinian gradualistic theory of the Anglo-American world. It has to do with predictability of the future.

According to Darwin and most Anglo-American thinkers, the future of the evolutionary process, in either biological nature or society, is beyond any present scientific determination or prediction. According to Darwin the factors within man and his environment determining the future are countless in number. Also, slight, minute and exceptional variational items are so decisive in determining what happens that it is obviously beyond the power of present human knowledge to prescribe what the new species or the future state of society will be. One cannot, therefore, blueprint the future structure of one's own or any other society in a thesis or doctrine. Instead, one must feel one's way into the future, dealing with new facts and new problems inductively and pragmatically as they arise, remodeling one's legal norms and one's social habits by way of community-authorized judicial decisions in concrete cases before the courts in which all the old and the novel factors in the social situation are allowed to bring themselves to bear.

For Hegel and Marx, however, not only is evolutionary development dialectical rather than gradualistic, but its future is absolutely determined. The final synthesis which will resolve the present conflict of theses and antitheses is, according to these dialectical thinkers, known now with certainty, exactly as Thomistic and Aristotelian Roman Catholics are sure they now know the final cause of all temporal creation.* This is why Hegel's dialectical idealism and the Marxist Communist's dialectical materialism both describe themselves as dialectical determinism. Here we have the source of the Communist confidence in his own particular, doctrinaire, dialectically materialistic ideology as the pattern not merely for himself today but for the entire world tomorrow. From a standpoint of both Hegel and Marx, due to their determinism, the inevitable, supposedly objective *Khrushchev* scientific laws governing evolutionary change are on their side. Each regarded or regards himself as riding the historical bandwagon.

Curiously enough, however, these Hegelian and Marxist dialectical determinists were in complete disagreement about what the final goal of the evolutionary process in society will be. For late nineteenth century Hegelians, it tended to be identified with the *Kultur* of Kaiser Wilhelm's Germany. For the Marxist Communist dialectical materialists, it is that state of the world which will occur when, by revolutionary and forceful means, the small group of leaders of the Communist party, in the name of "the dictatorship of the proletariat," takes over the administration of the entire world.

Needless to say the determinism of both the Hegelians and the Marxists is scientifically spurious. This judgment follows from the nature of the dialectical theory of evolution itself. The heart of dialectic is the logical operation of negation. It is by negation that any thesis in an earlier stage of evolution generates its opposite or antithesis; and it is, in turn, by negation of both the thesis and the antithesis, that the synthesis which defines the future state arises. For the latter process to be deterministic the logical operation of negation must be such that when applied to any thesis and its corresponding

---

* The difference between the Aristotelian and Thomistic Roman Catholic determinism and that of the Hegelians and Marxists is that the former is teleologically governed by the logic of identity and the latter by the dialectical logic of negation.

antithesis one and only one synthesis is possible. The most elementary consideration of any two theses is sufficient to show that either one, or both, can be negated in more than one way. Thus, by its very nature, an evolutionary process governed by the logic of negation cannot be deterministic.

The important point to note, however, is that both the dialectically idealistic Hegelians and the contemporary dialectical materialistic Marxist Communists *believe* the contrary; the future state of society is absolutely determined. The first two wars of this century have pretty thoroughly removed the Hegelian idealists from positions of political influence in today's world. The Marxist Communists, however, still remain in positions of absolute power in both Moscow and Peking, all thoroughly convinced, because of their belief in dialectical determinism, that the future is theirs. This being the case, American and Communist political oratory of the moment to the contrary notwithstanding, the Cold War is likely to remain with us for some time to come.*

Such is the relevance of nineteenth century evolutionary thought to this first major event of our time. Its second major event—the release of atomic energy—goes back also to the nineteenth century. In this case, however, it is mathematical physics rather than biological and social science which provides the key.

The release of atomic energy and the atomic bomb would not have been dreamed of, even as an imaginative possibility, were it not for Einstein's special theory of relativity of 1905. In formulating the latter theory Einstein had no concern for engineering or the construction of practical technological instruments. Instead he was troubled by a theoretical difficulty in the basic assumptions of the electromagnetic theory of the nineteenth century. This theory was formulated by the great British theoretical physicist Clerk Maxwell, in 1873, when his classic *Treatise on Electricity and Magnetism* first appeared. In this treatise Maxwell brought electrical, magnetic and optical phenomena, and all the experimentally verified laws governing their behavior, together under a single, deductively formulated set

---

* This was first written at the time of President Eisenhower's and Premier Khrushchev's speeches at their first Summit Conference. The writer sees no need for revision in the light of Premier Khrushchev's recent (1959) visit to the United States.

of theoretical assumptions, thereby founding the science of electromagnetics, or what, in more popular language, is called field physics. Maxwell's electromagnetic theory had one consequence which distinguished it from the deductively formulated science of mechanics founded by Newton in the seventeenth century.

The theoretical assumptions of Newton's physics with respect to the relation of a non-accelerated mass to space and time were such that no observation or experiment performed on such a mass, assuming no reference to another mass outside it, would permit one to detect whether the mass were at rest or moving at a uniform velocity in a straight line. Observation and experiment confirms this Newtonian thesis. In other words, the observable facts concerning mechanical bodies are such that they permit one to interpret the body either as at rest or as moving with a uniform velocity in a straight line. In short, in Newton's mechanics, for all non-accelerated motions, there is no experiment that will detect absolute rest or absolute motion. When this condition is satisfied, the principle of relativity is affirmed to hold for such bodies.

In Maxwell's electromagnetic theory, however, this was not the case. It followed from its basic assumptions that it was possible to perform an electromagnetic, as opposed to a mechanical, experiment which would determine whether a body was at absolute rest or in absolute motion with an experimentally measurable absolute velocity. In other words, whereas the principle of relativity for non-accelerated masses held in seventeenth century Newtonian mechanics, it was not valid in nineteenth century Maxwellian electromagnetics. In 1885, consequently, two physicists named Michaelson and Morley performed the electromagnetic experiment, in the basement of the Case Institute of Technology in Cleveland, which was to confirm this unique theoretical consequence of nineteenth century electromagnetic theory. The experimental result was not what the theory required.

It was this discrepancy between fact and theory in nineteenth century electromagnetics that led Einstein to the discovery of the special theory of relativity in 1905.

Curiously enough Einstein's analysis showed that the difficulty in nineteenth century electromagnetic theory could be corrected only by modifying the theory of space and time of Newton's seventeenth century mechanics as well. The modification consisted in shifting from the absolute theory of space and time, held in common by Newton and Maxwell, to a relational theory. Put crudely, the absolute theory of space and of time is the thesis that they are two independent containers within which the masses of physical objects of nature are located, after the manner in which peas are contained within a can, except that in the Newtonian and Maxwellian theory there would be two cans containing the peas—one the container called space, and the other the non-cyclical linear continuum called time. On the relational theory, however, of Einstein's special and general theories of relativity not only are space and time united into a single continuum called space-time, but instead of space-time being regarded as a container within which matter is located, space-time is conceived to be the relatedness of matter or of the events resulting from the collocations and collisions of matter.

These considerations reveal the exceedingly theoretical, and even philosophical, character of contemporary physics. So excessively theoretical and philosophical are the assumptions in Newton's and Maxwell's physics, which Einstein's special theory of relativity finds it necessary to reject, that one has to go to a footnote in the Introduction to Newton's *Principia* to discover what the erroneous assumptions of classical physics were. Similarly, the alternative assumptions introduced by Einstein are even more theoretical, and completely shocked common sense when they were first proposed.

Nevertheless this very theoretical, and even philosophical, alteration in the basic assumptions of mathematical physics makes all the difference in the world of our daily lives. For the engineer it means the atomic bomb and atomic reactor, for the doctor it provides tracer elements to track down the sources of disease within the human body, and for everyone everywhere it means living under the threat of an atomic holocaust in an atomic age unless or until international relations are brought under the rule of law.

The manner in which Einstein's abstract theory has brought about these practical changes can be put very precisely. After he had reconstructed the foundations of nineteenth, and even seventeenth, century physics with his formulation of the special theory of relativity, thereby solving the problem raised by the Michaelson-Morley experiment of 1885, he then proceeded to deduce the mathematical consequences of his new, exceedingly theoretical and philosophical assumptions concerning the relation between space, time and light propagation. When he did this, a specific mathematical formula became evident which has to apply to the systems of nature if the special theory of relativity is true. This formula bears the name "the mass-energy equation." It is this equation which gave physicists and engineers the idea that it was possible to derive energy in prodigious quantities directly from the disintegration of the mass of the chemist's atoms. Forthwith came Los Alamos, Hiroshima and the explosion of the hydrogen bomb. To get Einstein's abstract theory and to apply it is to be where we are today.

Needless to say, our politics as well as our medicine, our engineering and our psychological hopes and fears are affected. Every public official and every citizen on the surface of this planet lives at the present moment under the risk of destruction in an atomic war and must make his military and political decisions and plans accordingly. Moreover, in these decisions and plans, the evolutionary, biological and social thought of the nineteenth century and its theory and experimentation in mathematical physics have come together.

This merging occurs because of the two major nations with the largest stockpiles, quantitatively and qualitatively, of atomic bombs —the one, the Soviet Union, is dominated by the Marxist dialectical materialistic revolutionary theory of evolutionary change and social reform; and the other, the United States, is guided by the more Darwinian, gradualistic and pragmatic theory of evolution of both natural objects and social systems. Unfortunately these two evolutionary theories and the corresponding values which they tend to generate are incompatible the one with the other if applied universally as guiding principles for the entire world. Hence it is that to the fears generated by the existence of the atomic bomb there have been added the anxieties of the Cold War. Such is the manner in which the thought and deeds of the biologists, philosophers, social scientists and physicists of the nineteenth century have contributed to make the events of today what they are.

Three conclusions for the future are to be drawn. First, the biological and social assumptions of the Communist and liberal democratic portions of the world are so different that we must reconcile ourselves to a life of international tension in the days ahead. Until we have objective evidence coming from the Communist countries that, in their official teaching and in their school instruction, they are rejecting their nineteenth century dialectical materialistic Marxist ways of thinking by introducing men who are opposition party members into their own domestic and foreign policy decisions, professions of co-existence and peace must be taken, as Marx, Lenin and Stalin in their writings tell us they are to be taken, merely as temporary tactics rather than as a fundamental change in basic aim. Ideas for them, as for us, really matter, and such is the nature of both their ideas and their diplomatic activity. Second, this does not mean that war is inevitable. It does mean, however, that a sufficient majority morale backed with military police power must be maintained in the United Nations and in the world community to stand as both an idealistic and a realistic deterrent to the theoretical inclination and avowed practical purpose of the Communists to make their mid-nineteenth century Marxist philosophical doctrine the rule for the entire world.

The third implication has to do with the value we place on theoretical inquiry within our own country. We pride ourselves upon being a very practical people. This pride may well be our downfall. If we fail, it will be probably more from errors committed from within than from dangers from without. Our most likely domestic error is that in a shortsighted worship of the practical we shall become impractical. The foregoing analysis of the abstract theory of physics in its bearing on the practical affairs of this atomic age shows conclusively that we are now living at a time in scientific and human history in which only the pursuit of the most abstractly theoretical and even philosophical will enable us to be truly practical. Those industrialists or military leaders who pull the brains of our universities away into the solution of temporary and immediate practical problems, thereby leaving our universities and engineering schools without the Newtons, Maxwells, Gibbs, Einsteins, Schroedingers and Heisenbergs necessary to pursue scientific theory for its own sake and to develop the fundamental theory upon which practical leadership now depends, may well be killing the goose that lays the golden egg. More than one chairman of a scientific department in our universities is worried about the sense of values of a general public which so underrates and underpays theoretical scholars, as compared with pseudopractical men, or even practical plumbers, that our nation runs the grave risk in another generation of having no first-rate theoretical scientists in our universities to train the military and industrial engineers of the future.

Similarly, in the political sphere, may not our American inclination to underestimate the necessity of expert theoretical knowledge be exemplified by those politicians and their followers who deprecate the presence of what they term "eggheads" in government and affirm that only "practical" business and military men are to be trusted to preserve our democratic institutions in a world that contains Communists? Our foregoing analysis of nineteenth century biological, philosophical and social theory in its bearing on the Cold War shows that it may in fact be a very dangerous thing to have our major domestic and foreign policy decisions made by men who do not know this theory. More specifically, without a knowledge of Marxist evolutionary and social theory, the present statements of Soviet officials may be misconstrued in a way that is positively dangerous for democracy. But if this theoretical knowledge is to be possessed by our public officials, they must be either technically expert in the basic beliefs behind both Communism and free democracy or advised by experts from our universities who do have this indispensable theoretical knowledge. In either event, there must be theoreticians in government if government today is to be truly practical.

Must not also those of us who are educators, or who have children taught by educators, ask ourselves whether we are not committing the same error of underestimating the indispensable role of philosophical as well as scientific theory in today's world? Is this not precisely what is happening when we permit and urge the schoolteachers of our country to load the curriculum with specific applied subjects and pseudopractical courses in contemporary events and social problems to the neglect of the discipline in formal mathematical, logical and normative philosophical thinking and in the writing of clear and grammatical prose, without which the construction of the theory necessary for effective practice today is impossible? To these questions we shall return in Chapter 17.

In any event, one general conclusion is clear: To see the way in

154   *Philosophical Anthropology and Practical Politics*

which the technical scientific and philosophical beliefs of the intellectual leaders of the nineteenth century have made the major events
and practical political problems of our day in considerable part what
they are is to realize that the practical man neglects scientific and
philosophical theory at his peril.

10

Asian Mentality and United States Foreign Policy *

Any American who arrived in Pakistan or India in October of 1950 underwent a severe shock. Newspapers, whether Muslim or Hindu, whether British- or Indian-owned, in both their reports and their editorials described the police action of the United Nations as a greedy struggle between the two major powers of the world, in which the interests of Asians were largely overlooked, and with respect to which the United States was, if anything, slightly the worse of the two disturbers of the peace. There was little to choose between the attitudes of the British-owned *Statesman* and the Indian-owned *Hindustan Times* or *Times of India*. Had Premier Stalin himself selected the headlines and written the editorials, they could hardly have been more to Moscow's liking. The fact that they were written with apparent objectivity, not taking sides, made the effect all the more telling.

The Communist invasion of Tibet altered this appraisal momentarily. The morning after the invasion was announced officially by Peiping, the *Hindustan Times,* with which Devadas Gandhi, Mahatma Gandhi's son, was then associated, and which is usually a reliable clue to the opinion of at least one portion of Prime Minister Nehru's government, raised editorially the question whether India should not change its policy in the United Nations of urging the admission of Communist China. The newspaper even prepared for a re-

* This chapter is reprinted with permission from *The Annals of the American Academy of Political and Social Science,* July, 1951, Vol. 276, pp. 118–127.

education of the Indian people with respect to the United States by running that same morning, opposite its editorial page, an article "from a correspondent in London" describing how President Franklin D. Roosevelt had worked for the independence of India and urged his friend Prime Minister Winston Churchill to grant it.

This change of attitude with respect to the role of the United States in the world was, however, of very short duration. By December the newspapers owned by Indians were back on the old theme, again suggesting that the United States was aggressively militaristic and imperialistic, insane because of its own power, a threat along with Soviet Russia to the peace of the world. Following the Tibetan invasion only the more British-minded *Statesman,* among the major newspapers of India, underwent a lasting change of mind, persistently portraying the Korean affair as an officially authorized police action of the United Nations necessary to stop aggression, to which the United States was making the major contribution. When, however, the latter attitude towards the United Nations and the United States was urged upon the Indian Government by certain members of India's Parliament in a debate upon foreign policy, it was met with sarcasm by India's Prime Minister.

Nor was this response restricted merely to the official governmental position and to most of the press. In a small community of tea pickers far from any city on the slopes of the Himalayas in Northern Bengal, a humble lower-caste Hindu, who as a houseboy had picked up English, said to me with a rolling of his shoulders as if trying to shake off some pollution, "We here in the village do not like this Korean War." His intonation was clearly one which had within it the query, "Why are you doing it?" Upon another occasion he asked, "When is everyone here in India going to be able to read and write and have an education as in America?" There is admiration for America in India, even though in 1950 it did not extend to its foreign policy.

This shows perhaps most pointedly in those Indian leaders in strongest opposition to Prime Minister Nehru—people like Acharya Kripalani then within the Congress party, and Ashoka Mehta and Jai Prakash Narayan of the Socialist party. The latter in particular have no wishful thinking about Communists. They know Communist doctrine technically, its strong points and its errors. Hence by intellectual and moral conviction its way is not theirs. Also, they have passed through the experience of trying to cooperate with Communists in a common program against what both oppose, only to find the common trust betrayed. As one provincial leader of the Socialist party said, "We found that they want, not success for a common venture, but chaos." Even so, all these men in opposition to Prime Minister Nehru are for a foreign policy of neutrality. While unequivocally opposed to Communism, they hesitate to join with the United States in a United Nations program of collective security backed with the police force necessary to make it effective.

Other peoples in South Asia and the Middle East hold a similar position. Siam provides the only exception. Notwithstanding the dangerous impasse between Pakistan and India over Kashmir, there was no difference in October of 1950 in attitude towards the United States between Pakistan's *Civil and Military Gazette* and the newspapers in India. Trustworthy reports from Muslim Indonesia describe a similar attitude. Even as far west in the Muslim world as Cairo, Prime Minister Nehru, upon his stop there en route home from the London Commonwealth Ministers' Conference in 1951 received an ovation and was hailed as a great world leader. Coming immediately after the failure of Muslim and Hindu to find a common domestic policy in India, notwithstanding centuries of social life together, this agreement of Muslim and Hindu on foreign policy is all the more remarkable.

Clearly, something is present in the Middle East and Southeast Asia which must be understood and taken into account if one's role in the United Nations program of collective security is to be effective and if the foreign policy of the United States is not to defeat its own purposes.

Why, we must ask ourselves, is the attitude of a large portion of the non-Western peoples of the world so much what Moscow must want it to be? Or, to put the matter more specifically, What has persuaded the Indian peoples that the United States, instead of being a preserver of the peace of the world through the avoidance of an Asian Munich, is a power-intoxicated, economic and militaristic imperialistic nation, which, to use Prime Minister Nehru's language of 1950 has deflected the United Nations from its original intent as a peace-preserving instrument into a war-making machine?

Cannot the Asian see that if the United States really wanted to further aggression and imperialism, little and far-distant South Korea would hardly be the place to begin? Can they not understand that, if Korea falls, then Indochina, Burma, Siam, the Malay Peninsula, Indonesia, and even India may well follow in turn? Having given their sons in Korea in order that the Asians and peoples everywhere might not be intimidated by outsiders but might instead enjoy the right to build their cultural and political institutions in their own way, why must the people of the United States bear the additional agony of being branded as imperialistic and aggressive by the leaders of the very Asiatic people their Korean efforts and sacrifices were designed to save?

When the latter question was put to a priest of the important Ramakrishna Order in India, he gave the following reply: "You say you are in Asia for our good. But if you give me what to you is food, and to me is a poison, do you accomplish your purpose?" This response is important for two reasons. First, it shows that we have been going about what we are attempting in a way which strikes the Hindu Indian as wrong. Second, it shows that our aim, which to us seems good for Asia, appears to Hindu India as a poison, and evil. Something in the way we have handled the North Korean Communist invasion of South Korea has offended the Hindu Indian's criterion of proper moral and political conduct. That this is the case the next statement by the priest demonstrates: "There are factors in the nature of man which the action of your President Truman has not taken into account."

At this point a difference between the Gandhian Hindu Indian attitude towards the United States and that of the Islamic peoples appears. Whereas with followers of Islam one receives the impression that their failure wholeheartedly to take the American side centers in more purely practical political considerations, the Indian reaction to the United States' and United Nations' Korean policy cuts deeply into the unconscious and the emotional and is definitely accompanied by moral indignation. Or, to put the Indian attitude in a more positive way, there is no escape from the conclusion that Premier Nehru's stand against support of the United States gives expression to something deep and satisfying in the moral and spiritual consciousness of the Indian people. The Hindus feel that almost for the first time in modern history the moral and spiritual riches of India are being brought to bear in the world of practical politics.

What is this deep-rooted moral value in the Gandhian Hindu outlook which the United States and the United Nations have failed to take into account in their foreign policy? A clue to it will be gained if we turn aside from international politics at the national level to the legal method for settling disputes in Asian communities. The word "Asian" rather than "Hindu" is used deliberately, since it happens that the criterion of high moral and social leadership which exhibits itself in the settling of domestic disputes is, for present purposes, the same in a Confucian Chinese society, a Buddhist Siamese society, and a Gandhian Hindu Indian community. In short, we are confronted here with a moral factor, embodied in century-old practices for settling disputes, which is common to any culture which is Confucian, Buddhist, or Gandhian Hindu.[1]

The experience of my former colleague in the Yale Law School, Mr. Francis Liu, will guide us to this crucial moral factor.[2] Recall from Chapter 6 that the practice of law in the Western manner in Chiang Kai-shek's Shanghai led to the loss of his Chinese clients. As he put it in his quiet Chinese manner: "This caused me to reflect." These reflections guided him to the cause and the cure. "I won the confidence of my clients," he said, "when I showed them that I was not a lawyer in the Western meaning of the word, but was a moral man in the Confucian sense of the word 'moral.'"

The point is that the vast majority of the Chinese people were still impregnated with Confucian philosophy and its living legal customs according to which the moral man and social leader is always a peacemaker, not a litigation maker. Consequently to them the Western method of obtaining moral and social justice by sharpening issues and bringing a concrete dispute under abstract general rules seemed to be litigation making instead of peacemaking, and hence not to be trusted. This showed itself in Mr. Liu's practice in the following way: After the new client has described his case, he followed it with the question, "To how much, in the light of the facts, do you think I am entitled under the code?" At first Mr. Liu took this as a straightforward legal question. If he knew the statute most likely in question, he gave the answer; if not, he looked it up and then gave the answer. What he observed was that forthwith the client showed no further interest, politely withdrew, and often went out and settled the dispute with the other party for less than the statute provided. This happened sometimes even when the code to which appeal was made was a pre-Western ancient Chinese one.

Later when Mr. Liu looked at the client's initial question from the Confucian moral rather than the Western ethical and legal standpoint, he saw that the question, instead of being the straightforward legal query it seemed to be, was instead a moral examination of the lawyer which was going to be measured by Confucian rather than Western standards. From that time on, when the inevitable question came, "To how much am I entitled under the code?" Mr. Liu did not hear it. Instead he countered with another question: "Have you got together with your adversary?" Immediately a look of understanding appeared on the client's face. Mr. Liu had passed the moral examination in the Confucian, and, one may add, Asiatic, meaning of the word "moral." He was proceeding with his client like a peacemaker, not like a litigation maker. Clients felt, "This is a man in whose hands one can put one's difficulties with confidence." Forthwith Mr. Liu kept his Chinese clients.

He found that when the lawyers of the two parties in a dispute under the classical Chinese procedure fail to bring their clients to agreement between themselves either through a middle man or directly, and the dispute goes to a judge, the judge in turn uses the same procedure. He has interest neither in evidence nor in witnesses, nor in statutes, codes or precedents. He asks the disputants instead if they have got together, and when they reply, "Yes, many times to no avail," he often answers, "Then go back and try it again."

Even though Confucian society has ancient codes, they are regarded only as an evil last resort when the regular methods fail. In other words, it is immoral in the Confucian first-best morality to settle disputes by appeal to general rules. Contrast this with the West where it is usually taken for granted that the only fair and just way to settle a dispute is by bringing it under a general rule, thereby making all men equal before the law.

What is true of Confucian China is true also of Buddhist and Gandhian Hindu societies in this matter.[3] Notwithstanding the Western type of national law on the French model which Siam has adopted, one finds that not merely at the village level where Western influence has less effect, but even at the top Supreme Court level, the Chief Justice in 1950, before he would open a trial between Thais in the Western manner, would often first attempt to get the disputants to leave the court and settle their differences by themselves.

Is not this conception of social leadership and moral conduct as peacemaking without particular regard to specific facts or determinate principles precisely what Pandit Nehru epitomizes for Gandhian Hindu India in his attitude towards the North Koreans' invasion of South Korea and the determinate policy voted by the contractual legally constituted United Nations? And was it not precisely because of the awareness of this inclination of the Confucian, the Buddhist, and the Gandhian Hindu to mediate and compromise that Moscow encouraged New Delhi to initiate mediation early in the Korean affair in the hope that the United States, goaded by the McCarthys and the MacArthurs, and mindful of Munich, would turn it down and thereby establish itself in the Oriental mind as an uncompromising dispute-to-the-death-maker rather than as a peacemaker to be trusted by Asians as a partner in international affairs?

Was it a mistake then to go into Korea? Was the entire Korean action and the United Nations official policy with respect to it a mistake? Or if the policy was correct, is the refusal to compromise that policy an error?

To these questions the answer is unequivocally "No." Communistic doctrine and deeds, being what they are, the North Korean Communist invasion of South Korea if unstopped would truly have become an Asian Munich. Furthermore Communist ideology which affirms that ideals are not merely neutral and impotent, but morally evil unless they are backed with all the materialistic might they can muster, could hardly be stopped with words uttered by Prime Minister Nehru or the President of the United States or by a mere overwhelming majority positive legal vote of the United Nations. Police action, as well as official words, was necessary.

Furthermore, notwithstanding the initially demoralizing retreat of the United Nations forces from North Korea, the Korean policy achieved a major aim. When in Bangkok in 1950, I met an elder Siamese of Chinese stock who had returned the previous day from a meeting with Chiang Kai-shek on Formosa. This Siamese reported it to be Chiang Kai-shek's opinion that the Korean police action by the United Nations troops had thrown off the whole Communist timetable for Asia. The entrance of the United Nations troops into South Korea forced the Chinese Communists to move divisions of their army from central and southern China to northern China. Had this move not occurred, Chiang Kai-shek affirmed that the Communists would have taken Indochina. Interviews with American newspapermen who had spent weeks on the spot in Indonesia confirm this judgment.

If the United Nations policy in Korea was correct, and if the principles defining that policy should not be compromised, is there anything else that could have been done or can now be done to win rather than to alienate the moral judgment of India and East Asia? The answer to this question is affirmative and definite. We must do what we have done, but in a way that takes into account Asian moral and living law values, as well as those of the West and the lessons of Munich.

Again and again while pondering this problem in India and experiencing the negative attitude towards the United States and United Nations policy, the analogy of the football quarterback came back to me. It is as if the right play were called, but because it was not accompanied by other plays designed to take Asian mentality and moral values into account, the play was turned against us as far as the support of our Asian associates among the free nations is concerned.

Upon first thought it might occur to some that such support is not too important; that the important thing is that the right decision was made with respect to Korea even if the United States has been misunderstood in Asia. Such a thought, true though it might be as far as it goes, overlooks the fact that the United States is a democracy, and that for a democracy there is no such thing as a correct foreign policy with respect to Asia that does not win the spontaneous, heartfelt moral support of Asians. If this support is to be won, the character of Asian moral values and attendant Asian methods for handling disputes must be taken into account, as well as the lessons of Munich and the materialistic and expansive character of Communism. To do this is by no means easy. Moreover, a policy which accords with Asian mentality and values is likely to err in the opposite direction unless European ethical standards, the nature of Communism, and even other characteristics of the peoples east of Suez are considered with equal care.

Policy makers must remember that in addition to Munich and Moscow there are also Cairo, Karachi, Jakarta and the entire Muslim world to consider. As we have noted, the Arab States have also tended to side with Pandit Nehru and Hindu India against the United States and United Nations policy.

It would be a mistake to suppose that the Arabs side with Pandit Nehru for the same reasons which are behind the moral indignation of Gandhian Hindu India. If one examines the method of settling local disputes in a Muslim village outside of Cairo, one finds the same type of village leaders as in China, Siam or Hindu India, but they proceed in a radically different manner. Instead of urging the disputants to settle the case themselves, the village leader listens to the evidence and then himself gives a verdict, which is final and from which there is no appeal. This occurs even in Spanish Valencia in a water court for settling disputes over irrigation supply, which was founded there by the Arabs in the tenth century and still operates today. It is as if Allah speaks. Justice is sharp, definite and final.

This means that President Truman's rejection of mediation or compromise under Prime Minister Nehru's initiation, which placed us in such an unfortunate light as judged by Hindu, Buddhist, or Confucian Asian moral precepts and mentality, would appear to Islam more like a virtue than like an evil. For the Islamic world there are definite, determinate codes or rules of conduct specified by the Prophet or announced by his present earthly representatives, and good conduct consists in accordance with them. It does not consist in mediation and compromise and fuzziness with respect to facts or principles after the peacemaking manner of the mediating Asian.

In this respect Islamic mentality and values are more in accordance with those in the Western legal and moral tradition. Nor is this an accident, for Mohammedanism is one of the Semitic religions of the West and Near East, of which Judaism and Christianity are the other two.

Unless the difference in the fundamental beliefs and attendant values of nations and peoples rooted in the theistic religions of the West and those of nations and peoples nurtured in the intuitive religions of Asia such as Confucianism, Gandhian Hinduism and Buddhism are grasped, the problem of mutual understanding necessary for an effective collective security in international affairs cannot be appreciated. At bottom the basic difference is this: According to the intuitive philosophy and religion of Asia, whether Confucian, Gandhian Hindu or Buddhist, the ultimate factor in man and things, which is timeless and hence such that conduct based upon it will be trustworthy under all circumstances, is indeterminate in character; or, to put the matter negatively, all determinate things are transitory and hence not qualified to be made a basis for judgment or conduct under any circumstances and for all people. Precisely from this belief stems the Confucian, Buddhist and Gandhian Hindu tendency to foster a vague fellow feeling expressing itself in mediation and compromise and to forego determinate legal codes except as a last resort.

The Semitic theist on the other hand, whether Hebrew, Christian or Muslim, tends to regard the ultimate and eternal in human nature or things as an ideal determinate pattern or logos introducing determinate order and perfection into an otherwise chaotic and confused world. Hence his tendency is to regard the moral man as the man of determinate principles and to conceive of the correct method of settling disputes and rendering justice as the bringing of all men and cases under a determinate code, moral principle or general rule, whether this code be of the law-of-status or the law-of-contract type.

In this connection it is interesting to note that the Communists, with their determinate doctrinaire economic and political blueprint for society, belong in the theistic Western rather than in the intuitive mediative Eastern tradition. In fact, of all the moral and political philosophies of the Semitic theistic and Western world, Protestant Anglo-American liberalism with its recognition of diverse determinate forms of belief as reasonable and its doctrine of toleration comes nearer the values of Asia than any other. Because we have not taken Asian values into account in our foreign policy, we have failed fully to capitalize on this fact. There was no word uttered more often by India's Ambassador to Moscow, Sir Sarvapalli Radhakrishnan, at the Indian Philosophical Congress held in December of 1950 at Calcutta, when talking either publicly or privately on these matters, than the word "toleration." Conversely, because Russia has kept Asian mentality and values continuously in mind (notwithstanding the almost complete antithesis between her determinate doctrinaire naïve materialistic philosophy and that of the traditional Far East), she has been able to jockey the Western free nations into the position of appearing to Asians as stubborn, uncompromising folk who are warmakers rather than preservers of the peace.

The basic difference in beliefs and moral attitudes between theistic cultures of the Hebrew, Christian or Muslim religious type and the Confucian, Buddhist [4] or Gandhian Hindu species is important for another reason. It explains the fact noted earlier in this paper that the Indian failure to go along with the United States has been accompanied by moral indignation whereas the Islamic attitude is more one of a difference of opinion with respect to practical expediency. That the latter is the case was illustrated by one Muslim who, after defending the Arab policy of joining Pandit Nehru's India in an independent line with respect to the United Nations policy in Korea urged and supported by the United States, added, "But if you think you are ready to fight a victorious war now, then go ahead with it." Clearly, this man's attitude towards the United States policy at the time was not one of moral indignation.

Upon what consideration, then, is the similarity of attitude towards the United States in the Islamic and Indian press based? This brings us to a major factor motivating Islamic peoples and a second important element behind India's attitude. Practically every country in the Middle East and Asia, with the notable exception of Siam, is emerging from imperialistic domination by Western European powers, during which legal forms derived from Western European cultures had been imposed on its society. Any policy therefore has a great appeal if it sets up any or all of these countries in international affairs as a third force in the world, independent of either the Communistic West or the traditional democratic West.*

Furthermore, it is natural for people in the Middle East and in Asia, especially those like the Pakistanis, the Hindus, and the Indonesians who have been under the rule of Westerners, to conceive of the West in terms of what they have experienced it to be. This experience has been that the West has always meant imperialism

---

* In world affairs the reference to the democracy-Communism issue as an East-West issue is a misnomer. Communism is a creation of a European West German, Karl Marx, and stems directly from Hegel and the problems left by modern Western thought. Only with respect to Europe is it appropriate to refer to Communism as Eastern, since it was developed in West Germany and flourished first in Eastern Europe.

under the control of the strongest Western power of the moment. When therefore two world wars have depleted Great Britain's former strength as the leading Western power and the United States has become in fact the most powerful free Western nation, it becomes easy for Middle Easterners and Asians to conclude that Western imperialism has merely shifted to the United States the power through which it expresses itself.

Nor did statements by President Truman that the United States is in Korea merely to prevent aggression and to permit Asians to run their affairs in their own way suffice to alter this judgment. The Middle Eastern and Asian peoples have been accustomed in the past to Western imperialistic nations that have moral and political arguments convincing to themselves for maintaining Western troops and political administrators on Middle Eastern or Asiatic soil. Nor is the Korean affair the first time in history that people in Asia have been told that both a selfish interest in their own future independence and their moral obligation require them to side with the Asian foreign policy of some Western nation.

Also, again with the exception of Siam, there is hardly a present political leader in any Islamic or Far Eastern country who has not come to power on the thesis that the ills of his countrymen are largely due to foreign interference and imperialism. This is as true of Islamic Pakistan, Egypt and Indonesia as it is of predominantly Hindu India. In short, in these vast areas of the world imperialism is the politician's main stock in trade.

These factors common to India and Islam add up to one thing: a spirit of cultural and political independence—one might even call it provincialism—dominates this vast area of the world. The consequence is that any Westerner initiating anything of a political or military nature in this area is suspect. The Asians want things from America and from the West, but they have learned from experience that the West ties strings to its gifts.

It appears therefore that the negative attitude towards American foreign policy with respect to Korea which one met in 1950 from Cairo eastward has its basis in at least two factors—one peculiar to the cultures of Gandhian India and those rooted in the intuitive religions and philosophy of the Far East, the other common both to Islam and to the cultures of India and the Far East. The former factor, exhibiting itself in the moral indignation accompanying India's negative attitude towards the United States, and towards the United Nations' legally authorized police action in Korea, seems to have its source in the concept of the moral man as a dispute settler by mediation rather than by the measurement of specific acts against determinate principles, a moral attitude which in turn derives from the belief that the timeless, hence dependable and divine factor in man and things, is indeterminate in character, not expressible in any proposition or code. The factor common to Islam and Asia is less passionately moral and more political and expedient in character. It is a spirit of cultural and political independence, which is a reaction from the intimate connection of the West with imperialism, as experienced during the very recent past.

This being the attitude, and these being at least some of the reasons for it, what are the implications with respect to a policy which will not defeat its own purposes in Islam, Africa and Asia? This is a question taking us beyond the limits of this chapter.

A few observations may, however, be briefly noted here. So far as the Middle East and Asia are concerned, America will do well to pursue an American rather than a European or Western policy, giving the clear impression that she is not taking over Holland, Britain or France's role in the tradition of Western imperialism but is instead pursuing the way of the United States of 1776 and the Mexico of 1810.

When any proposal comes from the leaders of any people in the Gandhian Hindu, Confucian or Buddhist cultural tradition, it would be well to keep in mind their moral concept of the peacemaker as a mediator. It will also be well not to allow one to be jockeyed into the position of turning the mediation down, however justified such conduct may seem as a matter of principle from the Western standpoint; instead the proposal should be so handled that the other party appears as the uncompromising one.

In expressing this sensitivity to the different moral values and to the independent aspirations of cultures and peoples other than our own, our leaders must reiterate that our aim is the achievement of an international order rooted in every culture and ideology of the world and that our military and political influence will be brought to bear in a foreign country only in the name of the United Nations when some nation has violated the right of some other people to build their social institutions in the light of their own traditions and values in their own way. This means that threats to overthrow a country or to throw one faction of it against another because we do not like one faction's ideology must be avoided. United Nations and United States military action when necessary to prevent aggression from being successful must be called and kept a defensive police action.

Only then can the Western free nations avoid Asian and Islamic suspicion that United States action in the United Nations is a cloak for Western imperialism. And, what is more important, only then can the mutual respect and confidence between the free nations of the world be fostered, which is necessary if an international organization is to be achieved for settling disputes by legal rather than warful means, with the police support necessary to make it effective.

One final caution is to be noted. It would be an error in the opposite direction to take these Asian and Middle Eastern attitudes into account in our foreign policy to the neglect of the European ones, the lessons of Munich, and the dangers and errors in Communist doctrine and policy. We are confronted with a problem the correct solution of which requires attention directed upon a large number of different factors. The task is that of determining the character of each factor and then of formulating a policy in the light of all.

One further caution is to be noted. The foregoing description of Asian mentality restricts itself, especially in the case of Hindu India, to but one factor in it. This factor is the mediational type of dispute settling and the ethic of the middle path which characterizes Confucian and Buddhist peoples and also the Buddhist non-dualistic Vedantic-Gandhian portion of Hindu India. The legal codes of Aryan Hindu India show that its living and positive law contains another exceptionally important factor which was brought into India by the ancient Aryan conquerors. This factor in pre-Western and pre-Muslim Hindu India has been shown by recent Indian scholars to express the Mimamsa system of Hindu Indian philosophy.[5] Actual Hindu India is, therefore, a systematically related complex culture which combines non-dualistic Vedantic with Mimamsa philosophy. The latter non-Gandhian and non-mediational component of Hindu and Hindu-Buddhist Asian mentality will concern us in later chapters.

11

---

*Neutralism and United States Foreign Policy**

Neutralism can be best approached through its historical and ideological context. Its historical context is both immediate, since World War II, and of wider scope, reaching back in the case of the United States to the days of its Founding Fathers. In the case of other nations, it goes back to the fifteenth century when Vasco da Gama sailed from Lisbon around Africa to southwestern India where he inaugurated the Western imperialistic domination of Asia, Africa and Middle Eastern Islam. The ideological context of neutralism is equally complex, involving at least five factors: (1) The political, economic, and religious or antireligious philosophies of (a) Communism and (b) contractual modern constitutional democracy. (2) The religious and social philosophies of the African tribesmen; of Buddhist, Hindu, Confucian, or Shinto Asia and of Islam, which differ not merely within and among themselves, but also from the Stoic Roman legal or the Judaic-Christian West in either its Byzantine Communist or its liberal democratic modern variants. (3) The European theories of foreign policy in the imperialistic era. (4) The classical theory of United States foreign policy of its Founding Fathers, as given later positive application in accordance with its basic contractual democratic philosophy by President McKinley and Congress in Cuba in 1898 and by President Truman and Congress in

* This chapter is reprinted with permission from *The Annals of the American Academy of Political and Social Science,* July, 1957, Vol. 312, pp. 42–68.

Korea in 1950. (5) The subsequent confusions and contradictions resulting from the Europeanization of (4) by (3).

The theory of United States foreign policy laid down by its Founding Fathers was usually described as neutralism. Washington's prescription of no "entangling alliances" is too well known to need further documentation here. Nowhere does the radical difference between the foreign policy of present and past United States military and political leaders become more evident than in the letter to President Monroe in which Jefferson wrote that "nothing should ever be accepted [by way of commitment outside the United States] which would require a navy to defend it." [1] Although they differed on almost every domestic issue, Hamilton and Jefferson agreed on the "neutralist" theory of United States foreign policy. Noting that the key to British and French foreign policy was the quest for colonial possessions, Hamilton wrote:

Why then should we, by a close political connection with any Power of Europe, expose our peace and interest, as a matter of course, to all the shocks with which their mad rivalship and wicked ambition so frequently convulse the earth? [2]

As late as 1885 President Cleveland added:

Maintaining, as I do, the tenets of a line of precedents from Washington's day which proscribe entangling alliances with foreign states, I do not favor a policy of acquisition of new and distant territory, or the incorporation of remote interests with our own.[3]

Perhaps the first apparent break in this classical doctrine came with the doctrine of America's "manifest destiny" uttered by President Eliot of Harvard with respect to the domestic frontier and extended beyond the borders of the nation by President Theodore Roosevelt. Even he, however, in 1904 applied the traditional United States doctrine in declaring the United States neutral in the war between Japan and Russia. Recently a British student of comparative international law, Mr. N. C. H. Dunbar, has listed some twenty-one major proclamations by Presidents of the United States with respect to specific wars or invasions between Jefferson in 1806 and Theodore Roosevelt in the Russo-Japanese crisis of 1904 in which the "neutralist" theory of United States foreign policy was explicitly appealed to and applied. After contrasting this theory of United States foreign policy with those of Europe, he concludes: "The most important contribution which the United States has made to international law is undoubtedly the doctrine of neutrality." He adds that the period before Presidents Cleveland, McKinley and Theodore Roosevelt "marked the lowest point in the quality of United States diplomacy, and in the amount of popular attention devoted to it"; but that, nevertheless, in its "control of diplomacy [the United States] has always been more democratic than any other country." [4] It never had a self-perpetuating foreign service élite, even though in Jefferson it had, as the Declaration of Independence which he wrote shows, perhaps the greatest foreign policy maker the free world has ever possessed.

To describe the theory which dominated United States foreign policy from the Founding Fathers until at least the opening of the twentieth century as neutralism is, however, to describe it only partially. It was not an unqualified doctrinaire neutralism that ignored what the issues in any foreign war were; it was, instead, a concrete qualified neutralism directed explicitly against one specific thing—namely, military invasions and wars arising from the theories of foreign policy of the European nations in the imperialistic era. Always when they urged their countrymen to be neutral, Washington, Jefferson and Hamilton referred to the wars arising between the European powers due to their imperialistic foreign policies vis-à-vis their colonial peoples. Why this specificity in their neutralism? Is not the answer clear? They had just had the concrete experience of being a colonial people under European dominance and had fought and won a revolutionary war to throw it off. Obviously, therefore, they did not want to side with their European oppressors to prevent other colonial people from doing the same thing. Furthermore, in justifying and consolidating their revolution, the Founding Fathers had written a Declaration of Independence and Bills of Rights to both state and federal Constitutions which affirmed that "all men," not merely Americans, are born *in principle* not merely free but also democratically equal before the law and have the inalienable right to such democratic freedom and equality.

In short, their neutralism with respect to any alliance with European powers rested neither on the expediency of the moment nor on the doctrinaire notion that entrance into *any* foreign alliance or war is an error. It rested instead upon the principles of their basic religious and political philosophy, that, namely, of Locke and Jefferson. Since this moral and political philosophy affirmed the natural right of everyone to freedom, it proscribed the siding with one or another of the European powers in the wars arising from their conflicting imperialistic conquests of other people. It did not follow from this, however, that this same philosophy in the case of a war between a European imperialist and a native people might not prescribe the sending of troops abroad on the side of the native people. This is precisely what occurred in 1898 with the United States military intervention in the war between the Spanish and the Cubans. President McKinley spoke of this decision as the action "of a neutral" made only after Spain had refused the mediation offered by President Cleveland two years earlier to settle the Spanish-Cuban war "on the basis of self-government for Cuba under the flag and sovereignty of Spain." [5] Immediately Congress added in its Joint Resolution: "First, that the people of Cuba are, and of right ought to be, free and independent." President McKinley's reference to his dispatch of American troops abroad as the act "of a neutral" shows that he did not regard the act as a departure from the classical United States foreign policy of the Founding Fathers. He was merely applying the basic Lockean-Jeffersonian natural-rights philosophy of the Declaration of Independence and the Bill of Rights to a foreign war in which one of the parties was a European imperialist power and the other party was a much weaker native people whose natural right to run their own affairs was being violated; then intervention in support of the native people was both just and called for. That Congress interpreted President McKinley's action in the same way is proved by the fact that the first sentence of its Joint Resolution states and applies to the Cuban people the basic moral and political principle of the philosophy in the Declaration of Independence. When the foreign war is one between imperialists conflicting over their conquests of native people, this philosophy of United States foreign policy prescribes neutralism; when the foreign war is between an imperialist and a native people, then the classical United States theory of foreign policy justifies entrance on the side of the native people.

As previously noted, the traditional European theories of foreign policy are the accompaniments of the Western imperialistic era. In fact, they produced it. Hence, instead of looking to imperialism as their explanations, we must look to them as the explanation of imperialism.

Our reference to the traditional European foreign policy has been in the plural. There are two theories. One is moral, teleological and monistic, and, hence, may be appropriately termed the monistic morally based theory of foreign policy. A moral theory of foreign policy is monistic when it is based on religious and moral norms of one's own nation alone. The other is materialistic, mechanistic and pluralistic, and, hence, may be termed the pluralistic power-politics theory of foreign policy. In European history, civilization and politics, the former derived from Aristotle—in the case of England by way of Hooker, Shakespeare, the Church of England and Sir Robert Filmer—and in the case of France and the other predominantly Roman Catholic European nations and some contemporary Holy-War-inclined American Roman Catholic cardinals by way of St. Thomas Aquinas. The second of the two European theories derives on the Continent from Machiavelli, Guicciardini and the pluralism of the Italian tribal- and family-centered city states; and in Great Britain from Harrington, Hobbes, and the nineteenth century jurist Austin.

In Aristotelian physics and metaphysics, not merely man but all things were governed by teleological causality, that is, by purposeful causality in which the content of the purpose was identified with the *telos,* or inevitable future state of the system. This led Aristotle to identify the words "good" and "God" with the organically and internally related final causes of all things. Since this organically related final cause of all particular individual things was one rather than many, it followed that there was but one possible good aim for any person or any nation. Hence, the monism of this morally based theory of foreign policy as defined and made known to morally principled statesmen by Aristotle. The criterion, therefore, of any good foreign as well as domestic policy meant in practice the bringing into being everywhere of this Aristotelian Spanish, French, Portuguese or American Roman Catholic or Tudor Elizabethan Church of England Conformist Protestant Christian way of life. Consequently, in bringing their particular Christian and Western domestic ways of life to bear in the political, economic and cultural conquests and domination of non-Western civilizations and people, the Western European Spanish, Portuguese, French, British and German conquerors sincerely believed that they were doing what was religiously and morally good.

To this belief the Protestant Reformation made its unique contribution. As used by both the Lutheran Germans and Henry VIII, it broke the Christian universal man of Cicero and the Stoic Roman legal scientists loose from universal cosmopolitan man to identify him with modern nationalistic Protestant Prussian German chauvinistic or Church of England English man. This, combined with the French Revolution which was rooted in modern secular philosophy, produced modern Western political nationalism. This modern nationalism reversed the trend towards effective international law and the concept of moral man as any man whatever, which Cicero and the Stoic Roman legal scientists had introduced and which the later Roman Empire and its inheritor, the Holy Roman Empire, had tried and partially succeeded in making effective. At this point, the Protestantized monistic morally based theory of foreign policy and the pluralistic power-politics theory became identical; and the modern power states, each possessed of supposedly absolute and unlimited sovereignty, arose.

Aristotelian Christianity, whether Roman Catholic or Shakespearean and Elizabethan Church of England, also affirmed that it was in the natural-law nature of all things that certain people were born to be moral, religious and political leaders and that others were born to be both their responsibility and their servants. Aristotle before them, under the influence of the law-of-status living law of his time, took it for granted that certain people are born to be slaves. In short, both Roman Catholic Christian society on the Continent and Ireland and Conformist Church of England Christian society in Great Britain conceived a legal and theocratic hierarchical, rather than an egalitarian democratic type of society, in which church and state are kept separate politically, as the good one—not merely for Africans, Middle Easterners and Asians—but also for Westerners. A democratic egalitarianism in politics, religion or education, to say nothing about ideological, religious and cultural pluralism, was not contained in their concept of the religiously, politically, morally and educationally good. Thus, at Oxford and Cambridge, for example, it was taken for granted—as with the Filmerian First Families of Virginia—that the best education would be given, with minor exceptions, to those who in the divine dispensation and hierarchy of all things carry the greatest responsibility—namely, the sons of the First Families. Macaulay gave expression to this idea of the good of the monistic morally based theory of national foreign policy when, with respect to India, he said that it was the ideal of the British government in India "to form a class of persons Indian in blood and color but English in taste, opinions, morals and intellect." [6] With this ideal, the conception of British policy in India as that of carrying "the white man's burden" became self-evident. The idea of a Foreign Office aristocratic, self-perpetuating élite making foreign policy decisions unmolested by unrestrained democratic legislative debates and control became equally self-evident. In a recent study of the leaders of the British government, its foreign ministers, and its foreign officers, the Britisher N. C. H. Dunbar has shown that until recently a preponderant number of them came from the aristocratic families and were trained in the Aristotelian philosophy at Eton, Harrow, and the other Church of England "public schools" and at Oxford and Cambridge. Thus, just as the classical theory of United States foreign policy was rooted in the Stoic-cosmopolitan and the Lockean-Jeffersonian democratic and egalitarian idea of the morally, politically and legally good and just man, so the morally based theory of foreign policy of England and its Empire was rooted in its monistic Aristotelian hierarchical and regal Conformist Protestant Christianity.

The pluralistic Machiavellian-Hobbesian-Austinian theory of European foreign policy seems initially to be the direct antithesis of this Aristotelian monistic morally based theory. Hobbes's philosophy of physics followed that of Descartes, which, like that of Newton, was mechanistic rather than teleological in its causality. Hence, no room apparently was left for teleological purpose and its morality. Consequently, war resulting from the conflict of material inertial forces described men in their state of nature. Since this state, according to Hobbes, is self-defeating and self-destroying, it became necessary if men were not going to destroy one another in their domestic relations to hand over their pluralistic, personal, material powers to one undivided sovereign power whose will was absolute.

At this point notwithstanding their initial apparent opposition, the European monistic Aristotelian morally based and the pluralistic Hobbesian power-political theories of foreign policy become identical in practice. For both there is no international law since there is no *de facto* sovereign in the international community with the physical power to enforce its will. The normal, even the good—good being identified with Protestant Reformation *Volk* or national man—relation between nations is that of war, except insofar as the monistic moral imperialism and unilaterally guided power-political maneuvering of one's own nation succeeds temporarily in dominating the situation. To this somber consignment of humanity in this atomic age, some contemporary Protestant theologians add another argument deriving from the original sin committed by Adam and Eve in the Garden of Eden, a sin so irreparable as it is handed down from generation to generation that it becomes unreasonable and even irreverent with respect to the ways of God in history for anyone to suppose that religiously moral or even secularly legal considerations can operate in international affairs. Thus do the Reverend Reinhold Niebuhr and the power politician Mr. George Kennan join their spiritual and material hands to make Hobbes and Jesus lie down together. Mr. Arnold Toynbee's general induction from history of the law of "challenge and response" comes near to the same thing taken erroneously as a prescription of what must be in the future, rather than merely as a description of what has been most of the time in the imperialistic past. It is hardly an accident that power-politics-minded generals and foreign policy "experts" quote the Reverend Mr. Niebuhr and Mr. Toynbee so frequently. Such a combination of Christianity with Machiavelli and Hobbes has been the traditional European theory of foreign policy.

The only surprise is to find this theory embraced by Americans as spiritually sensitive and professionally able as Mr. Kennan and Professor Niebuhr. The fact, however, is that they bespeak a modification in the theory of United States foreign policy, embracing Republicans and Democrats alike, that occurred in the first half of the twentieth century. To this phenomenon we must now turn. Otherwise, the development of neutralism cannot be understood with respect to United States foreign policy in Asia during Mr. Kennan's, Secretary Acheson's, Mr. Paul Nitze's and President Truman's decision making and its spread to Europe under the foreign policy of their opposite numbers Mr. Robert Bowie, Secretary Dulles, Admiral Radford, and President Eisenhower.

Reference has already been made to President Theodore Roosevelt's doctrine of America's manifest destiny. At the same time, the American Mahan was developing his theory of sea power. This new Republicanism put a novel and more militant interpretation on the meaning of the Spanish-American War. Centered in New York State, it expressed the effect of Europe on the Eastern United States. As such it was vigorously opposed by the Republican machines of President McKinley's Ohio, Senator Robert La Follette's Wisconsin, and the Chicago *Tribune*'s Illinois. The symbol of this New York State Republicianism was the Bull Moose carrying "the big stick." It was the mood of a Republican United States which, accepting its power-laden imperialistic destiny, would forsake neutralism with respect to European wars to take on Europe at Europe's own power-politics game. The practical result was a securing of land for the Panama Canal by methods for which a later Democratic administration guided by President Woodrow Wilson's more classical theory of United States foreign policy found it necessary in all conscience to make amends.

The present relevance of this past history is that it is in this Theodore Rooseveltian New York Republicanism that General Douglas MacArthur received his political nourishment; from which Secretary of State Dulles derived; and to which, rather than the isolationist Republicanism of his home state of Kansas,* General Eisenhower decided to attach himself as a voting citizen before he was called to be the Republican candidate for the Presidency. In fact, the battle at Chicago in 1950 between General Eisenhower and Senator Taft, which still goes on, as yet undecided, in the Republican party was an issue between the more Europeanized, still persisting Theodore Roosevelt New York Republican machine and the differently Euro-

---

* The *New York Times* of September 21, 1959, reported that "The State Department proposed [to Premier Khrushchev] a visit to the . . . President's home town of Abilene, Kansas."

peanized Middle Western Republican machines aided by Republican House floor leader Representative Joseph Martin from Massachusetts and Senator Styles Bridges from New Hampshire.

It is not correct to leave the impression, however, that the latter Middle Western and right-wing Republican theory of United States foreign policy is identical with the classical theory of the Founding Fathers, particularly as the latter theory was applied by President McKinley in Cuba. For Senator Taft of Ohio, like the older Senator La Follette of Wisconsin and Representative Joseph Martin of Massachusetts, also expressed and represented a Europeanization of the classical theory of American foreign policy. Their Europeanization is, however, different from that of President Theodore Roosevelt and his New York Republicanism since it results from the emigration to the United States of the Irish from a then British-dominated Ireland and the German liberals fleeing from the defeated liberal revolution in Germany in 1848. Unlike Theodore Roosevelt who wanted the United States to carry a big military stick, these Europeans came to avoid military service; their mentality was quite other, therefore, than that of General Washington, Hamilton or Jefferson. Hence, they wanted not even a small stick and nothing of United States troops abroad under any circumstances. The Irish settled heavily in Boston; the Germans in Cincinnati, Chicago and Milwaukee. It is the Cincinnati group who were Senator Taft's constituents. It was to the Milwaukee group that Senator La Follette, notwithstanding his liberal domestic policy, went for his isolationist foreign policy support. Hence, for Middle Western Republicans, whether La Follette economic liberals or Taft-Chicago *Tribune* conservatives, the classical theory of United States foreign policy became transformed into unqualified doctrinaire go-it-alone isolationism.

Thus it happened that the Europeanization of Republican foreign policy thinking in two opposite ways during the twentieth century brought the Republicans up to World War II with two diametrically opposed theories of foreign policy, both of which were incompatible with the classical American theory. The effect of both of these Europeanizations was to break United States foreign policy loose from the basic Lockean-Jeffersonian and later Lincolnian liberal democratic Declaration of Independence and Bill of Rights philosophy which makes the nation that is the United States unique.

But this is by no means the end of the Europeanization story. The legal profession and, hence, the Secretaries of State in both the Democratic and the Republican parties were also affected, as were the military leaders at West Point and Annapolis and the professors of international relations in the oldest universities. In fact, most of the latter came from Europe and, hence, unconsciously, and to this extent uncritically, brought European theories and ways in international relations with them.

Consider the present elder members of the American legal profession first. Its law is that of the English common law. At the end of the nineteenth century the Hobbesian theory of law as the will of an absolute sovereign who had the physical power to make his will effective passed over by way of the English jurist Austin through Thayer of the Harvard Law School to spread throughout the law schools of the United States and capture minds like those of Judges Learned Hand and Thomas Swan, Mr. Justice Frankfurter, Secretaries of State Dean Acheson and John Foster Dulles and their legally-educated foreign policy advisers Mr. Paul Nitze and Mr. Robert Bowie. The story of how this Europeanization of the classical natural-rights theory of United States law occurred has been told by Judge Learned Hand in his eulogy to Justice Stone in the *Columbia Law Review* of September, 1946, and to Judge Thomas Swan in the *Yale Law Journal* of December, 1947.

According to this English-Austinian legal philosophy, international law is not law, since there is no absolute *de facto* sovereign with the physical power to enforce its commands upon the pluralistic power-politics nationalistic states—each with its unilaterally controlled absolutely unqualified sovereignty. This is the reason why both the British and Secretary of State Dulles were so weak with respect to President Nasser's insistence upon Egypt's absolutely unqualified sovereignty over what goes on in the Suez Canal. The Egyptian leader was giving the British Prime Minister and the American Secretary a good dose of their own Hobbesian-Austinian philosophy of law and international politics. If anyone thinks this is unreasonable, then he must also conclude that the legal and political philosophy not merely of the British and Mr. Dulles, but also of Dean Acheson, Judge Hand, Justice Frankfurter and all the countless other Hobbesian-Austinian posivitists in high judicial and executive places in the United States is unreasonable also. Hobbes was quite clear on this point. Since for him and Austinians following him, law and justice are defined as the will of an absolute sovereign who has the physical power to make his will effective, Hobbes pointed out that on this theory there is no such thing as an unjust sovereign.

Nor is this all. According to this positivistic legal philosophy, law derives its effectiveness not from its moral content, but from the independent *de facto* Hobbesian physical power which the sovereign who wills it applies. This has the implicit effect of making physical power rather than moral principle the criterion of what happens in practice even under law when law is effective. Then one uses the moral content of the legal norms to condemn one's enemies but believes according to positivistic legal theory, and hence in principle, that power alone is the criterion of any law's effectiveness. At this point the morally based theory of foreign policy, even when filled in with liberal democratic, rather than Aristotelian aristocratic and medieval theocratic content, becomes indistinguishable from the most materialistic power politics. Hobbes, there at the beginning in the legal positivists' definition of law, triumphs in the end and clubs become trumps.

Furthermore, as the legally positivist Judge Learned Hand has recently made clear in the aforementioned articles, according to this Hobbes-Austinian-Harvard Law School-Thayerian philosophy, the Declaration of Independence and the Bill of Rights are not to be taken, after the manner of the Founding Fathers, as immutable natural law principles to be used by the courts in the judicial review of legislative statutes; instead, the Declaration of Independence and the Bill of Rights are to be interpreted merely as "admonitions to forbearance" to the legislators and the electorate. It follows that if the legislature passes statutes or the Executive and his Secretary of State pursue a foreign policy that violates the Declaration of Independence for all men, this is quite proper legally. The sovereign will being what the legal positivist means by justice, it follows by definition that anything any sovereign state wills is just. Forthwith the Lockean natural law and contractual legal philosophy at the basis of the classical theory of United States foreign policy is removed, and the way is made open in positivistically minded legally trained United States decision makers such as Secretaries Acheson and

Dulles, Mr. Paul Nitze, and the one-time Republican Chairman of the Planning Board of the State Department, Under Secretary Bowie, to make United States foreign policy identical with that of traditional Europe.

While this legally positivistic Hobbesian-Austinian Europeanization of the American legal profession was going on, the future generals and admirals at West Point and Annapolis were pondering Theodore Roosevelt's America's "manifest destiny" and reading Mahan and the German Clausewitz on national strategy. Also, two world wars threw them into collaborations with the military minds and political decision makers of Europe. They would hardly have been human if, quite apart from the Theodore Roosevelt-Mahan influence, they had not unconsciously come to take European theory and practice with respect to national policy in some part at least for granted.

After World War I a young officer in the Foreign Service found his duties taking him to Europe. There in his formative years he saw the European type of foreign service in which both long-range planning and day-to-day decisions are made (not subject to vigorous democratic legislative debate) by a self-perpetuative foreign service élite who followed the European theories of foreign policy. The young man was impressed. After World War II he wrote two books attacking the moral and international-legal mentality in international relations and arguing for the power-political theory.[7] At about the same time he found himself as Secretary of State Acheson's and President Truman's Ambassador to the Soviet Union and later as Head of the Planning Board of the State Department. *Who's Who in America* (Vol. 29) reports that in 1949–1950 he was "dep[artmen]t counselor and chief long-range adv[iser] to the Sec[retary] of State." In Secretary Acheson and Mr. George F. Kennan, the Hobbesian-Austinian positivistic legal mentality and the Hobbesian power-political diplomatic mentality had come together. Let it be recalled that Mr. Dulles and Mr. Bowie brought the same Hobbesian-Austinian positivistic legal mentality to the Secretaryship and the Planning Board of the State Department as did their Democratic predecessors. Senator Taft was a legal positivist also. This is why with strict legally positivistic integrity he later opposed the Nuremberg trials.

Mr. Kennan's appointment to Moscow was an exceedingly good

one for a European-minded power politician, provided he departed sufficiently, as he did, from his power philosophy—to the effect that the ideological and the morally and internationally legal mentality had best be kept out of international relations—to pay attention to the Communist ideology as well as to Soviet military power, thereby avoiding the mistaken and costly judgments about the meaning of Moscow's occasional smiles into which his Republican successors later fell. The assignment in Washington was not so good a place, however, to put a European-minded power politician if one's aim was to present to the peoples of Africa, the Middle East and Asia, just revolting from European domination, an image of America as the nation of a people who once issued their Declaration of Independence from European domination and (in terms of the Lockean-Jeffersonian philosophy written into that Declaration) created a novel theory of foreign policy dedicated to the following propositions: (1) All men, not merely Americans or the physically strongest men, have the God-given natural right to be free. (2) The United States will be negatively neutral to wars between nations guided by a power-political foreign policy, but positively on the side—even with physical support as occurred in the Cuban war against Spain—of people fighting for their independence against nations guided by power politics. (3) A legal system or a nation achieves lasting influence and effectiveness, not from the policeman's club it must have and sometimes use, but from the freely accepted and shared moral principles in the hearts and minds of its people and of people the world over. Hence (4) it is not, as Machiavelli, Hobbes, Austin and their contemporary followers think, physical power that makes morality and law effective; but law freely assented to and morally based and shared in the hearts and minds of the people that make a legal system's or a nation's use of force just and effective. Consequently, (5) no use of force abroad by any nation is justified or likely in the long run to be anything other than self-defeating, unless it is subservient to democratically grounded moral and legal principles and procedures and dedicated to the mission of guaranteeing to another people, again only with their free consent, their natural and contractually legal and political right to run their own affairs.

Paradoxically, while the Europeanization of military, legal and diplomatic leaders and teachers in institutes of international relations went on in the United States during the early decades of the twentieth century, a converse classical Americanization of foreign policy thinking and practice developed in Europe. If the rise of neutralism in Asia under President Truman's administrations and its spread to Europe under President Eisenhower's administrations are to be understood, the reason for the latter remarkable development must be examined.

Following World War I, the British turned from foreign philosophy to modern British philosophy. More specifically, they pushed the monistic, morally teleological Church of England and Aristotle and the monistic, morally and historically deterministic German Hegel into the background at Oxford and Cambridge to concentrate attention upon the more empirical modern British thinkers Locke and Hume. With Hume ontological metaphysics received a rough jolt, and out went the metaphysically materialistic Hobbes also. This meant that even the aristocratic élite coming from Eton and Harrow to Oxford and Cambridge on their way to the Foreign Office became like the Founding Fathers of the United States in their domestic and foreign policy thinking. Forthwith abstract moralizing about Britain's carrying the white man's burden around the world or power-politics musing about any other nation's manifest destiny began to lose their former glamour. Other people, according to Locke and Hume, had as much right to freedom as Britishers. Also, people other than Aristotelian or Church of England aristocrats had the right to make domestic and foreign policy decisions for Britishers. Immediately the notion of an aristocratic self-perpetuative foreign policy élite began to look a bit woolly, not to say stuffy. With time these sons of British Conservatives began to make their influence felt in the Conservative party. Mr. Butler is their present leader.

Even in the nineteenth century the British Liberal party had rooted itself in Locke and Hume and their non-Hobbesian successors. The *Economist* of London is their present spokesman. This is why, believing still that the classical America is the authentic United States, this sober and remarkably well-informed British weekly was consistently pro United States through the recent crisis in British-American relations over Suez.

The British Labour party was made up mainly of trade-union leaders. Unlike their Continental opposites, they did not immerse themselves in the socialistic philosophical doctrines of Saint-Simon,

Proudhon, Marx and Engels; nor did they have the privilege of attending West Point to read Mahan or Clausewitz, or of going through the Inns of Court or the Thayerian Harvard Law School to absorb unconsciously Hobbes and Austin. In this respect they were not unlike a contemporaneous young American named Harry from the state of Missouri, just out of the National Guard Regiment in World War I. Undoubtedly, if recent reports can be trusted, the State Militia and the National Guard have their weaknesses; but none of them is that of an awesome regard for the dying élite of Europe or an unconscious and uncritical absorption of the legal and political philosophy of Hobbes and Austin. The British Labour party and their leaders were of a like mind.

This did not mean that they had no moral or religious convictions. Quite the contrary. The late Lord Lindsay of Birker has recently described what they are.[8] These moral and religious convictions are not those of the aristocratic Conformist Protestant Church of England with its hierarchical ideal for society and its in part theocratic theory of the good state; instead, they are those of the non-Conformist Protestant Christian sects, the same kind of non-Conformist Protestant Christians who constituted the religious and secular living law majority in the United States when its federal government was founded.

The consequence was that even before World War II, Britain had already decided to return India to the Indians as their due, and career diplomats in the foreign and civil services were working to do the same thing in Africa. Only in those colonies such as the Union of South Africa where British and Dutch of the old European mentality had ensconced themselves in the government were they blocked. At this same time the British Empire was being transformed into the British Commonwealth in which all members stand on an equal democratic basis.

On the European Continent, a similar classical Americanization of European foreign policy was occurring. In some ways it is less fully advanced than in Great Britain; in other ways, more. With respect to foreign policy affecting non-European people, the French were not so far along as the British at the end of World War II. With respect to the European nations they were further along.

The former fact shows in their holding on to Indochina and Bao

Dai too long—thanks in part, no doubt, to the power-political minds in the United States Department of State and the Pentagon—and in the recent unpleasant news from Algeria. In the latter connection, however, it is important to note that the French people and an exceptionally large proportion of French statesmen are morally shocked. Were they still dominated in their value judgments by European monistic morally based imperialistic theory or the Machiavellian and Hobbesian power-politics mentality, there would be little that is shocking to them in recent reports from Algeria.

The sense in which the French and other Continental European nations have gone further than the British in the Americanization of their foreign policy shows in their achievement of Continental European union for coal and steel and in all likelihood for atomic energy. That the European statesmen themselves consciously regard this is an Americanization of their foreign policy is shown by the name which they give to this development. They call it the movement towards a United States of Europe. This does not mean that the present nations of Europe are likely to become similar to the states of the United States with respect to the United States federal government. Such an extreme localization of traditional national sovereignty in the international Continental European community would probably not be wise or practical. This movement does mean, however— and this is the truly remarkable thing about it—that realistic, experienced statesmen and parliaments in six Continental European nations have actually transferred part of their traditional Hobbesian and nationalistic sovereignty to an international community under a common international constitutional law. Gone is the absolutely unlimited national sovereignty of Hobbes and Austin.

It would be a grave error to leave the impression that the classical American theory of foreign policy is now taken seriously only in Europe. Not even the musing over abstract nouns like "manifest destiny" and "original sin"; or the emotive thrill that comes from the contemplation of a big stick; or the awe and envy which any sensitive person must feel before the self-assurance (now slightly tarnished) of the traditional European Foreign Service Office official; nor the instrumentally valid truths in Mahan and Clausewitz; nor even the unconscious, and, hence, uncritical, absorption of Hobbes and Austin in the Harvard Law School of Thayer and his present successors or in the Columbia, Yale and other United States law schools of 1920 can transform able diplomats and theologians like Mr. George Kennan and the Reverend Reinhold Niebuhr; military men like General Eisenhower, Bradley, Ridgway and Twining; or lawyers like Mr. Dean Acheson, Mr. John Foster Dulles, Mr. Paul Nitze, Mr. Robert Bowie or Mr. Christian Herter into 100 per cent imitations of Hobbes, Austin and Machiavelli. The living law and traditions of their own country, the non-Conformist egalitarian and democratic Protestant and the Lockean philosophy of Jefferson, Adams and the other Founding Fathers and the heritage of Lincoln, together with its foreign policy implications, are in them in part in spite of themselves and of the questionable philosophy taught in the professional schools in which circumstance placed them in their impressionable youth. Hence, the confusions, contradictions, vacillations and the broken image of America which their foreign policy decisions were to present to the world later on—a broken image not entirely unconnected with the development of neutralism.

Fortunately, other Americans during the first half of the twentieth century were not so easily impressed by Hobbes, Austin, and Machiavelli and the traditional European theories and ways in foreign affairs. One of them was President Woodrow Wilson. He and some of the aforementioned Americanized European statesmen took the positive portion of the classical theory of United States foreign policy, as exemplified by McKinley in his intervention on the side of the Cubans in the Spanish-American War, and generalized it to create a few years later the League of Nations. Thus, in his War Message of 1917, President Wilson said:

It is a fearful thing to lead this great peaceful people into war, into the most terrible and disastrous of all wars, civilization itself seeming to be in the balance. But the right is more precious than peace, and we shall fight for the things which we have always carried nearest our hearts— for democracy, for the right of those who submit to authority to have a voice in their own Government, for the rights and liberties of small nations, for a universal dominion of right by such a concert of free peoples as shall bring peace and safety to all nations and make the world itself at last free.[9]

The response from the masses of people thronging the streets when he went to Paris at the end of World War I is something which those who experienced it will never forget. The response from the peoples of distant Africa, the Middle East and Asia was similar. A new hope engulfed the imagination of men the world over.

Another American Roosevelt, whose first name was not Theodore, was to do the same thing in World War II. Winston Churchill as war Prime Minister built on this same Lockean-Jeffersonian classical British-American philosophy also. It should never be forgotten that John Locke as well as the Tory Church of England, aristocratic Elizabethan Woman of Empire, is in him and in part of his Conservative party also. Hence, his persistent insistence on British-United States collaboration.

But let us return to the 100 per cent classical American Woodrow Wilson. He saw that the spirit of the Lockean-Jeffersonian natural-rights egalitarian and democratic philosophy at the basis of the classical United States theory of foreign policy ran grave risk of being misinterpreted and even violated if the decision as to when a nation is justified in sending its troops abroad to protect the freedom of another people is left to the unilaterally authorized judgment of that nation alone. The only way, therefore, to ensure that the sending of a nation's troops abroad, to protect another nation's Lockean-Jeffersonian-Lincolnian natural rights to run their affairs, will not be misinterpreted by the very people one proposes to help, is to have it authorized, as under domestic law, by the legally processed decisions and rules of the world community. Hence, the absolute necessity of the League of Nations, if the Lockean-Jeffersonian-Lincolnian-based classical American theory of foreign policy is not to be misinterpreted abroad or used by power politicians at home as an excuse for throwing one's unilaterally authorized power-politics weight about. But Woodrow Wilson was more than a black-letter lawyer. He knew very well that more than the writing of an international constitution for the League was required. If people weak in physical power were to achieve by means of the League the right to run their own affairs to which the Lockean-Jeffersonian-Lincolnian natural-rights philosophy tells them they are entitled; if even Woodrow Wilson's own nation is to have the advantage of such help and protection, then the right to this protection must be accompanied by a correlative responsibility—the responsibility, namely, to contribute automatically to the world-community authorized legally processed police action in the case of any violation of the right of a people anywhere to run their own affairs. Hence the necessity not merely of the Charter of the League of Nations, but also of its Article 10, which was Wilson's own Article and in his opinion a Monroe Doctrine for every nation of the world. Article 10 committed members of the League "to respect and preserve as against external aggression the territorial integrity and existing political independence of all Members of the League." [10]

One important qualification must be noted. As Professor James T. Shotwell has written,

The Covenant of the League of Nations did not prohibit war as a last resort if the Council of the League failed to settle a dispute. In that case, it provided that "the Members of the League reserve to themselves the right to take such action as they shall consider necessary for the maintenance of right and justice." [11]

This qualification is of a special contemporary interest, since the British and French governments, before the Suez affair and before they at Secretary of State Dulles' request took the matter to the Security Council of the United Nations, made it clear that if the United States and the United Nations failed to settle the matter, they, Britain and France, would deem themselves justified in acting unilaterally.

As is well known, it was President Wilson's insistence on Article 10 which brought down upon his head the wrath of the unilaterally acting Theodore Rooseveltian Eastern Republicans led by Senator Henry Cabot Lodge, Sr., and the equally unilaterally minded doctrinaire neutralist and isolationist Republicans; the isolationists objecting because any use of American troops abroad under any circumstances was anathema to them, the Eastern Republicans objecting because they wanted no legally processed world community restricting them in the way in which with their big stick they proposed to take over the traditional role of Europe. Thus Woodrow Wilson and the League of Nations were defeated in the Senate of the United States.

But the validity of the Lockean-Jeffersonian-Lincolnian philosophy, the conviction in the hearts and minds of men that they *do* have the right to run their own affairs; that where a people is weak the world community does have the responsibility to see that this right is protected—this philosophy and conviction in the hearts and minds of men does not die so easily. Later evidence showed that two young men at the time were impressed. One was the aforementioned young man from Missouri just back with his National Guard Regiment from Europe. The other was a young man in the regular Army who had graduated from West Point. After World War II, each of these men found himself the President of the United States.

Unfortunately, however, they had to work with the military, legal and diplomatic advisers whose minds had been immersed in Mahan, Clausewitz, Hobbes, Austin, Thayer and Machiavelli and impressed by the foreign policy ways of traditional Europe. Such was the situation when World War II ended.

One other inheritance must be noted. Following the defeat of the League of Nations and the Republican victory of isolationist Ohio's President Harding, one exceedingly important thing occurred. The Washington Naval Conference was held, and the traditional power-politics-minded British-Japanese Alliance for the imperialistic aggrandizement of China was broken. The classical American policy of China for the Chinese and the "open door" for all to trade with China was applied. For this, however, one unfortunate price was paid. The United States took on with Britain, France and Japan the traditional non-Chinese military control of the port cities of China. The result was that when, following World War II, the Asians saw the imperialistic era of the Western European nations come to its end with the departure of European troops from Peking and from Chinese soil, they saw United States troops depart with the European ones. This left the impression upon Asian minds, not overlooked or unreported to his countrymen by India's Ambassador to Peking at the time, that the United States was as imperialistic as the British and the French.[12]

World War II ended when atomic bombs, then possessed only by the United States, were dropped on Hiroshima and Nagasaki. This did not improve the Asians' image of America. Its big stick had now become the biggest bomb. President Eisenhower later described the situation as meaning also that man now has it in his power to destroy mankind. Forthwith the meeting of an international crisis by any nation's unilateral use of physical force lost most of the plausibility it may ever have had.

Furthermore, man's capacity to destroy mankind which this atomic age has made possible requires even the followers of Hobbes to carry the Hobbesian thesis to its logical consequence. This thesis, let it be recalled, is that it is necessary for people to transfer personal sovereignty in the state of nature to a sovereign power having the physical power to enforce its will upon them, because, their state of nature being one of mutual physical conflict and war, they would be self-destructive if they did not make such an unqualified and unreturnable transfer of sovereignty to the modern sovereign power state. But the amount of self-destruction that men would bring to bear upon one another with the little popguns they possessed in Hobbes' seventeenth century when women and children were left unmolested in war is as nothing compared to the self-destruction that the modern Hobbesian power states with their absolute unilaterally used sovereignties can bring to bear upon themselves and the whole of mankind in this atomic age. Hence, if the Hobbesian logic which required a real transfer of each and every person's individual sovereignty to the modern nationalistic power states is at all valid, then the necessity of the latter states in turn making a similar transfer today to the world community is even more valid.

World War II ended also with two major powers rather than the normal one. This meant that neither dominated the world situation by his own unilateral use of physical power.

The situation was further complicated because the philosophical ideologies of the two major powers were incompatible if taken by each power acting unilaterally as monistic moral standards for civilizing the rest of mankind. This meant that the unilateral monistic morally based theory of national foreign policy was as self-defeating as the power-political theory since its pursuit by both major powers would not merely hasten the coming of war by adding morality and religion to the power conflict, but would also bring annihilation rather than civilization, as conceived by either power, to mankind.

Nevertheless, the nature of the Communist ideology, its aims and its theoretically specified ways of implementing those aims had to be reckoned with. To take the Communists, their changing tactics and their periods of smiling for something other than what the Marxist-Leninist-Stalinist philosophy specifies that they mean was not merely to live in a fool's paradise, but to brook disaster for every free nation in the world. But to pay attention to Communistic ideas and philosophy was to admit that, after all, ideas and ideals—good or not so good—really do matter in a realistic theory and practice of international relations.

Physical power in another nation is dangerous or not dangerous, something to be prepared for, or not to be prepared for, not because it is so much power, but because of the ideas, the philosophy of domestic and foreign policy of the decision makers who have the power. It was one of the great and fortunate merits of Mr. Kennan, when he was Head of the Planning Board of the State Department, that he recognized this ideological factor and acted upon this recognition in the case of the Soviet Union; but in doing so, he demonstrated that his practice was wiser and more realistic than his power-politics theory. This is pointed out by Mr. James Reston in a review of Mr. Kennan's Hobbesian philosophical theorizing about history in the *New York Times* of September 30, 1951. In short, not merely the Lockean-Jeffersonian philosophy which makes the culture of the United States unique and without attention to which a foreign policy fitting the United States cannot be built, but also the philosophical nature of the Communist ideology and its theory of the necessity of resorting to force rather than merely to persuasion to implement that ideological world-embracing aim make the shift from the power-politics to the pluralistic ideological theory of international relations imperative. Both the unilaterally dictated power-political theory and the unilaterally determined monistic morally based theory of national foreign policy are obsolete.

To be sure, the Lockean-Jeffersonian basic philosophy of one's own nation which because of Lincoln is as Republican as it is Democratic, must be understood and used to determine the United States factor in one's foreign policy. To be sure, also, Communist ideology being what it is, power must be present in taxation-costly quantities. Nevertheless, we can only know that the latter costly need for power is the case if we believe in the Lockean-Jeffersonian worth of our own way of life and also know the Communists' philosophically specified aims and ways. The same is true of the cultural philosophies of all the other nations of the world. The native traditions of no two of them are exactly alike. These differing social habits and cultural traditions of the many peoples and nations of the world express and embody differing cultural philosophies—Buddhist, Hindu, Confucian, Islamic, Judaic, African intuitive and tribal. Clearly, an international policy that is going to draw the physical power to itself necessary to be effective before the Communists' ideologically crusading, power-implemented threat must fulfill the cultural and philosophical traditions of other free peoples as well as those of one's own nation. This means that after first fitting one's foreign policy to the unique philosophical tradition of one's own nation, one must then know with objectivity the many different religious and philosophical traditions and present guiding principles of other nations. In short, an effective national foreign policy must come to terms with ideological and cultural pluralism which includes factors in common as well as those which differentiate. For this the foreign office or state department of any nation must have a planning board headed by a civilian expert trained in the descriptive and evaluative scientific methods of comparative cultural anthropology and the comparative philosophy of the world's nations and cultures.

The economic approach to politics has its limitations also. In its issue of May 11, 1957, the *New York Times* described Premier Habib Bourguiba, Jr., of Tunisia as "one of the staunchest supporters of the United States in the Arab world," and then quoted as follows from a speech he made in Tunis the day before on economic aid from the United States:

It is well that Americans should know that peoples who have achieved their independence are more careful to safeguard their dignity than to satisfy their immediate needs. Dignity before bread is a basic principle. By ignoring, by having wanted to wound human dignity the occident has lost precious positions in the Far and Near East.

This observation points up the fact that a foreign policy based primarily on economic aid is likely to be self-defeating, since by ignoring spiritual and cultural factors it fails to see that any nation is a nation because it has spiritual goal values, as well as material, military and economic instrumental needs, and that these spiritual goal values are defined by their respective philosophical, religious and cultural traditions. This, in fact, is the moral merit of nationalism, never to be forgotten: Nationalism expresses the spiritual fact that various peoples on the earth's surface have formulated their goal values with respect to the purposes of God for man and the meaning of the secular facts of human experience in different ways. The planning board of any state department which is objective and realistic about its own nation and other nations will first inform itself about the goal values of all. This is necessary so that it knows what it is doing in framing a foreign policy that relates the particular goal values and instrumental technologies of one's own unique cultural tradition to the different, equally unique and cherished cultural philosophies and material instruments of other nations.

A third and the most important development after World War II was the resurgence of the common people of Africa, Israel, Islam and Asia. This resurgence expresses itself in the existence of the new nations of Israel, Free India, Pakistan and Ghana, the Arab League and the Bandung Conference. It bespeaks, however, more than the insistence of the masses of mankind upon the Lockean-Jeffersonian-Lincolnian kind of right to run their own secular affairs. The resurgence is cultural and spiritual as well as material and instrumentally secular. Consequently, they are insisting not merely on running their own affairs, and, hence, democratically throwing out the traditional Hindu maharajas, as in India, but also in doing so in the light of their own unique spiritual and cultural traditions. This means that, notwithstanding their acceptance and insistence upon what amounts to the classical United States Lockean-Jeffersonian-Lincolnian philosophy—that is, the right to run their own affairs themselves—a United States foreign policy based on carrying Christian civilization and the American way of life to the world is doomed to generate the neutralism it has in fact generated, and thereby be self-defeating. In addition to their deep respect for and acceptance of the Lockean-Jeffersonian-Lincolnian component of United States culture, the masses of men throughout the world have an equal pride in and respect for the different spiritual traditions of their own particular religions and institutions. Hence, only a national foreign policy based on (a) the Lockean-Jeffersonian natural-rights-of-*all*-men philosophy and (b) ideological, religious and cultural pluralism can hope to succeed in the contemporary world.

Into this technologically, ideologically and internationally revolutionary post-World War II world came the North Korean Communists' military invasion of South Korea. The UN police action followed immediately.

In ordering General MacArthur to leave Japan with United States troops, President Truman and his advisers were not content to base their decision on a unilateral action of the United States alone. Instantly he raised the matter in the Security Council of the UN; and, thanks in part to the abstinence of the Soviet Union's representative, had the entire affair transformed into a legally processed and world-community authorized *police action* under the international law of the UN Charter.

The importance of this precedent is yet to be fully appreciated. First, it meant that in the application of the classic United States theory of foreign policy to a foreign people whose right to run their own affairs is being violated, two conditions, rather than merely one, must be satisfied before the United States or any other nation is justified in departing from neutralism to send its troops abroad. Not only must it meet the requirement specified by President McKinley and his Congress in coming to the aid of the Cuban people against Spain, but it must also meet the Wilsonian condition of being authorized by the world community under international legal rules and made a part of the world community's police action. Second, notice was given to prospective aggressors anywhere that the UN, if the United States could prevent it, was not going the way of the League before Mussolini's aggression. Membership in the UN was being taken as entailing the responsibility to share in policing the right of other people to run their own affairs as well as the insistence upon such a right for one's own people. Third, and most important of all, as subsequent events were to show, the United States and other troops in the UN police action were removed from the status of being one belligerent on the same footing as the opposing belligerent in a *war* and were placed, instead, in the quite different status of being a peace-preserving police force in a world-community authorized *police action*—precisely like the local policeman who has to use physical force under legal rules in any Asian, African or Western domestic community.

This meant that in any subsequent ending of the police action, the UN representatives would not come together on the same basis as the North Korean Communist aggressors' representatives, sitting about a round table as equal disturbers of the peace with Asian neutralists as the only "peacemakers" present. Instead, it meant that the representatives of the UN police force would sit beneath the international law of the world community, before which the North Korean representatives, sitting on the opposite side of a rectangular table, would come as culprits brought by the world community's policeman to be judged, with the neutralists remaining at home where in their unilaterally decided isolationism they had placed themselves. There they could contemplate the somewhat tarnished peacemaking professions of one who as a member of the UN insists upon its rights for one's own people, but then unilaterally isolates oneself from one's UN policing responsibilities by taking a holier-than-thou attitude towards the world community's policemen when those same rights are violated in the case of another people.

But why, if President Truman had been so careful to place his dispatch of United States troops to Korea upon such a world-community authorized morally and legally impeccable basis, did so many Asians, in the face of the most blatant Communist aggression there, turn neutralist during his administration? It will help us to understand and, in part, but not wholly, condone this development of neutralism if the following things are kept in mind: (1) the traditional Confucian, Buddhist and Gandhian-Hindu Asian conception of the moral and political leader as a mediator.[13] (2) The neutralism of the United States after its first break from European imperialism, when considered as a blind mechanical rule apart from its underlying moral and political philosophy. (3) The aforementioned European-minded appointees and advisers and their deeds which the Asians saw associated with President Truman and his successor President Eisenhower and the resultant broken image of America which they produced. (4) The astute Soviet play upon (3).

It did not take the Moscow officials long to realize that if the Communist invasion of South Korea was not to turn, in the face of the UN police action, into an irreparable defeat ideologically as well as physically, the image of America in Asian, African and Middle Eastern eyes as that of Locke, Jefferson and Lincoln, of the McKinley of Cuba, and of Wilson must be broken. They sent Mr. Jacob Malik, therefore, rushing back to the Security Council of the UN. His remarks were most illuminating. He said that the presence of the United States and other Western European military troops in South Korea was not the UN world-community authorized police action which President Truman and the European statesmen had tried to make it out to be; but was, instead, a power-political politician's excuse for covering up the old European power game of getting Western troops on Asian soil, into which some non-Western members of the United Nations had been duped to participate.

When the Head of the Planning Board of President Truman's own State Department himself says that the moral and international legal mentality is misplaced in foreign policy and affirms publicly in print that power is what matters internationally, this thesis by the Soviet Union's Ambassador to the UN is not easy to answer. When, moreover, beginning with President Truman and continuing with his Republican successor, one sees the control of foreign policy decisions taken more and more out of the hands of the civilians of the State Department where classically it was centered and shifted to the National Security Council where the military as well as civilians make the major decisions, outsiders in Asia who are not Communists may be excused if they conclude that perhaps the Soviet Ambassador is in part right. When, furthermore, United States government military and press officials feed pictures of United States military planes and weapons continuously into the press of the United States and the world, thereby creating abroad an impression of America in which the military instruments are thrust into the forefront of the image of America—so that the Lockean-Jeffersonian-Lincolnian philosophical heart and mind of America and America's respect for the different ideals and cherished traditions of others are covered up—need one wonder if those who want freedom themselves and want to believe in the liberty-loving and freedom-protecting principles of the United States conclude that perhaps, after all, the Soviet's Mr. Jacob Malik is right, at least sufficiently so to warrant one in going neutral? Again the words of the Tunisian Premier in the *New York Times* of May 11, 1957, are illuminating:

The only danger that threatens the occidental camp, which flatters itself to be the camp of liberty, exists precisely in the surviving tendencies or the support given these imperialist tendencies for opportunistic con-

Koecots

siderations. . . . As long as dissonance exists between words and acts, between the broad principles that bind the Western democracies and the incoherent opportunism of these same democracies . . . peoples newly arrived at independence have a right to doubt the sincerity of the free world. . . .

The shift from President Truman to President Eisenhower did not help matters. In fact, neutralism increased, spreading from Asia to Europe and resulting in a completely divided free West before the Soviet penetration of the Middle East in the Suez crisis. The lack of improvement under President Eisenhower should not surprise us, since, as previously shown, the same Europeanization of classical United States foreign policy characterizes the officials in key posts under him as under President Truman. As far as the traditional European Hobbesian-Austinian legal mentality with respect to the futility of international law is concerned, only the faces and party labels became different in shifting from Mr. Acheson to Mr. Dulles, and from Mr. Kennan and Mr. Nitze to Mr. Bowie and Mr. Cutler. But why, then, did matters get worse so far as the breakdown of free-world collaboration and the spread of neutralism were concerned? The answer is that President Eisenhower and his Secretary of State preserved all the Hobbesian-Austinian-mentality weaknesses of the Truman administration, while introducing certain additional novelties of their own.

The first and most serious novelty occurred when in the 1952 election campaign General Eisenhower insisted against President Truman that the United States boys in Korea were in a war and not in a police action. Few others than President Truman yet appreciate the seriousness of that remark by the man who a few weeks later was to be President of the United States, and who, because of his election promises to get the boys home from a "war," was to have to negotiate with the Communists in Korea. The difference between American boys being in Korea in a war or in a police action is the difference between being there on the unilateral authorization of the nation using force alone or being there under international law with the authorization of a legally processed decision of the world community. It is precisely the difference under domestic law between a man who kills somebody in a local village upon his own unilateral decision and the policeman who kills somebody else in pursuing his line of

official duty in accordance with the community- and legally authorized requirements of his task. The former type of killing is a
crime called murder; the latter is a peacemaking police action. President Truman had made sure before the American boys arrived in
Korea that they were there not on the unilateral decision of the
United States alone, but as authorized under international law by the
world community. He was right, therefore, in the 1952 election when
he insisted against General Eisenhower that the American boys in
Korea were not in a war but in a police action. CAETOE

This matter is of more than academic interest as the following
consideration shows. Why did the Soviet's Mr. Jacob Malik hasten
back to the Security Council on the dispatch of the UN police action
to the aid and protection of the South Koreans' right to run their
own affairs? We already know the answer: It was to persuade the
world that American and other UN soldiers in Korea were in a war
and not in a police action and hence were just as responsible for the
loss of life there as were the North Korean aggressors. Hence, when
General Eisenhower maintained against President Truman that the
American boys were in a war rather than in a police action, the man
who a few weeks later was to be President of the United States unwittingly made the Soviet representative's case for him. The last
vestige of Lockean-Jeffersonian-Lincolnian community-authorized
legality and principle beneath the presence of American or any other
UN soldiers in Korea had been removed. The moral quagmire was
thereby created in which the moral and legal principles justifying the
loss of life in the UN police action became muddied and then engulfed. Also, there ensued those troubles concerning round and square
tables experienced later by Ambassador Lodge in the UN when the
Asian neutralists insisted upon placing the UN and North Korean
representatives together around a round table as equally guilty war
makers, with the neutralists as the only "peacemakers." These events
show that more than an exceptionally successful military record and
a rare talent as an intuitively good human being are necessary if one
is not to commit tragically *bad* errors as a statesman concerned with
United States foreign policy. A clear comprehension of the difference
between a war and a police action, rooted in the classical Lockean-
Jeffersonian-Lincolnian theory of United States foreign policy as
applied positively by President McKinley in the Cuban affair, by

President Wilson in his Article 10 and by President Truman at the outset of the Korean crisis, is also essential. In the Suez crisis, President Eisenhower showed that he had the latter theory of United States foreign policy in him. It is too bad that it took so long to come out. Otherwise, the muddying of the moral issue in Korea and the breakdown of free-world unity in the West which produced the Suez crisis would not have had to be.

There was a second novelty in the foreign policy of President Eisenhower's administration. It showed in the issue between Secretary Dulles and Mr. Kennan, but included President Eisenhower also. In the 1952 election campaign, both General Eisenhower and Mr. Dulles expressed their personal moral and religious convictions. Reacting from the blatant Hobbesianism of Mr. Kennan's theorizing about foreign policy, they affirmed that United States foreign policy must be morally based so that its allies can know where the United States stands and so that no compromise with or appeasement of Communism and its fellow travelers will occur. Unfortunately, however, they failed to specify whether this moral basis was to be monistic or pluralistic; and, if monistic, whether it was to be implemented with military force. Thus, instead of making it clear where the United States was to stand, the effect was to leave its allies completely in the dark.

This uncertainty disturbed them for the following reasons: If the new United States foreign policy was to be morally monistic, based on the Christian religion and the American way of life, and was to be used in a crusade to roll back Communism, there was a danger that it might proceed in the Theodore Roosevelt big-stick Republican manner unilaterally and impetuously without consulting its free-world allies. Europeans noted also that both the Theodore Roosevelt big-stick military showdown-with-Communism Republicans such as General MacArthur, Admiral Radford, the late Senator McCarthy and Senator Knowland and the Middle West isolationist Republicans such as Senators Taft and Bricker agreed in wanting a go-it-alone unilaterally determined United States foreign policy. Either alternative would be fatal to the North Atlantic Treaty Organization and to free-world collaboration generally. Naturally, European statesmen found themselves looking around for ways by which they could neutralize themselves with respect to these uncertainties.

European fears were not decreased when they recalled that General Eisenhower had described an objective military campaign in Europe as a crusade, that upon acceptance of the Republican nomination for President in Chicago, the first sentences in his acceptance speech were:

You have summoned me . . . to lead a great crusade—for freedom in America and freedom in the world. I know something of the solemn responsibility of leading a crusade. I have led one. . . . I will lead this crusade.

More than any other word in the English language, the word "crusade" which combines the intuitive religious and the military mind seemed to mesmerize the President.

Mr. John Foster Dulles' 1952 election campaign references to rolling back Communism did not still Europe's rising fears. European statesmen and laymen reasoned that it is bad enough to have one of the two major powers off on a holy-war crusade to build the world over in terms of its own ideological image, but that it is absolutely fatal to peace if the other power indulges in this same moral monism also. Near the end of the election campaign in 1952, the Republican presidential candidate gave a major address on foreign policy. On September 4th of that year the *Listener* of London reported the European reaction as follows:

Commentators in Western Europe, for the most part, were critical of Mr. Eisenhower's speech. . . . This disapproval centered on the fact that the western nations were united under the Atlantic Pact to resist Soviet imperialism in a military *defensive* alliance, and not one committed to the liberation of the enslaved nations by war. Other commentators pointed out that Mr. Eisenhower was not advocating their liberation by war, but that his policy—if put into operation and not considered merely as electioneering—would seem to involve the risk of war.[14]

When some years later Secretary of State Dulles, in a major foreign policy address, announced his "brink of war" threat of "massive retaliation at places and times of one's own choosing," again the definition of the word "one's" was left ambiguous. Immediately, Mr. Arnold Toynbee appealed to the Lockean-Jeffersonian philosophy of domestic and foreign policy to affirm, "No annihilation without representation."

Even in the United States at the very beginning of President Eisenhower's first administration, the moral emphasis in their foreign policy had expressed itself in the issue between Secretary Dulles and Mr. Kennan concerning how the threat of Communist aggression was to be handled. Mr. Kennan, with his knowledge of the Communist ideology and his justified misgivings about monistic morally based holy-war crusades in national foreign policy, and President Truman following him, had stood for the containment of Communism. Mr. Dulles and other Republicans attacked this as appeasement and said that the new policy would be that of rolling back Communism. Again, he failed to specify whether this rolling back, which because of its monistic moral basis accepted no mere containment of Communism, was to be militarily backed or not. So incompatible were these two policies conceived to be by both Mr. Kennan and Secretary of State Dulles that even though the former was a career diplomat entitled to remain within the Foreign Service, both he and Secretary Dulles thought it wise to part ways. Mr. Kennan resigned to pursue his reflections upon foreign policy within the cloistered calm and politically innocuous confines of the Institute for Advanced Studies at Princeton, New Jersey.

The crucial event so far as Europe was concerned came with the defeat of the European Defense Community in the French Chamber of Deputies. It has been customary in the United States to attribute this defeat, not to the shift under the Republican administration from power-political containment to the monistic morally based rolling back of Communism, but to the French fear of rearming the Germans. Why, then, but a few weeks later, did the French Chamber of Deputies vote for rearming the Germans, even under a German general staff, within the Brussels Treaty Organization? If it was German rearmament which they feared, certainly this would never have occurred; if anything, they would have preferred EDC, since EDC proposed to rearm the Germans under a European general staff, whereas the Brussels Treaty rearmed Germany under a German general staff.

Clearly, there must be another factor that was present in the EDC Treaty and not present in the later Brussels Treaty. What is this other factor? It is that the United States is not a member of the Brussels Treaty. The latter treaty, unlike the NATO Treaty, is restricted wholly to European nations. In other words, the French preferred a rearmed Germany under a German general staff and under a treaty that was restricted to Europeans and quarterbacked by Great Britain to a rearmed Germany, even under a European general staff, that, under the EDC protocol to the NATO Treaty was quarterbacked by the military-minded Pentagon under Admiral Radford, President Eisenhower and his Secretary of State Dulles and their monistic morally based theory of United States foreign policy.

Forthwith the movement towards European union took on a new meaning. Initially it had been conceived as an essential part of United States and United Nations collaboration in the policing of the peace of the world, not merely in Europe, but also in Asia: Henceforth it was to mean for Europeans the implementation of the neutralization of Europe with respect to United States foreign policy.

In his aforementioned stand within the UN in the fall of 1956 with respect to the invasion of Egypt by Israel, Great Britain and France, President Eisenhower returned the compliment by disassociating the United States from the foreign policy of Great Britain and France with respect to Communism in the Middle East and in Africa. In this event, the neutralism with respect to collaboration throughout the free world which began in Asia under Mr. Kennan's power-political containment policy and which spread to Europe under the Republican monistic morally based rolling-back-of-Communism crusade spread to embrace the United States also.

The tragic irony of the situation is that as far as deeds, rather than words, were concerned, the morally based crusading rolling-back-of-Communism theory of foreign policy of President Eisenhower and his Secretary of State and the power-political containment foreign policy of the Democratic Mr. Kennan turned out to be almost identical, with, if anything, the Republican policy the weaker. Two decisions made by President Eisenhower suffice to make this unequivocally clear. The first decision occurred when the French faced defeat in Indochina unless air force aid came from the United States. President Eisenhower decided not even to contain the threatened Communist defeat of the French, to say nothing about rolling it back, thereby allowing the French to go down to one of the worst and most humiliating defeats in their history. The second momentous decision came in the Hungarian revolution. Again, President Eisenhower and his Secretary decided against rolling back Communism and allowed the Hungarian patriots to be smashed by a ruthless Soviet military attack. Nevertheless, as far as the growth of neutralism in Europe and the breakdown of allied collaboration in NATO and in the Middle East were concerned, the crusading roll-back words had done their damage.

In the unilaterally prepared and announced military White Paper of April 4, 1957, in which Great Britain declared her intention— probably for more than financial reasons—to withdraw ground troops from the Continent and, depending largely on rockets with atomic war heads, to withdraw into something that suggests a Fortress Britain, the unilateralism which bespeaks an increase of neutralism reappeared. The pro United States *Economist* of London reports NATO officials on the Continent to have been shocked more by the unilateral way in which they were informed than by even the contents of the information itself.[15]

The free world in 1954 was not far from the situation in which each nation was attempting to isolate itself with respect to the foreign policy of other nations. Yet both President Eisenhower and the British White Paper affirm that no nation in today's world can protect itself alone. Clearly, isolationism under such circumstances is a self-contradictory and self-defeating policy.

What is the way out of this impasse into which free-world policy under United States leadership, first Democratic and then Republican, has led everyone?

In the Suez crisis, President Eisenhower returned United States and UN policy to the sound basis from which his unfortunate statement about American boys in Korea had removed it. This occurred when he and the majority in the UN declared the *unilaterally* initiated invasions of Egypt by Israel, Great Britain and France to be an aggression and to be a violation of the world-community authorized international law upon which the UN rests and upon which the only constructive hope for peace can be reared. This amounts to a return to the classical United States theory of foreign policy as applied by the Republican President McKinley and the Democratic Presidents Wilson and Truman. This theory affirms any use of a nation's forces abroad to be immoral and unjust unless it meets the two following conditions: (1) It must be dedicated to the task of protecting a foreign native people in their right to run their own affairs and (2) it must be authorized not merely by the legally processed decision of the nation sending the troops, but also by the legally processed international legal rules and decisions of the world community, thereby making the status of troops abroad that of participation in a morally based, legally sanctioned peacemaking police action, rather than in a war.

To this conclusion, the analysis of the causes of neutralism made in this paper adds one additional requirement. This requirement is that the moral and international legal basis of national and UN policy must be pluralistic rather than monistic. The reason is that people the world over are not merely demanding protection from the world community in the right to avoid annihilation in an atomic age and in the Lockean-Jeffersonian-Lincolnian right to run their own affairs; but they are insisting also upon the right to run them in the light of their own philosophical, religious and cultural traditions. They simply do not believe that any one religion, church or nation has a monopoly on either God or civilization.

The following considerations make clear that such a theory of foreign policy meets the difficulties and has a real chance of succeeding. First, it puts the moral mind and heart of the people of the United States in the forefront of the image of itself which America presents to other people, thereby removing the broken image caused by the traditional Europeanization of United States foreign policy that has produced so much isolationism. Second, because of its moral pluralism, drawing on all the spiritual resources of the world, such a United States and UN policy has the chance to draw unto itself the collaborative physical police power sufficient to keep even the most blatant and powerful aggressor under control. Third, it puts the United States and the UN unequivocally on the side of the masses of men in Africa, Israel, Islam and Asia who are declaring their independence and who constitute an overwhelming majority of the people of the world. Fourth, it undercuts the whole purpose of the Soviet cold war which is to dupe the United States into putting her military fist, rather than her Lockean-Jeffersonian-Lincolnian heart and mind, into the forefront of the image she presents to the world, thereby generating neutralism and leaving the UN impotent before Communist aggression. Fifth, even for Middle West Republican doctrinaire isolationists, it offers the best option they have since it requires more conditions to be met before American boys are sent abroad than does any other policy. Sixth, the Suez affair shows that the Lockean-Jeffersonian-Lincolnian morally pluralistic theory of foreign policy has the support even of the very European nations which it condemned in that crisis. This fact became evident when the British, French and Israelis bowed to President Eisenhower and the UN action. Consider in the British case why this occurred. The reason was that Prime Minister Eden found on the President's and the UN's side not merely the Labour party and the Liberals as represented by the *Economist,* but also the aforementioned Americanized Conservatives of his own party, led by Mr. Butler. Furthermore, Winston Churchill immediately insisted that his Conservative party return to a foreign policy of British and United States collaboration.

Looking at the constructive developments since World War II, it appears, notwithstanding the omnipresent neutralism, that the causes of this neutralism can be removed. Four major precedents for doing so have been set and accepted. The first was President Truman's decision in the Korean crisis to forego the right of all traditional major powers to act unilaterally and to process, instead, the dispatch of American boys abroad through the UN. The second was his decision, when an issue arose between what the UN field commander in all sincerity thought to be wise in Korea and what the majority in the UN decided to be best. Again President Truman decided to forego the traditional Hobbesian power-political right to act unilaterally, and so withdrew General MacArthur from his command and accepted the world community's judgment. Moreover, the Republican *New York Herald Tribune* in an unequivocal editorial supported President Truman's decision, thereby repudiating both (1) Taft-Bricker-Hoover-Republican-go-it-alone isolationism in foreign policy on the one hand and (2) MacArthur-McCarthy-Knowland-Admiral Radford go-it-alone, show-down-war Republican foreign policy on the other hand, for a (3) Locke-Jefferson-Lincoln Democratic and Republican bipartisan go-it-together-with-one's-allies-in-the-United Nations policy. The third precedent was evident in the Suez crisis when President Eisenhower, forced to choose between siding with his best friends or putting his nation unequivocally against the unilateral use of force and on the side of the world community's international law, chose the latter course, as did the majority of nations in the UN.

Never since World War II has African, Middle Eastern and Asian respect for United States foreign policy been as high. The Lockean-Jeffersonian-Lincolnian philosophy of foreign policy does remove neutralism when followed 100 per cent. The fourth important precedent, the most important of all, occurred when the British, French and Israelis accepted the judgment of the world community and when a majority of the British people showed themselves to be against their own government and on the side of the United States classical foreign policy and an effective world law.

The victory for moral and legal international principle in national foreign policy has by no means been won. The roughest shoals lie immediately ahead. One present temptation is to say that, because the UN Assembly in the Suez crisis produced initially no permanent positive solution of the Israeli-Arab problem, therefore, the Assembly has demonstrated its perpetual incompetence and that the matter must be left to the old power-politics maneuvering of the major powers in the Security Council. This thesis completely overlooks the fact that the latter policy, precisely because of the neutralism and divided free world which it produced, had failed even more lamentably. As the London *Economist* pointedly notes, "To jump out of the fire into the frying-pan may be instinctive, but it confers no immunity. . . . The [powers in the] Council . . . had failed to solve the problem in eight years." [16] It was precisely because of this failure that the Suez crisis arose. The UN Assembly may therefore be excused if, after putting an end to the Suez war and placing its token forces between the combatants, it did not find a permanent solution in a few weeks.

Nevertheless, a UN which merely slaps down those who resort to force unilaterally will fail, unless a majority of its members pour in the moral will sufficient to enable it to solve the injustices which brought the unilateral actions forth. It needs to be made unequivocally clear that the responsibility for policing the world's peace is that of the world community and not that of any member of that community, however strong economically and militarily that member may be. Only if the peoples of the world are as vigorous in taking on the responsibility of freedom as they are in insisting upon its rights can either freedom or peace be obtained. To insist upon the right to freedom while not assuming the responsibility to police freedom is like insisting on drawing money from a bank in which one refuses to make a deposit. Obviously there can be nothing to draw out if first nothing is put in. Hence, the United States and other nations need to throw all their energies into the UN to ensure that its responsibilities are assumed. Too quickly, perhaps, after his epoch-making and correct decision in the Suez crisis, President Eisenhower rushed to Congress with a plan authorizing him to send money and arms to the aid of individual nations in the Middle East who ask for such aid. This had the unfortunate effect of giving the Soviet Union a similar right to accept another Middle Eastern nation's invitation to do the same thing. Such a result could have been avoided had President Eisenhower worked, instead, through the UN to get it to come to the aid of any Middle Eastern nation calling for help and had then asked the Congress of the United States to give him the authority to provide such aid along with other nations in the UN were the majority in that body to authorize it. Again we see the importance of Wilson's second condition being met before the departure from neutralism upon the part of any nation is justified, the condition, namely that no use of a nation's military or other physical power abroad is justified unless it is authorized by the world community.

This principle being established with respect to any nation's dispatch of military troops abroad, how is it to be implemented through the UN Assembly so that the latter body provides constructive positive solutions to the crises that confront it? The *Economist* of London has given the most practical answer yet offered to this question. This answer is that the gulf between the Secretary General with his staff and the eighty-one members of the Assembly needs to be filled by the appointment of "small, manageable bodies which, for lack of a better name, might be termed select committees." These committees being

carefully tailored to meet several vital requirements . . . should be small, to permit of quick and precise decisions and, if necessary, of mobility; . . . sufficiently representative of the various groups and interests in the Assembly to make it unlikely that the parent body would reject their findings; . . . given as much authority as the Assembly can muster . . . [and] a strict rule of privacy for all their proceedings . . . to screen out [publicity hunters] and leave a clearer field for the solid citizens who are actually concerned to get results.

Some such development, the *Economist* suggests, would give responsible scope to "the powers of the second rank, and other states that are ready to put more power to UNO's elbow," thereby making "for a sense of individual responsibility." [17]

In any event, the four aforementioned precedents constitute the hard cases in the international field out of which effective law can be made. It appears, therefore, that the escape from neutralism is not merely possible, but also, in these hard cases and in the foregoing practical suggestion of the London *Economist,* in part under way.

Even so, much more is involved. To demand and to be entitled to the Lockean-Jeffersonian-Lincolnian right to run one's own affairs under its contractual positive legal and political principles is one thing. To be able to do it effectively, however, in the face of old customs is quite another, as the events described in Chapter 1 at Little Rock, Accra, Karachi, Rangoon and elsewhere show. The time has come to face some of these concrete domestic political problems and difficulties.

12

Modern Ways in Medieval Societies

Medieval societies exist everywhere, even in the more modern nations. Many of the people who live in the small towns and farming areas of the Province of Quebec in Canada still think in terms of the religious and social beliefs and act according to the patriarchal familial customs of a medieval society. The same is true of most of the patriarchal families of the peasants who make up the villages of France. Any group of people are medieval if the covert or overt trapped impulses in their brains are the epistemic correlates of the introspected elemental concepts of a medieval or ancient religion, science and philosophy. To be a Modern means to be guided in one's moral, legal, political and other decisions by the elemental concepts and propositions of either modern science and philosophy or Stoic Roman legal science when its substantive content is made consistent with its most basic, i.e., elementary, proposition.[1] Chapter 18 will show why this is the case. Since the scientific, ethical, philosophical and religious theories of Asia, before it was influenced by the modern West, were formulated with respect to their most elementary concept of the person, in many cases as early as the seventh century B.C., Oriental societies are medieval and even ancient. The Elizabethan Christian theocratic England of Canterbury, the Crown and early seventeenth century Kent and Essex, as described and defended philosophically in Sir Robert Filmer's *Patriarcha,* was also a medieval society and even an ancient law-of-patriarchal-status one. As noted previously, the contemporary English historian Mr. Peter Laslett has shown that the non-Jeffersonian component of the society of the Old South is the result of transferring to Virginia and the other Southern British colonies, by Sir Robert Filmer's own blood

brothers and cousins, of this medieval white man's Christian patriarchally aristocratic society of early seventeenth century England.
The difficulty of modernizing such societies, be they in Africa, Islam,
Asia, France, Canada or the United States, is the theme of this chapter. How to meet these difficulties, once we see clearly what they are,
will be the topic of the remainder of this book.

Modern Ways in Technologically Underdeveloped Areas *

The difficulty of introducing modern Western ways into old societies has not received the attention it deserves. It applies as much
to modern Western legal, political, economic, agricultural, medical
and even religious forms as it does to machinery and to other technological instruments.

The difficulty is not that Asian, African or other medieval-minded
people, when properly trained, cannot master these forms. India has
several efficient air lines, wholly under Indian operation. Her present
railways are owned by the government and operated by natives with
reasonable efficiency. There is also an Indian-owned and -operated
steel industry. One Chinese in Indochina manages, through his own
sons, a remarkable interlocking complex of modern commercial firms.
There are many outstanding Japanese, Chinese, Indian and Islamic
mathematical logicians, mathematical physicists and mathematically
minded engineers. These facts show that there is nothing in the inherited nature of non-Western peoples to prevent them from becoming proficient in the Western technological ways and the imageless
legal and formal way of thinking from which these ways derive. Apparently all men are born free and equal as far as the innate potential
capacity to think and behave in Western ways is concerned, just as
Westerners, through the cultivation of impressionistic painting, the
appreciation of existentialist philosophy and their interest in Zen
Buddhism, are now acquiring the intuitive approach to nature and
experience in which the Oriental is a past master.

Nevertheless, the following facts, and countless others like them,
have to be faced. After 1912, Sun Yat-sen and his successor, Presi-

---

* This section is reprinted from the British *1954 Yearbook of Education,* pp.
79–88, by permission of Evans Brothers, Ltd., London, and World Book Company,
Yonkers, N.Y.

dent Chiang Kai-shek, introduced Western liberal legal and political forms, Protestant Christian religious institutions and modern scientific ways into China. President Chiang Kai-shek's devoted follower and present colleague Chiang Monlin, the former Vice Chancellor of Peking National University, has described the legal and political result as a miserable failure.[2] Instead of achieving its aim, these free democratic Western ways produced a "corrupt National Assembly" which became "a headache to the entire country." [3] He indicates also that modern Western science and its machines underwent a similar corruption.[4] Even the most simple Western farm machinery or mechanical equipment tends to become ruined, when left in the hands of Asian, Middle Eastern, African or South American natives, because of their failure to oil it, operate it or repair it properly.[5]

The results of the introduction of Roman Catholic or Protestant Christianity into societies with non-Christian religious traditions are similar. The "rice Christians" of Asia are well known. The natives who become Christians in order to attend free classes in the English language and thereby obtain more lucrative governmental and business posts in those areas under Western imperialistic rule or under strong Western commercial influence are also not unknown. And even in the countless cases where acceptance of the Christian faith is sincere, as in China, the meager opposition which it offered after centuries of missionary effort to but three decades of indoctrination in the materialism and atheism of Communism gives little ground for believing that the natives really grasped what Christianity means. They probably had its forms and its spirit in an intuitive Asian way, rather than in its own terms.[6] The outcome was some very fine Asian Christian spirits but a native society in which neither Christianity nor modern contractual legal and political thinking had taken deep root.

Western medical men report similarly that they can lift the level of health of an Egyptian or Peruvian native village practically to the level of a modern European city and keep it there, even when directed by natives, as long as the Western supervisors remain. Unfortunately, however, all too frequently the village returns to its original condition when the Western adviser withdraws and it is left under native leadership alone. It does very little good to put a bottle of pasteurized milk on every doorstep throughout the world if the delivery boy thrusts his dirty, unwashed thumb, fresh from vegetables grown with "night soil," through the bottle's paper cap in placing it there. Nor does it avail to train the delivery boy properly if the housewife pours the uncontaminated pasteurized milk from a properly sealed bottle into a kitchen pan wet with water from the washing of such vegetables, or if the natives, through their normal habits during the remaining twenty-three hours of the day, reinfect themselves in some other way.

But if this corruption of Western legal, political, mechanical, religious and medical ways is the frequent result of their introduction into non-Western societies, why is it that some members of these societies can manage these ways without corruption? As we have noted, the difficulty is not one of innate and ineradicable incapacity.

In answering this question, two things must be distinguished. One is the expert technical training of the native mechanic, lawyer, politician or Christian in the practical application of Western institutions and skills. The other is the way of thinking about this expert technical, practical behavior, which is necessary if one is to understand why it is, what it is and why it must not be corrupted by short cuts that appear, to those with merely an intuitive mentality, as equally efficacious. It is this distinction between practical ways and the theoretical understanding of them that marks the difference between individuals in non-Western societies who can handle Western ways efficiently only as long as Westerners are beside them, and those natives who can manage these ways correctly when left to themselves.

It is one thing for a native to learn the practical expertness, under the supervision and tutelage of a top sergeant, necessary to repair an airplane motor in a trustworthy manner. Under such circumstances the ways of working, the morale enforcing the native to do precisely as instructed and the immediate penalties for deviation are such that the native by mere mimicking and by enforced habit, without understanding, will do an effective job. The trouble, however, with such merely practical training is that when the Westerner withdraws, the native way of thinking about the newly acquired practical skills takes over. From the standpoint of this native mentality, these newly acquired, practical habits seem to be without rhyme or reason, a mere hocus-pocus, introduced to satisfy an arbitrary ritual upon which gadget-minded Westerners, without a proper sense of values, insist. Inevitably the native proceeds to think about what he has been doing in terms of the only concepts for understanding it which he possesses, namely, those of his own tradition and culture. As Chiang Monlin and others have noted, these native ways of thinking are quite inadequate to make the new, precise, practical skills meaningful, necessary or important.[7] Inevitably short cuts appear, or perhaps the old skills are carried on by habit, but other things, promoted by the native mentality, are also done which completely destroy the effectiveness of the habitual practices.

When this corruption of Western ways does not occur, it is because the top natives managing or supervising the entire process have spent the time and the money necessary to go to the West and acquire, in theoretically and mathematically grounded engineering, medical, military and theological schools, or in the departments of pure science and philosophy, the basic concepts and mentality necessary to understand the outward Western institutions and ways in the Western theoretical manner. Only the large, influential and more wealthy patriarchal joint families of the native, non-Western societies can afford such training for native sons. This is why Western industries and ways that are efficiently operated by natives tend to be owned in the end by a few patriarchal families such as the Soongs in China, the Oeis in Indonesia,[8] and the Berlas in contemporary India.

The political implications of this phenomenon are important. The major popular demand throughout the undeveloped areas of the world is for a lifting of the economic and medical well-being of the masses to the level of that of the modern Western societies. This political demand takes on two forms: one negative, the other positive. The negative demand is for the dismissal of all Western supervision. Such supervision, whether political, economic or religious, is called imperialism. The positive demand is to run their societies themselves.

These demands are not so easy to reconcile as non-Western natives or Western liberals have supposed. The natives' negative demand is anti-Western, yet the major reason for this demand is the observation of economic, medical and other advantages of Western ways. In short, the native wants the advantages of being Western while remaining himself and being anti-Western.

His positive demand to run his affairs in his own way is equally paradoxical. By his own way he means—because of his desire for a standard of living for everyone comparable to that of Westerners— the running of his native society by and for all the people, that is by the hundreds of millions in the villages rather than by a few top nationally privileged families. Moreover, this is what Western idealism has taught him to be the idea of the good. Nevertheless the fact is that his own society's way of running society is not thus liberally democratic, locating the source of political authority on an egalitarian basis in the masses of the people who express themselves through democratically elected and constitutionally guided officials at the national level. Instead, all these non-Western native societies are family-centered and tribal-centered rather than nation-centered and contractually guided in their binding social organization and in their moral and religious loyalties. Not only is the family and the tribe the basic locus and transmitter of moral, political and even religious authority and value, but within the family the rule of the elder, as determined by biological birth, often constitutes the good.

By its very nature the social ethics of a patriarchal or matriarchal joint family society is hierarchical and non-egalitarian. Its social, political and religious authority centers in the eldest member of each family and the village elders of the many families.

Practically, this means that primogeniture is the law of inheritance in such a society and that filial piety or family loyalty is its highest moral and social obligation. This makes the interfamily use of finance capital, necessary to run a modern Western technological industrial society in anything approximating an egalitarian democratic way, morally difficult if not impossible. Even in Westernized commercial Hong Kong, with its large Chinese population, one found in 1919 few if any interfamily Chinese business firms of any consequence. This is why a native-run Westernized society begins so often with a Western constitution and a democratic economic and political program, only to end with a family-run government and the Westernized native industries owned by a few families. The Soong family in President Chiang Kai-shek's National China was one example. The right-wing millionaire families in present Free India are another. Witness also Prime Minister Nehru's difficulty of passing the Hindu Reform bill which, after the manner of Jefferson in early Virginia, outlaws primogeniture and begins to break the old family ties and loyalties.

Even when native leaders succeed in changing the old patriarchal law of status to the ethics of a positive law of contract in which moral man is universal man rather than family or tribal man, the patriarchal living law habits of the masses change exceedingly slowly.[9] The present persisting influence of the ethics of family status of Sir Robert Filmer's *Patriarcha* in the First Families of Virginia [10] and the present Dixiecrats shows how long it takes the living law to catch up with the ethics of the Western positive law of contract even in the most modern nations of the West.

Danger joins difficulty when the new positive ethics and law, which would reform the ethics of the native living law, comes from abroad. The danger is that both the new foreign values and ways and the old native ones become corrupted. The local leader learns enough of the modern West on the outward practical side to become disabused about the forms and practices of his own culture. Forthwith he ceases to be himself, thereby cutting himself off from the underlying spiritual roots of his own society and from the masses of his own people. At the same time he has not gone deeply enough beneath the Western instruments and institutions to discover the unique mentality and spiritual roots which they require for their nourishment. Thus he runs the tragic risk of falling between both moral worlds. As noted in Chapter 1, sociological jurisprudence has a description for this situation.[11] It is one in which the positive law or leadership of a society is ineffective because its norms do not conform to those of its underlying living law.

What must be realized in combining modern Western ways with those of non-Western societies is that the living legal norms of these two types of societies frequently involve incompatible loyalties. The native societies entail patriarchal or matriarchal family loyalty as the highest social obligation. Modern Western personal and social ethics and all its technological institutions derive from a way of thinking about man which breaks his moral nature loose from the inductively felt family ties of a law of biologically bred status and identifies his moral, political, economic and religious personality instead with an axiomatically constructed, legalistically and constitutionally expressed law of contract before which all persons, regardless of family or tribal status, are equal. The problem of putting together these two different living laws and their, in part conflicting, spiritual values is the heart of the task of introducing Western ways —be they medical, legal, mechanical, economic, political or religious —into non-Western societies or even medievally-minded Western communities.

So far the result, whether attempted by Westerners or by natives, has been a failure. Chiang Kai-shek failed in China. The British failed in India. The French failed in Indochina. The Dutch failed in Indonesia. The Japanese succeeded perhaps better than anyone else —yet Pearl Harbor and its aftermath is the monument to their defeat. Mr. Chester Bowles is forced to write in his *Ambassador's Report* of "the frightening gap between the educated Indians and the villages." [12] The leaders of Turkey, notwithstanding the optimistically described modern European reforms of Ataturk, are confronted similarly today with what may well turn out to be a serious impasse between the modern Western legal, political and economic program which they have for their people and the reaction of the millions of Turks in the villages to medieval Islamic moral and religious social loyalties and ways.

The frequent result of such situations is the weakening of both the modern Western reforms and the traditional institutions and values, so that demagoguery becomes rampant and effective political movements to either the old or the new are impossible. Then, to prevent chaos, a military dictatorship takes over under the verbal façade of a constitutional democracy. Wonderful democratic speeches are made in the United Nations while a general, in office because of a military coup, rules at home. Lebanon, with its sensitive and able, Western-minded Dr. Charles Malik in the United Nations, came very close recently to being one contemporary example. Thailand comes very close to being another. Chile is a third. Egypt is a fourth. And so one could go on around most of the non-modern Western world.

But to see this prevalent political disease in all its stark realism from the standpoint of sociological jurisprudence and philosophical anthropology is also to become aware of its cure. Since Western ways presuppose Western living law values, and since the natives of the undeveloped areas want the democratic, economic and political fruits of these Western ways, we and their native leaders must not encourage the native people to introduce Western practices without at the same time bringing in the Western mentality and philosophy that are necessary to make the Western ways effective. The scientific and philosophical concepts of the ethics of the Western law of contract must be put, by their free choice, into their minds and hearts while Western practical ways are made habitual in the muscular responses of their bodies.

Practically this means that native political, religious and philosophical leaders in India and other non-Western societies must reexamine one of their present opinions. This prevalent opinion is that these societies have the true spiritual values of the world and that the modern West has nothing novel to teach them in the realm of the spirit. As a consequence of this error, some of them believe that the only thing they have to learn from the modern West is its technological efficiency. By combining these supposedly merely instrumental modern values with Indian and other non-Western ultimate goal values, India's present Vice President, Professor S. Radhakrishnan, and many others like him, suppose that the ultimate good for our world will be found, and traditional India's true values will be achieved with greater efficiency, by means of the modern West's merely secondary instrumental values.[13] What this overlooks is that the West's practical economic and political forms and technological instruments are the by-products of a unique set of ultimate beliefs and values, and that without the latter the former will not succeed; moreover, with only the traditional Indian or Asian values the Western instrumental efficiency will be corrupted.

Were the Indian and other non-Western or the medieval Western spiritual values able to generate the modern Western democratic law of contract with its more egalitarian type of economic and political community and its technological efficiency, these Asian, Islamic and African spiritual values would have done so long ago. Instead, they generated family-, caste- and tribe-centered, rather than constitutionally guided egalitarian nation-focused communities and family, tribal and even caste loyalties rather than the loyalty to contractually constructed, constitutional utopian doctrine before which all men, regardless of family, caste (color) or tribe, are equal. Western ways are unique because the mentality and ultimate goal values from which they derive are unique. The one will not be effective without the other. Indigenous, ultimate values of Hindu India, Islam,

Confucian China, native Africa and native Indian Latin America, while necessary and true in part, will not suffice.

The converse mistake will occur, as so frequently happens, if Western and native leaders go to the other extreme by regarding the indigenous living law and its unique values in undeveloped areas as outmoded, erroneous or unimportant. No people can slough off their cultural past completely, since their living law—its mentality and its social ways—has been built into them over centuries to form their inner personalities as well as their outer social practices. Nor is it wise that they should do so. There are factors in any man's experience anywhere which these native living beliefs and forms take into account, in many ways better and more empirically and scientifically even, than do the mentality, values and ways of the modern West. As has been suggested above, in aesthetic sensitivity to impressionistic immediacy and in existentialism, the modern West is discovering meanings and values that are native to non-Western cultures. Science and philosophy, therefore, as well as practical wisdom, require that men the world over see their task in the contemporary world as that of creating a fresh synthesis of the native and the modern mentalities and ways.

But if, as has been noted, these differing ways are in part at least incompatible, how is this to be done? Two things are necessary. The first is an international legal and political community which will give the native peoples the time to carry through such a long-range task. The second is that the native leadership draw a distinction between the basic, underlying living spirit and mentality of their own culture and its dead, outmoded applications. Often only the latter are incompatible with Western mentality.

To distinguish the dead, outmoded forms of one's traditional society from the valid portion of its underlying living spirit, native cultural and political leaders must, after the manner of Iqbal of Lahore, give as much attention to the basic religious and philosophical classics and mentality of their own culture and people as they give now to the democratic types of legal and political constitutions and five-year economic reconstruction programs which they copy from the modern West.[14] Moreover, after having, in this manner, found the lasting living beliefs in their own culture, these must be related to the equally ultimate basic beliefs and values of the modern

West in a fresh, consistent, creative synthesis which draws upon both as ultimate goal values.[15] Only thus can the demands of the masses of men throughout the world for political autonomy and a standard of living equal to that of peoples in the modern West be satisfied.

This is a tremendous undertaking. It requires depth of thought and breadth of feeling. It entails a stretching of the moral and intellectual imagination beyond traditional limits and the present demands for quick results. Nevertheless, this is what native leaders in undeveloped areas choose when they try to give to the millions of their fellow countrymen the democratically distributed medical, economic and political well-being they see their modern Western brothers in greater part enjoy. Nothing will be gained but bitterness and disillusionment by making them or ourselves believe the task is simpler or easier than it is. Everything in this world has its price, and such is the price of these things.

Communal Pluralism

In its issue of December 13, 1958, the *Economist* of London presented a thirty-six page descriptive study of contemporary Africa. This study arrives at the following conclusions: (1) "In no part of the world have constitutional lawyers and draftsmen had so much continuous work to do." [16] (2) The present African political leaders are trying to introduce modern technology and are pressing for democratic rather than the African tribal chieftain's control of their own affairs. (3) The "Africans are not prepared to take a modest advance in political influence and are tending to look more and more to their extremist leaders for guidance." [17] (4) It is by no means certain that they will gain the mentality and skills necessary to make the new technology work, assuming even that they can raise the capital, which is doubtful. Also, the extremists' haste may break down owing to "communal pluralism." This pluralism includes not merely the different living law norms of Negroes, whites and followers of Islam, but also the many different African tribes themselves, each of which tends to regard itself as an absolutely sovereign tribal nation.

Item (1) means that modern positivistically-minded lawyers are very busy in contemporary Africa. Items (2) and (3) indicate, however, that they and their modern-minded colleagues in politics, economics and engineering are very likely to fail in what they are trying to do because their way of going about it increases the gulf between their legal, political, economic and technological aims and instruments and the living law mentality and customs of their people. Item (4) demonstrates that the heart of their difficulty centers in not knowing how to deal with "communal pluralism."

A description of what the writer saw in Morocco in 1957 will help the reader to understand what the *Economist* means by "communal pluralism." In Morocco's capitol city of Rabat one finds today a remarkable modern French type of city, the apparent over-all living law of which is religiously Roman Catholic, socially, architecturally and aesthetically French and secularly commercial. In separate sections, however, in the heart of this otherwise modern city are two medieval religious communities whose eating and marriage as well as religious customs separate them from one another as if they were miles apart instead of being divided by the width of one street or the distance of a short block. In one of these localized religious communities live the medieval-minded Jews, in the other reside the medieval-minded followers of Islam.

Approximately one hundred miles to the east is the Moroccan city of Fez. As one approaches its suburbs the impression is similar to that of Rabat. Fez may best be described as possessing the shape of a doughnut, in the center of which is the old medieval walled Arab Islamic Moroccan Fez. Its surrounding doughnut is a French city, more modern than any city one can find in either France or the United States and, if anything, more French than the French. In the midst of this surrounding modernity at the large center of the doughnut is an Arab Islamic community packed with people, teeming with economic activity and handmade manufacturing skills, within the core of which is its medieval Islamic university and law school, older, these Arab Moroccans affirm, than that of El Azhar at Cairo. In its religious and legal teaching, its manufacturing and commercial practices, its mentality, its architecture and all its other customs, this medieval Arab Islamic Fez is completely uninfluenced by its engulfing modernity and might as well be five hundred years and ten thousand miles away.

At Marrakech to the south is a similar city which is the spiritual, political and commercial center of the Berber Moroccans who are also followers of Islam. Most of these Berber Muslims are patriarchal tribal folk who move about in the hot expanses of the desert or reside in the isolated valleys of the Atlas Mountains, each group tending to be a tribal nation unto itself. The writer resided for three weeks in 1957 beside two tribal groupings of these Berber Moroccans near the foot of one of these mountain valleys in the little city of Azrou.

This racial difference between the Fez-centered Arab Moroccan followers of Islam represents a communal pluralism even within the Islamic Moroccan community itself. The Berbers were the original Moroccans. They were converted to Islam many centuries ago when the Arabian followers of Islam conquered them and then settled culturally and politically at Fez. St. Augustine, for example, was a Berber. What frequently happens under such imperialistic religious conversions is that the religious faith and practices of the converts are changed but the old living, racially focused social and political customs go on as before. Hence not only are the present living law habits of the Berber Islamic Moroccans different from those of the Arabian Moroccans, as is their language, but there is even a patriarchically tribal communalism among the Berbers themselves. In some ways the living habits of the isolated Berber tribal groups are more conducive to democratic ways than is the case with the Arabian Moroccans. In other respects the opposite is the case. A modern-minded statesman, in introducing his Western contractual legal and political institutions, would use the descriptive method of philosophical anthropology to determine those respective living law factors that will support political democracy and then present his modern democracy as a better instrument for their fulfillment, thereby getting all the support for his new reforms that the old living law will provide.

In any event communal pluralism is something very real and very complex in Morocco. It contains medieval Jewish, medieval Arabian Islamic, medieval Berber Islamic and French Roman Catholic and secular communities, each with quite different and even incompatible living law customs. This is the reason for the psychological, political and cultural isolationism of each.

The first inclination of a modern-minded politician, especially one from the Protestant Christian or modern secular West, when con-

222 Philosophical Anthropology and Practical Politics

fronted with such communal pluralism in the living law is to introduce a modern secular state after the manner of Free India. Sociological jurisprudence, however, cautions one with respect to the practical wisdom of such a procedure, as does also the descriptive method of philosophical anthropology. For all of these religious communities of Morocco, the separation of church and state is completely foreign to their thinking. As the Muslim statesman and culturally-minded philosopher, Iqbal of Lahore, noted in the case of India, it is one thing to succeed politically in modernizing a medieval community with a positive legal and political system based on the secular state when the majority of the people in the community in question have passed through something equivalent to a Protestant Reformation and modern secular moral, economic, legal and political philosophy and have come to believe on moral and even religious grounds in the separation of politics and religion. It is quite a different thing, however, in communally plural nations when none of the communities have in their positive beliefs or their living law customs ever envisaged the idea of the separation of church and state. The practical legal and political experience of Ceylon since World War II will show what can happen politically when communal pluralism is ignored.

13

How Not to Do It; The Sinhalese Experiment

A few years ago the Swedish economist and parliamentarian Dr. Gunnar Myrdal was in Colombo as economic adviser to the government of Ceylon. He found that the task of modernizing such a society in a free democratic way could be managed if the problem were solely an economic one. But unfortunately, or perhaps fortunately, this is not the case. The reason is that the roadblock to modernization in medieval or ancient societies is not primarily the weakness of their economic instruments or the dirth of finance capital, great though these be. President Mao, for example, had remarkable success in modernizing China even though he received very little outside economic aid. In short, the obstacles to modernization are more political and cultural than they are economic or technological.

One of these political obstacles is that in many old societies, such as China, India, Lebanon and Morocco, to name but a few, there are two or more medieval-minded groups often geographically localized with different racial origins and religious faiths. Because of the law-of-status tribal focus of their marriage, medical, eating and other religiously sanctioned customs, these racial and religious communities are frequently incompatible politically when they are freed from foreign rule. Also, there is an even greater conflict between the customs and traditional political aims of any one of these medieval religious communities and the political ideals and practices of any modern nation, be it free democratic or Communistic. Hence, if freed from foreign rule and left to themselves politically, holy racial and religious wars break out which can be ended only by a military dictatorship or martial law, whereas if local modern-minded leaders attempt to democratize them, these medieval-minded religious fundamentalists tend to unite to oppose any change of their traditional ways.

To these political obstacles the writer would add the befuddled state of mind of many Western and Asian pseudomodern-minded political leaders concerning what the following words mean: (a) "liberal democracy," (b) "Communism" or, as many Africans and Asians today like to say, (c) "the best of both." How one can get the best of both of anything when one has no clear conception of what either means, many well-intentioned, but verbally bemused contemporary Asian, Middle Eastern, African and Western politicians never make clear to themselves or to anyone else.

Let us not, however, look down our long noses at such leaders. All too many "social scientists" who are doing what they call "Research in The Economics of The Underdeveloped Areas of the world" talk in much the same way. Not having been trained in the epistemological analysis of abstract nouns or in the construction of the incomplete symbols of deductively formulated scientific theory, even their description of political and other social facts is frequently questionable owing to their metaphorically nonsensical mixed-worlds-of-discourse prose and their confusion of abstract nouns with concrete entities. Being also devoid of training in the philosophical analysis of normative language and in the difference between the method for describing cultural and national norms and the method for evaluating them, such "social scientists" offer politicians "solutions" to inescapably evaluative political problems which (by the very nature of the factual evidence and the scientific method upon which the "solutions" rest) can only answer descriptive normative questions even when the "scientist" understands and practices the descriptive method for handling even the descriptive portion of the politician's problems. To enable politicians to avoid wasting their time, that of their Foreign Service officers abroad and the public funds on such politically irrelevant "research" is one of the reasons for Chapters 6 and 7 of this book.

Fortunately there are some political scientists, such as Professors Francis W. Coker, Karl Friedrich and Frederick M. Watkins, who know that the subject matter of politics is politics; that it has to do with nations, that nations are legal and political goal-value normative things, that alliances or wars are internormative things and that political problems, therefore, require knowledge of and evaluative choices between the respective cultural and positivistically legal goal-value norms of the world's many civilizations, political parties and nations. Since, moreover, no nation's goal-value norms are known until its particular legal and political philosophy is specified, such authentic experts in politics know that there is no such thing as political science which is not at the same time political philosophy, both comparatively descriptive and evaluative.

A rough operational test which the politician and the voter can use to distinguish authentic political scientists and research from spurious ones and the latter's "research institutes" is this: Ask the following question about what the "expert" specifies to be the subject matter which according to him provides the criterion of the correct political policy, "Is this 'expert' a professional expert in that subject matter?" If the answer is "No!" then the result of your political litmus test is clear. You are confronted with a faker who is trying to pass as a political scientist. For if he practiced what he preaches, he would close up his political science department, withdraw from his normative profession of black-letter lawyer and liquidate his expensive "research institutes in international relations" to become an economist, an atomic scientist, a theoretical physicist who has specialized in interstellar missiles or a soldier who is similarly expert. If politics is economics or the physics of the equilibrium of physical forces or the military science of interstellar atomic weapons, then make it so and be done with political documents written by black-letter legally positivistically-minded lawyers such as Acheson, Nitze, Dulles and Gaither or by "political scientists" and "theorizing diplomats" who are mesmerized with abstract nouns, such as Hans Morgenthau and George F. Kennan, all of whom are ignoramuses in economics, physics or military science. If politics is equilibrium-of-forces physics, let us put it in the hands of physicists and send all the aforementioned gentlemen off to some quiet place of their own choosing to meditate in silence on their metaphysical abstract nouns such as "the great powers," "the national interest," or "the power vacuum in the Middle East."

The amusing paradox is that at least some topmost military men such as Generals Anderson and Wilson who were formerly Commandants of the United States Air War College and General Desmond Smith, former Commandant of the Canadian War College, know that they cannot make their military decisions until the politician has first made his non-military political decision. To be more precise, it is impossible for the military leaders of any nation to tell either the legislature or the chief executive how much of a military financial budget must be provided unless the foreign minister has first determined what the goal-value political policy of his nation is with respect to the similar and the different goal-value political philosophies of other nations. Clearly it is neither the science of the physics of the equilibrium of forces, nor military science whose subject matter is the comparative and evaluative legal and political philosophy of the diverse goal values, i.e., normative domestic and international political intentions of the world's nations. Furthermore, unless the political policy presented by the foreign minister is based on such objective and evaluative philosophically political information, no military general such as those named above will trust it. In the United States, at least since World War II, such trustworthy specification of their political goal-value foreign policy aim has rarely if ever been provided for the military leaders by any Democratic or Republican Secretary of State. The result has been that the military men have had to turn aside from their proper military job to do the Secretary of State and his assistants' non-military political job for them. In other words, the American war colleges, breaking from the tradition of West Point which required military men to remain neutral with respect to political questions, have had to introduce a year course for their topmost officers below the rank of generals in which a very large proportion of the time is given to the study of the cultural and national philosophies and mentalities of the major civilizations, nations, political parties and politicians of the world, Communistic and non-Communistic, Hebraic, Christian and Islamic, Buddhist, Hindu, Confucian Chinese and Shinto Japanese. In these courses cultural anthropologists and philosophers who are expert in different particular national and cultural philosophies are regular lecturers. Also, it is required in some at least of these war colleges that each graduating student of the course write a thesis on the political policy of the United States in the light of this kind of study and then design an instrumental economic and military policy to implement it. In the case of the Canadian National War College, it is customary also to take the graduates around the world to see the nations and national cultures and to meet the politicians whose philosophically cultural mentalities they have previously studied, thereby in part checking on their descriptive culturally anthropological politics operationally.

During one of his visits to one of the United States war colleges its commandant told the writer that they ought not to be doing this for two reasons: First, their expertness is in military science, not comparative cultural anthropology and comparative and evaluative political philosophy. Second, their military job is more than a full-time job. This general added that nevertheless the military had to do it because it had to be done before military plans could be made or military budgets drawn up, and the person who should be doing it, namely the Secretary of State, was not doing it.

That this military leader was correct in the latter judgment the following facts confirm: At the time there was no such course in the State Department. Since then, a three-month course only part of which has this content has been introduced in the Foreign Service Institute of the Department of State for returning mid-career Foreign Service officers. Never has any State Department official or experienced career diplomat, with a rank comparable to that of a general, regarded it as sufficiently important to give his time to the direction of this course. Moreover, continuously since World War II at least the heads of the Planning Board of the State Department, who should be doing this political job, have been black-letter-minded lawyers with the mentality of Acheson, Dulles, Herter, Nitze and Bowie, or theorizing power politicians such as Mr. Kennan. They are above such a vulgar non-power political or "non-legal" subject as sociological jurisprudence or philosophical anthropology, even though each of them has a covert culturally anthropological legal and political philosophy—and a most self-contradictory and questionable one—trapped epistemically in his brain—namely, that of the power-political theory of legal obligation and of international relations of Hobbes, Austin and Thayer.

The recommendations of President Eisenhower's Wriston Com-

mittee report on improving the morale of the State Department, after
the late Senator McCarthy had made a shambles of it, is little better,
moving almost entirely as it does on the instrumental linguistic and
administrative surface of the subject. The "Gaither report," with its
"top-secret" emphasis on power politics that is an open secret to the
similarly superficial and even more conceptually confused newspaper
columnists is equally useless as a foreign policy for the military
leaders to use as a political basis for making their military plans,
since it is to be presumed that they know more about throwing power
around than does either the Wriston Committee or the lawyer Mr.
Gaither.

Some other well-intentioned people would now have us commit
such political errors all over again by making economics rather than
physics what politics is about, thereby shifting the politician's attention from guns to butter. The result would be merely that both the
military men and the economists would have to do the politician's
job for him. Authentic economists such as Professor Oscar Morgenstern of Princeton University, Lionel Robbins of the London School
of Economics and Frank Knight of the University of Chicago who
have investigated the elementary concepts and postulates of their
science and analyzed the method by which they are empirically confirmed, make it clear that their science, like military science, is instrumental to moral, legal and political science. The Swedish parliamentarian and economist Gunnar Myrdal knows this also and
found it confirmed at firsthand when he was in Ceylon as the economic adviser to the government of Ceylon. What he found there
was not "the economic factor which is the key to the political problems of the underdeveloped areas of the world," but a specific group
of particular people between whom the daily economic exchange of
goods was disrupted and for whom a free democratic constitution
and its political practices had been replaced by a state of martial
law. The very evident reason was that the Hindus of the Tamil tribal
community, whose ancestors came to Ceylon from South India several centuries ago, and the tribally different people of the Buddhist
Sinhalese community were self-expressing themselves most democratically by cutting one another's throats in a bloody racial and religious war. Also, in terms of particular quantitatively measurable
economic quantities rather than philosophically unanalyzed abstract

nouns, the total production of goods and services was continuously decreasing even though (a) both the government officials and the bankers undoubtedly had finance capital available which, under such circumstances, was not being used, and (b) there was an expert Western economist at their elbow, who knew the difference between an abstract noun with the word "the" before it and concrete entities, to tell them how to spend their capital with the greatest instrumental economic efficiency.

Ceylon is not an exceptional case, as the Ford Foundation learned *perhaps* at the conference of American, European, African and Asian economic and political experts, including Gunnar Myrdal, which it financed and arranged on the Isle of Rhodes in 1958. The interested reader will find a report of the substance of what happened there in the *New Yorker* of November 10, 1958. The contents of the report would be uproariously funny were they not also so tragic with respect to the fate of free democracy in the African, Middle Eastern and Asian world and the waste of hundreds of millions of dollars on pseudoscientific research by the wealthy American foundations, not to mention the taxpayers' money which has been funneled into culturally and politically ill-conceived or non-conceived "economic aid."

By "ill-conceived" or "non-conceived" is meant "aid" that is pushed in lavishly and blindly at the instrumental level before the descriptive living law cultural and political goal-value customs and conflicts unique to each foreign people and nation are first determined objectively and then evaluated to define a specific positive legal and political policy for both drawing upon and reforming the old living law to achieve what is cognitively true in both the old and the new. This policy must tell one precisely what in the old living customs is to go and what is to be retained in bringing in the new modern mathematically physical scientific mentality with its unique technological instruments (Chapters 14 and 18) and the new legally contractual free democratic political institutions (Chapters 17 and 18) with their economic and military instruments.

In addition, this anthropologically political policy must be conveyed by political speeches to and education of the people in the villages to win their support for it and to trap epistemically in their brains the appropriate impulses for understanding it and its instruments and effectively using them. Otherwise, the majority of the people will not want the aid even if it is thrust upon them. As the immediate sequel will show, some of the most religious and morally principled of them may even assassinate the modern-minded political leader of their own faith who tries to make them use these new modern ways. Moreover, even if they take the aid, they are likely to misuse or corrupt it, as the previous chapter has indicated. Except as the cultural and political problems are answered first in philosophically anthropological, political and educational terms with the economic, military, agricultural, industrial and medical instruments made secondary to such a policy and designed to fit the *de facto* mentality and capacity for understanding of the people, the aid will not be economic.

To the economist Gunnar Myrdal's experiences in Ceylon and at the Rhodes Conference of the Ford Foundation may be added the earlier experiences of the writer in Ceylon in January of 1951. Then a British-minded and positivistic, legally educated Sinhalese party was in office. There were no racial or religious riots. All was peaceful, beautiful and calm. Economic trade was normal. Furthermore, it was clear that the executive and judicial leaders of the government, many if not most of whom had been through the English "public schools," Oxford or Cambridge, and even the Inns of Court in London, were philosophically, economically and legally clear in their own minds about what the word "democracy" means not merely in theory but also when it is brought down to particular legal and political judgments in a court of law or the day-to-day decisions of a politician. Undoubtedly they had read their Locke, Hume, Bentham, Mill and Austin and their modern free democratic British common law. What is even more important, this specific mentality had been consciously and unconsciously epistemically trapped as a basic way of thinking and behaving in the teleological mechanisms which were their respective brains and nervous systems.

One day in Colombo the writer and his wife were invited to luncheon by the Buddhist philosopher Professor Malalasekera and his wife. Present also was a leader of one of the opposition parties. The briefest conversation sufficed to show that this political leader had one political virtue and one political limitation.

His political virtue was that he was thinking about the Buddhist cultural philosophy and customs of his own people. This was the reason why Professor and Mrs. Malalasekera, being devout Buddhists and spiritually and culturally sensitive people, had invited him and were on his side against the British-minded Sinhalese political party which was then in office. Both this opposition leader and the Mala-lasekeras wanted a Buddhist Sinhalese Ceylon and not one which was a shabbily commercialized and a second- or third-rate imitation of the culture of Great Britain or the United States.

The political limitation of this Sinhalese opposition party leader (and, it must be added, of Professor Malalasekera also) showed when his conversation turned to the description of the modern philosophy of goal values which his political party would introduce if they came into office. His democracy was to be that of the Buddhist middle path in which "the best" of the Anglo-American Western free democratic and of the Russian and Chinese Communist democracies were to be combined. In specifying what the theoretical philosophical and the legal and political operational differences would be when such a "best-of-both democracy" was brought down to particular cases in the decisions of a judge or of the Prime Minister, my colleagues at the luncheon table were singularly vague. This was confirmed after Professor Malalasekera's Sinhalese guest had discussed at considerable length this new Buddhist Ceylonese Anglo-American-Communistic "best of both" way for his fellow countrymen, and was thrown into a silence which turned his attention to the delicious food on his plate when he was asked: What leads you to believe that a made-in-mid-nineteenth-century German political philosophy will merge harmoniously with your own culture to enable you to have a first-rate Buddhist-Sinhalese rather than a second-rate-mid-nineteenth century Marxist German Ceylon?

Clearly the answer to this question he did not know. In fact, it may well have been the first time that it had come home to his consciousness that either the Soviet or Mao's Communism might be a nineteenth century German way of life rather than a merely Asian "democratic people's movement." He is not, however, the first person to have lacked both the knowledge of technical Marxist philosophy and the imaginative mental capacity to distinguish its political consequences from those of an Asian peasants' reform movement.

In any event, facts are now teaching him the answer to the foregoing question. For a Buddhist Sinhalese political party was victorious a few years later. Furthermore, our host of that day became the Ambassador of Ceylon to the Soviet Union. The answers which the facts are speaking out for them are: (1) Buddhist Ceylon got the very worst of itself in a racial and religious civil war between tribally embittered Tamil Hindus and Sinhalese Buddhists, whose tribal loyalties and their caste segregation the Buddha unequivocally repudiated. (2) A permanent state of martial law made a mockery of the democratic legal and political system which the opposition party inherited from the previous government and which preserved the peaceful, economically vital and beautiful Ceylon of 1951. (3) A continuously declining total production of goods and services occurred, which is the very antithesis of the aim and the demonstrated achievement of either the Soviet Union or Anglo-American democracy.

The Sinhalese have, therefore, performed a very important political and social experiment. Its result is concrete and unequivocal. Furthermore, the findings are as important for contemporary social scientists and practical politicians as was the Michaelson-Morley experiment for recent mathematical physics and the making of the atomic bomb.

But the question is: Will either the politicians who performed the experiment or the "social scientists" in the modern West who talk so much about putting social subjects on an experimental basis note the kind of theory that was put to an operational test and look at the practical results of the use of such political and social "theory"? The theory tested by my Colombo luncheon companion and his political party was "the best of both" worlds' verbiage of any political or social theory or policy which does not give a philosophically precise set of criteria for defining the meaning of the abstract nouns it uses to give substance to the legal and political goal values the politician proposes to pursue. The result of any experiment which tests theories of politicians or social scientists that are stated in terms of vague, philosophically unanalyzed abstract nouns is precisely the result which exists now in Ceylon—namely, the failure of any social scientist or politician guided by such verbiage to succeed practically in what he tries to do.

The reason why this Colombo experiment holds for any non-philosophically analyzed and specified goal-value policy word is that the meaning of all non-philosophically analyzed abstract nouns is identical, regardless of what the abstract nouns are, since their meaning is that they have no cognitive or scientific meaning at all. Consequently it is not necessary to repeat the experiment performed by my Ceylonese luncheon companion, putting the philosophically unanalyzed policy words of many American social scientists in the place of my Sinhalese friend's "the best of both" worlds language, since their policy words and his are identical in their meaninglessness.

Even so the Colombo politicians of the opposition parties were correct in giving attention to the traditional beliefs and customs of the people. But they failed for two reasons. First, by not applying the descriptive method of philosophical anthropology to the living law of *all* of his own people, they did not take sufficient account of the two racially focused, incompatible law-of-status religious communities which Sinhalese living law contains. Hence, they were not prepared for what might happen when that religious community whose members were in the quantitative minority saw the religious community whose members were in the majority take over the national government and put themselves and their relatives in most if not all of the important religious, political, commercial, cultural and other decision-making posts. Nor were they prepared for the explosive reactions that might occur even among their own Buddhist Sinhalese because of the conflict between their ancient living law medical beliefs and customs and those of a modern government's Minister of Public Health. The second, and even more important reason for failure, was that they had no theoretically clear idea of what their best of everything political aim is, to say nothing about the particular operational procedures and economic and other instruments for achieving it.

Their modern British-minded Sinhalese predecessors made the opposite error. They were philosophically and theoretically clear about their modern free democratic political, economic and legal goal values, when applied to concrete cases, but committed the error of failing to pay equal attention to the indigenous goal-value beliefs and customs of their Sinhalese selves and their own people most of whom are in the countryside.

The writer had misgivings about the practicability of their policy when he interviewed in Colombo in 1951 several people who were in the Cabinet or Justices of the Supreme Court. He found some of the

Justices giving their time to a detailed codification of specific branches of their law in a purely British manner with no regard for the use of Buddhist or other Sinhalese symbols and beliefs that might tie this dull Western abstract law of contract and its mentality to the intuitive mentality and vivid customs of their people. When it was suggested that the codification wait until culturally-minded lawyers had found out how to do this, it was evident that too many of them were merely legalistically trained in modern Western positive law and that it had never entered their heads to think about their problem from the standpoint of anthropological and sociological jurisprudence.

This state of mind would not have been quite so dangerous had their legal education occurred somewhere other than in Great Britain or the British Commonwealth or in the Harvard and other law schools of the Thayer legally positivistic era in the United States. For British legal training explicitly teaches and unconsciously and covertly inculcates the legally positivistic philosophy of law, to which we referred in Chapter 11, which came into the United States about half a century ago through Thayer of the Harvard Law School. According to this positivistic British philosophy of law, the lawyer knows everything that he needs to know about his science if he studies nothing but the positive law, i.e., the constitution, the statutes, the judicial decisions, traditional cases, etc. This does little harm in Great Britain where the positive law has grown out of the living beliefs and customs of the people. Such a legal philosophy and mentality is, however, likely to be exceedingly impractical and even fatal to the positive legal system itself in a country such as Ceylon or any other non-British or non-Anglo-American culture which is introducing free democratic contractual normative goal values in its modernization program, but whose traditional living law of the majority of the people is not that of a relatively homogeneous, non-pluralistic modern democratic Anglo-American society. Such a positivistic legal philosophy also does not fit the political and legal system even of the United States, since, as Chapters 11 and 17 show, this system rests on "the separation of powers" under a system of checks and balances, instead of locating all political sovereignty in the legislative branch of government.

The danger of such judicial and executive political leaders is that, although they are clear about what they mean by the modern political, economic and legal goal values that they are trying to introduce, they, nevertheless, fail to be understood by the majority of their people. Hence they run the risk politically in a free democratic government of not being able to carry the majority of their people with them. Furthermore, they lay themselves open to their political opponents' charge that their government is a foreign British-minded, rather than a Sinhalese democratic government of either a Tamil Hindu or a Buddhist Asian people. Even the Christians in Ceylon, who are a significant community, may be alienated also, since these Christians are for the most part medieval-minded Portuguese-converted Roman Catholics instead of modern-minded British-converted Protestants. In fact, these are the charges that the parties of my two Sinhalese luncheon politicians hurled at their more British-minded Sinhalese political opponents. Also, it was because of these charges that the majority of the people of Ceylon voted one of the opposition parties into office to send our gracious Buddhist host of that day to Moscow as the Ambassador of Ceylon to the Soviet Union.

This Sinhalese experiment has an important lesson to teach those who plan the curriculum in Western universities for graduate or professional students from non-modern Western societies and nations. This lesson is that it is likely to be fatal for the leadership which these students provide for free democratic modern political institutions when they return home if, while in the modern Western universities of the democratic nations, they are taught merely the Western mentality and applied "know-how" of their own particular profession. In addition, they need to be given a sense of the sociological jurisprudential and philosophically anthropological dimensions of the particular professional problem that will confront each when he returns to his native land. Only if this is done are they likely to see their task as that (a) of objectively knowing and respecting both the deepest and best philosophical beliefs and ways of their own people and those of the modern, legally contractual mathematically technological free democratic West and then (b) learning the evaluative method and political art for putting these two factors together so that negatively political nitroglycerin does not explode and that positively the cognitively true in both their own people's culture and in the modern West is retained and consistently and harmoniously combined.

Chapters 6 and 7 have attempted to show that the descriptive and evaluative cognitive methods for doing this are at hand. The sequel will try to indicate in particular political situations and nations how to apply them.

With respect to the role of instrumental economic, technological and military factors in politics, one caution is necessary. The point of this chapter and of this book is not that these instrumental values are unimportant or unnecessary. It is, instead, that being instrumental values rather than goal values they are not, as so many now suppose, the answer to the politician's problems. The reason is twofold: First, political problems, especially when one is dealing with new ways in an old society, are descriptive and evaluative goal-value problems rather than merely instrumental-value problems. Second, goal-value problems are anthropologically cultural and philosophically political in character and must be met and solved at that level of analysis.

Consequently, before one has made the philosophically determinate political decision concerning the kind of political nation one wants, there is no meaning to saying that a particular instrument, whether it be money, guns or a modern drug, is economically, militarily or medically efficient or not; nor is it meaningful to say that any of these instruments is an aid to the people who receive it. For whether anything is efficient, effective or an aid to any people is a function of their goal-value wants.

Conversely, unless a given people themselves are captured (a) by the epistemological philosophy of natural science with its logically realistic constructs which make the technological instruments of modern mathematical physics both possible and meaningful, and (b) by the new psychological theory of the person which makes free democratic law of contract nations similarly possible and meaningful, they will hardly want to make the changes in their old living habits and beliefs necessary to use the economic, industrial, military and medical instruments that are necessary to actualize these new epistemological and psychological meanings, even if the instruments are put in their hands. Instead, one of two things is likely to happen. If the instrumental aid turns out to be compatible with the old, covertly trapped social and national customs, then the economic, military and technological aid will be welcomed but used to make a few tribal leaders or high caste, privileged patriarchal joint families very influential politically and very wealthy economically while the masses of the people remain in squalor and become easy game for foreign imperialists and revolutionists. If, on the other hand, the foreign aid requires the giving up of old medieval-minded customs, then the result is likely to be the liquidation of the dedicated, self-sacrificing native modern-minded political leader by some right-wing religious fanatic. The recent assassination of Premier Bandaranaike by a Buddhist who was opposed to the modern medicine of his officer of public health, because it upset and deviated from the old Buddhist medical customs, is a case in point.

Once, however, any people have clarified their philosophically political goal values and committed themselves to them, thereby trapping their neurological epistemic correlates as the inner target of their nervous systems, the teleological mechanics of that nervous system itself will necessitate behavioristically that they seek out and themselves create or obtain the instruments required to achieve those goal values. Mao's remarkable success in modernizing his Chinese, notwithstanding the fact that the free world blockaded him from the receipt of foreign aid and that the Communist Soviet Union sent him relatively little such aid, is an example. Why he succeeded using Marxist goal values where the Sinhalese using free democratic political goal values failed will concern us in Chapter 16.

14

Man's Relation to the Earth in Its Bearing on His Aesthetic, Ethical, Legal and Political Values *

Contemporary man is at once the creator and the captive of a technological civilization. Its instruments have related him to the earth in a new way. This new way has reflected back upon man himself, forming and altering his values. Of what do these modifications of the humanity of man consist? This, I take it, is our question.

Put more concretely, the question is: What effect has man's role in changing the face of the earth had on his aesthetic sensitivity and creativity, his ethical, political and legal standards for ordering his relations to his fellow men, his emotive relation to nature itself and to its creation, and his moral standards for determining whether his tools are used for good or for bad ends? The last factor suggests that the answer which the evidence and its analysis permit us to give to this question may well determine whether man remains the master or becomes the slave and perhaps even the murdered victim of his tools.

In selecting and analyzing the relevant evidence, what method are we to use? Clearly the method chosen will determine the character of the answer. It is important, therefore, that we allow the nature of

* This chapter is reprinted here from the symposium volume *Man's Role in Changing the Face of the Earth*, with the kind permission of its editor, William L. Thomas, Jr., its publisher, the University of Chicago Press, and its sponsor, the Wenner-Gren Foundation for Anthropological Research, Inc. © The University of Chicago, 1956.

the question to guide us to the relevant data for answering it. Our question implies two things: first, that man's relation to nature is different in a technological civilization from what it is in a non-technological one; second, that his cultural values differ correspondingly. Our first task, therefore, becomes that of finding the criterion which distinguishes a technological from a non-technological civilization. Having done this, we can then turn to the respective values of each.

Finding this difference is not easy. The difficulty becomes evident when one asks: Do not all men have tools, at least the tools of their natural hands and of natural objects, and hence are not all civilizations technological civilizations? An affirmative answer to this question would mean that the difference confronting us is merely one of quantitative degree or complexity and not a difference in kind. Then the point at which one draws the line between a technological and a non-technological society would be purely arbitrary. But, if so, why did the passage from the one civilization to the other result in a change in men's mentality and values? Why, when the instruments and legal norms of a technological civilization enter Africa and Southeast Asia, do the natives there feel that they are confronted with something baffling which they do not understand and which to them seems destructive of all values? These reactions could hardly occur if the difference between a non-technological and a technological civilization were merely one of complexity.

How is the suggested difference in kind to be found? Our question indicates the way. When it refers to a technological civilization, it clearly means one in which mechanical, chemical, electrical and the recently born communication engineering play a dominant role. From where does this type of toolmaking come?

Its source clearly is in physical chemistry and in physics. More specifically these engineering sciences derive from the mathematical acoustics of Democritus, the mathematical-physical chemistry of Willard Gibbs, the mathematical mechanics of Newton, Einstein, and Schroedinger, and the mathematical electromagnetics of Maxwell, Lorentz, and Planck.

These sciences are unique. Their basic elementary scientific objects and relations are not directly observable. Instead, they are axiomatically constructed entities and relations whose existence is verified only indirectly by way of experiments which confirm their deductive consequences. Einstein has told us [1] that this way of knowing nature arose with the ancient Greeks and adds that the person who has not been thrilled by Euclid does not understand contemporary mathematical physics. Chiang Monlin, former Vice Chancellor of Peking National University,[2] tells us also that the ancient Greeks discovered a unique way of knowing nature and of relating man to nature. After being trained in the way of knowing man and nature of a Confucian, Chinese non-technological civilization, he came, as a young man, to the University of California at Berkeley, where for the first time he was introduced to the abstract concepts of Greek philosophy and of Greek mathematical physics. He adds that he felt quite at home mentally in the Western, natural history, descriptive sciences of botany and zoölogy but that in Greek philosophy and in deductively formulated mathematical physics he found himself confronted with something completely foreign to his classical Chinese mind. Students of the history of mathematics confirm also that, while many people previous to the ancient Greeks had discovered isolated propositions of Euclid, such as the Pythagorean theorem, it was the Greeks who first grasped the idea of proving these otherwise isolated findings by deducing them rigorously from a very small number of axiomatically constructed entities and relations and then using this way of thinking and knowing to understand man and nature empirically.[3]

Here we come upon the difference in kind which distinguishes a technological civilization from a non-technological one. The nature to which a non-technological civilization relates man is completely exhausted by immediately apprehended, or by purely inductively sensed, entities and relations. Its scientific objects are defined in terms of directly sensed properties. As noted above by Chiang Monlin, such science exists in non-technological societies. It is the science of the purely descriptive, natural-history type. Natural-history biology, with its species and genera, is an example. Aristotle's physics, in which the terrestrial scientific object "water" was defined in terms of the sensed qualities "wet" and "cold," is another example. Early atomic theories of the Charvakian materialists and the Vaiseshika dualists of India are similar examples. The Chinese natural-history paintings of birds and bamboo are another instance.[4] Such science is strong descriptively but weak predictively. It is also weak in the tools which it generates. This occurs because, deriving its tools from sensed objects and materials, it obtains only such tools as come from modifying and manipulating such objects and materials.[5]

The science of a technological civilization takes this natural-history type of knowledge merely as its data. It does not suppose that adequate knowledge of man or of nature has been obtained until the gross sensed objects and their described relations can be deduced from a very small number of unobservable, more elementary, axiomatically constructed objects and relations such as electrons, electromagnetic waves, and their mathematical laws. From the axiomatically constructed postulates of the deductively formulated theory, which designates such elementary particles and their relations, theorems can be logically deduced. These theoretically deduced theorems specify the possibility of new tools—tools quite different from anything one would come upon merely by moving sensed materials about.

The atomic bomb is an example. It was not discovered by engineers moving sensed materials about, after the manner in which the tools of a non-technological civilization arise. If we had depended for it upon engineers alone working inductively and pragmatically, it would never have come into being. The idea of the possibility of releasing atomic energy came not from an engineer, or even from an experimental physicist, but from a very theoretical one—Albert Einstein— and the mass-energy equation of his special theory of relativity. This equation is not a relation which can be sensed. Instead, it is a theorem deduced from the very abstract and shockingly novel, axiomatically constructed postulates of Einstein's indirectly, and experimentally, verified special theory of relativity. The latter theory was discovered or introduced not in order to make a new tool but in order to clear up a theoretical difficulty in the foundations of modern mechanics and electromagnetics which was revealed by the Michelson-Morley experiment in 1885.

It is in this difference between tools made out of scientific objects of the purely inductively manipulated, immediately sensed type and tools derived from scientific objects and relations of the axiomatically constructed and deductively formulated type that the difference in kind between a non-technological and a technological civilization consists. Furthermore, it is in the difference in meanings and materials and their forms provided by immediately apprehended and immediately sensed man and nature as compared with the meanings, materials, and forms provided by axiomatically constructed, deductively conceived man and nature, with its more elementary and universal scientific objects and relations, that the difference in kind between the aesthetic, ethical and legal values of a non-technological civilization and those of a technological one has its basis.

We must put ourselves within the way of knowing one's self and nature from which the cultural values of a non-technological civilization derive. To this end, let us suppose that we know nothing about mathematical physics and its contemporary, unimaginable and unsensed, axiomatically constructed, scientific objects and equations. Let us try to imagine also that we have no concepts of the regular solids of Euclid's geometry or of Newtonian linear, infinitely extended time, or even of matter itself. Let us try, in other words, to approach nature and ourselves afresh, in a radically empirical and purely inductive manner. What do we immediately apprehend?

Must we not describe nature somewhat as follows: It is a vast, spread-out, going-on-ness, vague and indeterminate at its outer fringes, ablaze with diverse colors, and issuing forth manifold sounds, fragrances and flavors. This initial evidence of sounds, vivid colors, flavors and fragrances is of considerable relevance to our major question. Such entities are essentially aesthetic, at bottom indescribable and hence ineffable, the stuff of which art is made, especially impressionistic art in which the proportions of Euclid's geometry and the perspectives of geometrical optics are not present. We would expect, therefore, that so-called "primitive man" or man in a non-technological society, would have considerable aesthetic sensitivity and that his paintings would not embody the techniques of perspective and of three-dimensional geometrical proportions of classical Western sculpture and painting. The anthropologists who have studied him and the artists who have examined his paintings or music tell us that in these judgments we are correct.[6]

We have described our initial all-embracing experience as one from which sounds issue forth. Would it not be likely that we would be impressed more by the sounds issuing forth to us than from those issuing forth from us? This would be especially true if these sounds were those of the rolling thunder of the Himalayas. Then we might well speak, as do the early authors of the Hindu Vedic hymns, of the Maruts shouting their noisy terror at us from the sky.[7]

Furthermore, since we would experience the particular instance first and come only long afterward to the class of all similar particular instances, would it not be scientifically correct for us to describe the particular instance with a proper name? Non-proper names are appropriate only for abstract classes of particular things, when the particularity of each is neglected and their similarity only is seized upon. But this means that early man was not unscientific and guilty of a spurious anthropomorphism, as many of his observers have supposed, when he described particular events in inorganic nature with proper names. Proper names are the only accurate scientific names for describing individual events or things.

Actually, however, in our initial experience and description we have not yet arrived at the concept of a thing, least of all at the concept of a persisting, substantial thing. We sense the terrifying shout of the thunder. It does not, however, last. Thus, although it is a particular which is appropriately described with a proper name, it is a perishing particular, succeeded by different perishing aesthetic qualities or particulars. From this sensed sequence of perishing aesthetic particulars, we arrive at our first concept of time. This is sensed time. Each particular sensed sound, fragrance, or flavor comes into being and goes out of being to be replaced by its successor.

This sensed succession of perpetually created, perpetually perishing particulars is quite different from the mathematical time of Newton or Einstein's physics, with which the people in a technological civilization order their daily lives. The latter, theoretically constructed time, is an infinitely extending series which does not return upon itself. The sensed time given in a sequence of perpetually perishing sensed particulars does return on itself, as the following sensed facts make clear. There is the sensed brightness which comes into being at dawn, reaches its highest intensity at high noon and perishes at dusk. It is succeeded by the sensed darkness which begins with a minimum degree of intensity, reaches its maximum intensity at midnight and perishes at dawn. This cycle has continued as long as men have sensed nature. Within the sensed darkness there appears another cyclical sequence of perishing images. This cycle is composed of the two-dimensional, yellowish crescent called the new moon. It perishes and in a succeeding creation of darkness is succeeded by the two-dimensional, yellowish image called the quarter-moon, which in turn, in a later sensed particular darkness, is succeeded by the half-moon, and so on through the full moon and receding quarter-moon until the new crescent appears. Thus it is that the monthly cycle of perishing particulars is known.[8]

These cycles can be counted just as the cycles of day and night can be counted. In this manner an aesthetic and qualitative astronomy becomes quantitative, and the inductive concept of number arises. This inductive concept of number is, however, sensed number. It is not the axiomatically constructed concept of number of the Greek and of modern technological society.

Similarly, the sequence of brightness in the cycle of days and nights is also differentiated with localized two-dimensional images. The most importance of these is the two-dimensional, localized image called the sun. It appears first at dawn as a very thin, two-dimensional segment. This perishes and is succeeded by a thin portion of a bright yellow patch which is circular on one side and rectilinear on the other. This perishes and is succeeded immediately by a larger circle, then a still larger circle, and finally a fully rounded, two-dimensional, intensely bright, yellowish patch. Concomitantly, the differentiation between earth and sky becomes evident. The intense, round yellowish patch called the sun vanishes at one point in the sky and appears at a higher point. This goes on until high noon, when the cycle is reversed. In the next brightness of the following morning the sequence of images called the sun appears at a different point on the horizon. This point varies in successive diurnal and monthly cycles. Similarly, it also comes back on itself. This sensed cycle is called the year. This cycle also can be counted, and the number can be related to the sensed number of monthly cycles and the sensed number of daily cycles.

Within the daily, monthly and yearly succession of brightness, there are other sensed colors than those of the sun. There are the vivid greens of the initial growth of sensed plants, the golden yellows of their mature growth, the reddish browns of their decline, and the dull blacks and grays of their death, succeeded again by the vivid greens of the following spring.

All these directly sensed cyclical changes man feels within himself. He notes his introspected moods changing with these colorful cyclical sequences of the seasons. He notes also, for himself as for other animals and plants, that there is birth, youth, maturity, the fall of life, and its winter, or death, succeeded again by a new birth. And so, through the generations of the sensed biological family, the human cycle goes on as part and parcel of the interconnected, numerically countable cycles of nature.

Knowing himself and everything else thus in terms of emotively felt and immediately sensed aesthetic qualities, it never occurs to non-technological man to separate the aesthetic and emotive beauty of everything from the things themselves, after the manner of a technological civilization. Nor does it ever occur to him to think of himself as outside of nature or as an exploiter of nature. The earth is "Mother Earth." Are not her materials and the forests and other plants and animals which arise out of her, like himself, fellow members of an interconnected set of cycles? Taking this for granted, the concept of the good, common to Confucian, Buddhist, Hindu, Indonesian and all other non-technological societies, arises—the concept of the good for man as immersion within, aesthetic sensitivity to and harmony with nature.

Each immediately sensed thing has one other characteristic. It is a temporarily created and perishing particular. It comes into being only by its predecessor's dying. It dies that its successor can come into being. When at dusk the brightness which is day dies, the darkness which is night is born. When at dawn the darkness of night dies, the brightness of day is born. So it is with every sensed thing that is determinate and finite. Determinate, finite human beings are no exception to this rule. The doctrine of transmigration is nothing but the thesis that the cycle of sensed perishing particulars goes on for man as for other things. This doctrine does not mean that man persists as an eternal, determinate substance. Restricting one's knowledge thus to immediacy, one does not come upon the concept of substance. All that one finds is a succession of perishing particulars which return upon themselves cyclically.

The sensed fact that nothing comes into being without the death of its predecessor and that nothing goes out of being without its successor coming into being, the early native Indonesians expressed as the principle of the cosmic equilibrium. This principle affirms that nothing is ever received except as something else is taken away. To violate this principle is to be immoral in a non-technological civilization. This is why the early Indonesians and their present descendants do not feel that they can cut down a virgin forest to gain land for cultivation unless they express sympathy, through a ceremony, for the death of what they destroy and accept the trust of creating faithfully that which is new to replace the old. To exploit nature, taking from it while giving nothing back in return, is to act immorally. Similarly, when the young Indonesian takes a bride, he or his family must make a gift of a very considerable amount in return. The Dutch interpreted this as the purchase of a bride and outlawed it as slavery, thereby showing that they were looking at the values and social norms of a non-technological society from the conceptual standpoint and mentality of a technological one. The so-called "payment" of the groom for the bride is, from the standpoint of the native Indonesian, a moral requirement. Failure to give something in return for what is taken would be to violate the cosmic balance; it would be to act immorally.

This conception of man as immersed in the cyclical sequence of nature shows in the aesthetic values of a non-technological society. Instead of starting with the musical theme and countertheme, which move linearly toward their resolution in a climax, after the practice of Western music, the tonal sequences in the music of a non-technological society are cyclical in character. There are melody and rhythm but no harmony and counterpoint. Also, the music is not recorded or controlled by meticulous, mathematically ordered scales. Instead, it is mastered and directed wholly by ear and transmitted from generation to generation in this way. The standard with respect to which the notes of the melody are measured and ordered is also different. This standard in Hindu music is called the "drone." [9] The drone is a continuous background. It is against this constant background that the differentiated sounds of the melody rise and fall and succeed one another in time cyclically.

The drone also symbolizes something immediately experienced. We described our initial experience of nature as "a vast, spread-out, going-on-ness, . . . ablaze with diverse colors, and issuing forth manifold sounds, fragrances, and flavors." The drone expresses both the dynamism of the going-on-ness and the relatively undifferentiated character of the vast spread-out-ness. It symbolizes, therefore, the infinite timelessness out of which each sensed particular thing, including sensed particular man himself, arises and to which it returns at death.

Early in this century William James attempted to bring scientific and philosophic discourse back to radically empirical immediacy.[10] In doing this, he noted that it is only the portion which is at the focus of attention that is sharply differentiated into the determinate colors, sounds, fragrances, flavors and feelings; the periphery of immediacy is vague, formless, undifferentiated and indeterminate, one portion of it being no different from another. James suggested also that it is from this undifferentiated, indeterminate periphery that religious experience arises. This periphery is both the subject of consciousness and its object. But, being indeterminate and undifferentiated, there is nothing in it to distinguish subject from object. Thus it is both subject and object and neither subject nor object. These are the defining properties of what the Hindus call the "divine" or "true self," "Brahman" or "Atman," and the Buddhists call "Nirvana." It is also the factor in immediate experience with which the divine is identified in all non-technological societies. At this point the radical empiricism of William James and the radical empiricism of a non-technological society become identical.

This all-embracing, indeterminate consciousness within which the sensed differentiations come and go in cyclical sequence is called by Hindus the "*chit* consciousness" to distinguish it from the differentiated, sensuous consciousness.[11] Both types of consciousness give immediately apprehended objects. One does not, however, sense the undifferentiated or *chit* consciousness, since sensing always involves a distinction between the sensing percipient and the sensed object. One can sense only differentiated qualities within the *chit* consciousness; one cannot sense the *chit* consciousness itself. In the case of the *chit* consciousness, to apprehend it is to be it; hence, being undifferentiated, there is no distinction between subject and object in the knowing of it.

The Hindus and Buddhists of a non-technological society call the cyclical sequence of perpetually born and perpetually perishing particulars the "law of karma." This is the concept of causality in a non-technological society. The transmigration of sensed souls is a special case of it. Salvation comes for man, however, only by escaping the karma cycle. This occurs when man realizes that he is the time-less *chit* consciousness within which the perishing particulars of the karma cycle come and go. To realize this is to be able to accept with equanimity the death of one's sensed self in the karma cycle.

The drone of Hindu music is the minimally differentiated expression of the all-embracing, infinite formlessness and dynamism which the Hindu terms "Brahman" or "Atman." The measure of the differentiated sounds, in their cyclical temporal successions, against the continuous drone expresses the tension between the temporal and the eternal, the finite and the infinite, in man and in things for people in a non-technological civilization.

Its legal norms are of two types. One type derives from the all-embracing formlessness of things within which the conflicting, differentiated, sensed creatures come and go. Since all sensed objects are relative to perceivers, only the all-embracing formlessness is common to all men. Hence only it can provide an absolute norm for a common law. In a concrete, sensed dispute each participant's experience of that dispute is relative to him. Ethical and legal codes, therefore, which are defined in terms of sensed objects cannot give a common law, since sensed objects are one thing for one perceiver and another thing for another. How then is anything common going to be found for settling social disputes in a non-technological society?

The basic answer is that it can be found in the sole factor in immediate experience which is common to disputants—namely, in the all-embracing, immediately felt formlessness within which the relativistic objects of each particular disputant's experience come and go. This formlessness, precisely because it is a formlessness, cannot be expressed in codes. It has to be immediately experienced to be known. It is to be found, moreover, pragmatically, as the Buddha teaches, in the "middle way" between the conflicting claims arising from the relativistic sensed experiences of the disputants.[12] Mediation is the method of finding this middle way.[13] Consequently, as Confucius emphasizes, the moral man does not indulge in litigation. He does not settle disputes by resort to codes. Also, no dispute is settled until both parties, working through a mediator, are satisfied.[14] Expressed in musical terms, the moral man looks to the drone rather than to any determinate ordering of the melody for the solution of his intrapersonal legal and social problems.

There are, however, certain sensed objects and relationships which seem, to most people in a non-technological society, to exist, the same for all perceivers. At this point their epistemology shifts from radical empiricism to naïve realism. These realistic sensed objects and relationships are the biological objects and their heredity of a natural-history, descriptive biology. One basic rule governs their sequence through time. No child exists without parents. From this scientific law of sensed biological human life, there arises the basic, determinate, ethical rule and legal norm of a non-technological society—the tie of the family and the priority of the family to the individual. In Confucianism this is called "filial piety." Objectively, it appears as the patriarchal or matriarchal joint family.[15] From this natural-history, biological science of man, there arises the social ethics and codified law of what Sir Henry S. Maine called the "law of status." [16]

In such a society men are not equal before the law. Daughters do not inherit equally with sons, nor do the younger sons inherit equally with the eldest son. Nor are people of a different family or a different hereditary stock, or tribe, treated with the same moral rules that one uses for the members of one's own family or of one's own tribe or nation.

Having based one's social ethics and law in this manner on the sensed objects of natural-history biology, the sensed color of the skin of people becomes important ethically. Consequently, the idea that a good society has nothing to do with differences in color of skin is foreign to the ethics of a non-technological society. In classical Hinduism, for example, the word for caste is the word for color. Furthermore, in the Hindu *Laws of Manu* the penalty for the same crime differs, if the offender is of one caste, from what it would be if he belonged to a different caste.[17] The classical Chinese called all other people "barbarians." The ancient Hebrews, Greeks and Romans, in the ethics of their patriarchal law of status, judged similarly.

Since the family has a head, so the groups of families in the tribe and the nation tend to have a head. Hence, the political ethics of a non-technological society is hierarchical and monarchical. The codes of a law of status express these familial, tribal, hierarchical and regal relationships in common-sense terms.

It is to be remembered, however, that in non-technological societies the ethics of the law of status is combined with the ethics of the law of mediation. Moreover, the former is usually regarded as a second best, to be followed only in the middle stage of life when the family is being bred and nurtured and the state is being governed. Before this "householder stage," as the Hindus call it,[18] and afterwards, the ethics of mediation, of the musical drone and of the all-embracing formlessness take over.

Considered by itself, apart from the ethics of the law of status, the ethics of mediation is democratic rather than hierarchical and regal. This is the case because the *chit*-Nirvana consciousness, being undifferentiated, is the same in all men. Actually, however, even in the Buddhist society of Burma or Thailand, in which there is no hierarchal ordering of the patriarchal families according to caste, there is nevertheless a king. This is achieved in Buddhist Burma and Thailand by combining the raj, the law of status codes, and the literary epics of Hinduism with Buddhism.[19] It is this combination of the hierarchical ethics of the family of a naïvely realistic, natural-history, biological science and the ethics of equality and mediation of a radically empirical science that gives a non-technological civilization its codified law of status, expressed in common-sense terms, with its legal and hierarchical social values combined with a basic theory of the ultimate or true self which is egalitarian and democratic.[20]

We have already come upon these values by way of contrast in connection with the values of a non-technological society. We noted also that the differentiating character of a technological society is that, in it, man knows himself and nature in terms of the unsensed, indirectly verified, axiomatically constructed entities and relations of mathematical physics. This frees scientific objects and their relations from sensed properties, thereby giving determinate public meanings the same for all men. It also frees ethical and legal norms from the necessity of being expressed in terms of the sensed qualities. This frees moral and legal man from a definition of his ethical values in terms of the color of his skin and the biological stock of his family or his tribe. Forthwith, the law of status is replaced by the law of contract. Thereby, meaning is given for the thesis that moral, legal and political man is not family or tribal man but universal man.

This ethics of the law of contract generates a completely new ethics of inheritance in which inheritance rights are equal for all offspring regardless of sex or differences in age. It gives rise also to a new philosophy of education—that of equal opportunity for all. It also generates a completely new concept of the basis of political and moral obligation.

In the social ethics of the law of status of a non-technological society, the sanction for the legal codes is in the fact of one's birth within the family and in the status relationship of one's family within the tribe or the nation. The authority for such a law and the obligations to abide by it have nothing to do with the consent of those who were born into it. As Sir Robert Filmer pointed out in his *Patriarcha*,[21] the younger sons have never given their consent to the inheritance of the family manor house and the entire family estate by the eldest son; nor have the patriarchal families lower in the social hierarchy ever given their consent to the privileged social positions and governmental powers enjoyed by the patriarchal families near the top of the hierarchy and the royal family at the top.

In the ethics of the law of contract of a technological society, consent, however, is of the essence. Such a law, being axiomatically constructed and hence hypothetical, has no validity, obviously, unless those to whom it is applied give their consent. This is precisely why it is called the law of contract. In a contract, nothing is binding unless the parties to the contract have consented to accept it. Furthermore, with respect to consent, and hence with respect to the obligation to obey any law of contract, all men are born free and equal. It is in this legal and contractual sense of the authority of a law resting upon consent, and not in the biological sense, that the Declaration of Independence speaks the truth when it asserts that "all men are created equal." The frequent attempts, therefore, to discredit the Declaration of Independence by pointing to the biological, psychological and economic inequalities of men at the time of their birth is quite beside the point. Such criticism confuses the epistemological and natural-history scientific basis of the ethics of the law of status of a non-technological society with the different epistemological and scientific basis of the ethics of the law of contract of a technological civilization.

The epistemology of the axiomatically constructed, scientific knowledge of a technological society has one other cultural consequence. Being deductively formulated by means of imageless concepts by postulation, it defines inductively sensed, different classes of things in terms of a single class of common, elementary scientific objects. This is but another way of saying that it replaces ethical groups of men, defined in terms of differences in color of skin or of familial and tribal heredity, with the universal moral man of the law of contract.

The very prevalent notion, therefore, that technological society has destroyed human values is quite erroneous. Through the law of contract, which entails the definition of moral authority in terms of consent rather than in terms of family or tribal status, it generates the ethics and politics of democracy. Furthermore, not merely its technological instruments and their capacity to lift the standard of living of the masses but also its democratic ethics of its law of contract have captured the imaginations and the loyalty of the masses of men even in non-technological societies. This is why they are demanding today that they be treated equally before the law in education and politics regardless of their color of skin. When they demand this, they are rejecting the familial, hierarchical and regal ethics of their own traditional law-of-status societies.

An equally significant shift occurs in aesthetic values with the transition from a non-technological to a technological society. The standard for measuring the sequence of musical sounds in the music of a non-technological society has been noted to be the drone. The music of a technological society drops the drone as its standard. In its place it puts the ratios of the deductively formulated, mathematical acoustics of the Greek Pythagoreans and Democritus. But these relations for ordering the sounds of the melody are not sensed. They are intellectually grasped, axiomatically constructed relations. Furthermore, mathematical physics works with an infinitely extending, linear theory of time instead of with the sensed finite cyclical theory of time. This automatically frees the music of a technological society, not merely from the drone, but also from a cyclical, temporal ordering of the melody.

But if this melodic ordering is to be an order rather than a chaos, some relation must govern it. The ratios and uniform, axiomatically constructed flow of time define this ordering. With such intellectual ordering, harmony and counterpoint as well as melody can enter in. For all this, however, there must be a precise musical scale. Otherwise, again, there would be no standard, and the simultaneous ordering of sounds in harmony and counterpoint would become chaotic, as would also the uniform, temporal ordering of sound in melody. Such a music no longer describes cyclical sequences of perishing particulars against the tension created by the all-embracing, dynamic formlessness of the drone. Instead, the sensuous materials are subjected to a mathematically formal and intellectually prescribed logos of proportion and perfection. Thus it is that there arises in a technological society a new concept of the beautiful.

This more formal intellectual concept of the beautiful appeared first in the music of ancient Greece. It actualized new formal potentialities of itself with Palestrina and came to some of its richest formal fulfillments in Bach and in Beethoven.

The parallel transformation of aesthetic values appears in painting. For all its virtues, the painting of a non-technological society, when seen from the standpoint of classical Western art, is flat. Once, however, the artist grasps the intellectual, three-dimensional, mathematical proportions of the imageless axiomatically constructed Greek geometry of solids, the flat type of painting starts moving into the round. Thence arises Greek sculpture, with a beautiful sense of geometrical proportion, but with its lack of emotive, dynamic beauty, when viewed from the standpoint of the art of the Oriental, all-embracing, ineffable, infinite formlessness. With the coming of axiomatically constructed geometrical optics, the logos of the perspective combines with the logos of the regular solids to generate the painting of the giants of the Renaissance—Leonardo, Raphael and Michelangelo. This, again, is an intellectually guided aesthetic of the beautiful.

It is interesting to note that, when with Berkeley and Hume modern thinking returned to the epistemology of radical empiricism of a non-technological society, concomitantly, impressionistic painting arises in which blurred, vivid, sensuous differentiations become the subject matter of the painter, and the axiomatically guided, mathematical laws of perspective and of solid geometry drop out of his technique. The music of Debussy is a corresponding development in the aesthetics of modern Western music.

It is to be remembered, however, that for a period of over a thousand years, following the decline of the mathematical physics of

Pythagoras, Democritus, Eudoxus and Plato, Aristotle's physics dominated the Islamic and the Western world. This physics is partially a mathematical physicist's physics, since Aristotle had an axiomatically constructed geometry and astronomy. In his physics of terrestrial objects, however, he reverted to the epistemology of naïve realism, defining the physical and chemical elements in terms of their sensed qualities. Water, as previously noted, was defined as anything which one senses as wet and cold. This gave Aristotle's ethics and politics a law-of-contract form with a law-of-status terrestrial content.

The consequence was that the law of contract, as initially formulated by the Stoic Romans and accepted down to modern times, was in considerable part filled in with law-of-status content. This law-of-status content of a law of contract still dominates Roman Catholic and Episcopal thinking as formulated in Aristotelian epistemological and metaphysical terms by St. Thomas and by Thomas Hooker. This type of law of contract with law-of-status content went into the South through the First Families of Virginia, as Laslett has recently demonstrated.[22]

It was not, therefore, until Galilei and Newton returned Western physical science to an axiomatically constructed physics of terrestrial as well as astronomical objects that it was possible for Western man to have, for the first time, a law-of-contract ethics with a law-of-contract content. This happened when Jefferson, in writing the Declaration of Independence and insisting upon the Bill of Rights of the American Constitution, followed Locke's theory of natural law and the physics of Newton rather than Hooker, St. Thomas and Aristotle.

Immediately, a technological society burst forth with new vigor and new moral content. Also, the patriarchal, hierarchical and regal values of a non-technological society were replaced in the content of the law of contract by the egalitarian and democratic values of a purely technological society. Locke and Newton had replaced Hooker, St. Thomas and Aristotle in the specification of the content of the ethics of a law of contract. This is what Jefferson meant when he wrote that Bacon, Locke and Newton were his gods and affirmed that the United States was creating a political society which is unique in the history of the world.[23]

The axiomatically constructed terrestrial and celestial physics of Galilei and Newton has been replaced, however, by that of Einstein, Planck, Schroedinger and Dirac. The former physics, while axiomatically constructed, was one, like that of the Greeks, which could be imaginatively envisaged in terms of geometrical models. This is not true of the theory of relativity or of quantum mechanics. Nature as known through contemporary, axiomatically constructed, indirectly verified, deductively formulated theory not only cannot be sensed; it cannot even be imagined. The aesthetic implications of this characteristic of our contemporary technological society are already upon us. Both art and architecture have been released not merely from geometrical optics and its laws of perspectives but also from the geometrical models of Euclid's regular solids. The result in the realms of aesthetics is abstractionism and functionalism in both painting and architecture. Houses and business buildings need no longer be rigidly rectangular. The roofs of public buildings do not have to be spherical domes modeled on the circles and spheres of Euclid. Music can break loose from the restriction of ratios. Giedion, Frank Lloyd Wright and Le Corbusier; Orozco, Picasso and Kandinski are already here.[24] With them also have come the tools and the unprecedented high standard of living of a technological society. By means of the deeper understanding of nature and the more powerful instruments which imageless axiomatically constructed knowledge gives man, the work of the world and even its most difficult mental calculations are being lifted from the shoulders and the brains of men. Thus to moral, legal and political equality is being added the possibility of economic equality.

But with these aesthetic, ethical, legal, economic and even religious values of a technological society, rooted as they are in the logos of an axiomatically constructed, intellectually known relatedness, there has also come a price and a problem. The basing of human relations on the hypothetically constructed constitutions of the law of contract has opened up the possibility of more than one constitution and the actuality of incompatible constitutions. In this, as well as in the conflict between the values of technological and non-technological societies, the ideological problems and conflicts of the contemporary world find their political origin and their basis. It is of the essence of a contractually constructed constitution that it defines a social and ethical utopia. Utopias tend to turn themselves into crusades. When these crusades of a technological society become armed with its instrument, the atomic bomb, the possibilities are appalling. This is why the members of technological societies are filled today with both high hopes and deep fears. To understand the source of these fears is to discover the way to construct an international law which will give mankind the values of a technological society without its dangers.[25]

There is a second price which one pays for a technological civilization. Its traditional fault arises from the tendency to take the emotively moving, immediately sensed, radically empirical man and world, ablaze with aesthetic fragrances, colors and sounds as a bare starting point, to be dismissed as mere appearance when the axiomatically constructed, scientific objects and their relations are obtained and the ethics of its democratic law of contract is constitutionally formulated. This has created a modern man who has become so absorbed by the intellectual imagination, its technological tools and its abstract legal codes that he is starved emotionally and with respect to aesthetic immediacy. Out of this half-man has come the crowds of people housed in the rigidly, rectangularly ordered streets and dull gray buildings and slums of our huge cities. No one with aesthetic sensitivity to the immediacy of things and to the emotions within himself could ever have created or have tolerated such a thing. This is the aesthetic and emotive paradox of a technological society. Need one wonder that such a modern man, for all his abstract art, democratic laws and effective tools, is a frustrated, even often a schizophrenic individual?

But the ethics and aesthetics of a non-technological society have their paradox also. Notwithstanding the affection of its folk for trees and all other creatures of "Mother Earth," its people, owing to their emphasis on family values, tend to produce more people than their instruments or their natural resources enable them to provide for. The consequence is, notwithstanding their affection for trees, that they eat the green twigs of the trees in order to live. In this way China has become denuded of its forests, and the rich top soil of its "Mother Earth" has been washed into the sea. The result is, not merely that millions upon millions of its trees have been destroyed, never to be replaced, thereby violating the cosmic equilibrium, but also that millions of its people die each year by starvation. The story of the non-technological civilization of India is similar. Owing to prolific breeding and for want of food, its people have turned hundreds of thousands of square miles of its once-forested or food-producing territory, extending from south of the Ganges Valley to the southern portion of the peninsula, into almost a desert. Egypt, where the situation and the cure are even more hopeless, tells the same story. This is the paradox of the ethics and the tools of a non-technological civilization.

The resolution of both paradoxes would seem to be clear. To this resolution, moreover, the analysis of the philosophy of contemporary mathematical physics is now taking careful thinkers in our contemporary technological society. A full account of knowing in even mathematical physics reveals the irreducibility and the ultimacy of both the aesthetically immediate, with its all-embracing formlessness, and the axiomatically constructed.[26] Clearly, it is by specifying the relation between these two components of complete human knowledge, supplementing the one with the other, that the paradoxes of the traditional technological and the traditional non-technological civilizations are to be resolved.

Whitehead has worked out in great detail one way in which this can be done.[27] The writer has sketched another.[28] Contemporary sociological jurisprudence demonstrates also that an effective law for the contemporary world must root itself in the living beliefs, practices and values of its non-technological as well as its technological societies.[29] Recently, the artist Rudolf Ray, born and reared in the technological society of the West, has discovered the art of the all-embracing formlessness of a non-technological society. The scientific, philosophical, legal and aesthetic insights necessary to reconcile and preserve both types of civilization appear, therefore, to be at hand. In Chapter 19 we shall be concerned with the political art of merging them.

15

The Present and Likely Future Success of the Soviet Union

The first thing to realize about this modern nation and the culture which it would produce throughout the entire world is that its set of elementary concepts and universal propositions is defined by Continental Rationalistic modern philosophy stemming from Descartes, Newton, Leibniz and Kant, rather than by British empirical and American pragmatic philosophy which derives from Bacon, Newton, Locke, Berkeley, Hume, Mill, Bentham, Austin, Peirce, James and Dewey. When this Continental Rationalistic modern philosophy came into the mind of the Newtonian-minded mathematical physicist Kant in Königsberg and was combined there with British empirical modern philosophy after the latter had passed through the mind of Hume, modern mathematical physics was given an idealistic epistemological interpretation as was modern ethical, legal and political language. According to this idealistic epistemological meaning of any concept in any domain of human thought whatever, all assertions, whether they be in the non-normatively worded experimentally verified theories of the natural sciences (*Naturwissenschaften*) or in the normatively worded moral, legal, political, aesthetic and religious theories of the cultural sciences (*Geistenwissenschaften*), are the products of two different kinds of concepts, one of which obtains its meaning purely empirically by reference to data given by the senses or introspected, the other of which is implicit in the scientist or common-sense man as knower and brought by him to the empirical data. The former type of concept and the portion of human knowledge to which it referred, Kant called *"a posteriori"*; the latter type of concept and its theoretically introduced component of knowledge he called *"a priori."* Kant's *a posteriori* concepts are equivalent to what we in Part I called "concepts by intuition." They are concepts which find their entire meaning by empirical reference to directly sensed, introspected or experienced data. The concepts of Locke's *Essay Concerning Human Understanding* and all the concepts in Hume's philosophy and in the legal positivist's theory of economics, politics and law are of this concept by intuition or Kantian *a posteriori* type. In this sense Kant was as much a British radically empirical philosopher as are all modern Anglo-American empirical thinkers.

But in addition to the *a posteriori* concepts by intuition of British empirical philosophy there are also, as was shown in Chapter 2, imageless, formally and mathematically constructed theoretical concepts in modern experimentally verified natural science which do not reduce to and cannot be defined in terms of *a posteriori* sensory or introspected data. In short, there are concepts by postulation which are concepts by intellection as well as the *a posteriori* concepts by intuition. Kant, who was a mathematical physicist of notable competence before he turned to the philosophical analysis of the abstract nouns in Newton's mechanics, was the first modern scientist and philosopher to see this clearly. The only difference between Kant and contemporary philosophical analyses of the theories of modern mathematical physics is that Kant regarded these non-empirically given, cognitively meaningful concepts of mathematical physics, which are creatively added to the scientist's directly sensed data by the theoretical scientist himself, to be *categorically a priori;* whereas we now know, for reasons which were not so evident in Kant's day, that they are merely hypothetically *a priori.*[1] In other words, the non-empirically definable, theoretically meaningful concepts of mathematical physics are, as Einstein emphasized,[2] speculatively introduced formal constructs, i.e., concepts by postulation that are concepts by intellection, which cannot be verified directly since what they refer to is not directly observable and which, consequently, have to be tested empirically via their deduced theorems which are epistemically correlated with directly inspectable *a posteriori* data. They are not categorical necessities as Kant supposed.

The latter supposition led him to the conclusion that the elementary non-empirical, theoretically introduced concepts of mathematical physics do not refer to a realistic epistemological object of knowledge, but are instead necessities of human thought, brought by the scientist as knower to the *a posteriori* data given empirically through the senses or introspectively. This thesis is the idealistic theory of conceptual meaning.

Since all meanings were, for Kant, of this character, words such as "good," "ought," "right" and "political obligation" in the normative sciences of ethics, law and politics have to be also. They contain their imageless, formal, theoretically introduced type of meaning as well as their perceptual *a posteriori* references. With respect to the latter thesis, Kant was correct. As Chapter 18 will show, modern nations are the theoretic contractual constructs of Western legal science.

Kant observed also that theoretically constructed knowledge is always characterized by its treatment of any individual particular fact or entity as an instance of a universal law. Applied to morality and assuming, as Kant did, that the formal, theoretically constructed factor in knowledge is categorical, this gives Kant's famous categorical imperative: Act as if one were an instance of a universal law the same for all men.

Unfortunately any statement of this principle in ordinary prose, such as that of the last sentence or of Kant's German Aryan language, is ambiguous. Such prose fails to make it unequivocally clear that the universal validity for all people applies not merely to the law as a whole but also to its substantive content and hence rules out some universal laws as immoral and illegal even when they are passed by the majority. We shall find in Chapter 18 that the difference between a modern legal and political system whose norms are those of a "free democracy" and one whose norms are those of a dictatorship of either the political executive or the majority in the legislature turns around this point. Since Kant lived at Königsberg but a few miles from St. Petersburg and his writings had a prodigious effect upon the modern Eastern European as well as the Prussian German educational system, this ambiguous way of thinking about "democracy" became epistemically trapped in every modern-minded Russian and German brain a century and one-half before Lenin came upon the scene.

In addition, Kant left the Central and Eastern modern European mind with a gulf between its natural science and its cultural and moral philosophy. The first effect of this was German Romantic philosophy and its release of moral and normative political man from all cognitively verifiable control, thereby giving rise to German, Polish and Russian Romanticism, Fichtean voluntarism and the later Hitlerian arbitrarily willful demands of the tribally pure German *Volk*. From this post-Kantian Romanticism stems much of contemporary antiscientific humanism throughout the Anglo-American world, as well as the prevalent notion that science is neutral if not evil with respect to human values.

The Central and Eastern European reaction to this dogmatic anti-cognitive voluntaristic Romanticism came with Hegel who again brought the Central and Eastern European modern mind under thoughtful and logical control by keeping Kant's idealistic epistemology but replacing his logic of identity with the dialectical logic of negation which he (Hegel) erroneously concluded to be causally deterministic, thereby fallaciously identifying the "ought" for evaluating any correctly described humanistic or political "is" with the dialectically deterministic historical evolution of that "is." Forthwith both evolutionary thinking and evaluative political policy making became dialectically deterministic for modern-minded Prussian Germans, Poles and Russians alike.

The result was the basic epistemically trapped universal proposition common to (a) the Prussian German Kantian-Hegelian idealistic *Kultur* of the Kaiser's pre-World War I Germany, (b) pre-World War II modern Poland and Russia and (c) Marxist post-World War I Bolshevik Soviet Russia. This proposition is that not merely every concept of the human scientific knower and normative evaluator in every domain of conceptual discourse whatever, but also the evolutionary facts of both nature and culture are under the deterministic lawful control of a dialectically deterministic logic and "law of history" which prescribes the second-order factual, cultural and political "is" that ought to be and hence, with respect to which, the assent of individuals is irrelevant. This is the first elementary universal proposition of both Hegelian idealistic and Marxist materialistic natural, humanistic and political philosophy. It was common to the thinking of most modern-educated Prussian Germans, Poles and

Russians long before the middle of the nineteenth century when Marx formulated his philosophy.

Furthermore, even in that portion of modern French and Continental European democracy which was non-Cartesian, non-Kantian and non-Hegelian, the goal-value ideal norm of free democrats was not defined by Locke. He, like Jefferson who followed him, would have had a democracy protecting the rights of minority groups and dissenters against the tyranny of the legislative and political statutes of the majority with respect to religion and civil liberties. Instead, the ideal political goal-value philosophy was that of Rousseau and his political practitioners, who brought about the French Revolution and who are represented in French politics today by the misnamed political party called the "Radical Socialists." According to this Rousseauian philosophy of democracy, to dissent from the majority will is to behave illegally, unjustly and immorally. Needless to say, Germany, as well as France, and pre-Marxist Russia, as well as Marx, took over this Rousseauian idea of democracy.

This is one reason why the French Revolution was accompanied by so much bloodshed and terror compared to either the democratic revolution in England or that in the United States. It is also one of the major reasons why it is easier for a dictator to receive popular support in any Continental European nation than is the case in the Anglo-American cultural world or in the Scandinavian nations which, with the partial exception of Sweden, are much more influenced by the British empirical modern philosophy of the early Locke than they are by Continental European early Rousseauian democracy or by Cartesian, Kantian and later Hegelian rationalism.

Consequently, Marx in the middle of the nineteenth century and Lenin later in the midst of World War I could take for granted this earlier inclination to the repression of dissenting opinion which is common to Continental European political theory and practice generally. Also, in the Continental European cultures to the east of the Rhine he could take for granted the Hegelian dialectically logical theory of evolution in both natural and normative cultural social institutions. Whereas the defeat of the Kaiser in World War I ended Hegelian dialectical thinking in top political decision-making posts in Germany, Czechoslovakia and Western Continental Europe, it did not end such thinking in traditional Russia, or, in all likelihood, in Poland.

One has but to read Trotsky's autobiography, describing the content of his education from the primary grades through his graduation from the University of Odessa in the Ukraine, to realize that not merely the curriculum contained Continental Rationalistic mathematical physics and post-Kantian German philosophy, but also that many of his teachers in Russia were Germans and Russians who had studied in the University of Berlin which until the end of World War I was dominated by the philosophy of Hegel.

The prevalent recent assumption in the United States, therefore, that only the Americans could be first-rate in industrial engineering and military weapons and that the Soviet Russians are doomed to be bunglers, defeated by their Marxist philosophy, could never have entered the mind of anyone who looked at the present Soviet Union or the Russian educational system which Lenin inherited in World War I with the methods of descriptive philosophical anthropology. Seen with this method, it is the Americans and even the British who are far more likely to end up with third-rate technology and military engineering, since British empirical and American pragmatic philosophy do not prepare the American or the British mind to appreciate the importance of theoretically mathematical, as distinct from radically empirical pragmatic thinking in either science or philosophy or in effective practical politics and engineering. It is only a slight exaggeration to say that the United States has had but one first-rate American-born theoretical physicist who has discovered a major formally constructed mathematical physical theory comparable to the theories of Newton, Maxwell, Einstein, Schroedinger and Heisenberg. This American theoretically-minded mathematical physicist is Willard Gibbs. Without the aid of Continental European Jews, who appreciate the importance of theory as well as observation and experiment in modern mathematical physics and who came to the American continent, thanks largely to Hitler, the United States interstellar satellites would in all probability be even more inferior to those of the Russians than is now the case. The influence of Einstein upon President Franklin D. Roosevelt's decision to make an atomic bomb was noted in Chapter 9.

What must not be forgotten is that to be modern-minded in the sense of any Continental Western, Central or Eastern European means to share the elementary concepts and postulates of Continental Rationalistic modern philosophy beginning with Descartes, Leibniz and Kant, all of whom were mathematical physicists. Consequently, most people in these nations of Western, Central and Soviet Union Europe have an appreciation of the primacy of theory, as well as of facts in science and politics, which most Anglo-Americans whose modern culture embodies the assumptions of merely British empirical and American pragmatic practical philosophy do not fully appreciate.

Russian mathematicians and engineers were outstanding even before World War I. The mathematician who developed the final formula for most neatly stating Einstein's special theory of relativity discovered in 1905 was a Russian named Hermann Minkowski. The mathematical astronomer who gave the most systematic solution of the problems of relativistic cosmology arising from Einstein's general theory of relativity was another Eastern European named Friedmann. Similarly in law, some of the outstanding legal philosophers and theorists in the pre-World War I Western world were Russians such as Korkunov, Vinogradoff and Petrazycki. The Harvard sociologist Pitirim A. Sorokin studied law in St. Petersburg under Petrazycki who was his most influential teacher before he became a sociologist. England had no legal theorist until John Austin in the mid-nineteenth century. After Wythe and Jefferson, America had none until the appearance of Roscoe Pound in this century. Furthermore, long before the origin of the modern world, two things went into Russia from Constantinople. The first was Greek Orthodox Christianity; the second was the contractual legal science of Stoic Rome which came to its most perfect codified formulation under Justinian.

All this, therefore, by way of preparation for a technology derived from the precise theory of mathematical physics and a contractual legal and political system with modern philosophical content, Lenin had to start with when, in the midst of World War I, he received his opportunity, thanks in considerable fact to the Kaiser's German generals, to overthrow the tsarist regime and reconstruct Russian society in terms of Marxist-Hegelian dialectically materialistic modern philosophy instead of Hegelian dialectically idealistic modern goal-value philosophy. Also, many decades previously a German Christian theologian named Feuerbach had made the Germanic Eastern European world aware of the second elementary universal proposition, the neurological epistemic correlate of which is epistemically trapped in every clearheaded and dedicated Marxist Communist's brain. This second postulate is the Feuerbachian naïve realistic epistemological thesis that any concept whatever in any domain of human experience or discourse refers for its meaning to a conscious mental substance or to unconscious material substances, the scientific defining properties of which are directly introspected or sensed. The early British empirical mathematical scientist and philosopher John Locke held this theory also. If it be true, then all Marx had to do was to follow the materialistic Hobbes and the power politicians generally by conveniently ignoring consciousness and the mental substances in order to be left with immediately sensed materialism as the whole truth in science, philosophy, common sense and politics. Moreover, assuming the *naïvely* realistic Feuerbachian postulate, this directly sensed materialism is supposedly known to be true with absolute certainty by direct observation. This undoubtedly was covertly at least in their minds when many Russian students, when discussing non-political subjects such as painting or literature with the visiting Yale student Mr. K. R. Dove, in the summer of 1959, always passed judgment as if the Marxist conception of the person and of politics were plain common sense. Were the naïvely realistic epistemological theory of conceptual meaning true, rather than the confused mixed worlds-of-discourse nonsense which Part I has shown it to be, the judgment of these Russian students would be correct. For if the qualities, which we directly sense and know with certainty are, as naïve realism assumes, the permanent predicates of unconscious materialistic substances, then we know the substances with the same certainty that characterizes our knowledge of immediately sensed colors, memories, shapes, pushes and pulls.

In any event Lenin's political decision with respect to the educational curriculum of the Russian universities and the "trapped universals" in the mind and brains of all modern-minded Russians that he inherited near the end of World War I was relatively easy to make. He had merely to leave the Hegelian dialectically deterministic theory of nature and social evolution in precisely the position of the most basic elementary postulate that it had enjoyed previously under the non-Communistic modern-minded Russians, keep the previous idea of the importance of mathematical physics and contractual legal theory in the curriculum and merely change its content by removing the Kantian idealistic epistemological postulate concerning the meaning of all concepts from its previous place of primary importance, to put in its stead the naïve realistic premise which, owing to Feuerbach, was already in modern German, Polish and Russian minds, and in most peasants' minds, while also being careful, like the free democratic power politicians, to mention only the material substances of this naïve realism. No brainwashing of all the previously trapped universals was necessary.

Forthwith, the economic value of any material object or quantity of muscular labor became defined materialistically in terms of the number of foot-pounds of physical work that went into it. Moreover, this materialistic labor theory of economic science of Marx and his Communists derives not merely from the naïve realistic epistemology of Feuerbach but also from the material substance portion of the naïve realistic epistemology of the earlier John Locke. In fact, Marx learned the labor theory of economic value quite independently of Feuerbach from the English economist Ricardo who, in turn, had taken it over from Locke.

Before he died, John Locke saw the error in his earlier naïve realistic epistemological theory of conscious mental substances, each conceived as a blank tablet, and of unconscious material substances which in the aggregate at least was supposedly directly sensed. The consequence was that in his last major work, the *Essay Concerning Human Understanding,* he rejected his earlier naïve realistic epistemology with its nonsensical mixed worlds of discourse, causally interacting material and mental substances for the radically empirical epistemological thesis that all concepts in natural or normative subjects derive from ideas given solely through the senses. This conclusion followed also logically from his earlier naïve realistic theory of the mental substance as a blank tablet. Obviously for such a mind there can be no ideas except as the senses write them on each person's otherwise blank atomic consciousness, and the imagination compounds the simple ideas to derive defined ideas.

Berkeley and Hume then made it clear that since we do not sense or introspect the idea of substance and also do not introspect or sense either our consciousness or our sensed images as persistently fastened as predicates to the inside of a mental substance or to the outside of a material substance, both the materialist's thesis that we directly sense material substances and the spiritualist's thesis that we directly introspect mental substances is not merely empirically false but also theoretically meaningless. Forthwith the labor theory of economic value which the earlier naïvely realistic epistemology of Locke generated and which is the elementary postulate of Marxist Communist economic science became replaced by the radically empirical psychological theory of economic value which is the elementary postulate of the modern free world's economic science and economic policy making.

The latter postulate is that the economic value of any object is determined not by the physicist's foot-pounds of work that went into its manufacture, but by its relation to the psychological wants of individual particular people for the object, relative to the supply. That this radically empirical, introspective psychological philosophy of economic science, rather than the Marxist Communistic naïve realistic materialistic labor philosophy of economic science, is the correct one is cognitively confirmed by the fact that all the foot-pounds of physical work under heaven can go into the manufacturing of an object, yet if no one introspectively wants it, it is economically valueless.

This means that there is no such thing as an objective economic fact or the "economic factor." There are merely the private, introspective psychological wants of particular individual people for non-economic facts. Hence, economics is an introspective, psychological science; a science whose subject matter centers in the relation between objects or facts qua fact and particular people's introspective psychological wantings of those objects or facts. Hence, economics is not a materialistic science.

In fact, there is no such materialistic science even in mathematical physics, for what the latter science is talking about, as was shown in Part I, is not a directly sensed public material substance or aggregates of such substances possessing as accidental or essential predicates the colors, shapes, pushes and pulls which one senses. Otherwise, the colors, warmths and the simultaneity of the spatially separated events which we directly sense would not vary from one frame of reference to another, from observer to observer on the same frame of reference, or even from one sense organ to another of the same observer. Instead, as shown in Chapter 3, what one knows in mathematical physics is an imageless, theoretically conceived relatedness whose Euclidian or other scientific properties are specified by the imageless, formal properties of a particular set of symbolic logically or mathematically constructed postulates. Moreover, the objects and events in the theoretically known and indirectly confirmed imageless logically realistic relatedness, are, therefore, related to the sensed objects, events, pushes and pulls which, being immediately experienced, are in the concept by intuition, radically empirical epistemological mode of discourse, by relations that have to be epistemic in character, as Part I has shown.

In all likelihood, it was the naïve realistic confused notion that radically empirically sensed colors, warmth, pushes and pulls are the predicates of equally directly sensed realistic epistemological substances which led the free democratic Hobbesian power politicians and the Hegelian and Marxist dialectical determinists to confuse logic which, be it dialectical or that of identity, has to do with relations between propositions about facts, with metaphysical pushes, pulls and obligations in the facts themselves. Medieval Aristotelians, Jews, Muslims and Roman Catholic or Filmerian Protestant Christians, with their radically empirically introspected final cause conceived to be fastened as a predicate to the interior of even non-teleologically mechanical stones and planets, commit the same confused worlds-of-discourse nonsense, again due to their overt and covert naïve realistic theory of conceptual meaning. In any event, the set of cognitively testable elementary epistemological, logical and evolutionary postulates of the Marxist Communist philosophy of intrinsic political goal values is not merely empirically false but also mixed worlds-of-discourse nonsense so far as the Feuerbachian naïve realistic materialism and its use of dialectical logic to push around the first-order facts of nature, the second-order facts of cultural and political history and the political obligations of the Communistic politician's citizens, are concerned.

In *de facto* politics, however, it is not the truth or falsity of what a group of politicians or their followers believe that is decisive, but the fact that they believe it. As Part I has shown, there are no politicians, citizens or nations except as individual people have assented and committed themselves to particular, purportedly meaningful, elementary concepts and postulates, the epistemic correlates of which are trapped in their brains as inner targets that condition their behavior and living-law customs. Whether the elemental postulate set be true or false, cognitive or non-cognitive, or even confused mixed worlds-of-discourse nonsense, the one-one epistemic neurological correlates that are the inner, self-contained target of that person's nervous system, mechanically inhibit or reinforce motor neural firings to condition that person's behavior accordingly. Hence, until the common shared set of primitive postulates of the political leaders of any nation, required to be learned by every student in the educational system, are changed openly and overtly in ways that any foreign ambassador on the spot can not avoid knowing, even if he be a power politician, it follows of teleologically mechanical, behavioristic psychological necessity that that nation will behave according to that particular political philosophy. This is especially true if there is no opposition political party and no other political philosophy is allowed to be taught.

Some important political predictions follow with respect to whether Premier Khrushchev's Soviet Union is a different Soviet Union in its foreign policy for peace than that of his predecessors. In answering this very important present political question, what must not be overlooked is that the application, earlier in this chapter, of the descriptive method of philosophical anthropology to the modern culture of Central and Eastern Europe shows that prior to the Bolshevik Revolution the minds of Russian students, university alumni and secondary-school students as well as university teachers were not filled with non-Conformist Protestant or secular Anglo-American British empirical or pragmatic free democratic "trapped universals." Instead, every "trapped universal" that is in any Marxist East German, modern Polish or modern Russian Communist mind and brain today was in the minds of the modern-educated German, Polish, Russian students and teachers before Marx wrote his philosophical treatises in the middle of the last century. Let it be repeated again: *All that the Marxist Bolshevik Lenin had to do near the end of World War I when he took over absolute political control of the entire traditional modern Russian educational system was to re-shuffle slightly the set of postulates already epistemically trapped in the students' and the elder modern-minded Russians', Poles' and East Prussians' brains by substituting the naïve realistic epistemology of their own German Feuerbach for the idealistic epistemology of their own East Prussian Kant, while keeping as the most basic epistemically trapped universal proposition of all Hegel's dialectically logical deterministic theory of the evolution of both natural objects and social institutions.*

That the modern Russian or Polish mind, during the century and one half preceding World War I, was as German as the German mind is not surprising. Hegel flourished in Berlin and Kant in Königsberg, which is nearer Leningrad than it is to Berlin, and much nearer to Warsaw and Moscow than it is to John Locke's mental substance-minded London or Hume's Edinburgh, to say nothing about Thomas Jefferson's Monticello. The philosophically anthropological reason for Lenin's immediate and intermediate-run success in modernizing Russia with Marxist philosophical goal values and methods should now be clear.

The likely future success of the present Soviet leaders in holding their people with them is equally clear. There is not one shred of objective evidence that any brainwashing of the students or their elders has occurred in the Soviet Union to untrap the Hegelian-Feuerbachian-Marxist reshuffle of old "trapped universals" and replace them with the Anglo-American free democratic universals, to say nothing about the Tibetan Buddhist or the Gandhian Hindu mediational and pacifistic concepts by intuition. To suppose that a popular revolt in Russia is likely in the foreseeable future is, therefore, to indulge in the most fanciful daydreaming. This is true whether the one who indulges himself be the late Secretary of State Dulles with his "roll-back" crusade, the late Senator McCarthy, any American businessman or banker who visits Russia or anyone who criticized Dulles because of his well-warranted skepticism concerning the Communistic politicians' smiles and offers of peace. Moreover, there is positive evidence that the present students, at least, in the Soviet Union, know what the Soviet Marxist Communistic set of trapped universals is and find that it gives them a purpose and a satisfaction which they do not see students from or people in the non-Communistic West enjoying.

In the summer of 1959, Mr. K. R. Dove visited many larger and smaller cities of the Soviet Union as a member of the Yale Russian Chorus. This group made it their practice to assemble in the evening in parks or on city squares where they gave their impromptu concerts of American and Russian folk songs. Immediately many people and especially Russian students flocked around them. When the singing ended, the American and Russian students talked freely and frankly to one another about American and Soviet cultural life, economic theory and political structures. Mr. Dove reports the following findings: (1) Wherever he went, even in the smaller cities, he found a large number of students thinking about international political questions in a remarkably competent philosophical way. (2) All students (as well as numerous men-in-the-street) had a working knowledge of Marxist philosophy for the very good reason that in every university throughout the whole of the Soviet Union, regardless of the department in which the student specializes, he must take four sequential year courses in Marxist-Leninism. (3) The students know something also about the democratic values and pluralistic ideals of the free world. Many were critical of the normative and methodological relativism which they interpreted as a corollary of American political pluralism. Whenever this topic came to the forefront of discussion, someone invariably inquired how the American people could have any sense of a collective purpose or confidence under such a chaotic system of values. As the debate progressed, however, others suggested that they would even prefer the less rigid ideological structure of the Western world, but they added that the West's political leaders seemed to be unimaginative or incompetent in their efforts to convey and apply these ideals. It became clear to Mr. Dove also that (4) Communism's philosophically precise aim and operational procedures for implementing that aim gave these Russian students a purpose which many found satisfying.

Clearly, such students are not going to be turned against their political leaders by the present policies of the politicians of the free world. There is even less objective evidence that the present political leaders in the Kremlin, including their visitor to the United States,

Mr. Anastas Mikoyan, with his carefully undefined abstract nouns about taking a more conciliatory attitude, have washed their own brains of the Hegelian-Feuerbachian-Marxist "trapped universals" while leaving the brains of the students, alumni and teachers of the schools and the universities unwashed, thereby subjecting themselves to the very real risk of being liquidated, at the instigation of one of their own number, by a popular student uprising which charges them with betraying Marx, Lenin, Stalin, Malenkov, Grotewohl in East Berlin, Kardar in Hungary, Mao in China and perhaps even Tito in Yugoslavia.

It is therefore an error of a doubly serious kind to suppose, as some returning businessmen, social scientists and students now do, that the epistemic neurological correlates of a new state of mind have entered the brains of the Soviet Union's leaders and that the Cold War can be ended providing the skepticism with respect to their abstract nouns concerning peace, which was common to Secretaries Acheson and Dulles, Mr. George F. Kennan and President Truman, be dropped and the free nations merely indulge in the businessman's profit-motivated trade in which, incidentally, the Communists do not believe.

The objective justification for Mr. Dulles' skepticism still persists and is twofold—being both empirical and theoretical. The empirical reason is that a careful examination of the Soviet leader's request for a more conciliatory attitude upon the part of the Western free nations and for a top-level Summit Conference is always accompanied by a threat of war at some point in the world such as West Berlin, where peace existed before this threat was made. This is hardly a conciliatory, peacemaking state of mind. Furthermore, the Soviet precondition for their participation in such a Summit Conference is that it restrict itself to a political battlefield chosen by the Communists, such again as Berlin, and to the raising of no other political questions such as Tibet, Mao's Chinese at India's frontier, Hungary or the free elections in Poland to which the Soviet Union agreed in its officially signed Yalta Treaty.

The theoretical reason for skepticism is even more telling. The present Communists specify and still teach to all students not merely the two basic Hegelian-Feuerbachian materialistic premises of their thinking, but also the third and fourth level, more opportunistic procedural derivative applications which give the instrumental rules for applying the premises to particular circumstances of the moment. These derivative theorems prescribe that at times they will use conciliatory, peacemaking, undefined abstract nouns which will have very concrete meanings for them in order to confuse and confound their philosophically untutored political adversaries, thereby hoping to throw them off balance and into the acceptance of concessions which, step by step, will fatally undermine their political position. These derivate instrumental beliefs, the epistemic correlates of which are trapped in every dedicated Communist's brain, specify also that the use of such verbally deceptive tactics never means that they will change in one iota their basic premises which define their long-range goal-value intentions.

The reason for this becomes clear when one recalls the first universal proposition of their entire theory. This premise determines the meaning of everything else they say or do. This premise also requires them to think about any fact whatever and any problem in any field whatever in Hegelian dialectically logical deterministic terms. The core of such thinking is never to peacefully conciliate cultural or political normative conflicts or "antitheses," but to pick them up and intensify them. This is precisely the point of their instigation of the Cold War and their creation of a crisis yesterday at Quemoy, the day before yesterday in Syria, today in Berlin and tomorrow at some other particular, specific spot on the surface of the earth.

It is one of the major merits of the descriptive method of philosophically anthropological method in international relations that it enables one to understand and not to be fooled by what occurs or by any abstract noun uttered by anyone anywhere. The procedure which philosophical anthropology prescribes for handling any abstract noun of any foreign or domestic politician is precisely the one, described in Part I, which the cultural anthropologist Clyde Kluckhohn found it necessary to use if he were to have an objective rather than a fanciful conception of the meaning of the words and the factual behavior and ceremonies of the Navaho Indians. This method is to suppose that one does not have the foggiest idea of what they are doing or talking about until one has found the primitive "postulate set" which alone defines the meaning of every word they use and teleological mechanically conditions the behavior of not merely everything they say or do today, but everything they will do tomorrow unless, in the intervening period, that set of postulates is consciously and overtly repudiated or altered.

More specifically, with any foreign or domestic politician, one must immediately ask oneself the following questions: (1) To what political party in his own nation does he belong? (2) What are the elementary concepts and propositions which specify the goal-value political aims of this party? (3) To what extent is this set of philosophical beliefs taught universally throughout the educational system or inculcated emotively and covertly in religious or political ceremonies or by the public press? (4) What percentage of the people in his nation vote for his party? (5) Most important of all, what *was* the educational and cultural living law philosophy of the people of his nation and of its plural religious communities antecedent to his advent to political office?

With respect to the Soviet Union, the answer to these questions is easy to obtain since there is only one party and its normative goal-value philosophy has been so spelled out by Marx that anyone who has the philosophical training necessary to understand what Marxist words purport to mean can easily know the Soviet leaders' long-range aims and short-range tactics. Knowing this, he can understand what any word of any Marxist Communist official or any modern-minded educated person in Russia is most likely to mean. Only with medieval-minded devout Russian Greek Orthodox Christians would one expect the words of today's Russians to have a different meaning, and even this meaning in many cases would not be that of the free democratic West.

These considerations suggest that much more is required than the late Mr. Dulles' and his predecessors' skepticism and their use of the most powerful materialistic military deterrents, if an effective foreign policy with respect to the Soviet Union is to be constructed by the political leaders of the free world. The goal values for which these military weapons are the *necessary defensive instrument* must not merely be made evident and analytically clear, but they must also be put in the forefront of domestic and foreign policy instead of being left vaguely stated in the background where they are covered up by the brinkmanship-waving of atomic bombs in the faces of not merely the Marxist Communists but also those who want to be one's free democratic allies.

Notwithstanding everything that has been noted just above, it may well be the case that Premier Khrushchev is sincere in his proposals for disarmament. He would in all likelihood be doubly sincere could he distract the Americans' foreign policy in the direction of international trade, thereby causing the free world to postpone until a still later date the theoretical specification and operational economic and military defensive implementation of its ideological purposes and aims. The reason for this possibility was given in Chapter 1. Premier Khrushchev may well have concluded that Africa, the Middle East and Asia will fall into his lap without any use of aggressive military pressure on the part of the Communists, because the uncommitted nations in Africa, the Middle East and South Asia, having failed in so many cases in their experimental attempt to democratize and modernize their old societies with free democratic political ideals and methods, are now in the mood to conclude that free democracy does not work for them and that, therefore, the only way they can achieve the advantages of modern ways is to embrace the Communistic political ideal and accept its dictatorial methods. Of interest in this connection is the statement made by Premier Khrushchev in Moscow shortly after his visit to the United States in 1959. In an address given at the Polish Embassy, as reported by the *Economist* of London, after denying any intention to force the Communist political philosophy and its ways on other nations he added, "Why drag a man up to Paradise by a rope?" [3]

Whatever his meaning, it is clear that the fate of freedom throughout the world is not going to be determined by merely technological, military and commercial considerations. Instead, it is going to turn around whether the political leaders of the free nations the world over who still believe in free democracy can clarify its aims in a philosophically unambiguous and imaginatively captivating way and learn the practical political methods for making those ideals work in democratizing and modernizing old societies. It is in our own minds and brains that the problem centers and not in Berlin, Moscow, Peking or New Delhi.

That such is the case is confirmed by the following experience of the American anthropologist Professor Sol Tax of the University of Chicago. On an airplane flight from Russia to India he found himself with a group of Russian students. Owing to engine trouble, the plane was delayed at Aktyubinsk for more than forty-eight hours. In a letter to President Paul Fejos of the Wenner-Gren Foundation for Anthropological Research, Professor Tax describes his impressions as follows:

What an opportunity for getting a feeling for Soviet youth! Needless to say, I liked them all very much. But it became evident to me that we in the U.S. may misunderstand a great deal in thinking they feel repressed—or at least their loyalty suffers in any way. We did not talk politics, domestic or otherwise, at any time; but we did talk art and literature and the English language, and joke a lot. The most important thing that was said to me by one of them was that they work hard because they have a purpose. . . .[4]

In other words, they are perfectly clear about what the goal-value aim of their political leaders' domestic and foreign policy is and this clean-cut aim has both captured their imaginations and given their personal lives a meaning.

Professor Tax continues:

. . . of course they were "catching up" and industrializing and building socialism—and these things are a common goal that seems to be felt every moment of the day. . . . I got the feeling that they take the leadership of the regime without comment, as a group of soldiers must, because the regime is so obviously successful in directing their energies to the goal.[5]

Can as much be said for those of us in our free world and its students? Do our educational and political leaders give our youth a common purpose that captures their imagination, their jokeful enthusiasm and their loyalty? Professor Tax also asked himself the same question, for between the quotations above he put in parentheses the following question: "As I thought back on our students, what could I properly say is a common or social goal?" The Yale graduate student Mr. Dove's conversations with both Russian and American students confirm this query.

An attempt to give a constructive answer to this question will concern us in Part III. By way of preparation, our application of the descriptive method of philosophical anthropology to the post-Kantian culture and nations of modern Central and Eastern Europe makes certain things evident: (1) Why Lenin's modernization of Russia in terms of Marxist Communist dialectically materialistic goal values was so successful immediately and has increased its success since his time. (2) Why the Soviet Union is likely to last for a considerable time in the future and has provided Russian students with the obvious clear-cut purpose and sense of living for something bigger than themselves which they have.

It remains to apply the evaluative method of Chapter 7 to the elementary propositions defining the political properties of the Soviet Union, which the descriptive method of philosophical anthropology has just determined for us. These assumptions are: (1) Any modern nation is based on the law of contract rather than on the law of status. (2) Any word in any domain of human knowledge or experience whatever has a meaning which is that of a naïve realistic epistemology, and this epistemology (according to Marxists) warrants only knowledge of material substances whose defining properties are directly sensed and possessed by the object, quite independently of its relation to the observer. (3) The evolution of political and other social institutions has nothing to do with the free consent of the people but is "determined" completely by the "laws of historical change" according to a dialectical logic of negation in which the *thesis* is identified with the class of businessmen in any industrial society and the materialistic tools of production which they have in their fists; the *antithesis* is identified with the class of all the laborers in an industrial society; and the final *synthesis* is identified with a revolutionary dictatorship by a very small number of politicians who are not elected even by the people in the class of the laborers but are instead the self-appointing and self-perpetuating leaders of the very much smaller Marxist Communist Party.

It is hardly necessary to point out that even if Propositions (1), (2) and (3) were cognitively true, these particular identifications of the thesis, antithesis and synthesis in the Hegelian dialectical logic of negation would be quite arbitrary. Being arbitrary, there is no historical necessity in them. Quite apart from this arbitrariness, Propositions (1), (2) and (3) can be shown by our evaluative method to be false.

Proposition (1) is quite independent of Marxist Communist philosophy and was inherited by Lenin, as was shown earlier in this chapter, from Greek Orthodox Christian tsarist Russia, which derived it in turn from the Stoic Roman Western legal science and philosophy by way of Justinian. The writer has shown elsewhere [6] that any nation such as the Soviet Union, Great Britain or the United States of America whose law is contractual, entails the tautologically true first postulate of contractual legal science. As previously noted this postulate is the proposition declared to be self-evident in the American Declaration of Independence. Since the Soviet Union's Marxist Postulate (3) is incompatible with this tautologically true, elemental proposition of contractual legal science, it follows that the legal and political philosophy which defines the substantive content of their contractual legal nation's goal-value political ideal is incompatible with the first postulate upon which any contractual political nation rests and is, therefore, false on purely logical grounds. It is as if a pure mathematician put substantive content in a theorem of arithmetic, which is logically incompatible with Peano's Fifth Postulate concerning what any arithmetical number means.

The Marxist Postulate (2) is similarly self-contradictory. As shown in Part I, the naïve realistic epistemological theory of the meaning of any word is even worse than self-contradictory. Because of its treatment of items of knowledge in different epistemological worlds of discourse as if they were in the same world of discourse, it is a meaningless expression.

It was shown in Chapter 9 that Postulate (3), the dialectically deterministic theory of the evolution of both first-order factual natural creatures and second-order factual social and political institutions, is false also on purely logical grounds. The reason is that the negation of any thesis, which dialectical logic makes the initial thrust of any logical necessity, does not give one and only one antithesis; since any thesis can be negated in more than one way. Yet without a unique antithesis there is no determinism, and "the laws of history," at least as conceived by Marxists, do not exist. Their claim, therefore, to the right of political authority without the free consent of those over whom they exercise this political authority, because the dialectically deterministic causal laws of history make a revolt of the proletariat led by them inevitable, is, therefore, spurious on logical grounds. Since logical inconsistency in any other political philosophy is used by Marx, Engels and Lenin as an argument valid for anyone, which establishes the cognitive falsity of that philosophy,[7] it follows that the Communists' dialectically deterministic theory of natural and social evolution is false for reasons which hold for Marxists as much as they do for anyone else.

But even if a dialectical logic were a deterministic logic, leaving no possibilities open (after the manner in which the conclusions of a valid syllogism follow necessarily from its premises in the logic of identity), the deterministic evolution of natural creatures and political institutions would not follow. For, as just noted, logic, whether it be dialectical or that of identity, refers to propositions, not to facts. Hence, no logic is a metaphysical push or pull that drives facts, citizens and their politicians about. Note again the naïve realistic epistemological error of confusing a person's private, radical empirically sensed pushes and pulls with mystical metaphysical forces in nature and in history.

Propositions are by definition things of which it is significant to say that they are true or false. Where truth or falsity is present, assent is also. And where assent occurs, there also is moral, legal and political responsibility and its converse moral, legal and political rights and privileges. Facts give no one any normative authority of any kind. Only assent by the citizens to propositions openly announced by their prospective politicians give any politician any political authority whatever. In short, no propositions that are true or false, then no "oughts" or "ought nots"; also no political authority and no political rights and privileges.

Earlier in this chapter it was shown that the Marxist labor theory of economic value is false on empirical grounds in a sense which can be confirmed by anyone anywhere. The evaluative method of philosophical anthropology tells us, therefore, that the Marxist Communist theory of national goal values is false on both logical and factual grounds. Moreover, when considered either collectively or distributively the three most elementary propositions of this political philosophy are found to be false.

Has not the time come, therefore, for the politicians of the free nations to use the descriptive method of philosophical anthropology to acquaint mankind inside as well as outside the Iron Curtain with an objective description of the different sets of cognitively testable philosophical propositions that define the different political properties of both a modern Marxist Communist nation and a modern contractually legal democratic nation? Then the youth in the free world (as well as the students in the Soviet Union) will have a clearly stated purpose that is bigger than themselves, and will know in clean-cut theoretical terms (to be spelled out in Chapter 18) what that purpose is and in operational terms (to be indicated in Chapter 19) how to make it work. Isn't it also practically possible politically, after having done this, to put the evaluative method in the hands of all the world's people, or at least their political leaders, so that they themselves can determine which of these two conflicting political ideals is the cognitively correct one?

With the descriptive method, people and their politicians in old societies would possess an objective means of bringing out into the open the unique and in part cognitively true underlying, covert philosophical beliefs and properties of their old society and nation. Thereby the political problem of modernizing their ancient ways with either Marxist Communistic or free democratic political ideals and methods would be clearly and objectively seen in all its particular local domestic complexity. Were such an objective determination of the philosophically defined living law of each nation then brought together in the United Nations, an objective description of all the nations and the living law of the entire world would be at hand for the first time. By using its content as a guide it should then be possible to put content in a positive world law which would have both the qualitative and the high-frequency support of the living law necessary to be effective.

Even so, if law and order break down domestically they are likely to fail internationally also. Until we succeed in each domestic nation we are not likely to succeed internationally. Hence the remainder of this book will be concerned with national attempts to modernize ancient societies. One of the most remarkable cases is Mao's China.

16

The Remarkable Short-Run Success of Mao's China

President Mao's task in modernizing his fellow Chinese with Marxist Communistic goal values at the end of World War II was far more difficult than the similar task which faced Lenin when he attempted the same thing with his fellow Russians at the end of World War I. None of the elementary beliefs of post-Kantian and post-Hegelian Western Europe, of which Marxist Communism is merely a novel permutation, were in either the educational system or the mentalities of Mao's fellow Chinese. Nor was there the Western contractual legal science, which even tsarist Russia had inherited from Stoic Rome by way of Justinian at Constantinople. Insofar as the modern contractual legal and political mentality imported by Chiang Kai-shek's regime was concerned, everything in it was opposed to Marxist Communism. Also, the Confucian-Taoist-Buddhist mentality and ways of most of the Chinese people who are in the villages are equally alien to contractual legal and political institutions of any type, whether they be free democratic or Communistic in their normative content. Truly, therefore, Mao's present success is remarkable. What made it possible?

In answering this question we can dismiss the usual controversial political reasons that are given in the United States. To suppose that anything any American Secretary of State could have done, be he either a Democrat or a Republican or even a divinely inspired Monday-morning military quarterback, would have altered the outcome so far as Chiang Kai-shek's regime on the mainland was concerned is to ignore the universal mood of all Asians, be the latter freely democratic or Communistically-minded. This mood is that no foreign minister and least of all any military man of any other nation is going to decide the political fate of Asians if they can possibly help it.

The second consideration is that in the case of Chiang Kai-shek's Nationalistic China even the Western-educated Chinese leadership failed to introduce those courses in their modern educational curriculum which are necessary for success even with respect to modern instrumental values. Also, too many of the American-educated Chinese advisers and lieutenants of Chiang Kai-shek became so American in their mentality and so unmindful of traditional ways and ancestral institutions that they alienated their own Chinese people, much in the manner of the first British-minded government of free Ceylon.

The present Chairman of Chiang Kai-shek's very successful Commission on Economic Reconstruction on Formosa, Secretary of Chiang Kai-shek's mainland cabinet and previous Chancellor of Peking National University, Dr. Chiang Monlin, told the writer in the midst of World War II, when President Chiang Kai-shek was still on the mainland, that he (Chiang Monlin) and other American-minded Chinese intellectuals introduced modern scientific instruments and even modern science itself to their countrymen in the wrong way. Their error consisted in giving them the applied side of science without at the same time acquainting them with the imageless, formal way of thinking and its theoretical physics and philosophy that is at the basis of the experimental physics and the mathematically mechanical engineering from which these practical instruments derive. The result was that the Chinese thought about and used these instruments with the only meanings in their minds that they had—namely, those of their more intuitive, impressionistic and naïve observational ways of thinking of their Confucian-Taoist-Buddhist mentality and cultural background.[1]

As Chapter 12 has suggested, these modern instruments cannot be understood or, as experience shows, used without burning out their bearings or otherwise ruining them when they are approached in this way. For example, automobiles or other machinery when they break down, or do not run perfectly, are frequently merely patched up with odd pieces of wire, bits of tin cans or binding twine instead of being repaired. Similarly, many American missionary educators and agricultural experts, trained in the best American universities, made the mistake with the Chinese peasant farmers of assuming too uncritically that the American ways are the most efficient and of failing to enter into the minds of the Chinese villagers and farmers sufficiently to win their interest and confidence and to find means to convey the new Western scientific agricultural mentality to them in case it were more efficient economically with respect to cost as well as chemically and the farmers wanted to have it.

Pearl Buck makes this clear in her autobiography, *My Several Worlds*,[2] where she describes the frustrating experiences which her husband Peter and she went through when, after graduating from the School of Agriculture at Cornell University he attempted, in a North China village, to teach the Chinese peasant farmers the American "scientific" agricultural "know-how." That this "know-how" is scientifically "superior" to that of the Chinese is, of course, self-evident *a priori*. Otherwise it would not be scientific. But can scientific knowledge, when applied, be true *a priori?* Apparently for this American scientifically trained agriculturalist in North China the answer was No! For his wife tells us (if we can trust the objectivity of one who tried to live with and through such an emotionally disturbing experience) that he became frustrated after several years of the most conscientious work because of the indifference of the Chinese farmers to the *a priori* best Western science that he was bringing to them. The reason she suggests was that their *a posteriori* "unscientific" ways produced at least as much per acre if not more than his *a priorily* best scientific ways would have done had the peasants' confidence been won sufficiently to have followed them.

This experience of Pearl and Peter Buck in their early days in northern China may well be pondered by those politicians and research professors who investigate the economic solution of the political problems of the so-called "underdeveloped areas." Whatever may be the results of their reflections, two things are clear: First, *instrumental ways cannot solve goal-value political problems involving a difference in and conflict of cultural mentalities whether the instruments be economic, agricultural or military.* Second, *there is no meaning to effective instruments or aid apart from non-instru-mentally defined intrinsic normative goal values in the minds of the people to whom the instruments are given.*

Failure to note the latter principle has one of two effects. Either the people receive the instruments and aid without any real interest in possessing them and without having the motive to undergo the discipline that is required to use them properly and efficiently, or else out of idle curiosity they take the instruments apart and later reassemble them incorrectly so that they are ruined when they use them.

The prevalent notion, therefore, that Communist success in China or the Soviet Union is due to their concentration on "the economic factor" is as erroneous as is the supposition that additional military aid to Chiang Kai-shek or the introduction of additional American agricultural know-how could have kept him in Nanking. The experi-ence of the economist Gunnar Myrdal, in Ceylon, which was de-scribed in Chapter 13, confirms the two general rules that are itali-cized above. What, then, is the source of Mao's success?

In 1950 on their way to South Asia the writer and his wife had luncheon in London with Bertrand Russell at the home of a mutual friend, Mrs. Edward C. Dyason. He told us that in the early twenties when he was a Visiting Professor at Peking National University the ablest students to enter his philosophical seminars were already con-vinced orthodox Marxist Communists. It is to such a group of phil-osophically informed and personally convinced Chinese Marxist students that Mao belonged. His Communism is, therefore, both Marxist orthodox and not of recent origin. Furthermore, Chiang Kai-shek's purges of Marxist Communists in the days of Borodin, which shocked even his own followers because of their brutality, failed to knock the Marxist "trapped universals" out of the young Chinese Communists' brains. As von Neumann learned at firsthand from both theoretical investigations and practical experience, once a computing machine has information or non-normatively worded procedural rules trapped in it, that machine does not forget them easily. Nor does merely pounding its mechanical muscles with a hammer cause the machine to throw away the universals it has trapped. The human brain behaves in precisely the same manner with respect to the phys-iological correlates of any person's covert or overt ideas, except as the person tries out imaginatively and himself selects and critically examines the universals to which he gives assent before trapping them, or at least, in the case of creative minds, as one has the capacity to do this.

Once thoroughly trapped, the basic philosophical universals are then shoved down into the introspectively subconscious in order apparently to permit one's introspective conscious attention to be given entirely to the present incoming sensory signals and to one's conscious choice between possible motor responses to them. As indicated in Part I, this is the neurological and physiological reason both for the Freudian discovery of the importance of the subconscious and for Professor Kluckhohn's anthropological observation that in any culture most of its philosophical premises are not consciously known by the people in that culture but are, instead, "covert." Such is the case because most people receive the universals that are trapped in their brains through stories, poetry, religious hymns and newspaper editorials and education which frequently state them merely metaphorically rather than with scientific and philosophical literalness and clarity. Only the Buddhas, the Lockes, the Jeffersons and the Einsteins, who first discover the most basic "trapped universals," and their literally educated followers know the basic "trapped universals" in the minds of the people of a given culture overtly and consciously as well as subconsciously and covertly.

In any event, two things concerning Mao are clear. First, he is an orthodox Communist with his Marxist beliefs so basically trapped that Chiang Kai-shek's purges did not succeed in knocking them out of his brain. Second, he is philosophically trained and philosophically clear about what his political goal values are, and has been so since the early 1920's. Furthermore, the neurological physiological theory described in Part I tells us why it is difficult for old dogs to learn new tricks. By the time they get old, their initially trapped elementary epistemic correlates of ideas are completely unknown to them, being covert and having been so continuously reinforced by associating with old dogs who bark as they do that it is usually impossible for themselves or anyone else to untrap them. This general rule that "trapped universals" are not forgotten easily and that one cannot knock basically trapped universals out of the brains of old dogs with the use of force applies as much to General MacArthur, Admiral

Radford, former Senator Knowland and the late Senator McCarthy as it does to President Mao himself.

Even so, how were Mao and his small number of Marxist-minded colleagues able to be so successful so quickly, considering the incompatibility of his basic trapped universals with the basic Confucian-Taoist-Buddhist trapped universals in the minds of the hundreds and hundreds of millions of Chinese people? In short, why is he still in political command on the Chinese mainland?

One answer to this question is already evident. He was philosophically clear in his own mind about what his goal values were. He was guided by something more than woolly-worded good intentions and philosophically unanalyzed abstract nouns. The second reason is that he carried on what he calls "theoretic investigations" in which he formulated a theoretically worked-out policy that (1) took into account not merely his own theoretically and clearly formulated Marxist aim, but also, with just the same precision and realism, the traditional Confucian-Taoist-Buddhist aims as defined by the *de facto* "trapped universals" that were in the minds of his people, and (2) theoretically specified a procedure according to which, by appealing to beliefs and values that they cherished, he could take them towards his Marxist ideal. Furthermore, in doing this, as the sequel will show, he made a considerable number of his own Chinese people feel that his program was their program.

As compared with Mao, Chiang Kai-shek had no philosophically, politically or economically clear conception of what his aims were. More particularly, he was not a philosophically-minded scholar. In Confucian Chinese society such a weakness is fatal. The reason is that in premodern China the scholars stand at the top of the social system, and war-lord generals, such as Chiang Kai-shek, stand at the bottom. The writer recalls passing a Chinese village between Canton and Kowloon in 1920 in which a telephone-like pole, serving no physical purpose, towered above the mud-walled houses. This pole signified that a young man from that village had passed either the provincial or national examinations in the Confucian philosophical classics. It was, moreover, from such scholarly Confucian-minded young men that the public officials of premodern China had to be chosen. Mao's scholarly philosophical concern met this classical

Chinese popular conception of what the skills of a political leader must be.

Secondly, the modern revolution, which eliminated the Manchus at the end of the first decade of the present century, was led by Sun Yat-sen. He also was not clear about his goal values, as his acceptance of Communist as well as Western free democratic beliefs clearly demonstrates. His Western political ideas were derived in part at least from a New York dentist who, in all likelihood, wrote about political philosophy in order to assuage his boredom. When Sun Yat-sen, guided by such a philosophically amateurish conception of Western democracy, carried through his revolution he was inevitably left with no clear conception of what was to replace the old. When, as Pearl Buck has noted, he made the mistake of not keeping the Manchu king, at least in the nominal political status of the British Crown, the country was plunged into political anarchy. No one was left to symbolize the national unity of the people. It was in this political anarchy that the provincial Chinese war lords flourished. Chiang Kai-shek was one of them. Sun Yat-sen chose him as his general to found his military West Point at Whampoa on the river between Canton and Hong Kong, which the writer passed many times when he and his wife lived first in Hong Kong and then in Canton at the end of World War I. Instead of sending Chiang Kai-shek to the free West to obtain his Western military training, Sun Yat-sen sent him to Marxist Moscow. The consequence was that Chiang Kai-shek initially was associated with the Communists. Finally, with Sun Yat-sen's decline and death Chiang Kai-shek was able, and often less rather than more, to defeat the other Chinese war lords with the help of the Communists as well as the non-Communists and to come to a semblance of national political leadership. Later he indulged in the Borodin purge of the Communists which, as previously noted, shocked many of his Western-minded Chinese followers. It was only with his marriage to T. V. Soong's sister, the present Madame Chiang Kai-shek, that he acquired even a smattering of what a contractually free democratic philosophy of goal values really means. Furthermore, even then his government was fundamentally a war lord's military government combined with a T. V. Soong Chinese joint family government.

The so-called American-minded free democratic government of China was further confounded, with respect to what its leadership stood for and what its "modern" aims were, by the fact that Sun Yat-sen, who selected Chiang Kai-shek as his military commander, came out for Communism rather than for free democracy before he died. Sun Yat-sen's wife, a sister of Madame Chiang Kai-shek, became and still is a Marxist Communist.

Quite apart from all these complexities, contradictions and confusions with respect to what President and General Chiang Kai-shek's modern goal-value aims were, such military-minded and unscholarly-minded leadership was about as unsuited as any modern-inclined political leadership could be to appeal to the Confucian Chinese mind with its regard for scholars. In short, Mao, with his philosophically and scholarly defined Communism, fitted the traditional Confucian ideal of a topmost political leader, whereas Chiang Kai-shek, Madame Chiang Kai-shek and even T. V. Soong and his sister's husband, H. H. Kung, did so only partially.

One has only to look at what happened in any change of government during Chiang Kai-shek's administration on the mainland to note that there was never a two-party election. Little more really happened than that in the Soong family government, T. V. Soong shifted from the Treasury to the Foreign Office and H. H. Kung shifted in the converse direction. By no stretch of anybody's imagination, therefore, can the government of Chiang Kai-shek be regarded as a free democratic government. The best that can be said for it was that T. V. Soong, his sister Madame Chiang Kai-shek and his brother-in-law H. H. Kung, because of their Harvard, Wellesley and Yale education, wanted to make it such a government. Chiang Kai-shek in fact had no clear-headed conception of what free democracy means except as his wife, his wife's brother, Chiang Monlin and Hu Shih tried unsuccessfully to make it clear to him.

Another reason for Mao's success is that even the American-trained Chinese who had a somewhat clear conception of what free democracy means divorced themselves so much from the Chinese people, most of whom are in the villages, that they not merely failed to represent those people, but also actually embittered them. Pearl Buck, who was in China through all these years and who wanted above everything to see the new American-minded young Chinese succeed in what they were trying to do, describes what happened as early as 1927 as follows:

[T]he sad and frightening fact was that the young and uprooted Chinese, who had been trained in Western universities or in missionary schools and other modern schools in China, had lost the Chinese philosophy. They belonged neither to East nor to West, and they were pitiful, for they were dedicated to the improvement of their own country, and yet they could not understand that it was impossible for them to save their countrymen because they themselves were lost. They still did not know how to speak to their countrymen. I cringed when I heard an earnest young Chinese, the milk of his American doctorate still wet behind his ears, haranguing a Chinese crowd on a street in our city or in a village where I chanced to be. . . . Why? Because he spoke to the wise old people as though they were serfs, stupid and ignorant.[3]

[The climax came when one day the tailor] came to tell me that "they" [the American-minded Chinese] were pushing down the homes of the people with a monstrous machine.

"Please explain," I said, unbelieving.

"I cannot explain," he replied. "It is being done."

I put on my jacket and went out to see for myself. . . . There I saw the monster machine. . . . A man rode upon it, a young Chinese man, not a workingman but a Western-educated man, and he was guiding it slowly along one side of the street and then the other. What was he doing? He was pushing down the houses. Those old one-story houses, made of hand-shaped brick and cemented together with lime plaster, had stood well enough for shelter through hundreds of years, but they had been built long before such a machine had been conceived in the mind of Western man. . . . They crumbled into ruins. . . . I stood among the Chinese people, watching, silent, stricken. And the young man said not a word, not even when an old grandmother, who had lived in a house since she was born, began to cry wildly and aloud. . . . I knew that from that day on the new government was doomed in the end to fail. Why? Because it had failed already in understanding the people whom it purposed to govern. . . . And the Communists in China gained their first victory that day. . . .[4]

The philosophically clear and intellectually-minded Mao made no such mistake. He was not only a philosophically-minded scholar and theoretician, but also a practical politician. In the Chinese-Japanese War, he was helped in being practical by the necessity, in order to avoid being attacked and destroyed by both Chiang Kai-shek's forces and the Japanese forces, to retreat to the northwest frontier provinces of China. Here he had to live with and come to understand the Chinese who tilled the land and resided in the villages.

Having both a theoretical mind and an empirically informed and objectively realistic practical mind, he proceeded to devise a theoretically formulated policy and operational procedure which, taking his fellow Chinese in the villages with precisely the *de facto* Confucian-Taoist-Buddhist intuitions and emotive attachments which they have in their minds and in their habits, would win their loyalties in accepting his leadership for modernizing their country in terms of his philosophically clear Marxist ideals and goal values.

One precise procedure which he devised as a result of his "theoretical investigations" first became known to the writer in the following way. While at Canberra in 1949, the writer met a British anthropologist who was trained under the anthropologist Malinowski. This anthropologist had just arrived from Peking where he had witnessed the march of the Communist troops into Peking. A few years later, while lecturing at the Foreign Service Institute of the State Department of the United States, the writer chanced to have in his audience an American army officer who was a specialist in the Chinese language and who had also witnessed the same events. The following description is, therefore, independently confirmed by observers who were not aware of one another's presence at the events in question.

To appreciate the following description, one must first try to imagine what the marching of an army into Peking must mean to the Chinese people, most of whom were not Communists. Peking is known as the Heavenly City. Its Royal Palace compound is also called the Forbidden City. Hence, the marching of Communist Chinese troops into Peking to take over its Heavenly and Forbidden City was equivalent for the Chinese to what for Roman Catholics would be the marching of an Italian Communist army through the streets of Rome to take over St. Peter's and the Vatican City. Let us pause in silence for a moment with eyes closed to imagine what the expressions of horror on the faces of the Roman Catholics of Rome would be.

Nevertheless, both observers in Peking described the following facts with respect to what happened there. The first of these two facts only the United States army officer reported. It was that the first time the Communist army marched through the streets of Peking they marched with the most stern demeanors, in absolute silence with the utmost possible show of physical force. This is compatible with classical Confucian peacemaking arbitration since the classical Confucian always expects his adversary to give the impression of the strictest sternness in the initial statement of his demand with respect to a settlement of the dispute. The Chinese name for such ferocity is "the paper tiger."

Both observers confirmed the following event, which happened the second time that the Communist troops marched. Upon this day there was no show of horror whatever on the Chinese people's faces. Instead, they were held spellbound with almost a suggestion of relief by the fact that the marching Communist Chinese soldiers were all singing old Chinese folk songs.

The theoretically and practically astute Mao had wittingly or unwittingly used the method of philosophical anthropology for modernizing a non-modern culture. He had picked up childhood songs and symbols to which the emotions of the people were emotively attached and was thereby suggesting successfully to them that, in throwing out Chiang Kai-shek and his American-minded Chinese, they were throwing away something that was artificial for them, whereas in accepting Mao and his Chinese Communist leadership they were returning in part at least to their old and true Chinese selves.

By this means he won the time and the trust of his people sufficiently to be permitted to try out his modernization experiment with Marxist Communist goal values and methods. Having them in this mood, he could then give them a vision of his goal-value blueprint in all its Marxist "clarity" and "distinctness" rather than in wholly fuzzy, muddle-headed, abstract nouns or in the equally misleading intuitive mentality and symbolism of his own people.

Furthermore, his own previous theoretical investigations in all probability had led him to modify *derivatively* "the dictatorship of the proletariat" to read for himself, "the dictatorship of the peasants," and to read for the peasants, "the dictatorship of the unscrupulous moneylenders and the rich landowners." Thus he was able to deliver something to the peasants which was concrete, as well as to capture their emotive attachment to himself and his leadership by

reference to their childhood folk songs. The former of these two results of his theoretical research into the practical procedure for transforming the traditional Chinese Confucian-Taoist-Buddhist society
into a completely Marxist one, which is the very antithesis of what
the villagers believe and cherish, served two purposes. First, it won
the peasants to what he was doing. Second, it fooled the unphilosoph-
ically-minded non-analytic Western and Asian newspaper reporters
and anthropologists and the Asian cultural guests into believing that
Mao's Marxism was a sweet twentieth century peasants' revolt
against the landlords and not really a mid-nineteenth century German Marxist Communist revolution at all.

This shows that mere newspaper reporting, intercultural visiting
and naïvely descriptive anthropological observation are not enough.
The anthropologists, the visitors and the reporters who do the observing must be philosophically trained in the analysis of a politician's words in terms of the basic beliefs epistemically trapped in
his brain, so that they learn to seek out the basic trapped universals
in the minds of those who utter them, which give the political words
their specific theoretical meaning and their most likely present and
future practical social and political significance. Even cultural anthropologists, cultural visitors, American businessmen and bankers
and visiting students to any foreign culture, whether it be Communist or not, neglect philosophy and the philosophical analysis of abstract nouns at their peril. For this reason, before their findings can
be accepted as objectively and scientifically valid, much of what present cultural anthropologists have published as "described facts" will
have to be critically reexamined because of the catch-as-catch-can,
naïve Western common-sense prose which they have used so often in
the description of their "facts."

The reason why common-sense prose will not do in cultural anthropology is that the common-sense prose of one culture is the nonsense and the myth of another culture. Furthermore, even in one's
own culture the common sense of today is usually the outmoded
theory of yesterday. Consequently, philosophically critical cultural
anthropology is as necessary for the objective description of cultural
"facts" and "norms" as it is for evaluating them or for finding criteria
for choosing between different ones in their merging.

Notwithstanding President Mao's remarkable short-term success in so using old folk songs and undoubtedly countless other similar procedures to suggest to his fellow Chinese people that his Marxist modernization program will return them to the beliefs in their traditional selves, we know that this is a deception. For it can be shown by theoretical investigations appealing to the basic universal premises of Mao's own Marxist philosophy of goal values, by means, therefore, which are as valid for Mao as they are for us, that his basic and not merely his derivative trapped universals are incompatible with the most basic trapped universals of any other culture, whatever may be its specific set of trapped universals. This means that Marxist Communists who use, as Mao has done, our philosophically anthropological methods for merging two cultures without destroying all of the old in obtaining the new, can win in the short run but cannot do so in the intermediate or the long run. This short-run merging of the old and the new is precisely what Mao, with his philosophically-minded, culturally anthropological method has achieved and it is precisely why he has succeeded so far to such a remarkable degree.

It has been shown in the previous chapter that the quite long run is likely to be a successful run for the Marxists in Russia. The reason, let it be recalled, is that the traditional pre-Marxist modern Russian educational system and modern culture, with which Lenin began, had all the Marxist trapped universals in it. All both Marx and Lenin had to do, therefore, was to reshuffle the old. For the Chinese minds with which Mao began, this, however, was not the case. Consequently, in the intermediate run which is already upon him he is confronted with what may well be insuperable difficulties. These difficulties may already have become evident to the villagers of China who constitute most of the Chinese population and who have not been turned into lost souls by losing their traditional beliefs while also not understanding modern free democratic values at their deepest philosophical level. As Mao proceeds to make his own Marxist goal values more and more concrete in the behavioral responses of his people, the incompatibility between his goal-value ideals and the cherished traditional goal values to which the villagers' folk songs refer and from which they derive must become evident to the villagers themselves. Already this incompatibility has become evident to certain Asian cultural visitors to Mao's China. It is considerations

294   *Philosophical Anthropology and Practical Politics*

such as these which are leading Prime Minister Nehru to say that Marxist Communism has demonstrated its incapacity to fit the goal-value needs of an Asian people.*

It is likely also that this incompatibility of the Confucian-Taoist-Buddhist Chinese old beliefs and customs and the Marxist new ones, which Mao's fellow Chinese are now experiencing and expressing to him, has played a part in his recently announced decision to retire from the practical administration of his Marxist modernization of traditional Chinese culture in order to return, while remaining President, to what he calls "further theoretical investigations." Faced with the practical choice of choosing between two incompatible policies, President Mao has evident need to reflect.

It can be safely said, because of the logical contradictions between the basic trapped universal propositions of his Marxist Communism and the basic, quite different, intuitively moral and religious trapped universals of his Confucian-Buddhist-Taoist village people,† that his theoretical investigations will not help him in finding the necessary practical procedure which he must use if, like Chiang Kai-shek's modern-minded Chinese colleagues before him, he is not to alienate his fellow Chinese in the villages. His practical political problems would be easy to resolve theoretically, even within his dialectically logical mentality, were he able to regard (1) the Confucian-Taoist-Buddhist beliefs of his people, which his soldiers' folk songs expressed, as the *thesis,* and (2) his Communist Marxist belief system as its incompatible *antithesis,* which it in fact is. Then he could theoretically construct a higher synthesis from which (1) and (2) above derive as partial, limited special cases. But his Marxism prevents such a solution to his present practical political problems, since, according to Marxism, (2) is the final dialectically logical *synthesis.*

It is precisely at this point that an evaluative philosophical anthropology, which uses the objective method for choosing between two basically trapped goal-value theories as specified in Chapter 7, becomes relevant. By the use of this method, evaluatively-minded, as well as merely descriptively-minded political leaders of the free

---

* As reported by Professor Amiya Chakravarty of India at the SEATO Conference at Bangkok in January of 1958.

† What their most elementary philosophical concept is will become evident in Chapter 19.

nations might very well be able to put intellectual diplomats in Peking who could persuade even the intellectual Mao that the only way to resolve his present theoretical and practical political problem is by giving up the two elementary premises of his Marxist Communism and turning to a free democratic philosophy for modernizing his Chinese people in which the most basic trapped universal is free consent and in which its other more determinate basic trapped universal propositions are compatible with some but not all the basic "trapped universals" in every system of Confucian, Buddhist, Taoist and non-dualistic Hindu Asian religion and philosophy.

It remains to demonstrate that this is true. It remains also to state clearly the specific concepts in the philosophy of Confucian culture, in the philosophy of Buddhist culture and in the philosophy of Hindu culture which, with the aid of traditional folk songs used honestly rather than deceptively, the peoples of Asia can be won with their free consent to a modernization program which preserves the most basic, contractually true religious and moral beliefs and emotively cherished values in their traditional cultures while also gaining the cognitively true and best in the religious, legal and political philosophy of a clear-headed rather than epistemologically and psychologically confused free democratic West.

But even without such a constructive approach at the level of goal values to the international political problem that is raised by Mao's China, it is clear that both Mao and his people are at a fork in the road. The honeymoon during which both the elderly bride and the new young groom have held hands is over. The folk songs must be admitted now to have been a deceptive tactic or else the basic premises of Marxism must be rejected. Confucian-Taoist-Buddhist beliefs, still epistemically trapped in the brains of four hundred million village Chinese, are something to be reckoned with. The fact that he has already slain thousands of young and middle-aged Buddhist monks, leaving only the elderly whom nature will soon slay for him, proves that he realizes that his Marxism requires that not merely the outmoded applications but even the most elementary and basic concept of the person in any Taoist, Buddhist, Hindu or Confucian society must go. When, however, the most elementary concepts and postulates of any philosophy of any culture or society and its behavioristically conditioned customs have to go, then everything of the old has to go. The fact that President Mao and Premier Chou En-lai have torn daughters as well as sons out of their village homes to send them marching on parade grounds or exercising en masse on gymnastic grounds proves it also. The fact that he has torn husbands away from wives in the hope of breaking down the old Chinese familial loyalty which Confucius called "filial piety" proves it a third time. The logic of negation as applied to the self-contradictory is at work. The old bride has been thrown out of the carriage and the young groom is a typically Marxist young man.

But will this work? The mothers and the young wives in the villages still have to be reckoned with if even the Marxists are to have sons to succeed themselves. These older women and the children they rear at least to school age have not studied either Hegel or Marx, or, in all likelihood, even Mao. Nor would they understand what any of the three is saying even if they did.

Consequently, if President Mao continues to follow through with his insistence that his Marxist philosophically defined aim is the final synthesis, then, to be sure, he remains a Marxist, but the old China goes completely and he runs the very serious and real risk of failing to carry his people with him. Should this happen, the result will be a blood purge that will not be a paper tiger. If, on the other hand, his dialectical way of thinking, that he has learned from Hegel and Marx, triumphs over the determinism of his Marxism, which, as Chapters 9 and 15 have shown, is incompatible with it, then Marxism is but an antithesis rather than the final synthesis it claims to be, and his Marxist goal-value aim has to be thrown away.

Clearly, President Mao has good reasons for wanting more time to think. He has the philosophical knowledge, the brains and the conceptual discipline which is required in theoretical investigations and which is sufficient to enable him to think deeply. Such a good brain may still be able to save Mao the man from a very real tiger that can tear to pieces Mao the Marxist, thereby still saving what is cognitively true and normatively best in one of the world's wisest peoples and greatest civilizations.

Can the political leadership of the free world rise to the opportunity which President Mao's return to "theoretical investigations" presents?

PART THREE

The Meaning and Methods of
Any Free People

17

What Kind of Modern Civilization Do We Want? *

In 1958 the Cultural Division of the South East Asia Treaty Organization called a conference at Bangkok. Its concern was modern technology in Asian societies. Two facts were reported which make one ask whether we have the kind of civilization we want.

Mr. Tom Harrisson, representing Sarawak, reported that a more culturally isolated people than his neighbors on the island of Borneo do not exist. Little reaches them except a few radios and three broadcasts from Indonesia, Australia and Communist China. Since they know none of the languages spoken, what they hear from abroad is not understood. Nevertheless, these broadcasts have disrupted their folk dances of high quality. By capturing their ears and imaginations, the mere beat of boogie-woogie has corrupted their aesthetic standards and is destroying their customs.[1]

Ambassador W. R. Crocker, representing Australia, called attention to the English reading material from the free world available on street-corner stands in Bangkok. He testified that it is similar to what he found at Jakarta when he was Ambassador to Indonesia. He suggested that it is all too similar also to what exists in Australia, Canada, the United States and even Great Britain. Needless to say, it portrays young people of the most vulgar aesthetic taste with ap-

* Originally published as Chapter 1, "What Kind of an American Civilization Do We Want?" in "American Civilization and Its Leadership Needs, 1960–1990," Vol. 325, Sept., 1959, pp. 1–10 of the *Annals of the American Academy of Political and Social Science* and republished here under its present title with their kind permission.

parently no moral scruples whatever whose main concern is with sex
at its crudest, making money by any means, and whipping out a re-
volver upon the slightest of whims. Many mollifying factors though
there be, this is the image of the free world which the marriage of
mass communication with the businessman's *laissez-faire* profit motive is creating today both abroad and at home. It appears, Ambassador Crocker concluded, that there is a Gresham's law of culture as
well as of money at work by which everywhere the bad is driving out
the good.[2]

To appreciate the full effect abroad of this image, the classical
Asian, medieval European, and Latin American conception of proper
relations between the sexes in public must be understood. In Confucian China, as in many Mexican villages today, a husband and
wife do not walk down the street side by side. It is immoral also for
even an engaged couple to meet unless the parents of both are continuously present. Imagine the impact upon the people when they
see American movies, to say nothing about the "personal confessions"
in the paperbacks. In 1950 the British-educated editor of India's ex-
cellent magazine of art, *Marg,* said to the writer:

If you think some of your American movies are vulgar, you should see
some which are created by young Indians who are copying yours and
who know nothing of the artistic and other cultural standards and
achievements of the West. Having been thus led by the influence of
your movies to repudiate the aesthetic standards and social customs of
their own great civilization and knowing next to nothing of yours, they
have no standards whatever to guide them. The result often is that compared with some Indian movies, the most vulgar of yours are models
of aesthetic refinement and sensitivity.

The only moral and artistic standards they know being thus flouted,
the conclusion follows easily that the Americans have no aesthetic
or social good taste whatever and that for them "anything goes"
providing one makes money in the process.

The ill effects are political as well as cultural. Once this image of
America arises, it becomes natural for Mr. Arnold Toynbee to reply
to an American secretary of state's broadcast about "massive retaliation at a time and place of one's own choosing" with "No annihilation without representation!" and for Asian statesmen to conclude also that the Americans, like the youth in their movies and

paperbacks, are "trigger-happy" with the atomic bomb and hence not to be trusted as allies in protecting the free world.

This is the trouble with neglecting the cultural factor in international politics. Because a secretary of state neglected the advice of cultural officers and other career diplomats in his own Department who are experienced in sensing the diverse cultural and political mentalities of the nations to which they are assigned and are expert in reporting objectively on the most likely foreign response to anything America does, the late Mr. Dulles defeated his own purposes. Instead of winning—through experienced diplomatic negotiations, tailor-made to the unique cultural and political concerns of each European, Latin American, African, Middle Eastern and Asian nation—the assent of his allies to his "new" foreign policy before he announced it, thereby giving political and cultural leaders abroad the time to prepare the minds of their own people for what he "really meant" by "massive retaliation . . . at one's own choosing," he unwittingly and quite unnecessarily drove into positive anti-Americanism even people like Mr. Toynbee, Pandit Nehru, and hundreds of millions of Europeans and Asians behind them, who want to believe the best about the United States. With far less money given to the Cultural Division and career diplomats than it costs to replace with American soldiers and weapons the military support thus lost, such unfortunate political and military consequences of the neglect of the cultural image of ourselves which we create abroad, could have been avoided.

Nor were Secretary Dulles' opposite numbers in the previous Democratic administrations entirely different. The major foreign policy adviser and Chairman of the Planning Board of Secretary Acheson's State Department was Mr. George F. Kennan. Quite contrary to his practice in understanding the Soviet Union, Mr. Kennan in his foreign policy theorizing tells us that "the moral-legal state of mind," that is, the cultural approach, is quite misplaced in international relations and that "power-balancing" "should" be used instead. This is equally self-defeating, as the neutralism which it generated in South Asia following the Korean United Nations police action shows, since it made the Soviet Russians' Mr. Malik's point for him when he returned to the Security Council. This point was that the presence of American forces in Korea was not the United Nations morally and legally authorized police action that it purported to be but was instead a militaristic power move upon the part of the United States to get its troops on Asian soil, into which America had duped her Asian and European allies.

Republican Candidate Eisenhower fell into the same Hobbesian error as Mr. Kennan when, in an irresponsible appeal for votes in his first election campaign, the general insisted against President Truman that the American boys in Korea were "in a war" and not in a United Nations legally authorized police action.

This power-politics philosophy of American foreign policy of the Republican candidate of 1951 and the Kennan-minded Democrats inevitably had the effect of reinforcing the image of America abroad as a military- and power-minded people rather than a morally and legally principled nation. It also left America morally and legally impotent when the Soviet tanks crushed Hungary. It is probably because of the danger of such a broken American image of herself that our Founding Fathers warned us explicitly against following the Machiavellian and Hobbesian power politics of eighteenth and nineteenth century Europe in our foreign policy. Jefferson—to whom our Founding Fathers entrusted the major share of the writing of their first foreign policy document, the Declaration of Independence—had studied the legal and political philosophy of the ancient Greeks, the Stoic Roman lawyers and all the moderns, including Hobbes, Locke, Hume and Rousseau. Jefferson's letters make it unequivocally clear that in the type of legal and political system which they created and in their foreign policy, the Founding Fathers' choice was between the political philosophies of Hobbes and Locke—and that they followed Locke. This is the point of Jefferson's statement that in his opinion "the three greatest men the world had ever produced [were] Bacon, Newton, and Locke." [3] This, rather than isolationism, is the point also of the warning issued to us by Washington, Jefferson and Hamilton against "entangling alliances" with "the imperialistic nations of [eighteenth and nineteenth century] Europe."

Unfortunately this counsel has not been followed. The result is that due to a Kennan-minded Hobbesian Democratic foreign policy and an Eisenhower-minded Republican foreign policy which has oscillated between a Hobbesian interpretation of what happened in Korea and an international legal interpretation of British, French and Israeli behavior at Suez, American international leadership in both parties has made America present a broken image of herself abroad. This is doubly tragic since it has occurred at the very time when the majority of Continental Europeans, as Continental European Union shows, and the majority of Britishers, as the existence of the British Commonwealth demonstrates, have repudiated Hobbes for Locke.

The domestic consequences are equally reactionary and serious. Only yesterday we read about the absurdity which occurs when three present Democratic foreign policy makers—Messrs. Acheson, Nitze and King—whose expertness is that of the black-letter positive lawyer, wrote "a major foreign policy document" on military weapons, the efficiency of which they are obviously incompetent to judge. Also, this Democratic foreign policy makes the professional soldiers who select their own successors the only competent deciders of foreign policy. Thus, again, military men and instruments are given primary roles in the image of America which American civilians are creating, thereby continuing the defeat of her purposes. Also, military men whose expertness is in instrumental values are forced, often against their own best judgment and wishes, to divert their attention from their own more-than-full-time job, to decide cultural and political goal-value questions in which they have no experience and little first-hand competence. Thus civilians in the State Department would behave like amateurish third-rate soldiers, and soldiers in the White House, Pentagon and war colleges are forced to behave like amateurish second-rate politicians. The unfortunate *de facto* result—as seen objectively from abroad and as Sputnik has made evident within—is an America which in the realm of military instrumental values is dangerously close to being second rate and in the even more important domain of goal values is presenting a politically confused or crude and an aesthetically vulgar image of herself to the world. This image was not improved by Vice President Nixon's public exchange with Premier Khrushchev in Moscow, as the British reaction reported in the *New York Times* of July 26, 1959, clearly demonstrates.

But some will say: "Washington, Jefferson and Hamilton did not have the Communist divisions and hydrogen bombs to face. Conditions are different today. Security must come first."

Let us reflect on what this means. It means what it says, which is that physical power and physical security are more important than civilized human beings who are the sole reason for physical power and security. In short, it means a self-contradictory and a persistingly self-defeating America.

Also, instead of curbing and eventually civilizing the Communists, it ensures that we do precisely what Stalin designed the Cold War to do—namely, cause us to abdicate the Lockean foreign policy ideals of the Declaration of Independence and the domestic religious and civil liberties of our Lockean Bill of Rights, thereby enabling the Communists to be feted at Bandung as the sole defenders throughout Africa, the Middle East and Asia of the ideals for which the America of 1776 and 1791 stands. In short, the result is to hand the entire idealistic religious, legal and political goal-value battle for the imaginations and loyalties of the youth of the world over to the Communists with little if any competition from us at the ideological-cultural level.

We must not fool ourselves. The Communists do not present themselves to Africans and Asians in terms of pressure for military bases or for the receipt of economic handouts. They present themselves instead in terms of their goal-value philosophy of an ideal world. In 1950 on the street-corner stands of Bombay, for example, one could buy for a few pennies the technical philosophical classics of Marx, Engels and Lenin which define this ideal. On his return from India in 1950, the writer was told by informed people in Cairo that young Egyptian Communists were studying the Islamic classics in the world's leading Islamic university, thereby identifying themselves with the best in that great civilization, while also teaching their fellow Egyptian students the technical philosophical doctrines and ideals of the Communists. Consequently, the image which Stalin's Russia and Mao's China were then giving to the youth of Asia, Islam and Africa was not that of youthful social parasites obsessed with sex, moneymaking and gun play, but of a serious and poor Russian and Chinese youth, like themselves, who were working long hours in the classroom, the laboratory and the factory to master the Marxist philosophy, the mathematics, medicine and technology necessary to implement and protect the achievement of a specific philosophically defined goal-value ideal for all their people.

One looked in vain in 1950 in the street-corner stands of New

Delhi, Karachi or Cairo for the goal-value classics of America and the free world. Instead, the literature described later by Ambassador Crocker at Bangkok was in its place.

It is to be noted that Australia's political scientist and diplomat did not put the blame for the present operation of a Gresham's law of culture solely on modern technology and the emphasis upon quantity at the expense of quality which it makes possible. Ambassador Crocker noted that the veneration of the businessman's profit motive as the highest good is also responsible. Certainly it comes near to being in major part culpable because technological instruments are normatively neutral with respect to what they communicate. It appears, therefore, that the vulgar image of themselves which the peoples of the free world are exporting has its source in the false inversion of instrumental and goal values in which they have indulged at home.

Is this the kind of modern world we want? If not, then must we not ask ourselves the following more specific questions?

Does creative art and the cultivation of aesthetic sensitivity to the artistic standards of our own and other great civilizations enjoy the place of primacy in our educational system and in the civilizing of our movie producers, commercial publishers, television viewers and book buyers which a world of quality requires? Is the Cultural Division of the State Department listened to with sufficient seriousness when Congress examines the budget, or by our secretaries of state when they make major policy decisions and announcements? Do we possess a Cultural Division and Planning Board in the State Department composed of experienced diplomats, cultural anthropologists and experts in the world's various cultural and political philosophies, including our own, who are capable of framing a consistent and principled foreign policy that is (1) based on the fact that our Founding Fathers created an America in which both domestic legal and foreign policy is grounded in the religious and political philosophy of Locke and Jefferson and the later Lincoln rather than in the philosophy of Machiavelli and Hobbes; and (2) capable of winning the joyful support of men like Mr. Toynbee, Pandit Nehru, Premier Nkhumah and hundreds of millions of Europeans, Middle Easterners, Asians and Africans who are now making their own Lockean and Jeffersonian declarations of independence?

Finally, are men whose expertness is in the instrumental values of the soldier, the businessman, or the latter's corporation lawyer, or whose foreign policy philosophy is that of instrumental material power, likely to express in their specific practical political deeds the primacy of concern with goal-value cultural and philosophical ideals which is required if one is to be an effective diplomat or a non-self-defeating secretary of state? In short, has not the time come in both political parties to create a single, truly American foreign policy by putting it in the care of fresh and more philosophically specific and imaginative minds who believe that the Lockean philosophy of goal values of our Founding Fathers still has something to say for itself in both domestic law and foreign policy?

If the answer to the foregoing questions be Yes, certain additional questions follow immediately. Must not religious and political philosophy be given a place of primacy beside the cultivation of aesthetic sensitivity in the general education of everyone? More specifically, must not the religious philosophy of toleration and the separation of church and state of John Locke's *Letter Concerning Toleration* be required reading for every student? As the English social historian Trevelyan tells us, many people previously advocated toleration for reasons of religious or political expediency when they were in the minority or wanted freedom from religious wars, but it was with Locke for the first time that toleration became regarded as a positive good in and for itself even when one was in the majority. Must not also the legal and political philosophy of the Stoic Roman lawyers and Cicero, of Locke's *Lectures Concerning Natural Law* and *Of Civil Government,* together with the letters of Jefferson and the *Federalist Papers,* be given a place of primacy in the general educational system, the war colleges and the training of Foreign Service officers? Is there any reason also why these philosophical classics should not be made available in penny editions, translated into every native language and dialect for all the world to read?

Might it not be well also to acquaint everyone in the United States with Hobbes' *Leviathan,* the nineteenth century English jurist Austin's *Province of Jurisprudence Determined,* Judge Learned Hand's *The Spirit of Liberty,* and essays on *The Bill of Rights* which derive, by way of Thayer of the 1890 Harvard Law School and Austin, from Hobbes? Then everyone will know the difference between the type of legal and political system of "checks and balances" based on Locke which our Founding Fathers created and the type of democratic positive legal institutions based on Hobbes which the British created and into which Mr. Justice Frankfurter sometimes, and Judge Learned Hand always, would now have us transform the institutions created by our Founding Fathers. Were this done, there would certainly not now be the confusion concerning whether it is the Chief Justice Warren and Justices Black, Brennan and Douglas wing of the Supreme Court or the Justice Frankfurter-focused wing which represents the original conception of the Constitution and its Bill of Rights.

The heart of the difference between Locke and Hobbes is this. The former does not trust the locating of the entire political sovereignty of even a democratic government in any one branch of government. Consequently it divides political sovereignty between the three branches. It has a directly elected president who stays in office until the end of his term even when his party loses majority control of the legislative branch and who also has the power, which every American president has exercised, of vetoing majority-approved legislative statutes for any reason he may choose to give. Similarly, in order to give legal protection to the religious and political beliefs of dissenters and to locate part of the political sovereignty in the judicial branch, the Lockean philosophy of democratic government as applied by Jefferson, Madison, the Adamses and our other Founding Fathers adds a Bill of Rights which the federal judges are legally bound to interpret as law and use as a standard, not, as Judge Hand would have us believe, to "introduce a third legislature," but to measure the substantive content of the legislature's statutes in the legal protection of religious and civil liberties.

The first draft of the federal Constitution was sent by both Washington and Madison to Jefferson who was then Ambassador to France. Jefferson immediately replied that this Constitution would not do, since it did not contain a "declaration of rights." Madison in his reply to Jefferson agreed, while adding certain reasons put forward to the contrary. On March 15, 1789, Jefferson replied to Madison as follows: "In the arguments in favor of a declaration of rights . . . one which has great weight with me [is] the *legal* check which it puts into the hands of the judiciary." [4] (Italics mine).

The word "legal" in the foregoing quotation from Jefferson speaks for itself. It means that the Founding Fathers who were persuaded in part by Jefferson's arguments to add the Bill of Rights to the federal Constitution intended it to be interpreted as law by the federal courts. They did not construe it to mean what Judge Hand, following Thayer, Austin and Hobbes, would now have it mean, namely, mere "admonitions to forbearance" or "counsels of moderation" [5] which, if the legislators choose to ignore, a federal "judge of principle" will do nothing to redress. Making it doubly clear that the Bill of Rights is to be interpreted as law, Jefferson added in his letter of March 15, 1789, that "the executive, in our [state and federal] governments, is not the sole, it is scarcely the principal object of my jealousy. The tyranny of the legislatures is the most formidable dread at present, and will be for many years." [6]

In the Hobbesian theory of democracy on the other hand, which the positive portion of the British unwritten constitution follows (the living customs of Britain's unwritten constitution being Lockean), the whole of political sovereignty is placed in the legislative branch. Thus in Great Britain today, as in most of the other democracies of the contemporary world, the head of the executive branch of government is merely the leader of the majority party in the legislature, having no veto power over legislation approved by the majority and going out of office the moment his party loses majority control of the legislature. Similarly, no British court can declare a statute approved by the majority of the House of Commons to be illegal. The legal philosophy of Hobbes, Austin, Thayer and Judge Learned Hand fits the positive law of Great Britain's unwritten constitution, but does not fit the legal and political system of the United States. The practical effect, therefore, of accepting the legal philosophy of Judge Learned Hand and the Justice Frankfurter wing of the present Supreme Court will be to transform the American legal and political system, which was based on Locke rather than Hobbes, into the Hobbesian positive legal portion of the British system.

Again two more questions arise: Is the latter the kind of America we want? In other words, do we want to follow Hobbes in our domestic as well as foreign politics? Or do we want to win back the confidence of the majority of Britishers who are now Lockeans, the majority of Continental Europeans who are now Stoic Roman internationalists, and the majority of the people of the world generally who are now issuing their own Lockean and Jeffersonian declarations of independence, by returning to both the domestic legal and the foreign policy philosophy of our Founding Fathers?

Whatever our choice, one thing is clear. To be a civilized modern without knowing the religious, moral, legal and political philosophy which specifies what modern civilization and the world's freedom as we understand it mean, is to attempt the impossible. Hence, the philosophy of our goal values must take its place as primary beside the cultivation of aesthetic sensitivity in our entire educational system.

But even this is not enough. Sputnik has shown that in addition to the seeking of beauty and justice there must also be the seeking of mathematical truth.

Admiral Rickover has told us something which every general and admiral knows who may find himself carrying on a legally authorized international police action with second-rate weapons. American youth who are self-indulgent or concerned mainly with extracurricular activities during their schooling will not do. What has to be realized is that the practical man by himself is today the most impractical fellow on earth. Without the pioneer leadership in the frontier of human knowledge of the most formally-minded theorists in symbolic logic, pure mathematics, and theoretical as well as experimental physics, the practical man knows, if he is honest with himself, that he will be a failure. Devoid of the most mathematical and even the most philosophical theory of natural science which Einstein, Heisenberg and countless others, such as Willard Gibbs, Maxwell, Kant, Leibniz, Newton, Euclid, Eudoxus and Democritus pursued in and for its own sake, the practical instruments of today's world would not be. Moreover, unless today's and tomorrow's youth pioneer beyond Gibbs, Einstein and Heisenberg, the military and industrial instruments of tomorrow's so-called practical people are likely to be second rate. This is why one commits instrumental as well as moral suicide when one puts sensitivity to moneymaking in the market place ahead of the seeking and telling of truth for its own sake in theoretical natural science and its philosophy.

But the symbolic logic and the advanced mathematics that are required to keep ahead in one's military and industrial instruments and strategy cannot be learned on the spur of the moment when the defense of freedom may become urgently necessary. Nor can they be studied for a while and then dropped to be picked up a year or two later where one left them off. When the writer was on the Executive Committee of Yale College some twenty years ago, it became evident that able students of high standing in mathematics who, for sickness or any other reason, were forced to drop their studies for even a year, on returning to college frequently failed their next course in mathematics. The practical moral should be clear: training in formal thinking, including English grammar, symbolic logic and mathematics, must be given a place of continuous primacy in the educational system beside the seeking of beauty and tolerant religious, moral, legal and political philosophy. Only if these three things are done is it likely that America, Great Britain,[7] France,[8] Vietnam[9] or any other nation can keep her ideals in the forefront of what she is doing to win the confidence of free men everywhere and at the same time possess first-rate instruments for protecting and implementing these ideals.

It will be said that the addition of these subjects in the degree indicated to the present educational curriculum is impossible since it is already overcrowded. Such a judgment will not, however, stand careful analysis. The plain fact at present is that most of the subjects now taught in the curriculum are not understood. The reason is that most of them require one or more of the three basic disciplines noted above for their understanding. How, for example, can a student possibly understand anything if he is incapable, as is presently the case with many students entering college, of framing semantically clear and grammatical sentences for an attempted paper? How can a person possibly distinguish sensed fact from inferred theory in natural or social science if he does not have the aesthetic sensitivity to distinguish (1) the impressionistic sensuous images which the senses convey to him from (2) the directly unobservable, theoretically known and mathematically defined scientific objects which he infers from these impressionistic aesthetic sensed images? How can a student, a teacher or a statesman avoid being anything but confused about his normative religious, moral, legal and political ideals and decisions if he is unaware of normative philosophy and the difference between a statement concerning what ought to be and a non-normative statement about what is the case in fact? To put the three aforementioned basic subjects first in our educational system will be, therefore, to clarify the curriculum and to economize in the time it takes to civilize our citizens.

In any event, two things are clear: there is a modern civilization of quality. We can have it if we want it.

18

The Normative Ideals of
a Free People

The previous chapter showed that three subjects need to be made primary in education: (1) the cultivation of radically empirical sensitivity; (2) the formal imageless thinking of abstract grammar, symbolic logic, mathematics, mathematical physics and the constructs of Western contractual legal science; and (3) analytically precise normative philosophy, especially that of contractual legal and political science, together with its major medieval religious and secular contemporary rivals.

1. *Aesthetic Sensitivity*

Art provides the emotively moving and persuasive factor that is a necessary, but not a sufficient, condition for making contractual democracy work. It is also required if modern-minded free men are not to create a commercially cheap and aesthetically vulgar world. But even more important, the cultivation of aesthetic sensitivity will convey a cognitive truth which is immediately evident to all human beings everywhere.

Its truth-telling importance arises because it is the immediately experienced, emotively felt, aesthetically moving and consciously vivid component of oneself and nature which is the denotative reference for verifying directly the truth of all propositions whose cognitive concepts in Part I were called concepts by intuition, i.e., concepts that refer to emotively felt aesthetically immediate experience

312

for their meaning. Rarely for people so educated by impressionistic and Oriental art will the immediately apprehended continuum of radically empirical experience and its sequences of perpetually perishing sensations and images be confused with the unaesthetic material substances which the materialists suppose that they sense. Immediately experienced fact is an emotively and hence consciously laden continuum which, from moment to moment, is vibrant with different vivid aesthetically ineffable and indescribable colors, sounds, fragrances and flavors. Pure immediately experienced fact is, therefore, the stuff of which feeling, consciousness and the materials of the poet, the painter, the musician and the epicure are made.

For people thus trained to separate immediately experienced fact from theoretical inferences that transcend it, the standard for measuring achievement in the dance may well be something in addition to, or quite other than the theoretical combination of ancient Greek geometry and the physical culturalist's muscle building, always fighting gravitation, which, beautiful though it be, is the traditional ballet. The dance and music of Erick Hawkins and Lucia Dlugoszewski will be appreciated also as the much less muscularly artificial and the more immediately natural and beautiful standard of artistic measurement in the domain of the aesthetically immediate which it is. In short, concept by intuition contemporary dancing *as well as* the anti-gravitational Greek geometrically ordered dancing of medieval or modern Soviet bourgeois society will flourish.

Moreover, this separation of aesthetic immediacy from the outmoded past concepts by postulation that defined medieval theocratic and modern Soviet bourgeois standards for measuring the beautiful will reveal a factor in the living law of any non-modern Western society which is common to all men and hence a factor upon which all can agree. What this factor is has been indicated in Chapter 14. How it is to be made use of politically will concern us in the next chapter.

It sufficeth here to note two things, by way of preparation, concerning the nature of any human being's immediate experience. First, as noted above, immediate experience is emotively felt and hence conscious experience. This means that a free world based on the cultivation of sensitivity to aesthetic, emotively felt, conscious experience will never leave one with a legal and political person who is

314 Philosophical Anthropology and Practical Politics

regarded as nothing but an aggregate of unconscious material substances for which political freedom means the inevitability of physical collisions with other unconscious material substances after the manner of the legal and political person of Hobbes' state of nature and the materialistic Marxists. Second, this conscious immediacy of experience is an all-embracing continuum. In other words, it is a field consciousness including as differentia within itself the transitory, temporally successive sensed and imagined images that come and go. Otherwise these perpetually perishing, differentiated sensations, feelings and images of which one is immediately conscious would not be within immediate conscious experience. Moreover, the continuum is continuously present; only the differentia within it change to give one the sense of sensed time. This one unchanging, undifferentiated field consciousness is what the Orientals call the "Nirvana consciousness" or the "*chit* consciousness," i.e., the Divine consciousness.

Negatively, with respect to the West, what this means is that radically immediate experience shows anyone's consciousness to be a field consciousness embracing in its formlessness all immediately experienced, sensed or introspected persons and things. It is not a consciousness that is fastened like a predicate to the inside of a windowless spiritual atom or mental substance, as Berkeley, Leibniz, Lotze and others such as Batlle y Ordóñez supposed.

From the standpoint, therefore, of this intuitive field consciousness, both the unconscious material person of the Hobbesian power politicians and the Marxists and the conscious atomic spiritual substances of the spiritualists arise from an evident confusion. First, they confuse the structure of the grammar of the Aryan language with the immediately sensed or introspected character of the things this language is used to convey. Secondly, they make the error, described in detail in Part I, of producing nonsense by putting the word "conscious" or the words "hot" or "hard" (whose meanings are that of a radically empirical concept by intuition) in the same sentence with the word "substance" which, if it has any meaning at all, is a logically realistic epistemological concept by postulation. Hence, as shown in Part I, this traditional modern notion of only unconscious material substances being real, or only conscious mental substances being real, or a causal interaction of both being real, is the product of epistemological and phantasmic confusions. Finally it is false, as noted just above, to what one immediately, overtly and aesthetically experiences. What one immediately experiences is a field consciousness, neither a self-focused mental substance consciousness nor an immediately sensed object-focused materialistic substance.

But this field-consciousness conception of the religious, legal and political person, as Chapter 14 has indicated, is already present in the centuries-old belief system and the living law of all un-Westernized native people and especially in the living law of the classical Buddhist, Taoist and Hindu Asian moral, legal and religious communities. These people quantitatively represent a majority of the people on the surface of the earth. Providing, therefore, that we root our free democratic modernization program in this factor in their old living law, while, by means of the cultivation of radically empirical impressionistic aesthetic sensitivity in ourselves, we become aware of the field-consciousness, emotive nature of our own selves, the living law support necessary to make such an aesthetically sensitive and emotively compassionate modern democracy work politically throughout the entire world should be at hand. In all likelihood, also, this field-consciousness concept by intuition of the self is still in all the peasants of the Soviet Union. Without doubt also, it is still trapped in the brains of the mothers in Mao's China, however much he may have succeeded in killing the Buddhist monks and pulling the patriarchal joint-family husbands and sons away from their families to indoctrinate them with the thinking of the materialists' material substances.

It is not, however, beyond the bounds of neurophysiological possibility that this field-consciousness concept by intuition universal is still trapped in the cortex of Mao himself and even the proud peasant Khrushchev too. Perhaps by merely calling attention to the immediately experienced field-consciousness component of anyone's consciously experienced self, the epistemic correlate of this concept by intuition person can be reinforced in Mao and Khrushchev's brains. For this no super-rockets, but merely a few radios with their electromagnetic waves that travel 186,000 miles per second are all that are necessary to contact both of them. Even if Premier Khrushchev, smiling down his nose at our inferior weapons, goes off on one of his super-rockets to the moon, we can contact him by means of radio waves, without the need of a Summit Conference, even there.

In the case of Mao's Chinese, this aesthetically immediate truth-telling should be easy, for the Chinese are the world's leading epicures. They love the flavor of young bean sprouts and they live in the world of the aesthetically immediate. To recall their attention to the fact that these unconscious and unaesthetic material substances of the Hobbesians and the Marxists do not have the reality even of moonshine should be relatively easy.

But more than flavorful emotively moving concept by intuition, aesthetically immediate truth-telling is required if free men are to be politically practical. The people of the world want modern instruments and the higher and more democratically equal standards of living and of health which are made possible by the modern logically realistic, indirectly verified concept by postulation theory of Western mathematical physics and Western contractually legal and political institutions. These instruments require for their understanding, at least in those who make them and occasionally even for those who use them, knowledge of the basic assumptions of modern technology and its mathematics and symbolic logic. We must, therefore, specify also the elementary concepts and propositions of these subjects.

2. *The Primitive Ideas of Symbolic Logic and Pure Mathematics*

Before the middle of the last century, the mathematicians were aware consciously of the definable ideas and approximately proved, but sometimes not overtly and rigorously proved, theorems of their subject. They had not, however, brought into the open the logically primitive concepts and postulates which they used covertly in carrying through the proofs of their theorems even when those proofs were logically rigorous. This deficiency was gradually removed by a series of epoch-making philosophical analyses of the meaning of the symbols of mathematical language. This series of analytic discoveries began in mathematics, perhaps with Weierstrass' rigorous definition of the mathematical concept of "limit" and with Dedekind's classical *Essays on the Theory of Numbers*.[1] These investigations were followed by the Italian mathematician Peano's five postulates for arithmetic which were followed in turn by the *Principia Mathematica* of Whitehead and Russell and the formalist mathematics of Hilbert.[2]

In the two latter works, analytical evidence was given for believing that the technical concepts of mathematics become clear and precise only when they are formally constructed in terms of imageless logical concepts such as negation, disjunction, the entity variable of a relation, symmetry, reflexiveness, transitivity and isomorphism of relations and the range of the variable of a relation with such imageless postulationally constructed formal properties. The postulates of deductive reasoning present in all mathematical proofs and calculations also have to be assumed.

Certain paradoxes and other problems remained having to do with self-referential statements and the analysis of "strict implication," which were noted by Russell, Whitehead and G. E. Moore and have led to symbolic logical assumptions slightly different from those of *Principia Mathematica*. Three of the most notable of these are the theories of strict implication of (1) C. I. Lewis, (2) Nuel D. Belnap, Jr., and (3) the systematic symbolic logic of F. B. Fitch.[3] Thus even symbolic logic and mathematics as well as practical politics have their basic theoretical problems. The intuitive theory of mathematics is one attempt to clarify these difficulties. There are reasons for believing that it confuses, rather than clarifies, by putting concept by intuition introspected psychological acts of counting in the same sentence with logically realistic concept by postulation constructs. Such psychological acts belong in mathematical psychology and refer to the operational epistemic correlates of non-psychological mathematical constructs; they have no place in a theory of pure mathematics, i.e., of the meaning of the constructs themselves.

Notwithstanding these theoretical uncertainties that still remain, three things, however, are generally agreed upon by all who have investigated them. First, the concepts of symbolic logic and Western mathematics are imageless. Mill's theory that they define away in terms of concepts by intuition referring for their meaning to data given directly through the senses is not now taken seriously. In short, the concepts of symbolic logic and mathematics and its mathematical physics are, to use the writer's language of Part I, concepts by postulation which are concepts by intellection. Second, traditional mathematics, or at least much of it, is but the advanced chapters of symbolic logic. Third, all the concepts of the more advanced branches of mathematics having to do with fractions, irrational and other real numbers generally can be deduced from Peano's five postulates about the natural numbers.

The first of these three conclusions means that one can effectively introduce to the people of a given nation the mentality necessary to modernize their medieval thinking and their living law customs only if concepts by intellection are introduced simultaneously into the education of their top research scientists and engineers and even more generally into the entire educational system. Otherwise, as noted in Chapters 10 and 16, the people receiving the modern foreign economic aid, agricultural ways and technological instruments will think about them and use them with the only concepts they have for thinking about anything and using anything, namely, the old concepts by intuition or the confused, naïvely realistic notions, the epistemic correlates of which are still trapped in their brains.

Western experience confirms this conclusion. Many businessmen and military strategists today are finding symbolic logicians frequently to be of more practical usefulness to them than the traditional type of mathematician. Obviously one cannot make a calculating machine or an antiaircraft gun which, given some "information," must deduce certain logical consequences from this data if the logical rules for carrying through a rigorous calculation are not programmed or in part built into the machine.

The third conclusion upon which twentieth century mathematicians came to agree—namely, Peano's five postulates of arithmetic—raised, however, a serious difficulty. The difficulty centered in Peano's Fifth postulate. After stating that Peano's three elementary or undefined concepts are "zero," "number in the sense of integer" and the relation "successor of," Russell states this Fifth postulate as follows: "Any property which belongs to x_0, and belongs to x_{n+1} provided it belongs to x_n, belongs to all the x's,"[4] where x means any one natural number. This proposition seems, therefore, to affirm that merely upon the basis of knowing the mathematical properties of but two members of an infinite class, one can know that all its other members have these properties. Clearly this seems to be a logical *non sequitur*. Nevertheless, unless this is assumed, the propositions of mathematics cannot be proved. This problem has been called, by mathematicians and symbolic logicians, the problem of mathematical induction.

Its answer was suggested, if not stated, first by the German Frege's philosophical analysis of mathematical language, and discovered and stated first for the English-speaking mathematical world at least by Bertrand Russell. The answer is that the mathematical properties of zero and one are not known by examining zero as if it were an entity possessing all its arithmetical properties in isolation by itself, and then doing likewise with the number one considered in isolation in the same way, to find inductively that zero and one have some properties in common, and then indulging in the prodigious *non sequitur* of concluding that all the infinite number of natural numbers possess these common properties merely because zero and one do. This would be to assume that zero and one or any other natural number is a complete symbol, i.e., a symbol whose complete meaning is contained in that symbol considered in isolation by itself. Instead, any natural number is an incomplete symbol, i.e., a symbol which by itself is meaningless and gets its entire meaning from its formal syntactic relation to other symbols in a formally constructed imageless set of postulates. Once this is realized, then Peano's Fifth postulate is seen to be true tautologically since then what it means to be *any one* of the infinite series of natural numbers, including therefore zero and one, is to be an entity for which Peano's Fifth postulate holds.[5]

That this is the correct answer to the problem of mathematical induction is shown by the substantive mathematical fact that when one compares the imageless, formal properties of the relation of immediate successor, which give the mathematical properties of the series of all natural numbers, with the quite different formally constructed relation which defines the series of real numbers, it is precisely Peano's Fifth postulate which distinguishes the infinite class of natural numbers from the infinite class of real numbers. In short, substantive mathematical as well as epistemological considerations confirm Frege and Russell's solution to the problem of mathematical induction.

The concrete meaning can perhaps be brought home to the reader who is not versed in these commonplaces of contemporary symbolic

logic and mathematical science if we use again the writer's epistemological language of Part I. There, as throughout this book, we have
distinguished between two different types of conceptual meaning
which almost any word which we use has: namely, radical empirical
concept by intuition meaning and logically realistic concept by
postulation which (being imageless) is concept by intellection meaning.

Words conveying the former of these two types of meaning are
always complete symbols. This follows from the definitions of (1) a
complete symbol and (2) any concept by intuition. A complete symbol is one which, so to speak, contains its entire meaning within itself
quite independently of its syntactical or imageless formal logical
relations to other symbols. "Yellow" in the sense of the immediately
seen color of impressionistic painting is an example. A concept by
intuition is one the complete meaning of which is given by denotative
reference to some particular sensed, introspected or immediately experienced factor in existential empirical immediacy. As David Hume
noted, in immediate experience one never senses necessary connections. From this it follows that were the concepts of arithmetic
complete symbols or, in other words, concepts by intuition, then,
given what is true for the concept by intuition number "zero" and
its immediate successor the number "one," one could never get to
what is necessarily true for the infinite number of successors of
"one."

In the case, however, of concepts by postulation which are concepts
by intellection, this is not the case. For such concepts, any word
taken out of the imageless, formal, axiomatically constructed set of
postulates or relations which give it and all members of the class
satisfying that postulate their meaning, is an incomplete symbol and
hence is by itself meaningless. This is the case because for any
concept by postulation, its entire meaning is specified completely by
the imageless formal relation or determinate syntax specified in the
particular set of postulates that relate that term to other symbols
in the postulate set.

Hence, instead of the individual entities and their isolated complete symbolic properties determining the truth or falsity of the
postulate, it is the formal imageless properties of the universally
quantified, for any number, relation or law specified in the postulate

set which give the otherwise meaningless incomplete symbols 0, 1, 2, 3, 4, etc. the only mathematical meaning they have. In short, the problem of mathematical induction arose because one thought the numbers of Western mathematics were concepts by intuition, or naïve realistic epistemological concepts which, being defined in terms of concepts by intuition, are also complete symbols. The problem is solved when it is noted that they are instead concepts by postulation which are concepts by intellection. Then Peano's Fifth postulate is seen to be true tautologically. In other words, its truth is self-evident. The reason, let it be repeated, is that, because the expression "natural number" is an incomplete symbol, what it means to be any natural number is to be any entity for which Peano's Fifth postulate holds.

The concept by intuition images which we associate with some of the natural numbers are merely at most the epistemic correlates of their concept by postulation technical mathematical meanings, and quite irrelevant to those meanings or to the carrying through of rigorous purely mathematical deductions from them. As noted above, concepts by intuition denoting introspected psychological acts of counting are essential in mathematical physics and mathematical psychology. They are misplaced, however, within the non-empirical science of pure mathematics or symbolic logic.

Their importance in mathematical physics and mathematical neuropsychology has been shown in Part I. The pure mathematics of any mathematically physical set of postulates are propositions, like Peano's Fifth postulate, which are true because they are tautologies. For example, the affirmation "For the entity variable called the electron, the universally quantified laws of electromagnetics hold" seems to be a synthetic proposition, i.e., one in which the predicate of the proposition means more than is meant by the definition of the subject of the proposition. But this is a mere seeming, since being an incomplete symbol or concept by postulation, to be an "electron" means to be an entity variable for which the universally quantified laws of electromagnetics hold. Hence, as pure mathematics, the proposition is analytic and true tautologically.

What meaning, then, is there to saying that a specific theory of the electron in mathematical physics (as distinct from the pure mathematics of the theory) is empirically true or false? Without the recognition of the epistemic rules of correspondence in theories of scientific objects and the public self of the logically realistic concept by postulation type, this question is unanswerable. It is the epistemic correlation of terms in the purely mathematical propositions of electron theory, with radically empirical data and operations, which adds the concept by intuition meaning to the otherwise analytic propositions of the pure mathematics of electron theory to give mathematically empirical propositions which are both syntactic and empirically as well as mathematically meaningful. This permits one to say of them that they are empirically true or false as determinable by concept by intuition operational confirmation or disconfirmation by anyone anywhere.

The non-normatively worded philosophy which defines the inhibition or reinforcement of the behavior that *ought to be* in our freely inquiring and behaving human world is composed of the foregoing (1) aesthetic, (2) purely mathematical and (3) mathematically physical and neurophysiological elementary postulates. We say "ought to be" because, as shown in Chapter 7, the word "ought" refers to one's non-normatively worded philosophy in its bearing on conduct, when all the postulates of this philosophy are cognitively true in the sense of being (a) analytic propositions and hence true tautologically or (b) synthetic empirical propositions which can be confirmed or disconfirmed by appeal to first-order facts by anyone anywhere.

Our aesthetic postulate (1) meets this requirement since it is known with radically empirical immediacy when one neglects, abstracts away contemplatively or experimentally removes the differentiations within the field consciousness which is radically empirical immediacy. Our mathematical postulates (2) are true tautologically. The contemporary empirical synthetic propositions of mathematical physics (3) and of the mathematically neurophysiological self designated in Part I are meaningfully true or false because they are confirmable indirectly by way of epistemic correlations with operational experiments performable by anyone anywhere.

These postulates are, however, instances of the even more elementary epistemological postulate which was described as (4) radical empiricism related by epistemic rules of correspondence to logical realism. In Chapter 7 this epistemological proposition was shown to be empirically confirmable by anybody anywhere and to make meaningful the introduction and precise statement of an additional empirically confirmable psychological postulate. The latter postulate is that (5) objects in the logically realistic world of discourse which are objects other than the public self are epistemically correlated with radically empirically sensed and introspected data by epistemic rules of correspondence that are one-many; whereas in the case of the logically realistic public object which is one's own self, these epistemic rules of correspondence between radically empirically sensed and introspected data and events and those of one's public self are one-one. More specifically, these one-one epistemic correlations tell us that overt or covert elementary philosophical ideas in the introspected consciousness or covert unconsciousness of any person are correlated in one's public neurophysiological self with unique trapped impulses that make determinate the hierarchically trapped inner target of one's teleologically mechanically behaving nervous system and its bodily instruments and movements.

What about our political postulate? To ask this question is equivalent to asking for the elementary postulate of contractual legal science. The reason is that Western politics as we have known it since the time of the Stoic Romans and contemporary world politics are the result of the creation of this science and its living and positive law shift from status to contract.

The elementary postulate of this much neglected and exceedingly important science is well known the world over. Moreover, it is self-evident or tautologically true precisely in the same sense in which such is the case for Peano's Fifth postulate in mathematical science. Expressed in ordinary prose, it was not merely stated by Jefferson in the Declaration of Independence, but also affirmed there to be "self-evident." That people everywhere today agree is confirmed empirically by what is occurring politically in Latin America, Africa, the Middle East and Asia. Everywhere people are appealing to this principle to justify (a) their demand that foreign rulers leave and (b) the importation of modern Western contractual legal and political normative institutions to set up their own democratic control of their nations.

But it may be said: You are violating your own method of descriptive philosophical anthropology by taking the positive foreign and domestic political principle of the Founding Fathers of your own nation and generalizing it provincially and self-righteously for the rest of mankind. Upon a first impression, this seems to be the case. But consider the following facts: (1) This basic proposition of the Declaration of Independence is "We hold these truths to be self-evident, that all men are created equal . . ." As this proposition stands, it is clearly elliptical. When expanded to bring out its full meaning, it reads: "We hold these truths to be self-evident, that all men are born free and equal with respect to their religious, moral, legal and political rights, privileges, obligations and duties." Note that this is not affirmed to be true merely for the American people. Hence, as shown in greater detail in the last chapter of the writer's *The Complexity of Legal and Ethical Experience,* this basic universal proposition, now trapped in most people's minds the world over, is a legal and political truth that is international, rather than provincially national, in its meaning and validity. It holds for Americans only because it holds for *anyone* anywhere. Hence it is a principle of international law and not of provincially American national law.

But then it may well be asked, What makes this international legal and political proposition self-evident? As a proposition in biology, it is most obviously false. Some children are born permanently maimed while some others are born vigorous and healthy. Some few come into the world with the creative association areas in their brains of an Einstein, a Jesus, a Buddha, a Bacon, a Newton or a Locke; others with the mental and spiritual talents of a moron. Hence, considered as a proposition referring either to the realm of the introspectively spiritual or the neurological and publicly natural, it is demonstrably false. By what justification, then, can Jefferson or anyone else say that this legal and political principle is self-evident? The answer is, Because it is a proposition, not in biological, or introspective psychological science, but in contractual legal and political science. More specifically it is the basic tautologically true proposition of any contractual legal and political system whatever, Communistic or non-Communistic, dictatorial or freely democratic alike.

But how can this be? The reason is that in legal and political nations of the law-of-contract type, as distinct from the biologically defined patriarchal or matriarchal joint-familial religious communities and tribal nations of the law-of-status type, there are no legal or political obligations, duties, rights and privileges until with some specific set of covert or overt contractually specified postulates, the parties concerned specify these legal and political rights and duties. This cannot be done until after people are born and have reached maturity of brain and mind. Hence at birth they are all born equal with respect to any and all of their political obligations, duties, rights and privileges. In short, the Jeffersonian principle is empirically self-evident. Or put more exactly, just as Peano's Fifth postulate specifies the substantive property which differentiates the class of all natural numbers from the class of all real numbers in the science of mathematics, so Jefferson's principle gives the differentiating property of any legally contractual nation.

But this political principle is also, quite apart from empirical considerations, *theoretically* self-evident or tautologically true. For put briefly it is: No contract, then no contractual obligations; similarly conversely, no contractual rights.

The quantitative majority of the *de facto* living law commercial practices of mankind are now of the contractual legal type. Exchanges of goods are now being made throughout the world by any individual whatever regardless of sex, primogeniture of birth, color of skin or familial or racial breeding. Religion much more slowly is also beginning to be broken free from the racial gods of the tribal nations. Also, the positive constitutional law of all the modern nations of the world—African, Islamic, Israeli and Asian as well as Western—Communistic and free democratic alike—is of the contractual type. Hence, the basic contractual tautologically true, internationally meaningful and valid proposition is already covertly present in the positive constitutional law and the living commercial law practices of the majority of people on the earth's surface. When, therefore, the political leader of any nation, such as one of the Marxists, the medieval Buddhist tribal Sinhalese, the patriarchally familial white Christians of the Old South, or anyone else puts substantive content in any contractual political legislative statute that is incompatible with the basic, tautologically true premise of any contractual legal system, they are self-condemning themselves to having done something which, being self-contradictory, is false. It is as if a mathematician affirmed an arithmetical theorem to be valid which contradicts Peano's Fifth postulate.

Since, moreover, this basic tautologically true proposition of any contractually legal nation is valid for any particular nation only because it is valid for anyone anywhere, it follows similarly that any legal and political scientist, such as Hobbes or Austin, and any foreign policy maker, such as former Secretary of State Acheson after the Suez crisis, and Secretary of State Dulles, in a conversation with Professor William E. Hocking, who affirms that international law is a self-contradictory and meaningless notion and, therefore, non-existent or "spurious," is unwittingly self-condemning himself to having made a self-contradictory and hence false judgment. *With respect to the most basic postulate upon which any law-of-contract nation rests, any nation's national law is international law,* however much the additional substantive content of one nation's contractual laws may differ from that of another at other points.

Why haven't previous lawyers and political scientists noted this? The answer is that in analyzing legal and political language, they made the same mistake that the earlier mathematicians made when they examined Peano's Fifth postulate. Assuming either (1) a naïve realistic epistemology, as did Hobbes, Marx and the free democratic power politicians in their materialism, or (2) solely a radically empirical epistemology, as did the Locke of the *Essay,* Hume, Bentham, Austin, William James, Holmes and Judge Learned Hand, they were forced to the conclusion that all legal and political words are complete symbols, i.e., either concepts by intuition or substances defined in such terms. Then the Declaration of Independence principle is a synthetic proposition and not true tautologically.

Moreover, it is a completely arbitrary synthetic proposition which one nation whose law is contractual can prefer or choose to put in its overt written or covert unwritten constitution and which another nation, such as Hitler's Germany, the Soviet Union, Mao's China and the state legislatures of America's Old South, can choose to ignore. As Judge Hand has frequently put it, "Some prefer peppermint and others prefer wintergreen." Such is the inevitable consequence of any radically empirical subjective introspective psychological philosophy of ethics, law and politics. The self-evident character of the Jeffersonian principle is then made meaningless.

Then also any individual legal and political entity such as "citizen," "politician," "the General Motors Corporation" or "nation" is a complete symbolic entity possessing all its legal and political properties when considered, after the manner in which "zero" or "one" was first considered, in isolation by itself. Once this supposition is made, the legal and political properties of each become absolutely restricted solely to itself. Forthwith, the legal and political sovereignty of each nation becomes absolute and international law becomes meaningless, since the notion of an absolute political sovereign limiting his absolute political sovereignty to make it less than absolute is a self-contradictory notion, as Hobbes and Austin quite correctly noted.

When, however, this conception of all legal and political entities as complete symbols is applied in domestic corporation law (the field of the late Mr. Dulles and Mr. Acheson's expertness) to the legal entity called a "corporation," e.g., the General Motors Corporation, difficulties arise. If this legal entity is something denoted by legal words that are complete symbols, then we should be able by looking in the public world of concrete entities to find it. When we attempt to do this, however, we come merely upon some buildings called factories in Detroit and many other cities throughout the world and some bodily persons such as Mr. Charles Wilson. But clearly none, nor the aggregate of all these complete symbolic entities is what is meant by the legal entity called the General Motors Corporation. It is now being recognized by some lawyers who have been successful practitioners of corporation law in Wall Street and who have returned to law school to reflect more deeply upon and teach this subject, that the legal and political expression "the General Motors Corporation" is an incomplete symbol. To use the epistemological language of Part I, it is a construct or concept by postulation that is a concept by intellection. Hence a logically realistic rather than either a radically empirical or a naïve realistic epistemological theory of the meaning of legal and political concepts is required to understand it. Put more concretely, this entails that to find the meaning of the legal entity variable "corporation," one must examine the politician's statutes of the state legislatures which have, by those statutes, brought this legal construct into being. Apart from these contractually constructed postulates, the word "corporation" is meaningless.

In his inaugural lecture given upon becoming the Regius Professor of Jurisprudence at Oxford, Mr. H. L. A. Hart, a trained lawyer who has practiced, as well as an expert philosophical analyst, examined the expression "a right" in the sense in which it occurs in any con-

tract which affirms that a particular person or party "has a right." [6]
He notes that the Scandinavian jurists have shown conclusively that
if one takes the word "right" as either an elementary, isolated, self-
evidently meaningful concept or as a non-elementary concept that is
defined in terms of such elementary concepts, i.e., if one assumes
the word "right" to be a complete symbol, the result again is unsatisfactory exactly as in the case of the legal entity "corporation." The
result simply is not what the word means. But what then does the
expression a "legal right" mean? Professor Hart's answer is that the
difficulty arises because previous legal thinkers and practitioners
have asked for definitions of normative words in legal science and
that this is an error, for then the aforementioned unsatisfactory results
occur. The correct and precise meanings do, however, become evident
if we stop asking for the definition of normative words and locate
their meaning instead in their relation to other words in the statutes
or propositions of the particular legal system of the particular political nation in question. In short, normative legal words are incomplete
symbols. Pulled out of the contractually constructed and postulated
context in which they occur, like the natural numbers zero and one,
they are meaningless. When, however, the contractual statutes that
assign their meanings to them are specified, then their legal meanings
are made determinate.

Since the most elementary postulate of any contractual nation's
legal system is given by its covert unwritten or its overt written
constitutional law, this means that the legal and political word
"nation" is an incomplete symbol, i.e., a logically realistic concept
by postulation that is a concept by intellection also. But as noted,
there are many nations with their different constitutions differing
from one another in the substantive content of those constitutions.
Consequently, as the substantive content of any two nation's contractually constructed constitutions differ, so the political properties
of the two nations differ.

Is all law and politics then relative? Is there only absolute sovereign national law and no international law? Even according to the
logically realistic epistemological concept of any nation as an incomplete symbol, it would seem so.

Such, however, as noted above, is not the case, for within any
legally contractual nation's system of legal propositions there are

two classes of propositions. The one class contains propositions which vary from nation to nation. Following Kant's terminology, we shall call this class of constitutional, legislative and judicial propositions "maxims" or "hypothetically imperative" legal and political norms. They are hypothetical because it is for the parties to the constitutional, legislative or commercial contract to decide what their substantive content is. Consequently, such hypothetical legal and political propositions put no obligations upon anyone to whom they are applied to obey them unless everyone in the community or their representatives assent to what is in the contractually constructed hypothesis. Note, therefore, that in the logically realistic legal science of contract, assent plays exactly the same role with respect to the validation of hypothetical imperatives as do operational definitions and experiments with respect to the confirmation of the logically realistic hypotheses of mathematical physics. This means that even for maxims or hypothetical imperatives, contractual legal science is compatible only with a contractual legal system that has free democratic substantive content in its constitutional law. We conclude, therefore, that any type of dictatorship—whether it be Communistic or non-Communistic—is logically incompatible with any legally contractual political system.

Even so, within a free democratic political system different nations may contractually construct their nation with hypothetically imperative constitutional or legislative rules with different substantive content. Great Britain, when it locates the whole of political sovereignty of a free democratic nation in the legislative branch, and the United States, which divides it between the legislative, executive and judicial branches, are examples.

Nevertheless, there is another class of legal propositions in any contractual nation which is identical for all such nations and hence is an international legal and political system. This class of legal and political propositions has two characteristics: First, it contains only one member. Second, its solitary proposition is a categorical imperative rather than a maxim or merely hypothetical imperative that depends upon consent for its validity. In a categorical imperative, consent is secondary since, being categorically true, the legal and political proposition is valid irrespective of whether one realizes it or not, exactly as with Peano's Fifth postulate.

This unique legal and political proposition of any contractual nation and international law is not, however, a categorical imperative for the reason which Kant gave. Kant's erroneous reason was that this unique moral and legal proposition is a synthetic proposition *a priori*. This again is to suppose that "citizen," "nation," "legal system" and "moral person" are complete symbols. Were such the case, let it be recalled, normative propositions would be synthetic, i.e., propositions which affirm more in their predicate than is given in the definition of their subject term. Instead, the unique international legal and political proposition which holds for any particular nation or person now, because it holds for any nation or person anywhere and any time, is an analytic proposition, for in contractual legal science any legal and political entity such as "nation," "politician" or "citizen" is an incomplete symbol. Hence, what it means to be *any one* legally contractual "nation," "citizen" or "politician" is to be an entity variable all the scientific properties of which are assigned to it by the solitary elementary postulate of contractual legal science, i.e., the Jeffersonian principle; exactly as what it means to be "zero," "one" or any other natural number in the science of arithmetic means that all such arithmetical entities possess the formal logical relational properties specified in Peano's Fifth postulate. The Jeffersonian postulate is, therefore, an analytic proposition, true tautologically for any contractually legal nation, citizen or politician whatever, irrespective of his consent, and hence a categorical imperative of both national and international law.

Two things remain to be done before the major political implications of this conclusion become evident: First, we must examine the relation between this national and international categorical imperative and the respective maxims or hypothetical imperatives of different contractually legal nations irrespective of whether these constitutional or statutory hypothetical imperatives enjoy the assent of the majority of the people or not. Second, we must state this single national and international categorical legal and political imperative with analytic precision.

With respect to the first of these two tasks, one thing becomes evident immediately. Whenever the substantive content of any constitutional, legislative or executive hypothetical imperative is incompatible with the Jeffersonian principle, that substantive content is illegal on logical grounds, exactly as a theorem put forward in arithmetic is false on logical grounds if its substantive content is logically incompatible with Peano's Fifth postulate. Furthermore, the same is true of the substantive content of any minority group or religious dissenter's religious conscience. Certainly it is quite unfair for a judge to be forced by the Bill of Rights in his judicial review to declare the substantive content of majority-approved legislation to be illegal and then to be bound later by that same Bill of Rights to declare a religious dissenter's conscience, the substantive content of which is identical with that of the previous majority, to be legal. It is the outstanding merit of Mr. Justice Frankfurter's notable dissent in *West Virginia v. Barnette* to have noted this.[7] Certainly there is something wrong with a theory of judicial review which permits (a) the substantive content of a single religious dissenter's moral and religious intuition and conviction to sabotage as unjust and illegal the incompatible substantive content of a majority-approved legislative statute and which (b) at the same time requires the judge to declare a majority-approved statute of the legislature which has the same substantive content as that of the latter religious dissenter to be illegal and unjust because it is incompatible with the moral and religious intuitions and conscience of some different religious dissenter. Our criterion for the judicial review of the substantive content of hypothetical imperatives—both those of the majority and those of dissenters—avoids this unfortunate consequence which Mr. Justice Frankfurter has noted in the present theory and practice of judicial review in the United States.

Such is the case because the principle which it provides for judicial review does not turn around the quantity of majority assent versus the absoluteness of any individual religious dissenter's dissent, but around whether the substantive content of either or both is logically incompatible or logically compatible with the elementary tautologically true proposition, i.e., the categorical imperative, upon which any contractual legal and political system whatever rests. Whether the substantive content in question is the substantive content of the religious conscience of a dissenter, the majority-approved legislative statute or a constitutional provision is irrelevant. Hence, a clear understanding of the basic tautologically true, and hence categorically imperative, proposition of any contractual legal nation makes it exactly as necessary in judicial review to measure the substantive content of the dissenter's religious conscience against this tautologically true proposition as it is imperative to measure in this manner the substantive content of the majority-approved legislative statute and even the provisions of the Constitution itself. It appears, therefore, that the judge in judicial review is provided with what Mr. Justice Frankfurter saw to be needed when dissenting in *West Virginia State Board of Education v. Barnette* he wrote:

[T]o deny the political power of the majority to enact laws concerned with civil matters, simply because they may offend the consciences of a minority, really means that the consciences of a minority are more sacred and more enshrined in the Constitution than the consciences of a majority.[8]

It remains to state the elemental tautologically true and hence categorical imperative of any contractually legal nation in completely imageless formal terms. This is necessary. For were substantive terms used, after the manner of the traditional "Bills of Rights," we would have a merely hypothetical, and not a categorical, imperative. Then judicial review turns around whether a given judge prefers such and such substantive content or does not—a matter which clearly in a democracy is the province of the legislature and not of the courts— and the absurdity, noted by Mr. Justice Frankfurter, occurs of the Supreme Court of the land reversing itself from year to year with respect to the same case in the name of the Bill of Rights.

The cure for this situation is not, as he indicates in *West Virginia v. Barnette,* to quote from Thayer and allow the legislature to have its way most if not all of the time. This is merely to substitute his preferences for such and such substantive content for that of his colleagues, thereby increasing the very absurdity against which he inveighs. Instead, it is to realize that any modern legal and political nation is a contractually constructed entity, the product of contractual legal science and that in this science there is one proposition having nothing to do with substantive content (or with his preferences or those of anyone else) which is true tautologically and hence is a categorical imperative that provides the standard to be used in judicial review.

Since this proposition does not refer to any specific substantive content, it is not a question-begging standard (as is any Bill of Rights stated in terms of substantive content) for measuring the specific substantive content of any legislative statute, religious person's conscience or constitutional provision. Being purely formal, this elemental postulate of contractual legal and political science must be stated in terms of purely formal imageless concepts by postulation which are concepts by intellection. This has been done in the writer's *The Complexity of Legal and Ethical Experience.*

To ensure a purely formal imageless concept by postulation statement, some symbols of symbolic logic had to be used. Ordinary prose is the product of a naïve realistic way of thinking and covertly pulls one back into the nonsensical ways of thinking about law and politics, a "corporation" or "a right" noted in previous chapters and earlier in this chapter.

Let p, x, l and s be entity variables where p denotes any person whether he be a citizen or a political representative of the citizens; x any object of intrinsic goal-value legal and political judgment; l any law which is a maxim, i.e., a hypothetically normative imperative, and s is the substantive content of l whether l be a constitutional provision, a legislative statute, an executive order, a legislative committeeman's rules of procedure or the substantive content when universalized into a law of a particular religious person's conscience. The parentheses when put around any one of these variables to give (p) or (s) means "for any one p" or "for any one s." In symbolic logic when this occurs, the variable in question is said to be universally quantified and the ( ) alone is called "the universal quantifier." When on the other hand any entity variable is preceded by the symbol Ǝ it is said to be existentially quantified, and Ǝ is called "the existential quantifier." Thus Ǝ x means "There exists at least one instance of the entity variable x." The symbol $\equiv$ means the relation of equivalence between sentences.

Expressed in such symbols, the categorical imperative of contractual national and international law then becomes:

(6) (p) (s) (x) (l): x is intrinsically good or just $\equiv x$ is an instance of an l such that for $(p)l$ and $(p)s$ of l.

This is the tautologically true legal and political postulate not merely of any free man's world but of any legally contractual nation or United Nations whatever.

Note its concrete implications. The key factor is "$(p)s$" in the expression to the right of the equivalence sign. Its effect is to enlarge or clarify further the categorical imperative of Kant (Chapter 15). It does this by requiring that, before any majority or dissenter's approved substantive idea of what is good or just can be declared to be good or just, two conditions must be satisfied: First, that substantive content must be universalized into a law applying to any person whatever. This is the significance of "$(p)l$" in the expression to the right of the equivalence sign in (6). Second, if the substantive content of $(p)l$ confers specified rights, privileges, obligations and duties on one or some persons under the universal law $(p)l$, then any person whatever (who has the maturity to enter into and comprehend the contract) must be substitutable for that person with respect to the enjoyment of those rights and privileges and the responsibility to assume those obligations and duties.

Even though (6) is purely formally stated in terms of concepts by postulation that are concepts by intellection, thereby providing the judge with a non-specifically substantive and hence a non-question-begging standard to use in judicial review, it nevertheless has very concrete applications. Consider the desegregation issue in the United States and some provisions of the Constitution of the Union of Soviet Socialist Republics.

In the former case, the legislative statutes and living law customs of the states of the Old South meet the first of the two conditions for any good or just law. Clearly the laws and customs giving the best schools only to white children and poor schools to the children of Negroes apply to all the people in these states. The second condition required by (6), namely $(p)s$ of l, is, however, not satisfied. This becomes evident when one notes that this second requirement means that if any legislative or constitutional provision specifies substantive content that gives a high-grade education to the majority or those who passed the law, then $(p)s$ of l requires that any person whatever be substitutable for those of the majority with respect to those rights and privileges.

The same is true of certain provisions of some state and national constitutions. Note first that because the above proposition of contractual legal science is, like Peano's Fifth postulate for arithmetic, tautologically true and hence a categorical imperative (rather than a merely hypothetical imperative approved by a legislative majority or by a private dissenter), it belongs not inside of, or as amendments to, a constitution, but at its very beginning as the elementary postulate of the constitution itself. When so conceived it becomes a categorical imperative which may and must be used by the judge to measure the legal validity of the substantive content of even the provisions of the constitution itself.

When so used with respect to the substantive content of the Constitution of the Soviet Union, the invalidity of this document is easily demonstrable as follows: The Soviet Union's Constitution does not define the obligations and privileges of its public officials or citizens in terms of biology of birth. Hence its codified law is that of contractual legal science. The substantive content of its constitutional prescriptions gives the political privilege of deciding all the intrinsic, i.e., goal-value, political questions of the nation which are obligatory for everybody in the nation to the self-appointed and self-perpetuating heads of the very small Communist party's leaders, without permitting *any one* in the nation to be substitutable for the Communist party's leaders with respect to those substantive rights and privileges. Clearly such substantive content satisfies the first quantification for any person of any contractually just law, as given in its analytic formulation in Postulate (6) above, but fails to satisfy the second quantification for any person with respect to the substantive content of the Soviet Union's constitution itself. Hence Soviet Union constitutional law is self-contradictory constitutional law, violating the analytic tautologically true proposition upon which any legally contractual nation rests.

The same is true of the foreign policy of any secretary of state or foreign minister of any legally contractual nation who respects this elemental self-evident proposition in his domestic political decisions but pursues a unilaterally decided power politics in his nation's foreign policy. Then he is putting substantive content in the foreign-policy prescriptions which he universally quantifies as placing political obligations not merely on everyone in his own nation whom he officially represents, but also on everyone in all the other nations of the world that are affected by his foreign policy. Otherwise his prescriptions would be those of domestic and not of foreign policy. In other words, the substantive content of his *unilaterally decided* power-political foreign policy gives himself as the official representative of the government and people of his own nation the political privilege of imposing political obligations on anyone anywhere in other nations without allowing their official national foreign ministers to be substitutable for him with respect to this same privilege as affecting the people of his nation. To such a foreign minister Mr. Arnold Toynbee replied to the point when he said, "No annihilation with representation" (Chapter 17). This again, like Soviet domestic constitutional law, satisfies the first universal quantification of a political rule for any person anywhere which must be met if a nation's law and politics is to be just as defined by the tautologically true Proposition (6) upon which any contractual nation rests, but fails to satisfy its second requirement which is that the substantive content of the rule, $(p)s$ of l, as well as the rule as a whole, $(p)l$, must be universally quantified for any person whatever.

One surprising practical implication follows: When the domestic law of any contractually legal nation is thus understood, it may be instrumentally valuable, but there is no necessity that there be an international court of justice to decide international legal and political disputes. Appeal of a foreign nation which believes it has been treated unjustly by some other nation can be made to any nation's federal court, including even the federal court of the nation against whom the charge of warful aggression or "peaceful" unilaterally power-political foreign policy decision making is being lodged. For if the judges of the latter nation know the contractual legal science upon which their own nation rests and which defines its political properties, then they also know as part of their own nation's law and politics the tautologically true elementary postulate of contractual legal and political science valid for anyone anywhere. Moreover, being tautologically true, this proposition of the judge's own national legal system makes it categorically imperative for him to measure in judicial review the foreign policy pronouncements and deeds of his own nation by this principle, should appeal be made to him by some other nation with respect to the justice of his own nation's international political conduct. Hence, whether one gives this principle implementation merely through national courts, merely through the world court or through both, is a secondary matter, having to do with instrumental values but not with goal values. No appeal to the world court occurred, let it be recalled from Chapter 11, nor was it necessary, as this analysis shows, when President Eisenhower in the Suez crisis declared that Israel, Great Britain and France had violated international law, so widely is the self-evidence of the Jeffersonian principle now recognized—the principle, namely, "No contract entered into by me, therefore no right to impose political obligations upon me."

To say this positively, however, in a concise and complete way is not easy, as the ambiguities in Kant's categorical imperative show and as the requirement of a second universally quantified p, i.e., the $(p)s$, in Proposition (6) makes clear. There may be reasons for believing that our legal and political Postulate (6) is not a complete statement of the Jeffersonian principle. These reasons have to do with whether even with the second universally quantified p, it is strong enough to rule out as illegal certain things which the Jeffersonian principle requires to be ruled out. It may be that not merely the substantive content of any hypothetical maxim such as a majority-approved legislative statute must be universally quantified for any person whatever, but also that the substantive content s itself must be universally quantified to read (s). This, however, is entirely too complicated a question to pursue and settle here.

Another reason is that our evaluative method of Chapter 7 prescribes as cognitively true and hence as categorically imperative not merely this legal and political Postulate (6), but also the five other Postulates: (1) aesthetic, (2) epistemological, (3) psychological, (4) mathematical and (5) indirectly confirmed mathematical physics given earlier in this chapter. Of these five postulates only the mathematical proposition (4) and the legal and political postulate (6) are analytic statements and hence true tautologically. Postulates (1), (2), (3) and (5), being synthetic propositions, have to be verified empirically. This and previous chapters have shown that these empirical tests have been met. Postulates (1) through (5) might well be put immediately following the legal and political postulate (6) at the beginning of any nation's constitution, with the explicit provision added that the synthetic propositions (1), (2), (3) and (5) are subject to revision should further empirical observations and theoretical reconstructions, that are experimentally and cognitively confirmable by anyone anywhere, indicate this to be necessary.

It is appropriate also that a cognitively true political philosophy which gives art [Postulate (1)] a cognitive meaning and such a primary status in its prescribed set of postulates should relate cognitive truth to emotive and aesthetically moving persuasion, thereby making art in its non-cognitive persuasive function, along with economics, engineering and military science, one of the instruments of this scientifically confirmable philosophy of personal and political goal values. Persuasion conversely then becomes the more persuasive, because in addition to being emotively moving, it is also persuasive because of the cognitive truth which it conveys.

Certainly such an ideal for mankind gives anyone anywhere something bigger than oneself for which to live. Moreover, the challenge is greater than that of the political ideal offered by those whose method is that of the dictatorship of but one class in society and of but one party and its party leaders within that class. For freedom's philosophy cannot win its modernizing and democratic way by dictatorial methods or the definition of political obligation in terms of the physical power of the political sovereign to inflict "pain or evil" on those who dissent from his commands, as the Communists, Hobbes, Austin and the free world's power politicians and eschatological theologians [9] would have us believe. Instead, freedom's philosophy must proceed by persuasion with respect to what is true in a sense which can be confirmed by anyone anywhere. It must use freedom's methods. It cannot resort to shortsighted short cuts by forcing its way with warful aggression, dictatorial and inquisitorial methods or recourse to the Index; for this is to hope to achieve freedom by destroying it.

One final practical political question remains: Can this true and persuasive political philosophy, when applied to old societies, avoid the failures that happened to free democracy on the Chinese mainland under Chiang Kai-shek, in Ceylon as described in Chapter 13 and elsewhere as noted in Chapter 1? It does little good practically to be cognitively correct in one's political ideals if others holding cognitively self-contradictory, epistemologically confused and false ideals are more successful than we in applying them to the workaday practices of mankind.

19

Freedom's Way to Modernize an Old Society

The modernization of an old society must be tailor-made to each particular instance. Such societies differ greatly from one another because the religious or secular universals, epistemically trapped covertly for the most part in the brains and behavioristically conditioned customs of the people, vary from religious community to religious community and from nation to nation.

The most elementary concepts of any Judaic, Christian or Islamic community are conveyed in the stories of creation and the Garden of Eden. All three of these Semitic religions, however, take on more specific religious content by virtue of the number of prophets, in addition to those of the Talmud and the Old Testament, which they accept. Thus Christian communities give assent to the teachings and life of Jesus in a Holy Trinitarian sense in which Jewish and Islamic communities do not; and Islam accepts Jesus as a prophet like the Jewish prophets of the Old Testament but believes that only in Mohammad and his Quran is the Divine Will perfectly expressed. Each of these three Semitic religious communities takes on more specific scientific, philosophical and religious content because of the varying influences upon it of ancient Greek science and philosophy and Stoic Roman law. Islam, for example, was deeply influenced by Greek mathematical physics and philosophy, as the later discovery of geometrical optics and its laws of perspective by the Arabian Alhazen demonstrates. It was not influenced by Stoic Roman law of contract until modern times and then only in some Islamic nations such as

339

Turkey, Egypt and Lebanon. Hence, except as Western imperialists have made it otherwise, Islamic nations have been of a law-of-biological-status, rather than a law-of-contract, type. Also, their secular law is regarded by orthodox Muslims to be as sacred and literally the word of Allah as is the Quran. Consequently there are few medieval societies more difficult to modernize than a traditional Islamic one.

Except as Western imperialism has brought it there, or as in the rare cases of Thailand and Japan where it has been freely imported, the idea of a contractual legal and political nation is foreign to the thinking or the customs of Asian, African or even North African and medieval Jewish people. For such people, "nation" means a patriarchal or occasionally, as in pre-British Cochin-Travancore province of India, a matriarchal law of biologically bred status community with a privileged theocratic first royal family. In contemporary Israel, for example, the modern free democratic contractual norms, which prescribe majority rule, and the medieval patriarchal and tribal customs of the majority of the people conflict. The political difficulties become intensified because the modern-minded political leaders with a Continental European or American background need citizens who put the logically realistic contractually conceived nation above the patriarchal close-knit racially-minded Jewish joint family and who have the best possible modern mathematically scientific and contractual legal education. Hence they keep their families relatively small in order that all their children may have such a costly education. The medieval-minded Jews, however, exercise no such birth control and in fact now have a political incentive to increase the size of their families since this makes it more likely in a free democratic nation that they can take over the government and its educational system, thereby preserving their old naïve realistic medieval-minded law and patriarchal religious fundamentalism and its ways.

The official stand of the Aristotelian-Thomistic naïve realistic medieval-minded Roman Catholics with respect to birth control is interesting in this connection and has precisely the same political significance and reason. The claim that it is based on natural law, i.e., on a categorical imperative that is true for anyone and therefore an ought for everybody, is spurious. For being a norm that is defined in terms of empirical content it is clearly a merely hypothetical and not a categorical imperative. Furthermore, were it a natural law, it would be immoral for priests and nuns not to marry and have large families also.

The method for reforming any naïve realistic society, whether it be Thomistic Roman Catholic, Filmerian Protestant Christian, Jewish, or Islamic, is to drive a philosophical and political wedge between the cognitive truthfulness of its contractual logically realistic "catholicism" or "univeralism" and the cognitive errors and mixed-worlds-of-discourse nonsense of its naïve realism by returning it to its earlier logical realism of the epistemology of Democritus, Theaetetus, Plato, Eudoxous, St. Augustine and William of Champeaux. Then one has but to fill in this logically realistic epistemology with the aforementioned truly categorical imperative of contractual legal science and with the richer and more cognitively universal and confirmed content of the logically realistic theories of contemporary experimentally verified mathematical physics and its philosophy. Since this logically realistic epistemology was once Roman Catholic Christian orthodoxy, there should be no serious difficulty for Roman Catholic minds in making it so again. This would end the conflict between the theocratic Aristotelian Thomistic medievalism of Roman Catholic or Filmerian Protestant Christianity and free democratic modernity.

Nations in the Asian rather than the three Semitic religious traditions present similar political difficulties when one attempts to modernize them and to democratize them with freedom's ways. This is especially true of India. Originally it was a single nation, comprising the two nations which are now called Pakistan and Free India. It is unfortunate that the word "India" does not appear in Pakistan's name, for Karachi India is just as much India as is New Delhi India. India as a whole, antecedent to Portuguese, Dutch, French and British rule, was conquered and ruled by the Muslims. The present result is that even over-all India is one-third Muslim, with many of the states predominantly so. Even in New Delhi India, there are now at least 45 million followers of Islam. Hence all the difficulties in reforming any medieval-minded Hebrew, Christian or Islamic society exist today in both Pakistani India and Free India. The same is true of the Aryan Hindus who comprise the majority in over-all India and are an even greater majority in present New Delhi India. As the sequel shows, the problem of reforming an old Asian religious community must be carried through politically in a quite different way than the one we have suggested for reforming any medieval-minded Semitic religious people.

The political problem, therefore, of democratizing and modernizing over-all India, which arose when the British withdrew, was a very complicated one. Also, the solution for the predominantly Hindu states could not be the same as for the predominantly Muslim states. Unless this point is seen, and one does not see it if one looks at India from the standpoint of either a power politician or a modern Western secularist, the political reason for the breaking of over-all India into Pakistani India and New Delhi India will not be appreciated.

Even so, elsewhere the writer has given reasons for believing that had the advice of the Muslim Indian Iqbal been followed, by giving greater expression to states' rights cultural and religious communal pluralism, the need for the partition of British and Princely State India into Pakistan and present Free India could have been avoided.[1] The result would have been a federal constitution for India as a whole, modeled on that of Canada which gives state's rights cultural, religious and political autonomy to the Province of Quebec. It is to be noted that had the British Canadians, who were in the majority when free Canada was created, insisted, after the manner of Gandhi and Pandit Nehru, on a secular state for the whole of Canada, the latter community would in all likelihood today be two nations, namely, secular British Canada and Roman Catholic French Quebec, similar to present secular New Delhi India and Islamic contractually free Pakistan.

Hindu Indian society considered by itself is a remarkable combination of two incompatible philosophies which were prevented from creating schizophrenic Dr. Jekyll and Mr. Hyde individuals by being assigned (a) to different tribal castes and (b) to different stages of any Hindu's life. It is because the lowest caste—the Untouchables—are regarded as embodying only the second-best of these two incompatible philosophies that the top-caste Brahman, who embodies the first-best, is polluted if the shadow of any Untouchable falls upon him.

These two incompatible Hindu philosophies are: (1) the radically empirical early Vedic Hindu Brahman-that-is-Atman *chit* consciousness psychological theory of the person which was later stripped of the Aryan conqueror's philosophical additions by Sankara to be thereafter called unqualified non-dualistic Vedantic Hindu philosophy, and (2) the naïve realistic mental substance-material substance dualistic cognitive psychological theory of the person called "Mimamsa Hindu philosophy" which, because of its Aryan Sanskrit grammar and its major role in the legal codification of Aryan Hindu patriarchal and caste law of status politics, is the Aryan conqueror's contribution to Aryan Hindu India. The empirical evidence for the correctness of the latter statement is that the Aryan conqueror brought two things to ancient India, the Aryan Sanskrit language with its naïve realistic subject-predicate grammar and its naïve realistic tribal and caste-focused codified law of the biologically bred status type. Recently, two Indian scholars, Professors D. M. Datta and P. T. Raju, have shown that the codified law of Aryan Hindu India is the work of lawyers who were Mimamsa Dualistic philosophers.[2]

According to the first of these two Hindu philosophies, the truly known selves of all human beings are not merely equal before the divine Brahman-Atman consciousness, but they are in the *chit* consciousness field portion of themselves identical with one another and with the Divine consciousness. Hence, a politics which gives a perfect expression to this cognitive theory of what any person is would be democratic and anticaste.

This is precisely what the Buddha affirmed and practiced. After the Aryan Hindus' political conquest of Northern India and their coordination of the philosophies of (1) and (2) by assigning (1) and (2) to different castes and to different stages of the three topmost castes' Hindu life, the Buddha repudiated (2) the naïve realistic subject-predicate dualism and its political color of skin tribal and caste ways to take India back to (1) what it was before the Aryan conquerors. Moreover, he won politically, as the Buddhist Indian empire of Asoka and the spread of Buddhism to Ceylon, Burma, Thailand, Cambodia, Vietnam, Tibet and even throughout China, Korea and Japan clearly shows. In India it was not until medieval times, when the Hindu philosopher Sankara formulated the philosophical system called unqualified non-dualistic Vedanta in which the concept of the person and the good society and nation is identical with that of Buddhism and affirmed (2) the Mimamsa philosophy to be merely a second-best morality and politics for Untouchables and appropriate only for the householder stage of the first three stages of the top-caste Hindu's life, that the Aryan Hindu patriar-chally-bred first- and second-caste descendants of the tribe of the Aryan conquerors rewon religious and political control over India from the Buddhists.

It is to be emphasized also that even in the ancient Aryan Hindu's codified law-of-biological-status codes, which were the work of Mimamsa lawyers and philosophers whose philosophy is that of (2), the just legal and political nation is portrayed as a combination of (1) and (2) where (2) is assigned to the lowest caste and to only the second or householder stage of the Hindu's life. As the Laws of Manu, for example, show, in the first stage and in the last two stages of the Hindu's religious, moral and social life, one drops all one's tribally bred Aryan caste political and social privileges and material wealth to put on a loincloth or the dress and bowl of a beggar in order to prepare oneself to show that (2) the Mimamsa philosophy with its morality and politics of caste is, none the less, merely a second-best, though necessary, step on the way to the first-best religious, morality and conduct which is that of (1).

Let no one suppose that even today this is mere ancient history. The Vice President of Free India believes in and talks most fre-quently about this first-best unqualified non-dualistic philosophy, morality and politics. In 1950 when the writer was in Calcutta, a retiring maharaja, after turning over his Princely kingdom to his eldest son, did precisely what has just been described, departing to the stillness of the recesses of the forest to prepare himself to let go of his private differentiated transitory perishing self and become one with his equally consciously immediate Brahman-Atman *chit* con-sciousness divine self which is the same in all human beings. The Maharaja of Rajputana, whose capitol is at Jaipur, and the Maharaja of Mysore, who visited the United States in 1959, believe in and religiously practice this Aryan Hindu philosophy which combines (1) and (2) while also making (1) primary. Literature pouring out of cities and villages all over India indicates that this philosophical way of thinking is reinforcedly trapped, via its epistemically correlated impulses, in the brains of Hindus who continue to represent more than two-thirds of the population of Free India.

Visiting the larger cities of India gives a quantitatively distorted picture of its cultural and political living law situation. Furthermore, with even the professional secularists in high places in government or the commoners, more of them than the casual observer would ever suspect, including even Muslims, are practicing daily Hindu Yogic meditative exercises and reading the Hindu's literary gem, the Bhagavadgita. One of the officials of the Rockefeller Foundation, whose duties frequently take him to New Delhi to confer with many governmental officials, told the writer recently that, whereas on his first trip they were thinking in modern Western secular, political and economic terms, on his more recent visits they were turning to and reading and rereading the Bhagavadgita. No person, not even a practical politician, can escape the covert living law of his own people and culture; nor does he want to do so for very long.

Consider also Gandhi and what he did. Refusing to use physical force, he succeeded politically in persuading the British to turn British India over to the Indians notwithstanding the fact that the British military power was overwhelming. If realistic politics is balance of physical power, this is a mystery. Gandhi removed the mystery, however, when he said in his Autobiography that his politics derives from his religion and that his religion is that of the Buddha, the Sankara version of the Upanishads and his beloved Bhagavadgita.

But how could this religion of himself and his Buddhist and Hindu Indian people and their literary classics enable politicians to be so successful politically? The answer is that he used these religious and literary ideas and emotively moving symbols, covertly in the minds and outlook of hundreds upon hundreds of millions of the villagers, to win their confidence in and political loyalty to what he was doing. To this end he indulged in meditation, putting on the loincloth of the top-caste and most venerated teacher, dropping the commercial instrumental values of the third Hindu caste into which he was born. Also, after the manner suggested earlier in this chapter, he used the most elemental and basic assumption—that of the Brahman-Atman *chit* consciousness which is at the basis of the medieval and ancient beliefs and classics of the Aryan Hindu living law to drive a political and social wedge between this most basic living law as defined by the Buddhist-Hindu philosophy of (1) and the patriarchal tribal and caste Aryan values which derive philosophically from the Mimamsa philosophy of (2). Thereby he carried the masses of Indians with him politically in the palm of his political hand because he preserved (1) in rejecting (2).

Why did this wedge technique succeed? The major answer is because (1) is incompatible with (2) anyway, while also being compatible with modern free democratic political and social goal-value political ideals.

Even so, this political wedge between components (1) and (2) in Aryan Hindu living law does not explain why the British capitulated, for their living law philosophy is not that of (1). Moreover, in its Elizabethan and Filmerian religiously theocratic patriarchalism it is like that of (2). The wedge technique accounts merely for why Gandhi carried with him the masses of people in the villages while rejecting the caste portion of their traditional living law.

His additional philosophically anthropological political method was to appeal, just as did the American Founding Fathers, to something in the living law of the British. This factor is the political philosophy of John Locke as expressed in its American version by Jefferson in the Declaration of Independence, in which, as shown in Chapter 11, the majority of the British in even their Conservative party believe. In short, Gandhi used the equivalent of the descriptive method of philosophical anthropology as applied to both the living law of Buddhist Hindu India and to that of Great Britain to obtain the behavioristic political response from both his own village people and the British people and their politicians which he wanted.

Why, with respect to the political reform of any old society, does the wedge technique work politically? The reason centers in the distinction between (a) elemental concepts and postulates and (b) derivative or merely instrumental beliefs in any person's epistemically trapped set of universals. When the elemental postulate set is first assented to and trapped for any group of people, additional procedural rules relative to the environmental and cultural circumstances of the time become trapped and conditioned in reflex behavior also. With time, the latter harden and become as sacred as the former. Anyone tends to be regarded as an atheist or a political traitor who even suggests their alteration in order to permit the elemental postulate set to express itself more perfectly in today's different circumstances.

The mistake which most modern-minded reformers make is that when they see that the old applications must go, they conclude that everything in the old living law must go also. For free democracy this is fatal, since they put themselves in the positive legal and political position in which the majority of the people will not support them and in which the whole of the living law is against them. Theoretically, the distinction between elemental concepts and proposition or postulates and derivative and instrumental ones is not kept in mind. This is why we spent so much time in Part I in explaining and emphasizing the importance of this distinction. Without it, the political practicality of the wedge technique in the political reform of any medieval or ancient society will not be appreciated.

The cultural wedge which this distinction gave Gandhi for separating (1) from (2) in Hindu living law and then repudiating (2) more perfectly to realize (1) gave the Congress party, had they used it, a Hindu living law basis for making their modern secular contractually free democratic legal and political nation work more effectively. For, according to the cognitively testable and radically empirically true concept of the person of (1), not only are all persons equal before or in the Divine consciousness, the realization of which according to Hindus is the religious, moral and political purpose of human existence, but they are identical with it. What better basis already present in the deepest and most ancient living law beliefs and customs of three hundred million Hindu Indians is there for free democracy than this?

Clearly also one does not have to do to a great Asian civilization of high quality which, for all its naïve realistic law of status errors, is one of the glories of human history, what President Mao is now doing to Confucian-Taoist-Buddhist China in order to gain the advantages of modern ways. Nor, providing one uses the descriptive and evaluative methods of philosophical anthropology, does one have to turn every African, Middle Eastern or Asian people or nation into a second- or third-rate imitation of the United States, Great Britain or France. Instead, by applying these philosophically anthropological methods to the unique living law of each one of these peoples and nations to find which factor in each is cognitively true and therefore should remain and what is cognitively false and hence must go, and then by combining the true in the old with the contractually and postulationally new and true from the West, each particular people and their nation on this earth's surface can be themselves producing a synthesis of high quality that is unique.

What about the free democratic modernization of Confucian-Taoist-Buddhist China? The first point to note is that all modern nations, whether they be Communistic or freely democratic nations, are nations of the law-of-contract type. In the case of the Soviet Union or of Mao's China this is evident, since political leadership is not determined by biology of birth from a historically first tribal family. One of the most notable achievements of the Soviet Union is its capacity to free politics from racially and religiously divisive, warful political distinctions. Any consistently formulated law-of-contract nation rests on the principle of the American Declaration of Independence as its most elemental, empirically and tautologically true postulate. Marxist philosophy, owing to its self-contradictory, naïvely realistic epistemology and its spurious dialectically deterministic law of history, results in the putting of substantive content in the contractual law and politics without which there is no modern nation, which is logically incompatible with this most elementary, tautologically true proposition upon which any modern contractual nation rests. It is, therefore, only by modernizing any medieval or ancient society with contractual law of the free democratic type that a contractually self-consistent modern legal and political nation can be constructed.

A cognitively informed and realistically practical political leadership will not allow anyone anywhere on the surface of this earth to escape the political implications of this fact. Just as the living law customs and state legislative statutes of the Old South in the United States of America are incompatible with the most elementary and basic tautologically true proposition upon which any contractual legal and political nation whatever rests, so any modernization of any society, be it that of China, Russia, Africa, India or Islam, with Marxist substantive content in its legal and political national norms is similarly incompatible with contractual legal and political nationalism and internationalism. As suggested in Chapter 16, President

Mao may well be sufficiently trained as a philosopher to understand this point, were it clearly, soberly and objectively put to him in terms of the difference, well known in the science of mathematics and its technology which he venerates and encourages, between complete symbols, i.e., any word in its concept by intuition or naïve realistic epistemological meaning and that same word in its incomplete symbolic, i.e., contractual concept by postulation meaning.

The descriptive method of philosophical anthropology when applied to any Confucian society tells us also that the most basic concept in Chinese Confucian philosophy is *jen*. This word is difficult to translate into English. Lin Yutang translates it as "compassion." The British Sinologist, E. R. Hughes, renders it as "man-to-manness." [3] The latter seems to be the more literal translation since the Chinese character for *jen* is a combination of the character for "man" and the character for "two." But Lin Yutang's translation is also correct. For it tells us that the "two" of "man-to-manness" is not Russell, Whitehead and Frege's logically constructed natural number "two," but is an intuitively and immediately felt fellow feeling which cannot be expressed in axiomatically constructed, imageless, symbolic logical or mathematical concepts or any legal code be it one of status or contract. In short, *jen* is what any human being immediately feels with respect to any other human being whatever when the immediately felt differences are neglected. Note the intuitive *any-one-ness* that this expresses.

Hence, Confucius tells us that so far as his determinate conduct with respect to another person is concerned, his determinate morality will be relativistically fitted to the circumstances. Sometimes he will do this determinate thing and at other times he will do that. But Confucius also tells us there is one thing that the superior person will never do, and that is to deny *jen*. In other words, however much he may differ from another person about anything in any dispute, never will he fail to express indeterminate immediately felt compassionate fellow feeling. There is nothing of the dictatorship of the proletariat in this. Nor is there any sense of being pushed around by naïve realistically conceived abstract nouns in the name of "the laws of history" or "a power vacuum."

The one absolute value, therefore, which any two Confucian Chinese, Korean or Vietnamese in the villages will never deny in their disputes with one another is the intuitive fellow feeling, or continuum of consciousness within which both immediately experience themselves as immersed and which, consequently, though unstatable in any codified rule, they will never deny. If appealed to, what better basis for democracy is there than this?

Even though Western Stoic Roman and modern democratic law of contract is something that never existed in any un-Westernized Asian society, its basic belief that moral, religious, political and legal man is universal man is completely compatible with the most basic trapped universal in every Confucian and, it may be added, Taoist and Buddhist Chinese villager's mind. Furthermore, this fundamental intuition of *jen* is more practically and consistently implemented by free democratic contractual legal and political ways than can be the case in any dictatorship of the proletariat or than was the case when the *jen* fellow feeling was applied to the Chinese people by Confucius.

This becomes evident when one notes the second factor in Confucian philosophy and classical Chinese society. It is expressed in the basic determinate relations between human beings which Confucius taught. These five relations are: (1) The relation of father to son. This would be perhaps more accurately expressed as the relation of the father to his eldest son. (2) The relation of the patriarchal father to his wife. (3) The relation between the eldest son and his younger brothers. (4) The relation between sovereign and subject, and (5) the relation between friend and friend. Common to all these is *jen*. The first four of these five relations technically define the goal-value ideal of a Confucian law-of-status patriarchal joint familial society. Practically what the first four relations mean is that the relation between the father and his eldest son takes priority over the relation even between a husband and his wife. This shows in the morality of any patriarchal society's family law which makes it a moral obligation, if the wife does not produce a son, for the husband to take a second wife. The reason for this is that in a patriarchal society, familial and political authority pass only through the male line. Hence, without sons, all family morality and political authority in the next generation vanishes. In a matriarchal society, such as that of Cochin-Travancore province in India, the mother-eldest daughter relationship operates in precisely the same manner.

Literally, and also practically, therefore, the first four social relations in Confucian society are incompatible with its *jen* concept, since they require a greater emotive loyalty and man-to-manness compassion and fellow feeling in a father's moral regard for his eldest son than is the case for his younger sons, his daughters or even his wife. This is incompatible with *jen* person-to-personness.

The reason for this incompatibility is, the writer believes, that without Western law of contract which classical Asia did not have, it is impossible to establish political authority without anarchy resulting at the provincial and the national level, unless such a patriarchal or matriarchal, biologically lineal law-of-status political system is set up with a privileged first family in the national capitol or Heavenly City to act as the political head of the nation. Thus practically the only procedure Asian societies had was to combine a law-of-status biological first-familial patriarchal or matriarchal morality with their Confucian man-to-manness *jen*, their person-to-person Buddhist Nirvana "true self" and their unqualified non-dualistic Vedanta Hindu *chit* consciousness self.

A practical Asian politician who is guided by the method of philosophical anthropology with respect to his own specific people and their particular culture will not, therefore, present his new liberal democratic law-of-contract constitution as something secular and completely foreign that is artificially imported from abroad. Instead, he will present it initially as simply a law-of-contract expression and a more perfect application of the most basic moral and religious universal which is already epistemically trapped in the minds of all Confucian, Buddhist, Taoist and Hindu people.

More specifically, his modernization program will be presented not primarily as a modern Western secular policy, but as a Chinese Confucian *jen* policy, a Buddhist Chinese, Burmese, Thai and Vietnamese Nirvana or Zen-self policy or a Hindu-Buddhist unqualified non-dualistic Vedantic Indian policy which is being applied more perfectly and realized more effectively than was the case with the old distinctions of caste and the old maharajas or the Manchu Dynasty which were corruptions of it. Such an appeal to the traditional and present beliefs of the people in Asian villages would be one which is genuinely true, honest and long range, rather than merely a folk-song-singing, temporary expedient and tactical deception. Clearly such an attachment of modern free democratic goal values to the elementary concept in the Confucian-Taoist-Buddhist or Hindu belief system and customs of the Asian villagers cannot fail to be effective, since their epistemic correlates are already trapped in their brains and behavioristically conditioned in their customs.

Such a practical politics will win the time necessary to modernize an old society with the free consent of the masses of the people by democratic procedures. Moreover, it will last over the very long pull, perhaps even to eternity, since the Nirvana, Taoist, Hindu *chit* consciousness self and in all probability also the *jen* consciousness man-to-manness, at least in its indeterminateness, is a timeless self.

Recently the modern-minded Burmese Buddhist philosopher Khin Maung Win, in his thesis for the doctor's degree in philosophy at Yale University, applied the descriptive method of philosophical anthropology to (1) the linguistic symbols and the children's stories which he learned from his mother in his native village and (2) the relating of the modern contractual free democratic constitution to his nation's traditional Buddhist beliefs and customs.[4] Unwesternized Burmese people in the villages and even modern-minded Burmese, such as Mr. Win when he came to the United States, think largely, if not completely, in terms of the concepts by intuition of a radically empirical epistemology. With such a way of thinking, only the undifferentiated field-consciousness self called by the Burmese "Nirbanna" is identical for all persons and one's only persisting self. Since the latter self, like that of the Hindu's *chit* consciousness, is identical in all persons, Dr. Win noted that it provides a living law basis for free democracy that is already present in the intuitive consciousness of all the Burmese Buddhists in both the villages and the cities.

But Mr. Win found also, when the descriptive method of philosophical anthropology was applied by him to the modern Western positive and living law from which Burma's new contractual constitution and its political system derives, that the rooting of this contractual law and politics in the most basic trapped universal in the Buddhist people's minds, while politically correct and necessary, will not be sufficient. The reason is a somewhat lengthy one. Although the Nirvana self entails democracy when it is applied and lived consistently, it is a factor in knowledge which cannot be said in the codes of any constitution or any legislative statute, since it is indeterminate and hence indescribable and unstatable. To be known it has to be immediately experienced by being it with all differentiations of immediate experience neglected or removed. Furthermore, as noted above, his application of the method of descriptive philosophical anthropology to his own Buddhist Burmese people and their language showed that even with respect to the differentiated, describable properties, objects and relations which they know, the people think of them by means of a linguistic symbolism which is completely radically empirical, denotative and hence imageful in all its meanings. Also, as Mr. Win learned the very hard way when he came to the United States for graduate study, (a) Western philosophical systems such as that of Kant with his *a priori* non-radically empirical concepts and (b) the theories of Western mathematical physics with their formal constructs or concepts by postulation which are concepts by intellection are foreign to the Burmese mind.

He then learned that Western legal science, as the previous chapter has shown, is a legal and political system of contractually constructed entities such as the General Motors Corporation, the United States of America or the Government of Burma of the Burmese people's new contractual constitution and legal and political system. He noted therefore that if his Buddhist people and their legal and political officials are to learn to think of this contractual law as something binding one morally, emotively and politically as much as does the immediately experienced intuition of one's Nirvana self or one's denotatively felt feeling for the members of one's own family, the logically realistic type of concept formation and thinking of the imageless symbols of symbolic logic and pure mathematics must also be introduced at the very beginning into the Burmese educational system. Otherwise it is likely that neither modern technology nor modern free democratic contractual law will be understood or used without being corrupted.

It must be added, if later corruption and the failure of free democracy are not to occur, that the elementary tautologically true proposition of the law of contract which was analytically stated in the previous chapter must be taught to the people. Otherwise they will not realize that contractually free democratic social and political morality is a formally constructed, procedurally defined, imageless thing with very concrete epistemically correlated operational moral, social and political consequences, as well as an intuitively felt indeterminately emotive and mediational thing. In short, the people and their leaders everywhere must be taught the imageless formal ethic of the law of contract, thereby learning that they can perfectly realize their non-codifiable *jen,* Nirvana or Brahman goal value only if they combine its intuitive indeterminate and uncodifiable experience of the morally good, the politically just and religiously Divine with the more formal, imageless type of goal value which free democratic law-of-contract philosophy defines and of which the prophets and saints of the three Semitic religions of the Middle East and the West had a premonition in their concept of God as an imageless determinate *logos* who transcends and transforms differentiated intuitive immediacy.

By such means, the prayer of modern Hindu India's talented poet and one of the world's outstanding men of vision may come true:

Where the mind is without fear and the head is held high;
Where knowledge is free;
Where the world has not been broken up into fragments by narrow domestic walls;
Where words come out from the depth of truth;
Where tireless striving stretches its arms towards perfection;
Where the clear stream of reason has not lost its way into the dreary desert sand of dead habit;
Where the mind is led forward by thee into ever-widening thought and action—
Into that heaven of freedom, my Father, let my country awake.[5]

References

Chapter 1 (Pages 1–18)

[1] "Ghana's Guided Democracy," *The Economist*, Vol. CXC, March 14, 1959, p. 948. See "Autumn Thoughts for Democrats," *The Economist*, Vol. CXC, October 10, 1959, pp. 121–122, for a later appraisal of the world-wide state of democracy.

[2] Ehrlich, Eugen, *Fundamental Principles of the Sociology of Law*, Walter L. Moll, translator, Harvard Studies in Jurisprudence, Vol. V, Harvard Univ. Press, Cambridge, 1936, pp. 121–136.

[3] Hoebel, E. Adamson, *The Law of Primitive Man: A Study in Comparative Legal Dynamics*, Harvard Univ. Press, Cambridge, 1954.

[4] Maine, Sir Henry S., *Ancient Law: Its Connection with the Early History of Society and Its Relation to Modern Ideas*, John Murray, London, 1908.

[5] The description of precisely how and by whom this was done is to be found in E. Vernon Arnold's *Roman Stoicism*, Cambridge Univ. Press, Cambridge, 1911.

[6] McWhinney, Edward, *Judicial Review in the English-Speaking World*, Univ. of Toronto Press, Toronto, 1956.

[7] Austin, John, *The Province of Jurisprudence Determined and the Uses of the Study of Jurisprudence*, Weidenfeld and Nicolson, London, 1954, pp. 1, 14 and 246.

[8] Hobbes, Thomas, *Leviathan or the Matter, Forme and Power of a Commonwealth Ecclesiasticall and Civil*, with an Introduction by Michael Oakeshott, Basil Blackwell, Oxford, undated, Chapter 18, Section 4, p. 115.

[9] Pound, Roscoe, "Toward a New Jus Gentium," in Northrop, ed., *Ideological Differences and World Order*, Yale Univ. Press, New Haven, 1949, p. 7.

[10] See the Introduction by Peter Laslett to Sir Robert Filmer's *Patriarcha*, Basil Blackwell, Oxford, 1949. Also Laslett, Peter, "Sir Robert Filmer: The Man versus the Whig Myth," *William and Mary Quarterly*, Vol. 5, 1948, pp. 523–546.

[11] Fustel de Coulanges, Numa Denis, *The Ancient City, A Study on the Religions, Laws, and Institutions of Greece and Rome*, Doubleday, Garden City, 1956.

[12] Westrup, C. W., *Introduction to Early Roman Law*, Vol. III, *Patria Potestas*, Oxford Univ. Press, London, 1939.

[13] Smith, Boyd, *The Patriarch, A Play in Three Acts*, S. French, New York and Los Angeles, 1931.

[14] See Northrop, *The Taming of the Nations*, Macmillan, New York, 1952, Chapter 11, pp. 214–226.

[15] Northrop, *The Complexity of Legal and Ethical Experience*, Little, Brown, Boston, 1959, Chapter XXII.

[16] Northrop, *ibid.*

[17] "In or Out?" *The Economist,* Vol. CXCI, April 25, 1959, p. 309; "The Commonwealth and Europe," Vol. CXCI, April 4, 1959, p. 17; "The Commons and the Common Market," Vol. CXC, Feb. 21, 1959, p. 675; "The European Rift," Vol. CXC, Jan. 10, 1959, p. 133; "Partition of Europe," Vol. CLXXXIX, Dec. 20, 1958, p. 1053.

[18] Clark, Grenville, and Sohn, Louis B., *World Peace Through World Law,* Harvard Univ. Press, Cambridge, 1958.

[19] Northrop, *European Union and United States Foreign Policy,* Macmillan, New York, 1954.

[20] Northrop, *The Complexity of Legal and Ethical Experience,* pp. 125–142.

[21] For the case of Stalin, see Northrop, *The Taming of the Nations,* Chapter 12.

Chapter 2 (Pages 21–41)

[1] Filmer, Sir Robert, *Patriarcha,* edited with an Introduction by Peter Laslett, Basil Blackwell, Oxford, 1949, pp. 1–43.

[2] Ehrlich, Eugen, *Fundamental Principles of the Sociology of Law,* translated by Walter L. Moll, Harvard Univ. Press, Cambridge, 1936, Chapter 21.

[3] Ehrlich, *op. cit.,* p. 37.

[4] Sorokin, Pitirim A., *Social and Cultural Dynamics,* American Book, New York, 1937–1941, and *Society, Culture, and Personality,* Harper, New York, 1947.

[5] Heisenberg, Werner, *Physics and Philosophy,* Harper, New York, 1958.

[6] Northrop, "Complementary Emphases of Eastern Intuitive and Western Scientific Philosophy," in Charles A. Moore, ed., *Philosophy—East and West,* Princeton Univ. Press, Princeton, 1944, pp. 168–234. Also Northrop, *The Logic of the Sciences and the Humanities,* New York, 1947, Chapter V.

[7] Russell, Bertrand, and Whitehead, Alfred N., *Principia Mathematica,* Cambridge Univ. Press, Vol. 1, 1910, Chapter 3, pp. 66–86.

[8] Margenau, Henry, *The Nature of Physical Reality,* McGraw-Hill, New York, 1950, pp. 60–100.

[9] Northrop, *The Complexity of Legal and Ethical Experience,* Little, Brown, Boston, 1959, Chapters XVII and XXII.

[10] Northrop, *ibid.,* note 6.

[11] Margenau, *ibid.,* p. 103.

[12] Mach, Ernst, *The Science of Mechanics,* Open Court Pub. Co., Chicago, 1919, pp. ix, 6, 481.

[13] Paper read before the Unity of Science Congress at Harvard Univ.; see also Northrop, *The Logic of the Sciences etc.,* Chapter VII.

[14] Margenau, *ibid.*

[15] Reichenbach, Hans, *Philosophie der Raum-Zeit-Lehre,* Walter de Gruyter, Berlin and Leipzig, 1928, pp. 23–39.

[16] Hobbes, Thomas, *Leviathan or the Matter, Forme and Power of Commonwealth Ecclesiasticall and Civil,* with an Introduction by Michael Oakeshott, Basil Blackwell, Oxford, undated, Part 2, pp. 136–137. Italics mine.

[17] Kroeber, A. L., "Concluding Review" in Sol Tax, Loren C. Eiseley, Irving Rouse and Carl F. Voegelin, eds., *An Appraisal of Anthropology Today,* Univ. of Chicago Press, Chicago, 1953, p. 373.

[18] Khrushchev, Nikita S., "On Peaceful Coexistence," *Foreign Affairs,* Vol. 38, October, 1959, pp. 1–18.

[19] Kluckhohn, Clyde, "The Philosophy of the Navaho Indians" in Northrop, ed., *Ideological Differences and World Order,* Yale Univ. Press, New Haven, 1949, pp. 356–384.

[20] As quoted by Kluckhohn, Clyde, *op. cit.,* note 5, p. 356.

[21] *Ibid.,* p. 356.

[22] Northrop, *The Meeting of East and West,* Macmillan, New York, 1946.

Chapter 3 (Pages 42–63)

[1] Northrop, F. S. C., remarks made in the Symposium on Mind and Body, *Proceedings of the Association for Research in Nervous and Mental Disease,* Vol. XIX, 1939, pp. 99–104, and reprinted as Chapter X in Northrop, *The Logic of the Sciences and the Humanities,* Macmillan, New York, 1947.

[2] McCulloch, Warren S., and Walter Pitts, or conversely, "A Logical Calculus of the Ideas Immanent in Nervous Activity," *Bulletin of Mathematical Biophysics,* Vol. 5, 1943, pp. 115–133; with H. D. Landahl, "A Statistical Consequence of the Logical Calculus of Nervous Nets," *ibid.,* pp. 135–137; McCulloch, Warren S., and Walter Pitts, "How We Know Universals, the Perception of Auditory and Visual Forms," *Bulletin of Mathematical Biophysics,* Vol. 9, 1947, pp. 127–147. For later formulations, see: Kleene, S. C., "Representations of Events in Nerve Nets and Finite Automata," *Automata Studies,* edited by C. E. Shannon and J. McCarthy, Princeton Univ. Press, Princeton, 1956, pp. 3–41; Culbertson, James T., "Some Uneconomical Robots," *ibid.,* pp. 99–116; Moore, Edward F., "Gedanken-Experiments on Sequential Machines," *ibid.,* pp. 129–153; Fitch, F. B., "Representation of Sequential Circuits in Combinatory Logic," *Philosophy of Science,* Vol. 25, 1958, pp. 263–273; von Neumann, John, "Probabilistic Logics and the Synthesis of Reliable Organisms from Unreliable Components," *Automata Studies,* pp. 43–98.

[3] The Josiah Macy, Jr. Foundation Conferences on Circular, Causal and Feedback Mechanisms in Biology and Social Sciences, 1946–1953, only published proceedings under the title *Cybernetics* edited by Heinz von Foerster, Josiah Macy, Jr. Foundation, New York, 1949–1953 inclusive. Independent publications of members of these conferences include: Northrop, McCulloch and Pitts, notes 1 and 2 *supra.;* von Neumann, John and Oscar Morgenstern, *The Theory of Games,* Princeton Univ. Press, Princeton, 1944; Rosenblueth, Arturo, Norbert Wiener and Julian

Bigelow, "Behavior, Purpose and Teleology," *Philosophy of Science,* Vol. 10, 1943, pp. 18–24; Wiener, Norbert, *Cybernetics,* Wiley, New York, 1948; *The Human Use of Human Beings,* Doubleday, New York, 1950; von Neumann, John, *The Computer and the Brain,* Yale Univ. Press, New Haven, 1958; Northrop, "The Neurological and Behavioristic Psychological Basis of the Ordering of Society by Means of Ideas," *Science,* Vol. 107, 1948, pp. 411–417, republished in Northrop, ed., *Ideological Differences and World Order,* Yale Univ. Press, New Haven, 1949, Chapter XIX; Young, J. Z., *Doubt and Certainty in Science,* Clarendon Press, Oxford, 1951; Ashby, W. Ross, *Design for a Brain,* Wiley, New York, 1952; Walter, W. Grey, *The Living Brain,* Norton, New York, 1953; Frank, Lawrence K., *Society as the Patient,* Rutgers Univ. Press, 1948; "Teleological Mechanisms," *Annals of the New York Academy of Sciences,* Vol. 50, 1948; *Nature and Human Nature: Man's New Image of Himself,* Rutgers Univ. Press, 1951; "Tactile Communication," *General Psychology Monographs,* Vol. LVI, 1957; "Purposive Behavior" to be published.

[4] Fitch, F. B., *Symbolic Logic,* Ronald Press, New York, 1952; see also Fitch, "Representation of Sequential Circuits in Combinatory Logic," *op. cit.,* note 2. The latter paper is in part the result of a suggestion made by McCulloch to Fitch when McCulloch was in Fitch's lectures that Fitch apply a logical operator upon which he was lecturing to neural circuits. Thus the symbolic logician Fitch and the theoretically-minded experimental neurologist McCulloch influenced one another.

[5] For the early Macy Conference discussion of the digital character of the activity of the nervous system, see Ralph Gerard's comments in von Foerster, Heinz, ed., *Cybernetics, Transactions of the Seventh Conference, March 23–24, 1950,* Josiah Macy, Jr. Foundation, New York, 1951, pp. 11–57. Cf. von Neumann, *The Computer and the Brain,* pp. 6–28 and especially p. 43.

[6] Von Neumann, *ibid.,* p. 66.

[7] Gerard, Ralph, "What Is Memory?" *Scientific American,* Vol. 189, Sept. 1953, p. 118–126.

[8] Russell, Bertrand, "The World and the Observer," *The Listener,* Vol. LIX, Feb. 6, 1958, pp. 223–224.

[9] Northrop, *The Meeting of East and West,* Macmillan, New York, 1946, Chapter IX, especially pp. 335 ff.

[10] Whitehead, Alfred North, *Process and Reality,* Macmillan, New York, 1929, p. 32.

[11] Von Neumann, *The Computer and the Brain,* pp. 14 ff. and 33. Cf. also McCulloch, Warren S., "A Heterarchy of Values Determined by the Topology of Nervous Nets," *Bulletin of Mathematical Biophysics,* Vol. 7, 1945, pp. 89–93.

[12] Von Neumann, *The Computer and the Brain,* p. 19.

[13] McCulloch, Warren S., and Pitts, Walter, "How We Know Universals, the Perception of Auditory and Visual Forms."

[14] Einstein, Albert, *The World As I See It,* Covici Friede, New York, 1934, p. 60; see also, Northrop, "Einstein's Conception of Science," and Einstein's comments in Schilpp, Paul A., ed., *Albert Einstein: Philosopher-Scientist,* Library of Living

Philosophers, Evanston, 1949, pp. 385–408 and pp. 663–688. Cf. also Russell, Bertrand, "The World and the Observer."

[15] Russell, *ibid.*, p. 225.

Chapter 4 (Pages 64–72)

[1] Rosenblueth, Arturo, Norbert Wiener and Julian Bigelow, "Behavior, Purpose and Teleology," *Journal of the Philosophy of Science*, Vol. 10, 1943, pp. 18–24.

[2] Macy Foundation Conferences on Cybernetics. See Note 1 of Chapter 3; Wiener, Norbert, *Cybernetics*, Wiley, New York, 1948; *The Human Use of Human Beings*, Doubleday, New York, 1954.

[3] Northrop, "The Neurological and Behavioristic Psychological Basis of the Ordering of Society by Means of Ideas," *Science*, Vol. 107, April 23, 1948, pp. 411–417; also Northrop, ed., *Ideological Differences and World Order*, Chapter XIX.

Chapter 6 (Pages 89–97)

[1] Win, Khin Maung, "Some Philosophical Problems of Contemporary Burma," Ph.D. Thesis, 1958, Sterling Memorial Library, Yale University; "The Epistemological Analysis of the Burmese Language," to be published in *Main Currents*, 1960.

[2] Jevons, W. Stanley, *Theory of Political Economy*, Macmillan, London, 1911.

[3] Robbins, Lionel, *An Essay on the Nature and Significance of Economic Science*, Macmillan, London, 1935.

[4] *Ibid.*, pp. 122–135.

[5] *Ibid.* See also Northrop, *The Logic of the Sciences and the Humanities*, Macmillan, New York, 1947, Chapter XIII.

[6] *Ibid.*, Chapter XV. Moore, Underhill, and Charles C. Callahan, "Law and Learning Theory: A Study in Legal Control," *Yale Law Journal*, Vol. 53, 1943, pp. 1–136. See my "Underhill Moore's Legal Science: Its Nature and Significance," *Yale Law Journal*, Vol. 59, 1950, pp. 196–213. Hull, Clark L., "Moore and Callahan's Law and Learning Theory: A Psychologist's Impression," *Yale Law Journal*, Vol. 53, 1943, p. 330.

Chapter 7 (Pages 98–120)

[1] Ayer, A. J., *Language, Truth and Logic*, Victor Gollancz, London, 1948, p. 105.

[2] *Ibid.*

[3] *Ibid.*

[4] Dewey, John, *Logic, The Theory of Inquiry*, Henry Holt, New York, 1938, pp. 157–158 and Chapter IX. See also Blanshard, Brand, *The Nature of Thought*, Macmillan, New York, 1941, Vol. 1, Chapter X, "Pragmatism and Thought."

[5] Moore, G. E., *Principia Ethica,* Cambridge Univ. Press, 1903, Chapter II. Cohen, Felix S., *Ethical Systems and Legal Ideals,* Falcon Press, New York, 1933.

[6] Hand, Learned, *The Spirit of Liberty,* Knopf, New York, 1953, pp. 228–229.

[7] Newton, Isaac, *Mathematical Principles,* Cajori, Florian, ed., Univ. of California Press, Berkeley, 1934, p. 6.

[8] Whitehead, Alfred N., *The Concept of Nature,* Cambridge Univ. Press, 1920, Chapter IV. See also Northrop, "Whitehead's Philosophy of Science," in Schilpp, Paul A., ed., *The Philosophy of Alfred North Whitehead,* Northwestern Univ., Evanston and Chicago, 1941, pp. 165–208.

[9] Northrop, *The Complexity of Legal and Ethical Experience,* Little, Brown, Boston, 1959, Chapter XVI.

[10] *Ibid.,* Chapter XV. As applied to international relations, see Chang Hsin-hai, *Within The Four Seas,* Twayne Publishers, New York, 1958.

[11] Northrop, *The Taming of the Nations,* Macmillan, New York, 1952, pp. 56–65.

[12] *Ibid.*

[13] Northrop, "The Mathematical Background and Content of Greek Philosophy," in *Philosophical Essays for Alfred North Whitehead,* Longmans, Green, New York, 1936, pp. 1–40.

[14] Burtt, E. A., *The Metaphysical Foundations of Modern Physics,* Harcourt, Brace, New York, 1925, pp. 61–88; Northrop, *The Logic of the Sciences and the Humanities,* Macmillan, New York, 1947, Chapters IV, VI, VII and VIII.

Chapter 8 (Pages 123–142)

[1] Cf. Kluckhohn, Clyde, *Mirror for Man,* Whittlesey House, McGraw-Hill Book Co., New York, 1949, pp. 29 ff., and Kluckhohn, Clyde, "The Philosophy of the Navaho Indians" in Northrop, F. S. C., ed., *Ideological Differences and World Order,* Yale University Press, 1949, pp. 356–384.

[2] Northrop, F. S. C., *The Meeting of East and West,* Macmillan, New York, 1946, Chapter II and Plate 3.

[3] Northrop, F. S. C., *European Union and United States Foreign Policy,* Macmillan, New York, 1954, Chapter 7.

[4] Rangel, Nicolas, *Preliminar a los Precursores Ideológicos de la Independencia, 1789–1794,* Publicaciones del Archivo General de la Nación, Mexico, D.F., 1929; see also Ramos, Samuel, *El Perfil del Hombre y la Cultura en Mexico,* Editorial Pedro Robredo, Mexico, D.F., 1938; O'Gorman, Edmundo, *Fundamentos de la Historia de America,* Imprenta Universitaria, Mexico, D.F., 1942; Northrop, *The Meeting of East and West,* Chapter II; Ardao, Arturo, *Filosofia Pre-Universitaria en el Uruguay,* Claudio García & Cia, Montevideo, 1945, pp. 23, 49–85.

[5] Ardao, Arturo, *Batlle y Ordóñez y el Positivismo Filosófico,* Número, Montevideo, 1951, Chapter XII; Ardao, Arturo, *Espiritualismo y Positivismo en el Uruguay,* Fondo de Cultura Economica, Mexico, 1950; Zea, Leopoldo, *Dos Etapas del Pensamiento en Hispanoamerica,* El Colegio de Mexico, 1949; Zea, Leopoldo,

Apogeo y Decadencia del Positivismo en Mexico, El Colegio de Mexico, 1944; Zea Leopoldo, *El Positivismo en Mexico,* El Colegio de Mexico, 1943; Zea, Leopoldo, "Positivism and Porfirism in Latin America" in Northrop, ed., *Ideological Differences and World Order,* Chapter VIII; Francovich, Guillermo, *La Filosofía en Bolivia,* Editorial Losada, S.A., Buenos Aires, 1945, pp. 95–116.

[6] Ardao, Arturo, *Batlle y Ordóñez y el Positivismo Filosófico,* Chapters X to XII.

[7] Ardao, Arturo, *Espiritualismo y Positivismo en el Uruguay,* pp. 85–176.

[8] Ardao, Arturo, *Ibid.,* note 6, pp. 208–210.

[9] Eyzaguirre, Jaime, *Fisonomía Historica de Chile,* Fondo de Cultura Economica, Mexico, 1948, Chapter IX.

[10] Francovich, Guillermo, *op. cit. supra,* pp. 49–54.

[11] Cruz Costa, João, *O Desenvolvimento da Filosofía no Brasil no Século XIX e a Evoluçao Histórica Nacional,* São Paulo, 1950, pp. 176–286; Cruz Costa, João, "O Pensamento Brasileiro," *Boletins da Faculdade de Filosofía, Ciências e Letras,* São Paulo, Vol. LXVII, No. 2, 1946, pp. 5–35.

[12] Ardao, Arturo, *ibid.,* note 6, p. 205.

[13] Vasconcelos, José, *Historica del Pensamiento Filosofico,* Ediciones de la Universidad Nacional de Mexico, Mexico, 1937; Reyes, Alfonso, *La Critica en la Edad Ateniense,* El Colegio de Mexico, 1941; Reyes, Alfonso, *La Experiencia Literaria,* Editorial Losada, S.A., Buenos Aires, 1942; Reyes, Alfonso, translator, *La Iliada de Homero,* primera parte, "Aquiles Agraviado," Fondo de Cultura Economica, Mexico, 1951.

[14] Northrop, *The Meeting of East and West,* Chapter II.

[15] Romero, Francisco, "Man and Culture" in Northrop, ed., *Ideological Differences and World Order,* pp. 385–406, and Romero, Francisco, *Teoría del Hombre,* Editorial Losada, S.A., Buenos Aires, 1952.

[16] Ardao, Arturo, *Espiritualismo y Positivismo en el Uruguay,* p. 269, and *Batlle y Ordóñez y el Positivismo Filosófico.*

[17] Northrop, *The Meeting of East and West,* p. 55.

[18] *Ibid.,* Chapter II.

[19] Madariaga, Salvador de, *Englishmen, Frenchmen, Spaniards,* Oxford University Press, London, 1931.

[20] Northrop, *The Meeting of East and West,* Chapter II, and Unamuno, Miguel de, *The Agony of Christianity,* translated by Pierre Loving, Payson & Clarke, Ltd., New York, 1928; Unamuno, Miguel de, *Tragic Sense of Life,* translated by J. E. Crawford Flitch, Dover Publications, New York, 1954.

[21] Ardao, Arturo, *Batlle y Ordóñez y el Positivismo Filosófico* and *Espiritualismo y Positivismo en el Uruguay.*

[22] Vaz Ferreira, Carlos, *Logica viva,* Editorial Losada, S.A., Buenos Aires, 1945.

[23] Hanson, Simon G., *Utopia in Uruguay,* Oxford University Press, New York, 1938, and Fitzgibbon, Russell H., *Uruguay: Portrait of a Democracy,* Rutgers University Press, New Brunswick, 1954.

[24] Ardao, Arturo, *Batlle y Ordóñez y el Positivismo Filosófico,* p. 166.

[25] Belaunde, Victor Andrés, *La Sintesis Viviente,* Ediciones Cultura Hispanica, Madrid, 1950; Belaunde, Victor Andrés, *Inquietud, Serenidad, Plenitud,* Imprenta Santa Maria, Lima, 1951; Belaunde, Victor Andrés, *La realidad nacional,* Ediciones Mercurio Peruano, 2nd ed., Lima, 1945; Belaunde, Victor Andrés, *La crisis presenta,* 1914–1939, Ediciones Mercurio Peruano, Lima, 1940; Belaunde, Victor Andrés, *Palabras de fe,* Editorial Lumen, S.A., Lima, 1952. For a similar study by a Cuban, see: Aja, Pedro Vicente, *El Christianismo en la Crisis de Occidente y otros Temas,* Sociedad Cubana de Filosofia, La Habana, 1953.

Chapter 10 (Pages 155–168)

[1] For a lengthier documentation, see Northrop, *The Taming of the Nations,* Macmillan, New York, 1952, Chapters 3 through 8.

[2] Liu, Francis S. (Liu Shih-fang), "Westernized Administration of Justice and Chinese Racial Characteristics," as translated by Alfred Wang, Yale Law Library manuscripts.

[3] Northrop, *The Meeting of East and West,* Macmillan, New York, 1946, Chapters IX–XI.

[4] Takakusu, Junjiro, *The Essentials of Buddhist Philosophy,* University of Hawaii, Honolulu, 1947.

[5] See papers by Professors D. Datta and P. T. Raju written for the 1959 East-West Philosophers' Conference, Honolulu, to be published under the editorship of Charles A. Moore.

Chapter 11 (Pages 169–208)

[1] Jefferson, Thomas, *Works,* Ford, P. L., ed., Putnam's, New York and London, 1904–1905, p. 443.

[2] Hamilton, Alexander, *Horatius,* May, 1795.

[3] Cleveland, Grover, First Annual Message to Congress, 1885.

[4] Dunbar, N. C. H., *Two Theories of Bellum Justum in the 19th Century,* a thesis submitted for the J.S.D. degree in the Yale Law School, 1957, p. 257.

[5] *Ibid.,* p. 285.

[6] *Ibid.,* pp. 303–304.

[7] Kennan, George Frost, *American Diplomacy 1900–1950* (the dates are significant), Univ. of Chicago Press, Chicago, 1951, and *Realities of American Foreign Policy,* Princeton Univ. Press, Princeton, 1954.

[8] Lord Lindsay of Birker, "The Philosophy of the British Labour Government," in Northrop, ed., *Ideological Differences and World Order,* Yale Univ. Press, New Haven, 1949, pp. 250–268.

[9] Shotwell, J. T., *The United States in History,* Simon and Schuster, New York, 1956, p. 93.

[10] *Ibid.,* p. 108.

[11] *Ibid.,* p. 114.

[12] Pannikkar, K. M., *Asia and Western Dominance,* John Day, New York, 1953.

[13] Northrop, *The Taming of the Nations,* Macmillan, New York, 1952, Chapters III, IV, V and VII.

[14] For a further account of the development of neutralism in Europe see Northrop, *European Union and United States Foreign Policy,* Macmillan, New York, 1954, Chapters IX and X.

[15] "A Jolt for NATO," *The Economist,* April 13, 1957, pp. 149–150.

[16] *The Economist,* April 13, 1957, pp. 109–110.

[17] *Ibid.*

Chapter 12 (Pages 209–222)

[1] See Northrop, *The Complexity of Legal and Ethical Experience,* Little, Brown, Boston, 1959, Chapter XXII.

[2] Chiang Monlin, *Tides from the West,* Yale Univ. Press, New Haven, 1947, p. 252.

[3] *Ibid.,* p. 140.

[4] *Ibid.*

[5] Northrop, *The Taming of the Nations,* Yale Univ. Press, New Haven, 1952, Chapter 7. See also Chapter 10 of this book.

[6] Northrop, *The Meeting of East and West,* Macmillan, New York, 1946, p. 381.

[7] Chiang Monlin, *op. cit.* Also Northrop, *The Taming of the Nations,* especially Chapter 7.

[8] Michener, James, "Chinese Success Story," *Life* (special issue on Asia), Dec. 31, 1951, pp. 76–81.

[9] For the difference between the law of status and the law of contract, see Sir Henry S. Maine, *Ancient Law, Its Connection with the Early History of Society and Its Relation to Modern Ideas,* John Murray, London, 1908. For a third type of positive legal procedure in non-Western societies and the scientific and philosophical mentality that goes with each type, see Northrop, *The Complexity of Legal and Ethical Experience,* Chapter XV.

[10] Laslett, Peter, ed., "Introduction," *Patriarcha and Other Political Works of Sir Robert Filmer,* Blackwell, Oxford, 1949, pp. 1–43; also Laslett, "Sir Robert Filmer," *The William and Mary Quarterly,* Vol. V, No. 4, Series 3, pp. 523–546.

[11] Ehrlich, Eugen, *Fundamental Principles of the Sociology of Law,* Walter L. Moll, translator, Harvard Univ. Press, Cambridge, 1936.

[12] Bowles, Chester, *Ambassador's Report,* Harper & Bros., New York, 1954, p. 186.

[13] Radhakrishnan, S., "Presidential Address," *Silver Jubilee Commemoration Volume II,* The Indian Philosophical Congress, 1950, Madras, 1951, pp. 9–19; Schilpp, Paul A., ed., *The Philosophy of Sarvepalli Radhakrishnan,* Tudor, New York, 1952.

[14] Iqbal, Sir Mohammad, *The Reconstruction of Religious Thought in Islam,* Shaikh Muhammad Ashraf, Lahore, 1951; see also Northrop, *The Taming of the Nations,* Chapters 7 and 8.

[15] For another instance of how this can be done, see Northrop, *The Meeting of East and West,* Chapter XII.

[16] *The Economist,* Vol. CLXXXIX, No. 6016, Dec. 13, 1958, p. 6.

[17] *Ibid.,* p. 32.

Chapter 14 (Pages 238–257)

[1] Einstein, Albert, *The World As I See It,* Covici Friede, New York, 1934.

[2] Chiang Monlin, *Tides from the West,* Yale Univ. Press, New Haven, 1947.

[3] Cohen, Morris R., and Drabkin, I. E., *A Source Book in Greek Science,* McGraw-Hill, New York, 1948.

[4] Sowerby, Arthur de Carle, *Nature in Chinese Art,* John Day Co., New York, 1940.

[5] Singer, Charles, Holmyard, E. J., and Hall, A. R., eds., *A History of Technology,* Vol. I, *From Early Times to Fall of Ancient Empires,* Clarendon Press, Oxford, 1954, Chapters V, VI, XX–XXV.

[6] Thompson, Laura, "Logico-Aesthetic Integration in Hopi Culture," *American Anthropologist,* Vol. LVII, 1945, pp. 540–553; Mead, Margaret, "The Arts in Bali," *Yale Review,* Vol. XXX, No. 2, 1940, pp. 335–347; Adam, L., *Primitive Art,* Pelican Books (published by Allen Lane), Harmondsworth, Middlesex, 1940; Barrett, Charles L., and Kenyon, A. S., *Australian Aboriginal Art,* National Museum of Victoria, Melbourne, 1947; McPhee, Colin, *A House in Bali,* John Day Co., New York, 1946.

[7] Müller, F. Max, *The Sacred Books of the East,* Vol. XXXII, *Vedic Hymns,* Part I, Clarendon Press, Oxford, 1891, p. 81.

[8] Singer, Charles, *et al., op. cit.,* note 5, p. 114.

[9] Ranade, G. H., *Hindusthani Music: An Outline of Its Physics and Aesthetics,* G. H. Ranade, Poona, 2nd ed., revised and enlarged, 1951; Tagore, Sourindro M., *A Few Specimens of Indian Songs,* the Author, Calcutta, 1879.

[10] James, William, *The Principles of Psychology,* 2 vols., Henry Holt & Co., New York, 1923; James, William, *The Varieties of Religious Experience,* Longmans, Green, New York, 1928.

[11] Northrop, *The Meeting of East and West,* Macmillan, New York, 1946; Woodroffe, Sir John, *Shakti and Shâkta,* Ganesh & Co., Madras, 3rd ed., 1929, Chapter XIV.

[12] Warren, Henry Clarke, *Buddhism in Translations,* Harvard Oriental Series, Vol. III, Charles Rockwell Lenman, ed., Harvard Univ. Press, Cambridge, 1906.

[13] Northrop, *The Taming of the Nations,* Macmillan, New York, 1952.

[14] Liu, Francis S., "Some Observations on Judges, Lawyers and Court Administration in China," *National Reconstruction Journal,* Vol. VII, No. 4, 1947, pp. 3–16.

[15] Hu Hsien-chin, *The Common Descent Group in China and Its Functions,* Viking Fund Publications in Anthropology, No. 10, Viking Fund, New York, 1948.

[16] Maine, Sir Henry S., *Ancient Law,* John Murray, London, 1908, p. 151.

[17] Müller, F. Max, *The Sacred Books of the East,* Vol. XXV, *The Laws of Manu,* Clarendon Press, Oxford, 1886.

[18] Müller, F. Max, *ibid.,* pp. 75–128.

[19] Dhani, Prince, "The Old Siamese Conception of the Monarchy," *Journal of the Siam Society,* Vol. XXXVI, Part II, 1947, pp. 91–106; Le May, Reginald, *A Concise History of Buddhist Art in Siam,* Cambridge Univ. Press, Cambridge, 1938; Lingat, R., "Evolution of the Conception of Law in Burma and Siam," *Journal of the Siam Society,* Vol. XXXVIII, Part I, 1950, pp. 9–31; Müller, F. Max, *The Laws of Manu, op. cit.*

[20] Benerjea, Akshaya Kumar, "The Contribution of Saivism to the Spiritual Culture of India," *Bulletin of the Ramakrishna Mission Institute of Culture,* Vol. V, No. 10, 1954, pp. 227–234; Osgood, Cornelius, *The Koreans and Their Culture,* Ronald Press, New York, 1951.

[21] Laslett, Peter, ed., *Patriarcha and other Political Works of Sir Robert Filmer,* Basil Blackwell, Oxford, 1949.

[22] Laslett, Peter, *ibid.,* pp. 1–43.

[23] Dewey, John, ed., *The Living Thoughts of Thomas Jefferson,* Longmans, Green, New York, 1940, pp. 61–62; Koch, Adrienne, and Peden, William, *The Life and Selected Writings of Thomas Jefferson,* Modern Library, New York, 1944, p. 609.

[24] Giedion, Sigfried, *Space, Time and Architecture,* Harvard Univ. Press, Cambridge, 1954, 3rd ed.

[25] Northrop, *The Taming of the Nations,* 1952, and *European Union and United States Foreign Policy,* Macmillan, New York, 1954.

[26] Margenau, Henry, *The Nature of Physical Reality,* McGraw-Hill Book Co., New York, 1950; and Northrop, *The Logic of the Sciences and the Humanities,* Macmillan, New York, 1947.

[27] Northrop, and Gross, Mason, *Alfred North Whitehead: An Anthology,* Macmillan, New York, 1953.

[28] Northrop, *The Meeting of East and West,* pp. 436–478.

[29] Ehrlich, Eugen, *Fundamental Principles of the Sociology of Law,* Harvard Univ. Press, Cambridge, 1936; Northrop, *The Taming of the Nations.*

Chapter 15 (Pages 258–280)

[1] Northrop, *The Meeting of East and West,* Macmillan, New York, 1946, Chapters V and VIII; *The Logic of the Sciences and the Humanities,* Macmillan, New York, 1947, Chapter VIII; Russell, Bertrand, "The World and The Observer," *The Listener,* Vol. LIX, 1958, pp. 223–226.

[2] Einstein, Albert, *The World As I See It,* Covici, Friede, New York, 1934, p. 60.

[3] *The Economist,* Vol. CXCII, Sept. 12, 1959, p. 817.

[4] Tax, Sol, letter to Paul Fejos of January 5, 1959.

[5] *Ibid.*

[6] Northrop, *The Complexity of Legal and Ethical Experience,* Little, Brown, Boston, 1959, Chapter XXII.

[7] Their argument against the free democratic socialism of Proudhon is an example.

Chapter 16 (Pages 281–296)

[1] Chiang Monlin, *Tides from the West,* Yale Univ. Press, New Haven, 1947.

[2] Buck, Pearl S., *My Several Worlds,* Pocket Books, New York, 1956. Used by permission.

[3] *Ibid.,* p. 281.

[4] *Ibid.,* pp. 279–280.

Chapter 17 (Pages 299–311)

[1] Harrisson, Tom Harnett, D.S.O., in *The South-East Asian Round Table,* A Symposium on Traditional Cultures and Technological Progress in South-East Asia, held at Sala Santitham, Bangkok, Thailand, January 27 to February 2, 1958, under the sponsorship of the Southeast Asia Treaty Organization. Published by the latter organization, SEATO Headquarters, Bangkok, Thailand, undated. Abridgment of comments, p. 14.

[2] Crocker, Professor W. R., C.B.E., High Commissioner for Australia, Ottawa, Canada, *ibid.,* pp. 81, 43. See also Professor Amiya Chakravarty, *ibid.,* p. 13.

[3] Jefferson, Thomas, *The Life and Selected Writings of Thomas Jefferson,* edited and with an Introduction by Adrienne Koch and William Peden, Modern Library, New York, 1944, p. 609.

[4] *Ibid.,* p. 462. Italics mine.

[5] Hand, Learned, *The Spirit of Liberty,* Papers and Addresses Collected by Irving Dilliard, Knopf, New York, 1953, p. 204 and p. 73.

[6] Jefferson, Thomas, *The Life and Selected Writings of, op. cit.,* p. 464.

[7] Allen, Sir George, K.B.E., Secretary of the British Association for the Advancement of Science, in *The South-East Asian Round Table, op. cit.,* pp. 78–79, 15, 64–68.

[8] Northrop, F. S. C., and Senateur Henri Longchambon, Ancien Ministre, Paris, in *ibid.,* pp. 57–59, 38–41, 45–54, 83–84, 87–91.

[9] Pham-Tieu-Tam, Professor, Dean of the Faculty of Medicine and Pharmacy, Saigon, Vietnam, in *ibid.,* pp. 5–6, 84–85.

Chapter 18 (Pages 312–338)

[1] Dedekind, Richard, *Essays on the Theory of Numbers,* Open Court Publishing Co., Chicago and London, 1924.

[2] Whitehead, Alfred N., and Bertrand Russell, *Principia Mathematica,* Cambridge Univ. Press, 1925; Hilbert, D., *The Foundations of Geometry,* Open Court Publishing Co., Chicago, 1921; Hilbert, D., and W. Ackermann, *Grundzüge der Theoretischen Logic,* Springer, Berlin, 1928.

[3] Lewis, C. I., *A Survey of Symbolic Logic,* Univ. of California Press, Berkeley, 1918, pp. 291 ff.; Belnap, Jr., Nuel D., *A Formalization of Entailment,* Ph.D. Thesis, Yale University, 1960; Fitch, F. B., *Symbolic Logic,* Ronald Press, New York, 1952.

[4] Russell, Bertrand, *Introduction to Mathematical Philosophy,* George Allen & Unwin, London, 1920, p. 8.

[5] *Ibid.,* Chapter III, "Finitude and Mathematical Induction."

[6] Hart, H. L. A., "Definition and Theory in Jurisprudence," *The Law Quarterly Review,* Vol. 70, January, 1954, pp. 37–60.

[7] "West Virginia State Board of Education v. Barnette," *United States Reports,* Vol. 319, pp. 646–671.

[8] *Ibid.,* p. 662.

[9] Blanshard, Brand, "Theology of Power," *The Nation,* Vol. 186, March 22, 1958, pp. 253–257.

Chapter 19 (Pages 339–354)

[1] Northrop, *The Taming of the Nations,* Macmillan, New York, 1952, Chapters 6, 7 and 8.

[2] Datta, D. M., and P. T. Raju, papers in the forthcoming proceedings of the 1959 East-West Philosophers' Conference, University of Hawaii, under the editorship of Charles A. Moore.

[3] Lin Yutang, *The Wisdom of Confucius,* Modern Library, New York, 1938; Hughes, E. R., ed. and translator, *Chinese Philosophy in Classical Times,* Everyman's Library, London, 1942.

⁴ Win, Khin Maung, "Some Philosophical Problems of Contemporary Burma," Ph.D. Thesis, 1958, Sterling Memorial Library, Yale University; "The Epistemological Analysis of the Burmese Language," to be published in *Main Currents,* 1960.

⁵ Tagore, Rabindranath, "Gitanjali," in *Collected Poems and Plays of Rabindranath Tagore,* Macmillan, New York, 1951, Verse XXXV, p. 13.

Index

369

Confucian, 163–165, 295; Episcopal, 24, 254; Far Eastern, 166–167; Gandhian Hindu, 163–165; Greek Orthodox, 264, 274, 278; Hindu, 295, 344; Islamic, 34–35, 164–165, 220, 339, 341; Judaic, *see* Judaism; Lutheran, 174; Muslim, 163, 221; Protestant, 24, 126, 142, 173–175, 176, 211, 221, 254, 269, Filmerian, 268, German, 174, non-Conformist, 184; Semitic, 163, 339, 341–342; Taoist, 295
Renaissance, the, 253
Reston, James, 191
Reverberating circuit. *See* Circuit, reverberating
Reyes, Alfonso, 129, 361
Ricardo, 266
Rickover, Admiral, 309
Ridgway, General, 186
"a right" in law, 327–328
Rio de Janeiro, 128
Rio Grande, 124, 125, 142
Rió Grande do Sul, 128, 132, 135
Rivera, Diego, 124, 136
Robbins, Lionel, 228, 359
Rodó, José Enrique, 129
Roman Catholicism, 10, 24, 126, 142, 144, 173, 174, 211, 254, 268, 290, 340–341; American, 173; Aristotelian, 147, 340–341; European, 173; French, 221; Latin American, 124, 133–134, 141; Portuguese, 123–124, 126; Spanish, 123–124, 126, 141; Thomistic, 147, 340–341
Roman Empire, 11–12, 84, 174
Romans, the, 6
Romanticism, German, 127, 261; Polish, 261; post-Kantian, 261; Russian, 261
Rome, 9, 11, 141, 290
Romero, Francisco, 129, 361
Roosevelt, Franklin D., 156, 187, 263
Roosevelt, Theodore, 170–171, 177, 178, 181, 199
Rorschach tests, 90
Rosenblueth, Arturo, 42, 63, 64, 67, 71, 357, 359
Ross, Alf, 104, 113
Rouse, Irving, 357
Rousseau, 262, 302
"rules of correspondence," 30
Russell, Bertrand, 47, 53, 60, 61, 62, 118,

284, 316–317, 318, 319, 349, 356, 358, 366, 367
Russia, 260–263, 264, 266, 269–270, 278, 281; education in, 269, 293
Russo-Japanese War, 1904, 170

St. Augustine, 221, 341
St. Francis, 133
St. Peter's Church, 290
St. Petersburg, 260, 264
St. Thomas, 24, 61, 64, 66, 173, 254
Saint-Simon, 128, 183
San Francisco, 1
Sankara, 343, 345
Santayana, 141
São Paulo, 124, 142
Sarawak, 299
Sartre, 130
Schilpp, Paul A., 358, 360, 364
Schroedinger, 60, 152, 239, 255, 263
Schuman Plan for Coal and Steel, 13
Science, Democritean, 40, 252; Greek, 61, 240, 244, 252, 339; medieval, 61; natural history, 240–245, 249–250, 251; non-technological, 245–247; Oriental, 28, 40; Platonic, 40; Pythagorean, 252; in the United States, 263; Western, 28, 40, 211–213, 254
SEATO Conference, 294 *n.*, 299
Shakespeare, 25, 173, 174
Shanghai, 159
Shannon, C. E., 357
Sheffer, Henry M., 91
Shotwell, James T., 188, 363
Siam. *See* Thailand
Singer, Charles, 364
Siqueiros, 136
Smith, Boyd, 355
Smith, Desmond, 226
Social science, 143, 148, 151
Social theory, descriptive, 95; **normative**, 95
Society, non-technological, 242–243, 248–257; technological, 243–244, 250–257; technological *vs.* non-technological, 239–247, 254–255
sociological jurisprudence, v, 3, 4–6, 8, 9, 11, 21–22, 119–120, 215, 216, 222, 227, 257
Sociology, 95–96; French, 129